OISC Level 1 Immigration Law Manual

HJT Training is a company limited by guarantee. Registered in England and Wales.
Reg no. 4891943

HJT Training Ltd
25 Finsbury Circus
London
EC2M 7EE

enquiries@hjt-training.co.uk
hjt-training.co.uk

ISBN: 978-1-9164312-5-6

2nd Edition

Contents

Glossary of Terms

ADS agreement	Approved Destination Status agreement
ATAS	Academic Technology Approval Scheme
BOTCs	British Overseas Territories Citizen
BOC	British Overseas Citizen
BNA 1981	British Nationality Act 1981
CAS	Certificate of Acceptance for Studies
CESC	Council of Europe Social Charter
CEFR	Common European Framework of Reference for Languages
CJEU	Court of Justice of the European Union (previously the European Court of Justice or ECJ)
CoS	Certificate of Sponsorship
CUK	Conservatoires UK
CUKC	Citizen of the UK and Colonies
DRC	Derivative Residence Card
DVLA	Driver and Vehicle Licensing Agency
DWP	Department of Works and Pensions
EC	Entry Clearance
ECG	Entry Clearance Guidance
ECO	Entry Clearance Officer
ECHR	European Convention on Human Rights
ECHR	European Court of Human Rights
EIG	Enforcement Instructions and Guidance
EEA	European Economic Area
EEA Regs 2016	Immigration (European Economic Area) Regulations 2016
EU	European Union
HMRC	Her Majesty's Revenue and Customs
HO	Home Office
ICT	Intra Company Transfers
IDIs	Immigration Directorate Instructions

ILE	Indefinite Leave to Enter
ILR	Indefinite Leave to Remain
IHS	Immigration Health Surcharge
IO	Immigration Officer
JCWI	Joint Council for the Welfare of Immigrants
KoLL	Knowledge of Life and Language in the UK
LTR	Leave to Remain
NARIC	National Academic Recognition Information Centre
NHS	National Health Service
PBS	Points Based System
PTE	Permission to Enter
PTS	Permission to Stay
SSHD	Secretary of State for the Home Department
TFEU	Treaty on the Functioning of the European Union (sometimes known as the Lisbon Treaty)
UKVI	UK Visas and Immigration
UKVCAS	UK Visa and Citizenship Application Services
VAC	Visitor Application Centre

The OISC Registration Scheme

The Office of the Immigration Services Commissioner (OISC) was created by the Immigration Act 1999 and regulates immigration advisers who are not solicitors and barristers or supervised by them. The OISC also regulates the provision of immigration advice in the not-for-profit sector. (OISC who they are and what they do.)

The OISC has three levels of registration:

- level 1: basic immigration advice within the Immigration Rules
- level 2: more complex casework, including applications outside the Immigration Rules
- level 3: appeals

The OISC's Guidance on Competence (supplemented from time to time by OISC News) lays out the type of casework that can be undertaken by an adviser at each level of regulation. Note that OISC newsletters are not in one location so it is best to sign up to OISC's email alerts on this page, which lists all OISC documents as soon as they are published.

A person applying for regulation will also need to read and understand OISC Code of Standards (April 2016).

The assessments are administered and run directly by the OISC itself. HJT Training has a contract with the OISC to draft and mark the assessment papers.

Successful completion of this training course and the OISC Level 1 exam allows participants to carry out permitted work advice and assistance immigration and asylum work as detailed by the OISC here.

Passing the OISC Level 1 exam is also essential for candidates who wish to progress through the OISC competency scheme to the higher Levels 2 &3.

Giving Immigration Advice and Registering as an Immigration Adviser

Providing Immigration advice when not qualified to do so is a criminal offence under section 91 of the Immigration and Asylum Act 1999. The organisation and the individual adviser must be regulated to provide advice or supervised by a regulated person.

The designated bodies authorised to regulate advisers are the Law Society, the Bar Council, the Institute of Legal Executives and the OISC. Some advisers and organisations are regulated by two or more of these bodies.

For the purposes of this manual the focus is on the OISC and registration at Level 1.

As a fledgling immigration adviser it is also important to understand what is identified as providing immigration advice:

Immigration **advice** is defined in s.82 as advice which:

- Relates to a particular individual
- Is given in connection with one or more relevant matters
- Is given by a person who knows that he is giving it in relation to a particular individual and in connection with one or more relevant matters
- By a person in the UK (wherever the client is)
- In the course of a business carried on whether or not for profit, by him or another

AND

- Is not given in connection with representing an individual before a court in criminal proceedings or in matters ancillary to criminal proceedings.

Immigration **services** are defined as the making of representations on behalf of a particular individual:

- In connection with one or more relevant matters
- In civil proceedings before a judicial decision maker in the United Kingdom or
- In correspondence with a Minister of the crown or government department
- By a person in the UK (wherever the client is)
- In the course of a business carried on whether or not for profit, by him or another.

Relevant matters are – just about every kind of encounter with the UK immigration authorities including the Home Office that you could imagine: asylum, removal, deportation, and applications for entry clearance or for leave to enter or leave to remain.

The material has been divided into three distinct sections that are clearly marked.

The main body of the material is information that is essential to know about, and where to source it, to be able to undertake permitted work, advice and assistance at Level 1 of the OISC competency scheme. It is designed to cover knowledge that it is recommended be thoroughly understood and revised before sitting the Level 1 exam.

Further notes/information **Will be beyond the scope of Level 1 work**. These consist of further reading and information and is clearly marked. It helps to explain the context of the main material in relation to wider immigration law and principles.

It will be of value to anyone sitting the Level 1 exam as a prelude to continuing on to higher OISC Level exams or people interested in pursuing a career in the immigration field. **Any case that raises issues identified in these notes should be referred on to a suitable accredited advisor.**

The course takes place online through a mixture of references to relevant sources of law as detailed in the OISC Level 1 Exam Resource Book, written explanations, videos as well as self-marking quizzes, assignments and sample test questions.

You can access the course on all suitable electronic devices. You can learn at your own pace, whenever and wherever you like. You can repeat any section until you become fully confident in your understanding of that element of the course.

The course is designed to be accompanied by this unique, paperback copy manual of the information contained in HJT's Online OISC Level 1 Accreditation Course.

The course includes helpful tips for preparing for the OISC level 1 exam.

The OISC examination

The OISC has the responsibility to ensure that its regulated advisers understand the law and procedures of UK and EEA immigration control and how to apply it properly to their clients' cases. Consequently, the tests require examinees to clearly show their knowledge. They are not easy to pass. Many have underestimated their difficulty and the failure rate is high.

The level 1 assessment has 2 sections, section 1 consists of 20 multiple choice questions and section 2 consists of scenario-based questions which require written answers. If an applicant passes both sections in one or two attempts, they will pass the assessment overall.

If they have passed one section and failed the other, they will only be required to re-sit the failed section. This only applies in relation to each application for registration received, a single passed section cannot be used by an applicant for a future application. The pass mark is ~~65%~~. 60%

The assessment is 2.5 hours with a 30 min break between the sections. It is open book but with no access to the internet.

Further information on the assessment process, including some revision tips, sample papers, a mark scheme and detailed syllabuses are at:

https://www.gov.uk/government/collections/competence-assessments-immigration-and-asylum-advisers .

Neither HJT Training nor any other training provider can provide OISC accreditation or registration as this lies with the OISC alone. However, HJT does offer training that will assist a person seeking registration with the OISC and is an approved OISC training provider.

Please see here https://hjt-training.co.uk/public-training-courses/ for all our Public Training Courses

Be mark-orientated

Follow basic instructions

Module 1: Sources and Framework of Immigration Law

1.1 Sources of law

It is essential as an adviser to be able to understand the various pieces of law that govern UK and EU immigration control and how they relate to each other. This takes a lot of practice and will always remain a challenge. Immigration law is the fastest changing area of legislation in the UK.

Immigration control is maintained through primary legislation, secondary legislation, the Immigration Rules, Home Office policy, obligations under international conventions, and the discretion of the Secretary of State to admit a person who does not satisfy any of the above.

All of these sources are amended from time to time and it will only be the most recently amended versions which will represent the current state of the law. In some cases it will be the state of the law that was applicable at the date of application that will be relevant.

The Immigration Rules are updated several times a year; the Immigration (EEA) Regulations which governed the free movement regime were amended many times, then replaced in the last few years and now saved for certain purposes with yet further savings amendments; and statutes are regularly amended too. The parliamentary drafts people prefer to amend existing legislation rather than starting from scratch.

It is unrealistic to try and memorise all the applicable law (in case you were thinking about doing so). However, it is realistic to know which legislation deals with which major issue; then you can go to the contents page of the relevant legislation to see which part and which section deals with the issue that concerns you.

Because the system of rules and regulations that makes up immigration law is so changeable, it is important to always check what you are doing against the law **as it is today** (or, where you are looking at refusal reasons, the law as it was at date of refusal): never presume the law is still the same as when you last looked. And it is a very good idea to know where a particular principle on which you rely has its source, so you can cite it in the event of a dispute down the line.

For this reason, it is of vital importance that when advising a client at any level you always look up and refer to the relevant law applicable for each case. The same applies to sitting the OISC Level 1 exam.

EXAM HINT

OISC exam questions will always be set by reference to the law as at the date the OISC exam resource book state as its date of currency.

You can therefore safely rely on the OISC Level 1 exam resource book as your study resource without worrying about changes to the law shortly before your exam. They will not be examinable!

The latest OISC 1 exam resource booklet will always be found here:
https://www.gov.uk/government/publications/oisc-level-1-exam-resource-booklet

Mark up and label this and any other hard copy resource that you are going to take into the open book exam as you progress through the online course. Colour coding and extensive tabbing is highly recommended.

1.1.1 Primary legislation

Listed chronologically, the following pieces of Primary legislation are referred to on this course. Although only extracts, as detailed in the OISC Resource Book, will be relevant to the OISC level 1 exam, these are critical pieces of immigration legislation and so the main issues contained in each piece of legislation are listed below:

Immigration Act 1971

- Continues to provide the framework of immigration control
- All persons without a right of abode are subject to immigration control (s.1)
- The Secretary of State must lay down the rules to be followed (s.1(4))
- Defines who has a right of abode (amended by other legislation) (s.2)
- Provides that entry/stay is regulated by the grant of leave to enter or remain for either a limited or indefinite period (s.3), and that leave continues whilst an application is awaiting decision (s.3C)
- Provides for regulation and control of entry into and stay in the UK by the Secretary of State through powers (delegated to Entry Clearance Officers and Immigration Officers and under-secretaries at the Home Office) to grant (s.4):
    - entry clearance
    - leave to enter
    - leave to remain/further leave to remain, or make
    - a decision to remove,
    - a decision to deport,
    - a decision to revoke a deportation order
- Provides for when a person may become liable for deportation (s.3(5))
- Gives the power to remove only to certain countries or territories – specified in paragraph 8 of Schedule 2
- Defines various terms including illegal entrant (s.33)
- Provides for the power to examine passengers and detain passengers (Schedule 2)

British Nationality Act 1981

- Redefined nationality and citizenship and limited 'right of abode' to newly created 'British citizens' (replacing Citizens of the United Kingdom and Commonwealth with six new categories of nationality and citizenship). While the Act may at first glance appear indecipherable, patience will be rewarded:
    - s1 defines acquisition by birth or adoption
    - s2 defines acquisition by descent
    - s3 sets out the provisions for the registration of minors born outside the UK
    - s6 and Schedule 1 set out the criteria for acquisition by naturalisation
    - s4 to s.4J and s5 set out other registration provisions
    - s11 defines who acquired citizenship on commencement of the Act
    - s14 defines a 'British citizen by descent' and, in effect, also 'otherwise than by descent'. The distinction is important, as will be seen in the nationality law chapter.
    - s40 deprivation of citizenship

Immigration and Asylum Act 1999

Largely superseded, but still relevant in certain important respects:

- amends IA 1971 to provide for entry clearance to have effect as leave to enter (s1)
- provides powers of administrative removal for persons (s10)
- provides for the registration of immigration advisors through the Office of the Immigration Services Commissioner (OISC), including the introduction of related criminal offences and enforcement power
- provides for the support and dispersal of asylum seekers
- provides for suspicious marriages to be reported by registrars
- creates new offences relating to facilitating/harbouring illegal entrants and increases powers of arrest and power to search premises and persons

Nationality, Immigration and Asylum Act 2002

- sets out rights of appeal to the immigration tribunal
- provides for certain asylum and human rights claims to be certified as clearly unfounded. The right to challenge such decisions is to be exercised from abroad only (commonly referred to as non-suspensive appeals because the removal process is not suspended to allow the appeal to take place) (s94)+
- provides for establishment of accommodation centres and removal centres (ss16-42)
- allows for revocation of indefinite leave to remain (s76)
- grounds of appeal (s84)
- gives domestic life to Article 33(2) of the Refugee Convention (s72)
- provisions for juxtaposed controls with EEA countries
- Part 5A, commenced on 28 July 2014, which provides certain considerations as to the public interest that judges must have regard to when assessing an Article 8 claim
- The appeals provisions have been heavily amended, leaving only those who have made asylum or human rights claims with a right of appeal

Borders, Citizenship and Immigration Act 2009 Abolished

- New citizenship provisions were enacted, but the then coalition government stated that these provisions will never be commenced.
- Abolished Asylum and Immigration Tribunal and merged immigration adjudication into the unified tribunal structure.
- Power to transfer fresh claim judicial reviews to the Upper Tribunal (a process which reached its culmination on 1 November 2013 from when almost all immigration JRs are heard in the Upper Tribunal)
- Powers to restrict what studies a person can undertake in the UK
- Most importantly, a new duty to safeguard and promote the welfare of children: section 55

Immigration Health Charge Order 2015 £624

- Sets out the requirements to pay an Immigration Health Charge
  - when applying for entry clearance
  - when applying for limited leave to remain
- Where to find the amount of the charge
- When the charge has to be paid
- Consequences of not paying the charge
- Exemptions and reductions, waivers or refunds from the charge

Legislation can be amended. It is brought into force via Commencement Orders. Sometimes the government keeps legislation online up-to-date: see for example the promising *Changes to legislation* dateline for the British Nationality Act 1981 here. Sometimes it doesn't manage this.

You can check whether a provision has been brought into force if you look at the '*Note as to earlier commencement Regulations*' found at the end of the most recent Commencement Order. Try typing 'Immigration Act 2016 Commencement Order No *x*' into your internet browser. So for example, the *Note* attached to this Commencement Order (No 7) for the Immigration Act 2016 lists all the Sections in force at the time of that particular Order.

Example

You are trying to remember where most immigration offences involving immigration history are found.

Luckily for you it is possible just to look this up in this course (Module 12), or via the summary of relevant provisions above. However, even if you didn't have access to these resources, you could work your way through the *Contents* of each seminal piece of immigration legislation over the years. Presuming you went in date order you would quickly find the Immigration Act 1971 and the list of criminal offences in Part III http://www.legislation.gov.uk/ukpga/1971/77/contents.

1.1.2 Secondary legislation

Some of this material is available on http://www.legislation.gov.uk/, but never in the amended form, so it's usually necessary to look separately at the original regulations and then any amendments to those regulations.

Tribunal Procedure (First Tier Tribunal) Rules 2014

- Regulates appeal procedure in the Immigration and Asylum Chamber of the First-tier Tribunal, including time limits for lodging appeals. This is the place to start your search when look for anything relating to appeals procedure.

1.1.3 Immigration Rules (HC395)

- Referred to here as 'the Rules'
- https://www.gov.uk/guidance/immigration-rules
- Unique legal status different to secondary legislation
- Regulates who may and may not be granted entry clearance and/or leave to enter or remain
- HC395 is not actually law or secondary legislation as such and the SSHD retains discretion to allow entry outside the Rules. SSHD cannot act more restrictively than is set out in HC395 as, assuming there is a right of appeal, the decision will be overturned on appeal or failing that would be susceptible to judicial review. The Immigration Rules are made under section 3(2) of the 1971 Act. The Law Commission conducted a review into the structure and complexity of the Immigration Rules in September 2018 and began the process of simplifying the rules in late 2020.
- Where the Secretary of State stipulates that certain requirements must be met in order to succeed in an application made under the Immigration Rules, all those requirements, including the requirement to provide specified evidence in support of the application, must appear within the Immigration Rules themselves.

Statements of Changes

Statements of Changes, each with their own 'HC' number, amend the Immigration Rules. They are available on the GOV.UK website from a link on the Immigration Rules page: Immigration Rules: statement of changes.

Although detailed knowledge is not required for the OISC Level 1 exam, reference will also be made as appropriate to the following, because an overview of these provisions is part of the OISC Level 1 exam curriculum:

Human Rights Act 1988

- Incorporates the European Convention of Human Rights into UK law
- Provides for a domestic remedy (rather than having to go to the court in Strasbourg) for those asserting that a public official has breached their human rights protected under the ECHR

1951 Refugee Convention

Article 1 (A) (2)

- Gives the definition of a refugee

Citizens' Directive (EU 2004/38)

- The right of citizens of the European Union and their family members to move and reside freely within the territory of the EU and EEA member states.

EEA Free Movement Directive and the Immigration (European Economic Area) Regulations 2006 & 2016

- Transposes into domestic law the EU's freedom of movement regime and regulates residence, exclusion and appeal rights for EEA nationals and their family members. Repealed on 31 December 2020 (the end of Brexit transition) but saved with modifications for certain purposes.

Operational Guidance

The Home Office publishes the guidance it provides to its Immigration Officer on how the Immigration Rules and other provisions should be interpreted and applied both generally and in specific circumstances. These extremely important policy documents also contain concessions, outlining circumstances in which discretion might be exercised, exceptionally, to grant leave outside the Immigration Rules.

Further notes/ information

These extremely important policy documents also contain concessions, outlining circumstances in which discretion might be exercised, exceptionally, to grant leave outside the Immigration Rules. Please note this is not Level 1 work.

These documents, voluminous and regularly updated, are vital tools in the armoury of the immigration adviser. They outline most of the processes undertaken by the Home Office to control migration. They allow the adviser to step into the shoes of the Home Office decision maker to see, for example, how an application will be assessed against the Immigration Rules. Where the guidance is helpful to a case, it should be quoted in the covering letter or representations, and on appeal or judicial review.

Attention will be drawn to any Operational Guidance required for Level 1 work in the main material.

The Operational Guidance, previously referred to as 'Staff instructions', currently includes:

- Asylum policy (Asylum Policy Instructions, APIs)
- Business and commercial caseworker guidance
- Enforcement (remodelled section, formerly Enforcement Instructions and Guidance (EIG), archived here)
- Entry clearance guidance (ECG)
- Fees and forms
- Immigration Rules
- Immigration staff guidance (includes guidance on most visa categories)Nationality guidance (remodelled section, formerly Nationality Instructions NIs, archived here)
- Non-compliance with the biometric registration regulations
- Rights and responsibilities
- Stateless guidance
- Visitors
- Windrush scheme casework guidance

Top Tip

When representing an immigration client, always:

- Identify their objective
- Determine their immigration history

- Identify the relevant Immigration Rule
- Find any relevant Home Office Guidance

1.2 Key concepts

1.2.1 Exclusionary Principles

- The fundamental rule of immigration control is that it is exclusive in nature. That is, everyone is excluded from lawful entry or residence unless they are either exempted from control or have permission, called 'leave'.

General rule

- Everyone is excluded

Unless

- Not subject to immigration control, or
- Permission ('leave') is granted

- This basic rule, the founding principal of immigration law, is derived from s.1 Immigration Act 1971. The 1971 Act still provides the framework for the UK's system of immigration control despite heavy amendments over the intervening years:
  - s.1(1) All those who are in this Act expressed to have the right of abode in the United Kingdom shall be free to live in and to come and go into and from, the United Kingdom without let or hindrance...
  - (2) Those not having that right may live, work and settle in the United Kingdom by permission and subject to such regulation and control of their entry into, stay in and departure from the United Kingdom as is imposed by this Act...
  - Section 1(1) states that a person with 'the right of abode' will be free of immigration control, and section 1(2) that all others will need permission to come, stay, live, work, settle and depart.

1.2.2 Exemption from control

Sections 1(1) and 1(2) IA 1971 do not quite provide the full picture as to who is subject to or exempt from immigration control.

Those not subject to immigration control include those with the 'right of abode'. This group includes all British citizens, but a few others too, who may be British nationals (but not British citizens) or citizens of Commonwealth countries who were settled in the UK or married to men settled in the UK when the Immigration Act 1971 came into force.

Additionally, some foreign soldiers, members of international organisations and diplomats may also be exempt from immigration control.

EEA nationals and their family members were, until 31 December 2020, not subject to UK immigration control either, and they would usually have a right to admission and to reside in the UK under European Union law. There were still some restrictions on EEA nationals, where they were economically inactive or criminals or had abused EEA rights. So, EEA nationals and their family members did not have the right of abode, and were subject to some restrictions on their freedom of movement but did not usually need to seek the permission of UK immigration officers to come or stay in the UK. Since 1 January 2021, new arrivals are fully subject to immigration control, whereas those with prior UK residence and their family members have until 30 June 2021 to apply for EU settled status and are temporarily protected. These complicated transitional issues will be dealt with in Module 8.

Section 1 of the 1971 Act, enacted prior to the UK joining the European Union, made, at no time, any mention of any exception or carve out for European Union or European Economic Area ('EEA') citizens and their families. However, section 7 of the Immigration Act 1988 (repealed on 31 December 2020) exempted them from the requirement to hold leave to enter or remain. In fact, European Union law prohibited an Immigration Officer from even endorsing any form of immigration status in a passport of an EEA citizen, and they did not require passports to travel within the European Economic Area if they could otherwise prove that they were nationals of a member state.

Suffice it to say that the principles that apply to domestic UK immigration law had little or no place when considering the rights of EEA citizens.

You may wonder why we still consider free movement rights in this course. The simple answer is that despite the ending of free movement on 31 December 2020, some of these, and associated rights are retained in some circumstances, and they remain relevant to many situations in relation to which you may be asked to advise.

For example, you will still need to know whether your client's UK residence *was lawful in the past* as this may impact settlement or naturalisation applications and determine whether a child of an EEA national was born British. The legal provisions under which deportation of an EEA national or their family member will be dealt with in certain circumstances also derive from free movement law. The existence of past free movement rights will not be determined simply by asking whether residence documents were held, as these were not compulsory and rights arose by operation of law, where certain conditions were fulfilled. Therefore, when advising EEA nationals and their family members, an awareness of free movement law remains vital to avoid giving incorrect advice.

1.2.2.1 Right of abode

- The right of abode is an example of legacy terminology carried over from an earlier era of immigration control. As is discussed in Module 9: British Nationality law, before 1948 anyone born in the UK or in any of its many colonies was a British Subject. From 1948, most British Subjects became Citizens of the United Kingdom and Colonies ('CUKC'). That status persisted until the great reform of citizenship laws in the British Nationality Act 1981.
- For the two decades prior to the 1981 Act, however, politicians had sought to limit the right of residents of the colonies to live in the United Kingdom itself. The way in which this was achieved was to introduce the concept of the 'right of abode', which was independent from citizenship status. A person could therefore be a CUKC but not possess the right of abode, and therefore have no right to come to the UK itself unless they could meet certain requirements.
- When the right of abode was initially introduced it was linked to another new concept, that of 'patriality'. Put simply, the right of abode was acquired through one's male ancestors having been born in the territory of the United Kingdom (rather than its colonies).
- Today, British citizens hold the right of abode. Some individuals hold the right of abode but are not British citizens, but they are few in number and are addressed in Module 9 on nationality.

1.3 Forms of control

- In order to apply and enforce immigration laws, a number of forms of control have been introduced, operated by different officials. These officials work under the direction of the Secretary of State for the Home Department (SSHD). According to statute, it is the SSHD who makes immigration decisions, though s/he delegates the overwhelming majority of these to civil servants.
- As with everything that touches on UK immigration law and practice, understanding the organisations responsible for immigration control is difficult.
- From April 2013, at least on paper, immigration officials operate within a number of separate departments of the Home Office: UK Visas and Immigration (UKVI), the Immigration Enforcement Directorate (also called 'Home Office Immigration Enforcement'), and the UK Border Force. The first two previously operated as the UK Border Agency (UKBA). The UK Border Force was split off from the UKBA in March 2012.
- The UK Border Force is responsible for controls at the border such as passport checks, juxtaposed controls operating from various ports abroad, and customs.
- In earlier times, the functions of these three new entities were performed mainly by the Immigration and Nationality Directorate (IND) of the Home Office. This was then briefly re-constituted as the Border and Immigration Agency (BIA) before morphing into the UKBA.
- Entry clearance work abroad (see below) was in previous years carried out by an organisation called UK Visas, a joint operation between the Home Office and Foreign and Commonwealth Office. The separate identity for UK Visas has now been abandoned and the visa operation is carried out within the UKVI by Entry Clearance Officers (ECO).

- References to these predecessor organisations, particularly the UKBA, will still be encountered regularly (e.g. Home Office policies are often not updated with the appropriate terms). As the control of immigration is a direct function of the Home Office, we will usually refer to the body of immigration officials who make decisions on applications and enforce controls as 'the Home Office'(HO).
- There are additional controls on employers and educational institutions. The UKVI must authorise them to recruit overseas workers and students through the system of sponsor licences and can penalise them if those they recruit breach immigration laws. The Immigration Act 2014 introduced further controls, exercised by marriage registrars, private landlords, banks and the DVLA. Civil penalty schemes and criminal offences provide the incentive for these organisations to enforce immigration controls. These measures, referred to collectively as 'the hostile environment for illegal migrants' were given more force, with significantly higher penalties for their breach, under the Immigration Act 2016.
- Immigration officers are endowed by legislation with wide powers to enforce immigration laws. Most of these powers originate in the 1971 Act (as amended) and include the power to search, seize, detain, question, arrest and enforce departure. These powers are not restricted to use on foreign nationals without the right of abode: an Immigration Officer also has the power to detain and question a British citizen in order to establish that they are indeed a British citizen.

1.3.1 The Home Office

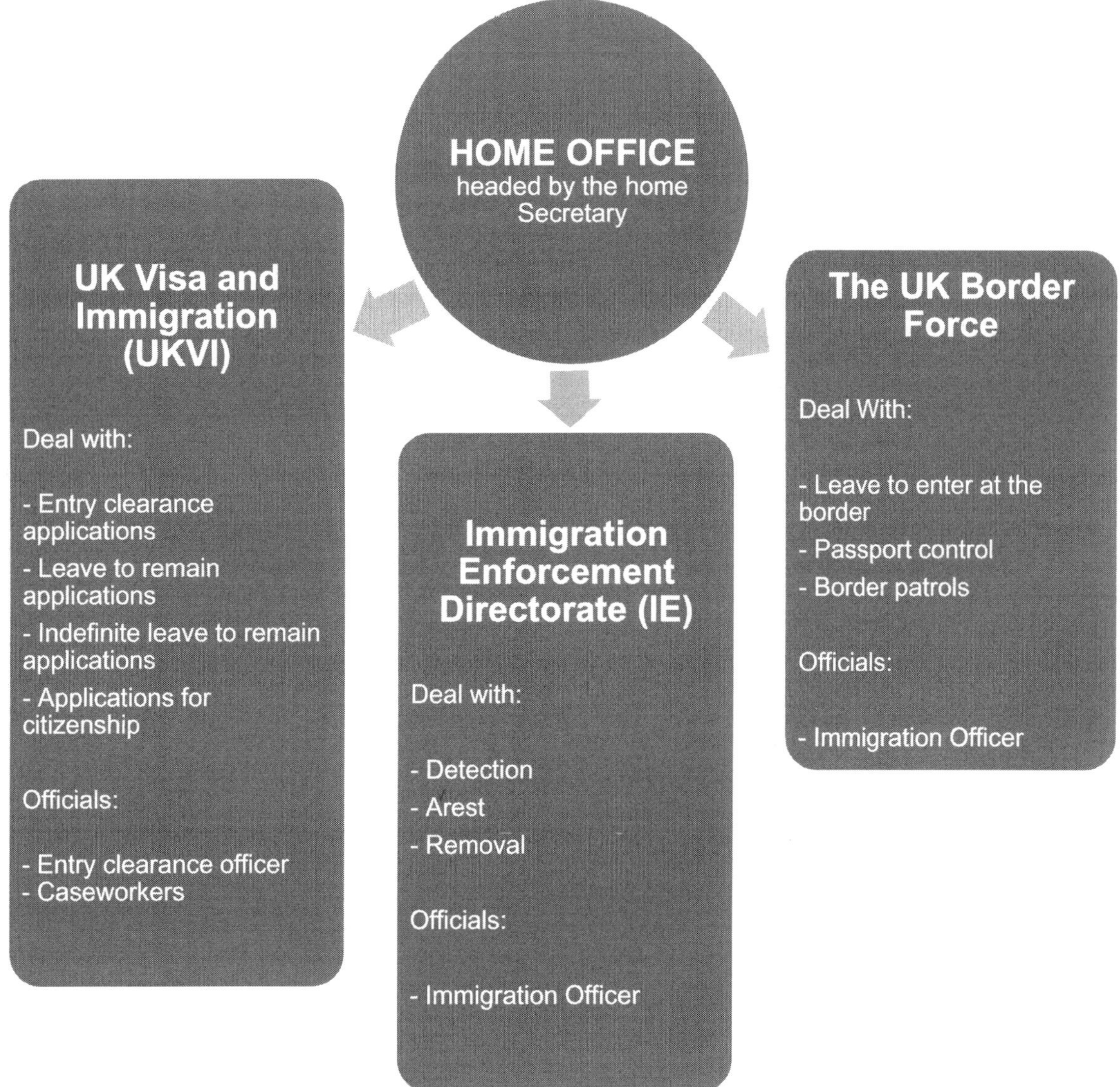

LEAVE = PERMISSION

1.4 Permission to travel, enter or remain

Those with a right of abode will be able to travel to and enter the UK with a British citizen passport, or another passport if stamped with 'right of abode' or a certificate of entitlement to the right of abode, without let or hindrance.

It can be also be seen from section 1 of the 1971 Act that for **those not exempt from UK immigration control i.e. anyone else**, their entry into, stay in and departure from the United Kingdom and their ability to live, work and settle in the UK is determined by the Act.

In short, they must **have permission** to do any of these things.

The word for **'permission'** used in immigration law throughout the Immigration Acts and Rules is usually that of **'leave'**, although we also need to mention the grant of permission to come to the UK before setting off, i.e. 'entry clearance'.

In the newly simplified immigration categories, many of which have been in force from late 2020, you will see the new terms "permission to enter" and "permission to stay" to take the place of "leave to enter" and "leave to remain", respectively.

People sometimes call their 'leave' a 'visa' (as when saying 'I want to extend my visa'): it is better for lawyers to use the correct legal term.

Here is a useful table of various types of permission that will be explored in greater detail below.

Entry clearance	• Pre-entry control, more commonly referred to as a 'visa'
Leave to enter /Permission to enter	• Permission to enter into the UK, either incorporated into the visa, or granted at port (to non-visa nationalsvisiting the UK)
Leave to remain /Permission to stay	• Leave to remain in the UK, usually granted in-country
Limited leave /temporary permission	• Time limited leave (to enter or remain), granted for a certain period with a specified expiry date
Indefinite leave to enter or remain	• Unlimited leave that has no expiry date (but which can be lost, see below)

1.4.1 Entry clearance

Entry clearance is a form of pre-arrival control.

Many of those seeking to enter the UK are required to possess entry clearance, a visa, before they physically arrive at an entry point to the UK.

This assists the Immigration Officer at a UK port. If everyone who arrived at a UK port had to seek entry at that stage it would require an Immigration Officer to make snap decisions on every case even if they were complex.

Also, the numbers concerned would make a detailed examination of each case impractical. For example, in the year ending September 2020 over 1.4 million entry clearance visas were granted for the UK (https://www.gov.uk/government/publications/immigration-statistics-year-ending-september-2020/summary-of-latest-statistics). This was a particularly low figure because of the impact of the COVID 19 pandemic – in 2018, for example, the figure was 2.7 million.

A person required to have entry clearance who does not have it must be refused entry (immigration rule 9.14.1 in Part 9).

The rules on who does and does not require entry clearance are as follows:

Immigration Rules Appendix Visitor: Visa national list

- Always required: Nationals of countries listed in Appendix 2 of Appendix V to the Immigration Rules

Stay of more than 6 months

- Always required: immigration rule 24

If category-specific rule says so

- Always required: check individual rules (e.g finace or marriage visitor)

A non-visa national can, optionally, apply for entry clearance to travel to the UK for a visit. This would substantially reduce the risk of being refused entry on arrival. This would be very useful advice to give to a person who is at risk of refusal on arrival, for example because of a poor prior immigration history, a criminal record or having less than concrete ties to their country of nationality (i.e. being young, footloose and fancy free, or for an elderly person whose family are all settled here in the UK – see Module 3: Visitors).

Entry clearance is sought from an Entry Clearance Officer (ECO) at a visa application centre in the country of origin usually via an online application process. If granted, it takes the form of a sticker or vignette in the holder's passport, which is then presented to an Immigration Officer on arrival. Those granted entry clearance/leave to enter for more than six months will be issued with a vignette in their passport which is valid for travel to the UK for 30 days. The person will then need to collect their Biometric Residence Permit within 10 days of arriving in the UK (from a nominated post-office or other location, e.g. a Tier 4 Student from their university). If they do not travel to the UK within this 30-day period they must apply for another 30-day vignette, for an additional fee (although a temporary COVID-19 concession is in place under which these should be issued free of charge and for up to 90 days).

Top Tip

British High Commissions exist in Commonwealth countries, British embassies in non-Commonwealth countries, and consulates are just smaller posts away from the main High Commission or embassy. They used to administer the visa process but now both the administration and the decision making, is outsourced to the 'commercial partners' of UKVI, namely either TLS Contact or VFS Global (depending on the country of application – check this page for country specific application guidance: https://www.gov.uk/find-a-visa-application-centre)

Although the UKVI still employs some ECOs outside the UK, much of the decision making now takes place in the UKVI's offices in Sheffield (UK).

Usually, by virtue of the Immigration (Leave to Enter and Remain) Order 2000, an entry clearance will also include the grant of leave to enter, which becomes effective on entry to the UK. However, on arrival an Immigration Officer may examine the leave to enter and has the power to cancel the entry clearance which contains the leave to enter under certain limited circumstances including (1971 Act, Schedule 2, paragraph 2A and immigration rule 9.16.2 and 9.20.1-2 in Part 9 of the Immigration Rules):

- False representations made or false documents submitted, whether or not material to the application, with or without knowledge, in writing or orally; material facts not disclosed in relation either to the application or in obtaining supporting documents, either from HO or from elsewhere
- Sufficiently significant change in circumstances since entry clearance issued
- Medical grounds, criminal record or conduct, subject to a deportation order or exclusion; SSHD considers exclusion conducive to public good

A person whose leave is cancelled at port may be able to lodge an administrative review application if the decision falls within Appendix AR 4.2&3 to challenge the decision.

> **Example**
>
> Tasneem applied for entry clearance as a student. The application was granted. While Tasneem was making arrangements to travel to the UK, though, her mother fell ill. She felt unable to leave her and did not travel.
>
> Her mother recovers and four months later Tasneem seeks entry to the UK. In the meantime, her course has started and her college has informed the Home Office that she has not enrolled.
>
> Even if the UKVI issues Tasneem a new 30-day vignette to travel to the UK, and they may not in these circumstances, when Tasneem arrives in the UK she can be stopped by an Immigration Officer and refused entry, even though she has a valid entry clearance. The basis of the refusal is para 9.20.1, because there has been a change of circumstances since the entry clearance was granted.
>
> She will be able to challenge the decision by way of Administrative Review (as the decision falls within AR4.2(a).

There are several other relevant provisions relating to entry clearance (see Part 1 of the Immigration Rules), including:

- Entry clearance applications for any purpose other than a visit or for short-term study must be made in the overseas post where the applicant resides or the nearest designated post if there is none: r28 (although Creative and Sporting workers can apply elsewhere: r28A).
- An application for entry clearance is to be decided in the light of the circumstances existing at the time of the decision. The one exception to that is where a child applicant (under rr296-316 in Part 8 or under the Appendix FM Child route) has turned 18 since the date of application: r27
- The obligation to determine an application based on present circumstances means that an ECO may refuse to grant a visa following a successful appeal, but only where genuine new information has come to light: they should not search for further information with a view to undermining the result of the appeal.
- The entry clearance application will not be treated as having been made until the correct fee is paid: para 30.

The visa application is made, usually online, to a Visa Application Centre (VAC) operated by VFS Global or TLS Connect, UKVIV's commercial partners. The applicant will then book an appointment via the relevant commercial partner's website (to which the end of the visa application form automatically routes), to attend the VAC in person. Between booking and attending the appointment, all supporting documents can be uploaded on the same website where the booking took place. However all documents must also be taken to the appointment where "biometrics" are "enrolled" (fingerprints and a biometric photo are taken). An applicant may be interviewed if necessary. Bar for a few exceptions (eg: EU Settlement Scheme family permits), an appointment booking fee will be payable, and the centre may charge an extra fee for scanning where documents are uploaded incorrectly. Extra "services" such as scanning, fast pass or passport return can be purchased when booking the appointment.

> **Example**
>
> Ayomide is applying for entry clearance as the daughter of her mother Alice who has ILR in the UK. The family has been saving up for the application with a view to making it whilst she remains a child. However they are worried that she will be an adult by the time it is decided because her 18th birthday is two weeks away and they have only just got the cash together.
>
> Applications for a minor child to join a settled parent are found in r297 in Part 8 of the Rules. Accordingly such an application benefits from the saving provision in r27: and must not be refused solely on the

basis of 'attaining the age of 18 years between receipt of his application and the date of the decision on it.' Good news!

The family revert to you a few months later. They had failed to complete the relevant payment authority and the application was invalidated.

This is a real problem. Under r30 the entry clearance application is not 'made until any fee required … has been paid.' So as the fee has not been paid, the application was not made before Ayomide's 18th birthday. As an adult child, Ayomide would suddenly move from the gentle climate of the entry clearance provisions for minor children to the harsh winter of Appendix FM for Adult Dependent Relatives, which requires the applicant to have unmet care needs to function properly which cannot be met by any alternative save for coming to the UK. Unfortunately, the procedural protection in r34B requiring a warning to be given before invalidating applications on some grounds only applies to 'leave to remain' applications, not entry clearance ones: see generally Module 1.5.3.1.

1.4.2 Leave to enter or remain

There is no real difference between leave/permission to enter and leave to remain/permission to stay other than where it is granted, either at port (e.g. Dover, Heathrow) or in-country (by letter or at a same-day appointment).

Leave to enter will be granted on initial entry, and then if a further period of leave is sought and granted it will be called leave to remain. Where limited leave to enter or remain has been granted and remains current, the holder can depart from and re-enter the UK using that leave (unless it was granted for a single entry as a visitor).

Leave can either be granted for a specific period, in which case it is referred to as limited leave/temporary permission, or can be granted for an indefinite period. Indefinite leave is usually encountered as Indefinite Leave to Remain, or ILR. This may also be referred to as 'settlement', as that is what it amounts to. There are a few immigration categories in which Indefinite Leave to Enter is granted right at the outset (for children of settled parents and Adult Dependent Relatives), though most migrants will need one or more periods of limited leave before being able to apply for settlement.

Please Note: although called **Indefinite** Leave to Remain, ILR can still lapse if the holder leaves the UK for more than two years. In these circumstances they must seek entry clearance as a returning resident if they want to come back to the UK. See Module 4.1 for further detail.

Top Tip

When immigration lawyers refer to **extensions of leave**, they are often referring to an extension of leave in the same immigration category. For example, a student will be granted a limited period of permission to enter the UK to undertake the course for which they have been sponsored and will then have to apply for further periods of permission to stay if undertaking further studies.

Immigration lawyers often refer to an application for an extension of leave in a different immigration category as a variation application or as **switching**. For example, a Tier 4 student might meet the love of their life, get married and want to apply for leave to remain as a spouse.

Whether in the same category, or a different one, both are extensions of leave (or **extensions of stay** as they are referred to in the Immigration Rules).

Technically, even an application for asylum for a person with leave is an application to vary leave e.g. from student to refugee.

Routes that leave lead to settlement are often called **settlement routes**.

Example

Washington comes to see you. He is planning to come to the UK and has options; he is finishing college in the USA where he is studying for a Doctorate in applied science. He is very keen to travel here as soon as possible as he is a phenomenal hockey talent and would enjoy playing sport in the UK for a few months. However his long-term goal is to secure British citizenship at the first opportunity.

It is always important to plan your client's possible options after first obtaining leave. Washington would need to choose a route that permitted him to obtain settlement. The two routes most obviously suggested by his facts are either an application under Appendix Skilled Worker or an application under Appendix T5 (Temporary Worker) Creative of Sporting Worker.

If we scroll through those two appendices we see that the Skilled Worker route has provision for grants of entry clearance as well as permission to stay, and culminates with the chance of ILR after 5 years.

But if you look at the temporary worker category, as the name implies, and the introductory paragraph states, this is not a settlement category. The provisions it cater for entry clearance and permission to stay, but only up to a total of 24 months, with no option to settle.

So the latter would put his aspirations for speedy British citizenship (for which ILR is the gateway) on hold.

1.4.3 Immigration categories or purposes

When entry clearance or a form of leave/permission is sought, it must be sought for a specific purpose, such as to visit, study, work or live with a family member in the UK. The Immigration Rules, a document forming a key part of the UK's system of immigration control, sets out the different purposes for which entry to the UK can be sought.

The Immigration Rules are a unique form of legislation that the Secretary of State is authorised to amend by a relatively simple Parliamentary process called the negative resolution procedure. Essentially, any change to the rules is simply laid before Parliament and then automatically becomes law. These changes are published in documents called Statements of Changes. An objection to an amendment can be made by a Member of Parliament, but the objection only triggers a debate, and does not actually prevent the rule changes being implemented.

The current set of Immigration Rules (the Rules) is officially called HC 395 (the reference number of the document in the House of Commons library). The current rules were first introduced in 1994 and have been very heavily amended in subsequent years, growing from some 30 pages to well over 1000 as successive governments have sought to limit immigration into the UK. Amendments are made several times a year: you can marvel at the sheer number over the years here. The plethora of amendments and drafting techniques used over the years make the rules difficult to navigate.

The following modules examine the specific categories in more detail. The most popular categories (and their locations in the Rules) include:

- Visitors (Appendix Visitor)
- Partners of British citizens or settled persons (Appendix FM)
- Parents of a child in the UK (Appendix FM)
- Children of settled parents (Part 8)
- Students (Appendices Student and Child Student)
- Workers (Appendix Skilled Worker and other Appendices containing the abbreviation T2 for settlement routes, and the Temporary Worker Appendices), and their dependents
- Investment and business (Tier 1 of the Points Based System, Part 6A)
- Asylum claims (Part 11)

However, there are many other categories under the rules, some of which only exist for a relatively small number of immigrants.

1.4.4 Multiple entry

The Immigration (Leave to Enter and Remain) Order 2000 (available in its original form online here) regulates standard scenarios involving entry clearances and the ability of migrants to leave and return to the United Kingdom.

Entry clearance takes effect as leave to enter if it specifies the purpose for which the holder wishes to enter the country and if it is endorsed with the applicable conditions – this means that it can generally be said, of anyone who travels to the United Kingdom arriving on a particular date with entry clearance, that on that day they were granted leave to enter (Article 3).

Multi-entry visit visas operate as leave to enter on an unlimited number of occasions for so long as they are valid (for six months if six months or more remain of the visa's period of validity; or for the visa's remaining period of validity, if less than six months) (Article 4).

1.4.4.1 Lapsing leave

Leave given for more than six months, or which was conferred by entry clearance (other than single-entry visit visas), does not normally lapse when a person leaves the Common Travel Area – but it does lapse where the holder has stayed outside the United Kingdom for a continuous period of more than two years (Article 13). **NB Such cases should be referred on to a suitably accredited advisor.**

Examples

Raymond has a visitor visa to come to the UK granted in advance of travelling here. It is valid from 18th May until 18th November. He arrives on 24th May. He is treated as having been granted leave to enter on 24th May.

Raymond travels to France on 16th June and returns on 20th June. He is comfortably within the duration of his visa. On his return to the UK he is treated as having been granted leave to enter for the remaining visa period.

Saffron is granted entry clearance as a spouse for 30 months. She arrives on 24th June. On 30th June she returns abroad to look after a parent who has had an accident. She ends up staying away for a long time. She returns to the UK on 29th June, two years after her arrival. She has returned within the currency of the leave she was granted. However her leave has lapsed, because of Article 13(4)(a) of the Order, stating 'that where the holder has stayed outside the United Kingdom … for a continuous period of more than two years, … any leave then remaining (where the leave is limited) shall thereupon lapse'.

This case must be referred on to a suitably accredited advisor.

1.4.5 The different stages of immigration control

The following flowcharts provide examples of the different stages of immigration control a migrant will pass through in various categories of the rules. The examples all assume that everything goes according to plan for the potential migrant – refusals, appeals and removals are not dealt with here.

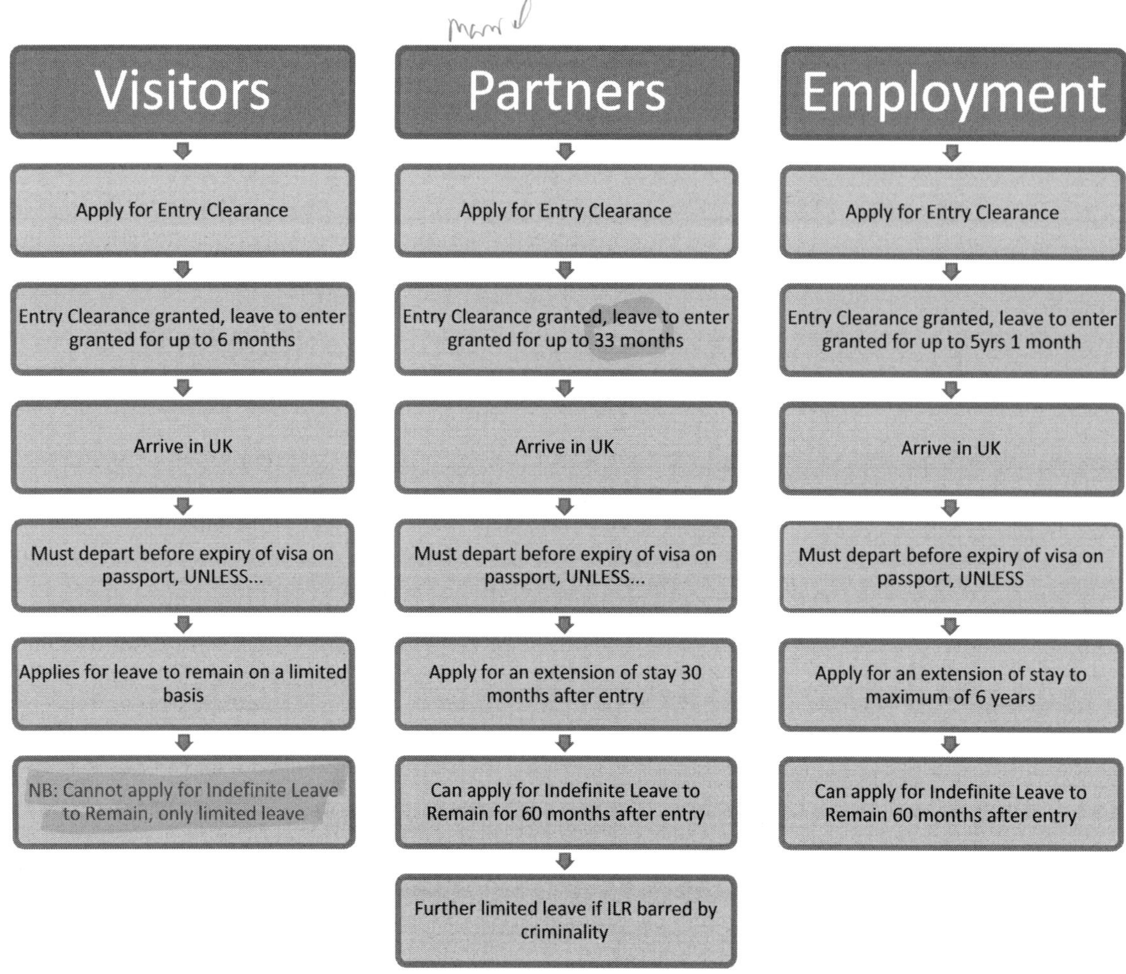

Brackets have been used around some of the stages as they may not apply in all cases (i.e. to non-visa nationals arriving in the UK as visitors).

The employment category above refers to Appendix Skilled Worker. As set out above, some work routes do not lead to settlement.

Further notes/ information

These categories are not to be dealt with by Level 1 advisors and must be referred on to a suitable accredited advisor.

1.4.6 Overstayers and illegal entrants (and the hostile environment)

Some people fall foul of various aspects of immigration control, which can have serious adverse consequences for them. These days Home Office refusal letters list the various misfortunes that they will visit upon people who do not leave the country when they lack permission to remain here. These measures, collectively referred to by the government as 'the hostile environment for illegal migrants', introduced in the most part under the Immigration Act 2014, apply to employers, banks, landlords, and the DVLA. The penalties for transgressors increase substantially under the Immigration Act 2016 (most of which has yet to come into force).

The measures include:

Under the Immigration Act 2016 (s34), as from 12 July 2016, it has become a criminal offence to work (which is widely defined) in the UK without permission, and the illegal worker's wages can be seized as the proceeds of crime. Employing someone without permission to work can lead to civil penalties for employers of up to £20,000, and prosecution and imprisonment. The HO has produced a plethora of guidance documents for employers who want to avoid penalties, the main volume of which seems to be *An employer's guide to right to work checks.*

From February 2016 landlords have been required to carry out document checks to identify if a potential tenant has the right to rent in the UK, before they grant a tenancy, and to keep appropriate records during the tenancy and for at least 12 months after the tenancy has ended. The Immigration Act 2016 (s39) provides for prison sentences of up to five years for landlords who knowingly allow their property to be occupied by someone who is disqualified because of their immigration status. S40 of the new Act provides for the eviction of tenants who lose their permission to rent, without the need for the landlord to obtain a court order and with no right of appeal. Measures that are as tough as this can be tested before the courts, and in 2019 JCWI brought a successful challenge to the 'right to rent' scheme, which was in part reversed by the Court of Appeal which found that the policy led to discrimination, but not intentionally. It found that the discrimination was indirect, possibly justified on grounds of public policy and in any case perpetrated by private persons rather than the state. Thus, the scheme itself was not unlawful. The subsequent appeal from that decision is ongoing at the time of writing.

The immigration service may share people's details with financial services agencies to restrict access to credit.

The DVLA will not issue a driving licence and may be asked to cancel any existing licence. The Immigration Act 2016 creates a new offence of driving when unlawfully in the UK, with imprisonment of up to six months. Guidance on the current rules on revoking driving licences is in Offender management section of the Enforcement section of UKVI operational guidance.

Undocumented migrants cannot open bank accounts. The 2016 Act went further and requires bank accounts to be frozen and then closed. This has an extremely more disruptive effect given that wages may be paid in and bills paid out. For how this is intended to be operated, see October 2017 guidance to banks and guidance for those whose accounts are affected. See also Codes of Practice on freezing orders.

The NHS (Charges to Overseas Visitors) 2015 Regulations (SI 2015/238) have tightened access to the NHS over time: they now provide for up-front payment; that immigration status checks must be made; and that information be kept on health records, from 23 October 2017. For detailed information, refer to this ILPA Briefing and Department of Health guidance on overseas visitors charging regulations. Employers and landlords may use the Home Office checking services to confirm the status of current and prospective employees and tenants/occupiers, though the information provided by the HO is not always accurate. The Chief Inspector of Borders and Immigration, David Bolt, published inspection reports on the 'hostile environment' in 2016, particularly looking at the measures relating to driving licences and bank accounts. It noted that hundreds of people per year had been wrongly affected and criticised the Home Office for its failure to appreciate the impact on the individuals concerned.

In April 2018 media exposure of the impact of the hostile environment on members of the Windrush generation and their descendants led to a public outcry, a change of Home Secretary and commencement of a review of the policy in general and the launch of the Windrush scheme on 30 May 2018. Despite early promises it is debateable whether the general approach by the Home Office has, since then, changed at all, as no hostile environment policies were deliberately withdrawn or significantly amended, unless litigation forced the issue.

1.4.6.1 Illegal entrants

An illegal entrant (identified as liable to the mandatory ban by r9.8.1 Part 9 of the Immigration Rules) is statutorily defined at section 33 of the Immigration Act 1971:

'illegal entrant' means a person

(a) unlawfully entering or seeking to enter in breach of a deportation order or of the immigration laws, **or**

(b) entering or seeking to enter by means which include deception by another person, and includes also a person who has entered as mentioned in paragraph (a) or (b) above;

So, the definition includes both a dishonest individual (e.g. who makes false representations in a visa application) and a clandestine entrant (who enters evading the immigration laws in the back of a lorry).

1.4.6.2 Overstayers

An overstayer is someone who has remained beyond their leave to enter/remain, either the original grant, or beyond a statutory extension under s3C Immigration Act 1971 (see the definitions at para 6 under 'Interpretation' in the Introduction part of the Immigration Rules).

When advising these individuals, always consider whether they may be better off leaving the United Kingdom and applying to return from abroad. Then there is less scope for bad immigration history to be held against them.

Remember though that it will always be necessary to take into account any relevant *Grounds for refusal* or *Suitability criteria* when doing so (see Module 3: *Grounds for refusal*). If they can avoid, for example, the mandatory one-year ban on return, by leaving the country before they have overstayed 90 days – or, where overstaying began on or after 6 April 2017, 30 days r9.8.2-7 Part 9 – then they should seriously consider so doing.

4.4.6.3 The Windrush scheme

The devastating impact of the hostile environment policy agenda (see Module 1) even on a generation of long term residents who were unable to document citizenship or settlement entitlements to the unreasonably high evidentiary standards applied in the preceding years, led to the 'Windrush scandal', resulting in a change of SSHD. A UKVI information page and helpline was set up and The Immigration and Nationality (Requirements for Naturalisation and Fees) (Amendment) Regulations 2018 were laid on 24 May 2018 and in force on 30 May 2018 to give effect to the Windrush scheme (see casework guidance and an application form). The intention behind the scheme is for the HO to assist applicants in gathering evidence of long term residence via various government departments. Citizenship- and settlement fees are dropped as well as some requirements such as KoLL. Those assisting applicants may wish to refer to outlines of the complex legal situation prepared by organisations such as SLC, ILPA (see ILPA Monthly, May 2018), HJT's own blog post on nationality sources, and may still wish to advise their clients to make the following requests for documentation themselves:

-Full Medical records request from GP max charge £50, can stretch back decades even where changed GPs as file travels with patients

-UKVI Subject Access Request – detailed request but can cover decades

-HMRC Subject Access Request – records for any taxes or national insurance contributions that may have been made. NICs records go back to the 1970s.

-In addition, the National Archives will assist in trying to locate old, lost naturalisation certificates (which may be relevant to questions of nationality for family members). If located, certified copies are provided at a cost of £27.40.

The scheme has worked relatively well although response times are much slower than promised, and many of those promised compensation are still waiting. The HO's own recent factsheet shows how little compensation was initially intended.

Example

Aimee enters the UK as a Tier 1 Investor. Due to spending too much time horse riding she forgets to extend her visa in time, and applies one day after her initial period of leave expired.

Aimee is an overstayer and within the hostile environment. So long as the SSHD accepts her equestrian activities as a 'good reason' which justifies her lateness (unlikely: it does not seem to be something beyond her control) then her immigration application would not face mandatory refusal. But she would still be an overstayer.

Anil enters the UK with a view to claiming asylum. He hides in the back of a lorry and claims asylum as soon as he is through the immigration controls at Dover.

Anil is an illegal entrant by clandestine conduct.

Fyodor enters the UK as a visitor. He fails to reveal the fact that his long-term partner, Anna, is present here with ILR.

Fyodor is liable to be declared an illegal entrant if this fact comes to the attention of the SSHD: the visa process asks one to identify family members in the UK and the presence of a settled partner is a factor that might well be deemed a material and dishonest non-disclosure.

1.5 Making applications for leave to enter and remain and Section 3C leave

Making an application for leave, whether from outside or within the UK, is always complex. The procedures for making the application are complex, and the substantive and evidential requirements of each application are complex too. None of this is helped by the constant changes to procedures, requirements, evidence and to the policies underpinning all of this.

Further notes/information

Extensive changes to Part 1 of 1 November 2018 were aimed at encouraging most in-country applicants henceforth to apply online, with assisted digital support where necessary. A process will also remain for receiving applications on paper for routes where there is no online application form, but paper forms can no longer be used for submission in person. The requirement for submission of passport photos was, also as part of those changes, dropped altogether.

1.5.1 Applications for a visa/entry clearance

Visa/entry clearance applications (terms which can be used interchangeably) must be made online (except in North Korea, where a paper application is still required), and since 1 November 2017 there has been a digital assist service available.

Information on entry clearance applications, processing times and local administrative arrangements for submitting an application can be found on the GOV.UK website at: Apply for a UK visa.

Each application form, on submission, provides links as necessary to the websites of the commercial partners who run the visa application centres. Visa processing times can be found at: https://www.gov.uk/visa-processing-times. For those who want quicker decisions, various priority services are available at an additional cost at some posts.

An application for entry clearance should be made from the country in which the applicant is living (i.e. not merely passing through). Visit and short-term study visas are an exception – they can be made at any post where entry clearance applications are considered (rule 28 and Appendix Visitor), as can Global Talent and some Temporary Worker categories (rule 28A).

The date of application may be important. An application is not legally made unless and until it is accompanied by the appropriate fee in local currency: rule 30. If the fee can be paid online, the application date will be the date the online application is submitted and payment is made. Otherwise, the fee will be paid when the applicant attends the VAC in person for the biometric appointment. Where the immigration rules that apply to the application have been amended between the date of the online application and the date the fee is paid, it will be the amended rule that will be applied to the application.

Under rule 27, a child applicant who applies before their 18th birthday will not then be refused solely on the basis that they are over 18 at the date of decision.

Visa fees in local currency can be found at: https://www.gov.uk/visa-fees. A list of all fees is available on the 'fees and forms' page on the UKVI.

Reduced fees sometimes apply for Council of Europe Social Charter (CESC) nationals.

Where the application is being made for leave of more than six months (but not for Indefinite Leave to Enter), there will usually be an immigration health surcharge to pay on top of the fee (see below).

For more on the entry clearance process, see the section on Entry clearance, above.

1.5.2 Applications for leave to remain/permission to stay/extension of stay

Applying for leave to remain had becoming an ever-more intimidating process until the introduction of the online application process for most applications, which brought with it its own problems but is generally more user friendly. The Home Office continued to invent new ways of refusing, rejecting and voiding applications, such that the process had become a minefield. And with the government's increasingly 'hostile environment' in full play, innocent mistakes by advisors could pitch their client headlong into disaster for minor mistakes such as submitting the wrong format passport photo or making one minor mistake when filling in payment details on a paper form. These issues no longer feature as passport photos are not generally required anymore and payment is done online, but there have been issues with the online processes and biometric appointments system too which are not yet fully resolved. ILPA regularly liaises with the HO about these, and problems, for example with lack of free appointment bookings, can be reported there directly via this form.

We consider below issues concerning the validity and timing of applications and further applications, including continuing leave under s3C of the Immigration Act 1971, and paragraphs 34 and 39E of the Immigration Rules. Understanding how these provisions operate together is difficult, but essential. To help you, there are some worked examples near the end of this module.

1.5.2.1 Timing of application

The question of when to make the extension application is critical. For applications made on or after 24 November 2016, the Rules (but for some narrow exceptions; see our section on r39E below) require that the applicant must be lawfully in the UK at the date of application. That means they must not have overstayed their leave before making the application, even by one day. If they have, their application can be refused for that reason alone.

The HO suggests a person applying for an extension/variation of stay makes the application no more than 28 days *before* their current leave expires. Although there is no prohibition on applying for an extension at any time during the person's leave, applying too early may not be a good idea as the person may lose out on the benefit of continuing leave under s3C should their application be refused very speedily before their leave expires (see section on 3C leave, below). **Individuals on settlement routes should bear in mind, when extending their leave, that the periods of leave they are granted are near enough completed before they are extended. Otherwise they may find themselves short of enough accumulated leave to reach the ILR requirement within the minimum possible period.** If they lack the right duration of residence, an additional extension application may be necessary to reach the settlement period.

The Rules tell us when an application is treated as having been made (r34G – as amended on 1 November 2018):

- A postal application by paper form is treated as having been made on the date of posting (r34G(1)). The HO will take the date of posting as the date shown on the tracking information provided by Royal Mail or, if not tracked, by the postmark date on the envelope (so an application will not be made merely by putting it in a post box).
- Where a paper form is sent by courier or other postal services provider, the date on which it is delivered to the Home Office (r34G(2))
- Where the online process is used, the date on which the online application is submitted (r34G(3)) or, where the application includes a fee waiver application, the date the fee waiver was submitted online, so long as the completed application for leave to remain is submitted within 10 days of the HO fee waiver decision being received by the applicant (r34G(4))

Note that paper forms can no longer be used for submission in person.

An extension of leave, if made by no later than the last day of a person's leave either online or sent by signed for delivery will be an 'in-time' application.

1.5.2.2 Automatic extension of leave (also known as 'continuing leave' or '3C leave')

The Home Office will take several weeks (at least) to decide an application for an extension of stay. For a person who has made an in-time application (i.e. before their leave ran out), this delay will usually result in their leave expiring after they have made the application, but before they receive the HO's decision on it. S3C of the Immigration Act 1971 deals with this problem. It provides that such a person will have 'continuing leave', which continues to run, automatically, when the person's leave that was granted to them has run out until that application is finally decided. The person's leave just continues, through the operation of the law, even though it will appear from a glance at BRP to have expired.

S3C extends a person's leave throughout *three separate stages* of the application and appeals process:

1. where the person's leave runs out before the HO has decided the application, s3C automatically extends that leave until the application is either decided or withdrawn
2. if the application is refused, s3C further extends that leave by the period in which the person can lodge an application for Administrative Review or (in-country) appeal:
   - An application for Administrative Review must be lodged within 14 days of the person receiving the HO's decision to refuse the application (r34(1)(a)).
   - An appeal must be lodged within 14 days of the HO decision being sent to the applicant (Rule 19, The Tribunal Procedure (First-tier Tribunal) (Immigration and Asylum Chamber) Rules 2014)
3. where an appeal or administrative review has been lodged in-time, 3C leave continues for as long as the appeal or administrative review remains pending (i.e. until it has been withdrawn or is finally decided).

In the special case of EUSS appeals, where first an Administrative Review, then *also* an appeal, (if AR is unsuccessful), can be brought, s3C leave is conferred:

- Under s3C(2)(ca) while an EUSS appeal can be brought and under (2)(cb) while it is pending
- Under s3C(2)(d)(i) while an EUSS AR could be brought and under (ii) while one is pending.
- An EUSS AR, under r34R(1A) must be lodged within 28 days, and if in detention within 7 days, of receipt of the decision notice
- An EUSS appeal must be lodged no later than 14 days after being sent the refusal decision notice or the dismissal of AR – Reg 19 (3B)(a)&(3D)(a) of the FTT Procedure Rules 2014.

Section 3C also extends the conditions attached to the previous grant of leave, so that a person who could previously work or study or claim benefits can continue to do so. Since December 2016 s3C leave can be cancelled under s3C(3A) for breaching conditions on leave or using deception (whether successfully or not).

Further Information

Note though that where an out of time appeal or administrative review is lodged, a decision by the Tribunal or Home Office to extend time will not, according to the Home Office, resurrect the person's s3C leave: so says their policy on 3C leave (as now provided in the current Home Office guidance: 3C and 3D leave in the Modernised Guidance).

This interpretation of the legislation will have to be tested in a legal challenge: one might read s3C differently.

Whilst a person is on the first kind of s3C leave before an application is determined, they may vary the application, by sending a new fee-paid application on the appropriate form (e.g. from an application as a partner under Appendix FM to an application under the ten years' long lawful residence route, if they clock up the relevant residence pending the first application's determination). However, it is not possible to vary the application once it has been refused: see JH (Zimbabwe)[2009] EWCA Civ 78.

Examples

Algernon was granted leave to enter as a student. He applies for further leave. He posts his application on the final day of his first grant of leave.

Algernon's leave is extended under section 3C(1), (2).

Bertha was granted leave to enter as a student. She applies for further leave 28 days before her leave expires. The application is refused 2 days before her leave expires.

Bertha's leave is not extended: leave did not expire without the application for variation being decided (section 3C(1)(c)). To avoid a gap in her lawful residence, she should consider making a new application.

Charlie was granted leave to enter as a student. He applies for further leave 28 days before his leave expires. Five days ago he receives a refusal two months after his leave was due to end.

Charlie's leave is extended under section 3C(2)(a) during the period the application was awaiting decision, and then is presently extended under section 3C(2)(d) as an administrative review application could be made.

David was granted leave as a Skilled Worker migrant. He made a timely extension application but it was refused three months ago. He made a timely application for administrative review and that was refused a week ago. He wants to know whether he can continue working if he lodges a judicial review application.

David's leave was extended under section 3C(2)(a) during the period the application was awaiting decision, and then was extended under section 3C(2)(d) during the administrative review process. It expired a week ago. A judicial review application will not bring section 3C leave into play and therefore he and any employer would be committing an offence were he to work. Were the judicial review to succeed in the future and the refusal decision to be set aside, then his section 3C leave should be treated as if resurrected.

Esther was granted leave as a Skilled Worker migrant. She applies for further leave before her last leave expired. Her application is rejected as invalid because mandatory documents were missing. She is given an opportunity to provide them by the Home Office and does so a week later. The application is treated as valid.

Esther's leave will be extended under section 3C(2)(a) because the Home Office policy is to treat the original application date as the relevant one where they subsequently validate an application.

Frank was granted leave as a student and remained a student migrant for nine years and ten months. He makes an application for further leave on private life grounds before his last leave expires. That application is not decided as at today's date when he visits you in the office, some four months after it was made.

Frank's leave is presently extended under section 3C(2)(a); he can accordingly make an application on 10 years long residence grounds by varying the application, as the original application may be varied (section 3C(5)) so long as it has not been refused (section 3C(4))

George has an outstanding application as a student. He wants to vary it to a spouse application under Appendix FM. He can do so whilst it remains outstanding. Once it is refused, there is no extant application to vary.

1.5.2.3 Confirming 3C leave

Those with s3C leave can easily fall victim to the hostile environment even though they remain lawfully resident in the UK. Some employers and landlords are now so nervous at the sanctions and penalties that can be levied against them if they get it wrong, that they may be resistant to continuing the person's employment or tenancy in these circumstances. Whilst they have access to HO guidance, which explains s3C leave to them and the circumstances in which they can rely on it to avoid HO sanctions, they may choose not to engage with it when dismissal or eviction appears the easier and safer option.

An adviser may need to help their client persuade an employer, landlord, bank or the DVLA that they are lawfully in the UK with continuing leave under s3C and, consequently, that their job, home, bank account, and car should not be taken away.

But problems can arise even where the employer does contact the HO checking service as the information available to HO staff can be out of date or inaccurate. Evidence that the application did reach the HO (recorded delivery tracking signature or proof of online submission) will be useful in these circumstances. Hopefully, in the face of a negative response from the HO, the employer can be persuaded to contact the HO again to clarify things with any new information you give them. One way of opening a channel of communication to the HO in these cases is for the person to contact their local MP's office, as the HO's MP Liaison Unit must respond within two weeks to the MP, whereas response times are usually much slower.

Where all else fails in such cases, the employer should be reminded that an action could be brought for wrongful dismissal and/or discrimination if your client is dismissed in these circumstances.

Top Tip

Remind the reluctant employer that the Right to work checks: an employer's guide states that:

'If on the date on which permission (as set out in the document checked) expires, you are reasonably satisfied that your employee has:

- submitted an in-time application to us to extend or vary their permission to be in the UK; or

- has made an appeal or an administrative review against a decision on that application;

- is unable to provide acceptable documentation but presents other information indicating they are a non-EEA long-term lawful resident of the UK who arrived here before 1988

Your statutory excuse will continue from the expiry date of your employee's permission for a further period of up to 28 days to enable you to obtain a positive verification from the Employer Checking Service'. This 'grace period' does not apply to checks carried out before employment commences. In such circumstances, you should delay employing the individual until you have received a Positive Verification Notice from our Employer Checking Service.

1.5.3 Making a valid application for an extension of stay

Applications for leave to remain are made from within the UK either online, or by post or courier and by appointment at the UK Visa and Citizenship Application Service (UKVCAS).

As well as being made in-time, the application must be 'valid'. If the application is not valid, the HO will *reject* it (rather than *refuse* it). They will return it to the applicant with a 'Notice of Invalidity' and treat it as if it had never been made. A rejected application cannot be challenged by appeal or administrative review. The cross-cutting validity requirements have thus far been contained in r34. From 1 December 2020, those Appendices, introduced on that day, to which new r34 will not apply (and which contain their own validity requirements) are listed in rA34. It is therefore essential to peruse the relevant new Appendix for its own validity requirements.

A decision that an application is invalid will bring the person's s3C leave to an end. The person may not then be able to make a further application. Consequently, if the decision on invalidity is incorrect, or the person has not been given an opportunity by the HO to correct the invalid application, the decision must be challenged (see more below).

A 'valid application' is defined in paragraph 6 of the Rules as an application made in accordance with the requirements of Part 1 of the Rules.

There are several elements to making a valid application:

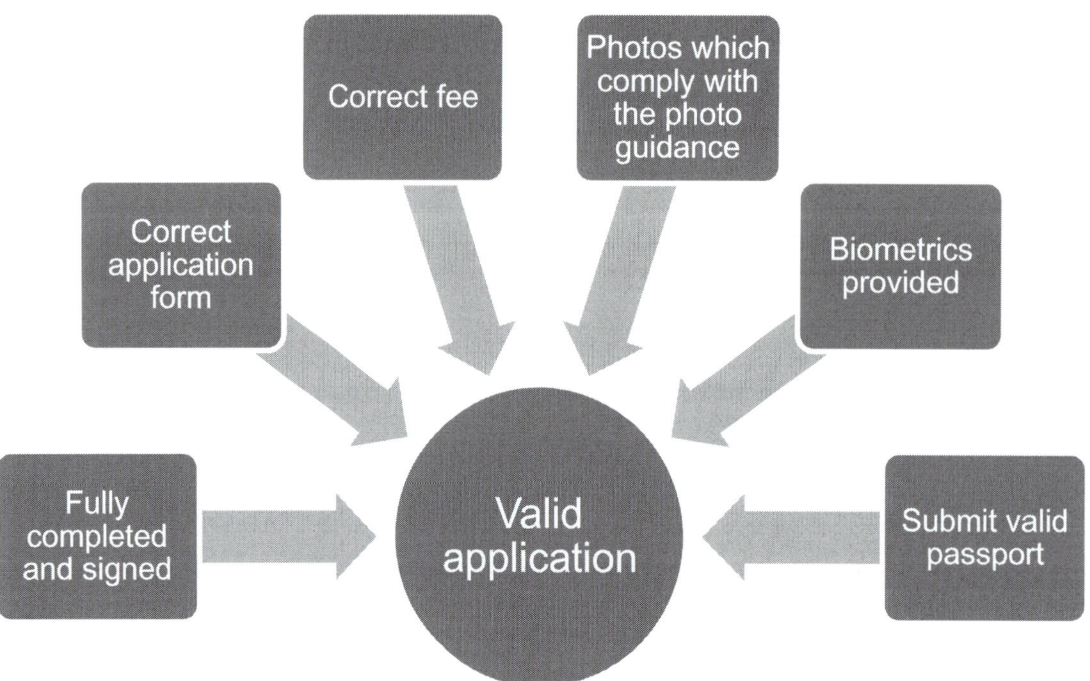

As alluded to above, the online forms ensure that forms are fully completed, that the correct fee is paid, and the biometrics appointment which forms part of every application means passport photos are no longer required.

However be aware that some of the newer Immigration Categories now include the above *as well as additional* validity requirements, such as previously were eligibility requirements, so the above infographic may not be the full picture.

Where they still apply, the cross-cutting provisions as to validity can be found at Immigration Rules 34 to 34E.

HO policy and guidance on these provisions is HO guidance Validation, variation and withdrawal (hereafter referred to as the 'Applications Guidance'). This represents a considerably less generous approach to validity than previous guidance.

The mandatory requirements are:

- **Use of the specified form**, **and the most up to date version of it** (see list of forms below). The forms state on their front page the types of applications for which they can be used, and the date of issue.

If the relevant form remains a paper form, always download the form directly from the UKVI 'fees and forms' page, and check that it is the correct form for the category of the Rules under which the application is being made. Before finalising and submitting the application, check again that it is still the most up to date version of the form available. Note though that rule 34(1)(c) allows for an old version of a form to be used for up to 21 days after a new version goes online, although the current fee must always be paid (not the fee showing on the superseded form, if they are different).

The Applications Guidance did, until recently, state;

If the application was received more than three months ago and does not meet the specified form requirements, you must use discretion and accept it as valid. This is because the applicant may be unfairly disadvantaged if you reject their application after this length of time

Further notes/ information

The implications of making an application on the wrong form are not clear cut. In JH (Zimbabwe)[2009] EWCA Civ 78 the Court of Appeal held that an application made on the wrong form (in that case, on a

SET form for ILR rather than an FLR form for further limited leave) may in fact be a valid immigration application, even though it was hopeless on its merits *as an application in the category for which the form is intended.* The application guidance on page 6 now states that the applicant *must* be informed of this and given 10 working days to make an application on the correct form. If they do, the date of the earlier application on the incorrect form is the date of application.

-The payment of a specified fee. Ensure, if the payment page of a paper form is used, that the account remains in funds until the fee is collected. You should also advise your client to contact their bank and let them know a large amount will be taken soon, to stop the bank's fraud prevention methods from stopping the payment going out. A full list of fees can be found at: https://www.gov.uk/government/publications/visa-regulations-revised-table

The payment of the Immigration Health Surcharge (IHS), where applicable, in accordance with the process set out on the GOV.UK website (https://www.gov.uk/healthcare-immigration-application/pay) – see section below on the his

Parental consent: where the main applicant is under the age of eighteen, their parent or legal guardian must provide written consent to the application

Two photographs as described in the photo guidance must be provided, but only where a paper form is used. Ensure you keep a photocopy of the photos paper clipped to the form, so you will be able to prove they have been sent with the application. Where the online process is used, the photo taken at the biometrics appointment will be the one that is used instead.

Completion of all the 'mandatory' sections of the form. If an online form is used, some fields may not be relevant to the applicant, or they may simply not know information required by a mandatory field. The workaround is to make an entry that will allow you to progress the application, take a careful note and address the information provided in your covering letter.

Compliance with biometric requirements, i.e. attending the Home Office or a post office for face and fingerprint scans within a specified timeframe. Biometric information must be provided in accordance with the process set out in the biometric enrolment letter and any subsequent warning letter issued in accordance with the Code of Practice about the sanctions for non-compliance with the biometric registration regulations.

Attendance at a UKVCAS- (or Service and Support) centre: where the application is made online, and the person must attend a UKVCAS centre as part of the process, they are 'encouraged to go to an appointment, which can be chosen within five working days of making the application, as soon as possible. A reminder will be sent after 15 working days if no attendance has taken place.

An original, valid passport, travel document or (unless the applicant is a Points Based System Migrant) national ID card issued to the applicant and to any dependant included in the application must be provided (Rule 34(5)). There are some exceptions, including (rule 34(5)(c)):
- those whose document is with the Home Office
- where it has been permanently lost or stolen and there is no functioning national government to issue a replacement
- where the applicant is a victim of trafficking, it has been retained by an employer or other person
- where the applicant has made an application under the destitute domestic violence (DDV) concession
- or as a stateless person or their family member or by a person in the UK with refugee leave or humanitarian protection
- or the applicant provides a good reason beyond their control why they cannot provide proof of their identity.

Home Office guidance on 'good reasons', in the Applications Guidance, says: reasons beyond the applicant or any dependant's control may include:
-if there is no longer a functioning national authority to approach and provide a new document, or because there is no Embassy or consular service in the UK
-if there is a national authority to apply for a document but they have run out of documents
-the applicant has made an application for a replacement document but the issuing authority was not able to provide it before the application was made

-if the applicant cannot obtain a document for reasons of national or personal security
-if the national authority is unreasonable and refuses to provide a document, for example: if the national authority will only provide a passport if they apply in person but there is no provision to apply in person in the UK, or if the national authority puts unreasonable barriers in place for the applicant.
Where an exception applies, the Home Office may ask the applicant to provide alternative satisfactory evidence of their identity and nationality; which can include, but is not limited to, a birth certificate, driving licence, national health card or national service document (r34(6) and Applications Guidance). **This work is outside the scope of level 1 work and should be referred on to a suitable accredited advisor**

1.5.3.1 Opportunity to correct an invalid application

Very importantly, where a person makes an invalid application, the Home Office *should* contact them before rejecting it as invalid, to give them an opportunity to correct the error or omission (r34B). An applicant will have 10 business days to correct the application from the date on which the notification was sent. They will only get one chance to correct it, so if they miss that opportunity the applicant will receive a Notice of Invalidity.

Although the rule states only that the HO *may* contact the applicant to give them this opportunity, the Application Guidance, states that they *must* do so in respect of informing the applicant about: having used an incorrect form; having paid an incorrect fee; having erroneously included a dependant where the form does not allow this; having attempted multiple applications; or a variation where no variation can be made. But where the HO has discretion, it must be exercised, unless there is a good reason for not doing so, e.g. if the HO decides to treat the application as valid despite the error. The *may* in the Rules, should therefore be read as *must*.

If the HO decide that the application is invalid and reject it *without having given the person the opportunity to correct it*, that decision may itself be unlawful for failure to apply the rules. Where the person has become an overstayer as a result, they must challenge the HO decision; firstly, because they will be subject to all the prohibitions of the *hostile environment*, including losing their employment (upon which they may have been relying for the application). And secondly, because they may not be able to make a further application in these circumstances!

As explained below, making an application as an overstayer is governed (in most categories of the rules) by the requirements of paragraph 39E (for applications made on or after 24 November 2016). Where a person who has become an overstayer because the application they made was rejected as invalid, it is unlikely that any fresh application will meet the requirements of para 39E. This is because that person is treated as having overstayed from the date their actual leave expired and not from the date the application was rejected as invalid (as noted in the guidance Applications from overstayers (non family routes) Guidance and the Supreme Court in Mirza [2016] UKSC 63).

By the time the person has been informed by the HO that the application is invalid, they will probably have overstayed more than the 14-day maximum period allowed for in para 39E. In any case, para 39E requires them to show that the application was made late for a good reason beyond the control of the person or their adviser. It is unlikely they will be able to persuade the HO that they made an invalid application for such reasons. If they cannot make a further application, they may have no option but to leave the UK. Note that in these circumstances a person who overstays more than 30 days before leaving the UK may face a re-entry ban when seeking to return (see Module 2.3 on Grounds for refusal in Module 2).

Examples

Anna makes an application for an extension of leave to remain. She forgets to include the payment details for her credit card authorisation on her paper form. Her application is returned to her as invalid.

Anna's application is invalid (R34(3)); payment is a fundamental requirement which cannot be waived.

James makes an application for an extension of leave to remain. He applied on the wrong form. His application is returned to him as invalid.

James's application is invalid (R34(1)(a)); the Home Office had a discretion to contact him and give him an opportunity to correct his mistake (R34B(1)). If no consideration was given to that possibility, it may be that their decision could be challenged as unlawful. However as administrative review is not available with regard to invalidity decisions, judicial review would be the only route of challenge.

Further notes/ information

1.5.3.2 How to challenge decisions on invalidity

The Home Office sometimes reject applications, claiming them to be invalid when they are in fact valid, e.g. where the HO loses an applicant's photos or passport, and then allege the applicant did not include them with the application. It can also happen where the HO claim that they have not been able to collect the fee from the applicant's bank, but the bank has no record of such an approach and the relevant account is in funds. These problems have been largely eliminated by the online procedures, which no longer require photographs and which require online payment by the applicant.

In the reported decision of *Basnet* [2012] UKUT 113 (IAC), the Upper Tribunal (IAC) looked at a case where the HO claimed that the applicant's bank refused to forward them the fee. The UT held that the burden of proof was on the HO to establish that the fault was with the applicant rather than with the HO (who, for example, might have mistyped the credit card number). The HO might be expected to produce records from the GCID casework information database.

So if you are faced with an allegation of invalidity, do all you can to work out who was at fault. Check:

- Can the client show that they had sufficient funds in the relevant account over the period during which payment authority was sought

- Any copy of the application that shows whether the right credit card details were given

If you can show that an invalidity application is not sustainable, your client's situation may suddenly change quite radically. Previously they would be treated as an overstayer, firmly within the hostile environment. But in reality it may be that the HO has made an unsustainable allegation undermining their own decision. So the application may have to be treated as still awaiting a lawful decision. Thus the client would remain on s3C leave.

Casework tip

Because of the implications of the hostile environment, the HO needs to be informed immediately of their mistake. That can be done by a letter of representations, or a letter submitted under the *pre-action protocol* for judicial reviews, which needs to be done by either a solicitor or an OISC Level 3 adviser specifically accredited and authorised to conduct judicial review matter.

1.5.4 Applying as an overstayer – Rule 39E

Rule 39 E comes in three sections (r39E(1) and (r39E(2) and (r39(3))

Level 1 work is limited to making applications under r39E (1).

r39E (1)

Whilst an applicant must normally apply for an extension of stay whilst their leave remains current, paragraph 39E of the Rules provides for two limited exceptions to this rule. Under the first exception (r39E(1)), an application made no later than 14 days after the person's leave has expired will be accepted and decided by the HO if the decision maker is satisfied that there was a *good reason beyond the control of the applicant or their representative*, provided in or with the application, why the application could not have been made in-time.

What is a *good reason beyond the control of the applicant or their representative*? Some examples are provided in the HO guidance, Applications from overstayers (non family routes) Guidance. These are:

- the applicant was admitted to hospital for emergency treatment (evidenced by an official letter verifying the dates of admission and discharge and the nature of the treatment)
- a close family bereavement
- an educational institution was not sufficiently prompt in issuing a Confirmation of Acceptance for Studies

When considering the reason given, the HO decision maker must give thought to:

- the plausibility of the reasons
- whether the reason was genuinely outside the applicant's control or whether the applicant is describing difficulties that could realistically have been surmounted
- the credibility of evidence provided.

Further notes/information

r39E (2)

This work is outside the scope of level 1 work and should be referred on to a suitable accredited advisor.
Under the second exception (r39E (2)), where an in-time application has been refused, a further extension application can be made within a 14-day period. On 6 July 2018 this rule was amended to clarify that it is not possible to benefit from the exceptions for over stayers twice in a row, i.e. that the refused application must itself have been an in-time application.

That 14-day period under para 39E (2) will begin on the day immediately following *one* of the events below:

-the refusal of a previous application, or

-the expiry of a period of 3C leave, or

-following the time limit for submitting an administrative review or appeal, or

-the conclusion of an administrative review or appeal

The question as to which one of the above events is relevant in any particular case is a complex one, but important for working out when the 14-day window for making a further application begins and ends. To answer it, you must understand how s3C leave operates in the context of the appeals and administrative review procedures. It is also important to understand that following a refusal of an extension application, a person cannot make a further application for an extension whilst they still have s3C leave. They *must* become an overstayer in order to make the application**. This may require a person to wait for their automatic 3C leave to expire before making the application**. An application made by a person who still has 3C leave in the period immediately following the refusal of their previous application will be a void application.

See below for some worked examples to help understand if and when, following a rejected or refused application, a further application can be made.

If the application was made *more than* 14 days after the person's leave expired, the HO will not be able to accept it under the Rules (although it always has discretion to do so outside the Rules in very exceptional circumstances). Note though that for applications made before 24 November 2016, the rules generally provided for late applications made up to 28 days after the person's leave had expired, without having to provide an explanation for the delay. The explanatory memorandum to HC667 explains:

This 28 day period was originally brought in so that people who had made an innocent mistake were not penalised, but retaining it sends a message which is inconsistent with the need to ensure compliance with the United Kingdom's immigration laws.

The withdrawal of the 28-day period reflects the government's ever toughening approach to irregular migrants (and to immigration generally).

Where accepted by the HO, the application made within the 14-day period will be considered under the Immigration Rules in the normal way. But the applicant will continue to be an overstayer until further leave is granted. They will have committed a criminal offence by overstaying, albeit one that seems rarely to be prosecuted (IA 1971 s 24(1)(b)).

They will also be vulnerable to the 'hostile environment', including (but not limited to):

-Losing their right to work and to receive benefits as they do not have the benefit of a statutory extension of leave under s3C of IA 1971

-Committing a further offence if they continue to work or drive

-Losing rental accommodation

-Vulnerability to detention and removal. They will be a person who requires leave but does not have it, and are liable to removal without notice under the 'single decision' procedure

-If they have a right to appeal a refusal, they may not get the chance to exercise it in the UK

The guidance to employers makes it clear that they cannot continue to employ a person who has overstayed, even if they have a current application awaiting consideration under the Immigration Rules. Every effort must therefore be made to make an in-time application, even if that means applying whilst the person awaits a new passport or before all the relevant documents are available. A person should be given time to correct an invalid application under para 34B, and missing documents can be submitted after the application is made if necessary (on the basis that the HO should consider all the documents they have at the date of decision). **The 14-day period of overstaying under the Rules should only be relied on where there is absolutely no other option.**

r39E (3)

This work is outside the scope of level 1 work and should be referred on to a suitable accredited advisor.
Under the third exception (r39E (3)), any overstaying which occurred between 24 January and 31 August 2020 is disregarded (in recognition of widespread disruption due to the COVID-19 pandemic). Obviously, this is no longer relevant for applications by overstayers but may be arguable when retrospectively challenging refusals during that period on the sole ground of overstaying.

Example 1

Barney is present as a student and wants to apply for an extension of leave. He was not able to submit his application on time because the college was late in forwarding his Confirmation of Acceptance of Studies (CAS). After repeatedly chasing the college, Barney now possesses the CAS, so wants to make the application. He is worried he may be late.

Barney will need to provide a good reason beyond his control justifying the lateness. He will need to show evidence that he tried to obtain the CAS in time and the efforts he has since made to chase up the missing document.

Example 2: An eligible decision

Socrates makes an initial in-time application to extend his stay. His leave runs out whilst waiting for a decision. He will have continuing leave under s3C from the date his leave runs out until the date of decision.

The application is refused. The refusal is an 'eligible' decision and therefore comes with a right of administrative review (AR). His s3C leave is automatically extended for a further 14-day period from the date he received the decision to allow him to apply for AR.

Socrates has several options now. To maintain his 3C leave, he will need to apply for AR before the deadline. If he does, 3C leave will cover him until he gets a decision from the AR. If the AR is refused, his 3C leave will end on the day after he receives the decision (presuming he has no right to bring a further AR). He will then have 14 days from the date of receiving the AR refusal to lodge a new application relying on para 39E(2).

Alternatively, if Socrates does not want to apply for an AR, he can make a further application (relying on para 39E(2)) during the 28-day period following receipt of the refusal. The 28-day period will be made up of the 14-day period his leave will be automatically extended under s3C, and the additional 14-day period of overstaying allowed for under para 39E(2).

Socrates can make a fresh application during the 14-day period in which his leave is extended under s3C because the Rules governing the AR process operate to bring that 3C leave to an end automatically on the lodging of a new application for leave. That provision is at Appendix AR2.10(b). The person's s3C leave will be treated as having ended on the day before the new application is lodged.

This provision does not apply to refusals which are appealable decisions. It is not possible to make an application whilst an appeal is proceeding, or during the period over which s3C leave applies during which an 'in-time' appeal could be brought. You cannot make a further application for leave during the 14-day period of 3C leave immediately following the refusal being sent to you. If the person tries to do so, it will be a 'void' application and will be rejected

Example 3: Eligible or appealable decision

Abdi makes an initial application to extend his stay, but makes it late, within the 14-day period following the expiry of his leave. The HO accepts that the delay was for good reason beyond his control, so applies para 39E(1) and decides the application. The application is refused for other reasons.

Abdi cannot make a further application without risking automatic refusal for excess overstaying. His leave had already expired when he made the last application; so of course it will have expired some time ago by the time he comes to make a new application

If he chooses instead to apply for AR or appeal, and those challenges are ultimately unsuccessful, or withdrawn, he will have 14 days from the date that the appeal or AR was no longer pending in order to make a fresh application.

Example 4: The rejection of an invalid application

Kiran makes an initial in-time application to extend her stay. Her leave runs out whilst waiting for a decision, so she has continuing leave under s3C from the date her leave runs out until the date of decision (or at least appears to have). But the application is found to be invalid (e.g. because she did not submit her passport).

She does not use the 10-day window provided by the HO to correct the omission. The HO serve on the applicant a Notice of Invalidity. That brings her 3C leave to an end, but the decision will apply retrospectively and she will be treated as never having had 3C leave.

So, by the time Kiran receives the Notice of Invalidity, she will probably have overstayed by more than 14 days, and will not be able to make a further application in reliance on para 39E(1). Nor will she be able to make a further application relying in para 39E(2) because it only allows a further application to be made following a refusal (and not following the application being rejected for invalidity).

If Kiran is seeking to extend her stay in a category to which para 39E applies, she will not be able to apply again from within the UK.

1.5.5 Prohibition on multiple applications

The Rules make it clear that a person can only have one outstanding application at a time. Thus multiple applications are now forbidden under Rule 34BB.

- An applicant may only have one outstanding application extant
- A further application will be treated as a variation of the existing one
- **If simultaneous applications are made on the same day, both are treated as invalid**; however the Home Office may give an opportunity to withdraw one or both within 10 days of the notification of potential invalidity being sent (the application guidance says they *must*)

The Home Office Guidance on Applications for leave to remain emphasises that a single form cannot be used for multiple applications.

Unless the application is made in respect of a human rights route (i.e. on the basis of family or private life), the HO policy is, unhelpfully, to ignore other issues raised in a covering letter or in a section 120 notice (see section 'Attempts to make multiple applications in a single form' in the Applications Guidance).

1.5.6 Withdrawing an application

Where an applicant applies for their passport's return for travel purposes outside the common travel area, the application is deemed withdrawn at the date of the request: r34J & r34K.

1.5.7 Applications forms and fees

Applications for an extension of stay/leave (terms which can be used interchangeably) can be made by post or courier or, sometimes, in person or online (see more below on these different processes).

The specified forms, and a list of current fees can be found on the GOV.UK website at:

https://www.gov.uk/immigration-operational-guidance/fees-forms

Dependants: Where explicitly stated on it, an application form can include dependants, including, where applicable, children over 18 (rule 34C). Otherwise, the dependant must use their own form.

In-country extension and regularisation applications

1.5.7.1 Forms

The main non-PBS, non-EEA application forms are as follows:

Form NTL (No Time Limit)

Use this online form to apply for a biometric residence permit confirming the person has indefinite leave. The same online form has also replaced previously paper Form TOC for limited leave. This will be necessary, for example, where the grant of leave was in a passport that has now expired.

Form FLR (M)

Use this online form to apply for an extension of stay as the partner (together with any dependent children) of a person present and settled in the UK, or of a person with limited leave in the UK with refugee leave or humanitarian protection (or of a person with pre-settled status or limited leave under Appendix ECAA extension of stay). This will usually be for a partner application under Appendix FM on the five-year route.

Form FLR (FP)

Use this online form to apply for an extension of stay for applications in any of the following categories:

- Private life in the UK
- Family life as a partner (10-year route)
- Family life as a parent of a child in the UK (five year and10-year routes)
- Dependent child of a person who has, or is at the same time applying for, limited leave to enter or remain in the UK other than under the points-based system or UK Ancestry (10-year route)
- Leave outside the Rules on the basis of family or private life

Form FLR (DL)

- This is an online form, and is intended for anyone who, following refusal of asylum, has been granted Discretionary Leave, and is now applying for a further period of Discretionary Leave or settlement, in accordance with the published Home Office Asylum Instruction on Discretionary Leave. Note that the refusal of asylum does not have to have been followed immediately by the initial grant of DL. There may have been many years between those decisions. This form must not be used by applicants applying for further leave on Article 3 medical grounds who must use form FLR(HRO).

Form FLR (HRO)

Use this online form to apply for these types of application:

- discretionary leave (DL) if you have previously been granted DL but have not previously been refused asylum, or have been granted less than four years exceptional leave
- medical grounds or ill health
- human rights claims (not to be used for claims on the grounds of family or private life, including on the basis of family dependencies between a parent and a child, or for protection (asylum) claims)
- leave outside the Rules under the policy concessions in the leave outside the Rules guidance claims for leave outside the Immigration Rules because of compassionate and compelling circumstances
- other claims not covered by another form

Form FLR (LR)

Use this online form to apply for an extension of stay in the UK under the 10-year long residence rule

Form FLR (IR)

Use this online form for these types of application:

- visitors (except transit, Approved Destination Status and Permitted Paid Engagements visitors)
- UK ancestry
- domestic worker in a private household
- domestic worker who is a victim of slavery or human trafficking
- parent of a Child student
- dependant joiners who are applying separately from the main applicant – dependants of a person who has limited leave to enter or remain in the UK, not including dependants of a person with leave under the points-based system or dependants of a person in the UK with leave on the basis of family or private life
- relevant civilian employee
- member of an Armed Force who is subject to immigration control (course F)
- dependant of a member of Armed Forces which are not HM Forces (dependants of a member of HM Forces should complete FLR(AF))
- representative of an overseas business

Form FLR (AF)

Use this online form to apply for an extension of stay for applications in any of the following categories:

- limited leave as a HM Forces member on discharge
- limited leave as the partner and child of a British or foreign or Commonwealth HM Forces sponsor under Appendix Armed Forces
- limited leave as the partner or child whose sponsor was discharged from HM Forces
- limited leave as the partner or child of a British HM forces sponsor applying under transitional arrangements under Part 8 of the Immigration Rules
- limited leave as the partner or child of a foreign or Commonwealth HM forces sponsor applying under transitional arrangements under Part 7 of the Immigration Rules

For settlement the form is SET(AF), which is now also an online form.

Form FLR (P)

Use this online form to apply for an extension of stay in the UK as a child under the age of 18 of a relative with limited leave to enter or remain in the UK as a refugee or beneficiary of humanitarian protection. Or as parents, grandparents or other dependent relatives aged over 18 of persons with limited leave to enter or remain in the UK as a refugee or beneficiary of humanitarian protection and for a biometric immigration document.

Form FLR (S)

This online form is to apply for leave to remain in the UK, and a biometric residence permit, as a stateless person

Form SET (M)

Use this form to apply for indefinite leave to remain in the United Kingdom as the spouse (husband or wife), civil partner or unmarried partner of a person who is present and settled in the UK.

Form SET (DV)

This online form is used specifically for applying for settlement under the Immigration Rules for victims of domestic violence or abuse whose relationships have broken down during the probationary period because of that domestic violence.

Form SET (F)

Use this online form to apply for indefinite leave to remain as the:

- child under age of 18 of a parent, of parents or a relative present and settled in the UK
- adopted child under the age of 18 of a parent or parents present and settled in the UK
- child aged over 18 of persons present and settled in the UK

Form SET (O)

Use this online form to apply for indefinite leave to remain in the United Kingdom when approaching five years of continuous leave to remain in the United Kingdom in one of the following categories:

- work permit holder
- dependant of work permit holder
- PBS dependant
- employment not requiring a work permit
- businessperson
- innovator
- investor

- self-employed lawyer
- writer, composer or artist
- Tier 1 (Entrepreneur) migrant
- Tier 1 (Entrepreneur) migrant – accelerated route
- Tier 1 (Investor) migrant
- Tier 1 (Investor) migrant – accelerated route
- Tier 2 migrant
- UK ancestry
- bereaved partner
- other purposes not covered by other application forms

Form SET (P)

Use this online form to apply for indefinite leave to remain in the United Kingdom when approaching five years of continuous leave to remain in the United Kingdom as a refugee or person granted humanitarian protection.

Form SET (LR)

Use this online form to apply for indefinite leave to remain (settlement) in the UK under the 10 year long residence rules. It is possible to extend leave for two years on this basis if not all requirements are met. The online version of former FLR(LR) is here.

Application process for the EU Settlement Scheme

This form has no name and is accessed via the "Apply" button on the page entitled "Apply to the EU Settlement Scheme (settled and pre-settled status)". The form for family permit applications is accessible via the same page under "if you're joining your EU, EEA or Swiss citizen family member".

Application process for EEA/Swiss citizens who are frontier workers

Both the form to apply from within the UK and from outside the UK have no name but are accessible via the "Apply now" buttons on page "Frontier Worker permit".

Application process for EEA/Swiss national S2 Healthcare Visitors

This online form is accessible via the page "Enter the UK as an S2 Healthcare Visitor"

Application process for Service Providers from Switzerland

This online form is accessible via the page "Apply for a Service providers from Switzerland visa"

Application process for entry clearance as a visitor

These are accessible via the basic guidance pages listed on page "Browse: Visit the UK"

Application process for work, study and family entry clearance

These are accessible via the following basic guidance page:

- https://www.gov.uk/browse/visas-immigration/work-visas
- https://www.gov.uk/browse/visas-immigration/student-visas
- https://www.gov.uk/browse/visas-immigration/family-visas

Citizenship application forms

These are found on this page https://www.gov.uk/government/collections/citizenship-application-forms

Other forms

All other forms are found on page https://www.gov.uk/government/collections/uk-visa-forms

Casework tip ***Always read the introduction of the Form you are about to use in order to ensure that you are using the right one.***

1.5.7.2 Fees and exemptions

These forms must be accompanied by the correct fee, where applicable, and current fee levels can be checked here. Fees are reduced, in some cases, for applications from citizens of countries that are signatory to the European Social Charter.

The fees must be paid for each applicant, including dependants.

The fees linked to above are for online applications. For applications made in person at the visa premium service centre (formerly the public enquiry office) there is an additional fee on top of the online application fee. For premium appointments, booked for early morning or evening (i.e. outside normal office hours), there is an additional fee. The Super Premium service, where a mobile Home Office unit comes to you, costs an additional amount again.

Some individuals are exempt from paying fees for applications:

- people applying for Indefinite Leave to Remain on the grounds of domestic violence where, at the time of making the application, the applicant appears to be destitute (or has been granted leave under the DDV concession);
- children under 18 and receiving local authority support;
- persons granted limited leave to remain whilst they were under 18 on the rejection of their claim for asylum and who are now applying for further leave to remain;
- nationals of Turkey and their dependants who are applying under Appendix ECAA Extension of Leave;
- applicants under the EU Settlement Scheme, including family permits
- applicants for frontier worker permits
- those applying for leave to remain where the basis of their claim is asylum or Article 3 ECHR.

1.5.7.3 Premium Service and Online Applications

It may be possible to pay for a faster decision on a visa or settlement ('indefinite leave to remain') application if the person is applying in the UK. This will depend on which visa is being applied for. There are two standards of service, Priority and Super Priority.

Whether this is possible depends on which visa is being applied for. This can be checked out by reading the guidance for the visa that is being applied for and the page "Get a faster decision on your visa or settlement application"

Priority Service – Decision within 5 working days

If eligible for the priority service you can chose the "priority service" when you apply. It costs an extra £500 on top of the normal application fee.

A decision will be made within 5 working days of the UK Visa and Citizen Application Services (UKVCAS) appointment.

Super Priority Service – Decision by the end of the next working day

If eligible for the super priority service you can chose the "super priority service" when you apply. It costs an extra £800 on top of the normal application fee.

A decision will be made:

- by the end of the next working day after your UKVCAS appointment if your appointment is on a weekday
- 2 working days after your UKVCAS appointment if your appointment is at the weekend

Working days are Monday to Friday, not including bank holidays

People using this service will receive an email when a decision has been made, followed by a decision letter in the post.

The email will only give the outcome of the application if it's been approved. If it's refused, the applicant will not find out until they receive letter.

Biometric Residence Permit

This will normally be received 7 – 10 days of the decision. It will be sent to the address that was given in the application.

There may be a longer wait for the decision if more information is required. They will be informed of how and when it should be provided.

1.5.7.4 Online Applications

Most visa applications can or should be made online. You can check out whether this is available or essential here https://www.gov.uk/apply-to-come-to-the-uk and here https://www.gov.uk/settle-in-the-uk

1.5.7.5 Fee waivers

The courts have held that there has to be a possibility of a fee waiver if the alternative would be a breach of a person's human rights. As explained in the Home Office Guidance Fee waiver: Human Rights-based and other specified applications, fee waivers are available for human rights applications generally, where further leave to remain is sought. However waivers are not available for other kinds of application, nor for settlement applications (even where predicated on a human rights claim).

Fee waiver application procedure

Before 1 November 2018 a fee waiver application raised a real practical problem: by the time it was decided, the applicant's leave might have expired. So if the fee was *not* waived, the application would be deemed invalid. This was a major disincentive to making waiver applications unless finances were truly desperate. There was then an interim fix, the HO allowing unsuccessful applicants caught in this situation 10 days to pay the fee. But if they could not, they would then become an overstayer and enter the hostile environment.

On 1 November 2018 r34G in Part 1 was amended and on 13 December 2018 the paper forms for all types of applications to which fee waivers apply, were withdrawn (see bottom of online form pages FLR(M); FLR(FP); FLR(DL) and FLR(HRO), which state 'you must now apply online'). Under this procedure, an applicant who wishes to apply for a fee waiver will have to submit it online (the previous paper form Appendix 1 also having been withdrawn) *before* the application for leave, and this will be considered first. The applicant will be notified of a decision on the request for a fee waiver and will have 10 working days from the date they receive this notification to submit an application for leave. If the substantive application is then made in time, i.e. within 10 working days of receiving the fee waiver decision, the *date of application will be the date the fee waiver request was submitted.* This is important because it protects an applicant's continuing leave whilst they make their application for further leave, mirroring the effect of s3C of the 1971 Act.

If the fee waiver request is granted, the applicant will be able to submit an application for leave without an accompanying application fee.

If the fee waiver request is refused, the applicant may still submit an application accompanied by the relevant fee within 10 working days, for the initial application date (the date of the fee waiver application) to preserve continuing leave under these provisions.

1.5.7.6 The Immigration Health Surcharge

The Immigration Health Surcharge (IHS) was introduced for all applications for entry clearance or leave to remain made on or after 6 April 2015.

This is payable for each dependent as well as the main applicant. There is guidance available here at Immigration Health Surcharge and on page "Pay for UK healthcare as part of your immigration application". This page sets out how much is payable in which category and it states, at the time of writing.

You'll have to pay:

- *£470 per year for a student or Youth Mobility Scheme visa, for example £940 for a 2-year visa*
- *£470 per year for visa and immigration applicants who are under the age of 18 at time of application*
- *£624 per year for all other visa and immigration applications, for example £3,120 for a 5-year visa*

Dependants usually need to pay the same amount as you.
The exact amount you have to pay depends on how much leave you're granted. Calculate how much you'll have to pay before you apply.
You'll pay half of the yearly amount if your application includes part of a year that is less than 6 months.
You'll pay for a whole year if your application includes part of a year that is more than 6 months.

You'll automatically get a partial refund if you paid the healthcare surcharge for more years than you were granted leave.

Liability for the charge is as follows:

- All applications for entry clearance *other than* those for indefinite leave to enter fiancés and visits of six months or less. Visitors will be expected to pay for NHS treatment at the point of use. NB: In some cases where the IHS should not apply, such as child settlement under Part 8, payment of the charge has been required at point of application, with a later refund if indefinite leave to enter (rather than a different, temporary form of leave) is granted.
- All applications from within the UK for any period of time other than indefinite leave to remain

If an application is made for ILR but limited leave is granted, the surcharge will become payable and the Home Office will require payment before the BRP is issued. The guidance sets out who needs to pay how much, and who is exempt. Some applicants must still use the service to obtain a reference number whereas others are exempt.

1.5.8 Decisions – professional skills and conduct relevant to dealing with decisions

A well prepared and properly evidenced application which meets the requirements of the Immigration Rules *should* be granted by the Home Office. **In practice, applications may be refused for all kinds of reasons**, many of which may be unexpected and unwarranted. Decision makers may overlook documents that have been submitted, ignore representations and witness statements, and adopt interpretations of the law that may be inconsistent with their own guidance.

Advisors should **always warn clients** that they may receive a disappointing decision and that appeals, where available, are routinely allowed by immigration judges. Where there is no right of appeal, an administrative Review may secure a favourable result.

Where an applicant may have the choice of **challenging a decision or applying again**, it will be necessary to **factor in** not only the relevant **costs and timescales**, but also a careful consideration of **s3C** of the

Immigration Act 1971, the **consequences of overstaying** and, where r39E applies, whether a further application can be made at all.

It will always **reduce the chance of a left-field decision if the application is well prepared**, **in form as well as in content**. The documentation should be easy to find and well ordered. Every application must be supported by a covering letter laying out the basic law relied upon, usually a category of the Immigration Rules or a provision of the Immigration (EEA) Regulations 2016, listing the enclosures, and explaining their purpose. Statements from the applicant (and other family members or others where relevant) are useful to explain the applicant's circumstances, put each document into context and show that each of the requirements of the rules is met.

Top Tip

A true legal professional never assumes that the law remains the same since they last made a similar application. A policy can be withdrawn at any moment, and Immigration Rules can be altered without very much notice at all. Remember:

Always check the legal framework as it is now (and remember that the legal framework may include HO guidance/policy documents)

Check whether any relevant Rules are about to be amended (and never let any client think the Rules are set in stone)

Further notes/information

Always check the legal framework as it was at the date of decision.

Legal professionals should always know the foundation for any legal principle that they rely upon, for example for many years there was a policy that applied to children allowing them to remain in this country if they had resided here for seven years and their removal would be unreasonable. This was withdrawn several years ago, and was not resurrected until Appendix FM was introduced. Now it has an even firmer footing, as it is found in section 117 of the NIA 2002.

Vague references to the 'seven-year rule' risk failing to appreciate the differing legal foundations of the principle over time, moving as it did from policy, then disappearing, then being resurrected via the Rules before moving onto the statute book.

Module 2: Navigating the Immigration Rules

The Immigration Rules (HC 395) set out the rules for entry to and stay in the UK for people who are subject to immigration control, and is the single most important document in immigration law. They must be consulted and strictly adhered to for all types of immigration applications for people subject to immigration control

The power to make the rules comes from section 3(2) of the Immigration Act 1971:

> The Secretary of State shall from time to time (and as soon as may be) lay before Parliament statements of the rules, or of any changes in the rules, laid down by him as to the practice to be followed in the administration of this Act for regulating the entry into and stay in the United Kingdom of persons required by this Act to have leave to enter, including any rules as to the period for which leave is to be given and the conditions to be attached in different circumstances...

The rules include a list of the purposes or categories under which people can enter and/or remain in the UK – e.g. for protection, to visit, to study, for employment, business and investment, and for family reasons. A few purposes though remain outside the rules.

Together with the government's policy of increasingly micro-managing immigration, this means that the Immigration Rules have become extremely long and convoluted. This manual can only really provide an overview of the Immigration Rules, which now run to more than 1000 pages. Indeed, no textbook or training course can substitute for consistent reference to the constantly changing and hugely complex matrix of Rules.

There is no alternative but for advisers to work directly from the Immigration Rules themselves. The only up to date and comprehensive version of the Immigration Rules is on the GOV.UK website here, in the form of a drop-down index.

The Immigration Rules are difficult to navigate. Critical information has been placed into the Immigration Rules in arbitrary places, and into an increasing number of appendices.

The employment of the term "Appendix" gives the impression that these contain merely additional information, but that is not the case. In fact, the main body of the immigration rules for work, study or family migration is currently contained in appendices to the rules. The reason for this is that the rules are currently undergoing a complete overhaul in an effort of simplification, and until most categories have been thus simplified, the overall structure will not be decided.

Advisers must avoid the temptation to work solely from the guidance to applicants provided on the GOV.UK website as this is neither comprehensive nor always accurate.

Each category of the Immigration Rules (e.g. visitors in Appendix Visitor, the main worker route in Appendix Skilled Worker, the remainder of the old Points Based system in Part 6A, family members in Appendix FM) has been drafted in different formats, but will generally contain;

- An outline of the purpose of the category
- A definition of criteria used in the category (though paragraph 6 of the Immigration Rules also contains important definitions of key words and phrases). It cannot be presumed that words in the Immigration Rules have their ordinary or common-sense meaning, so it is important to see how they are defined for the purpose of a particular rule.
- The specific requirements that must be met for entry clearance or leave/permission to enter, for an extension of stay, and for indefinite leave to remain where available. The requirements of the rules are different for each of these types of application
- Specified (i.e. mandatory) documents – detailing both their form and content – that must be submitted with the application
- The period of leave that will be granted
- The conditions that will be placed on the grant of leave (e.g. no recourse to public funds, prohibition on working – see more on conditions below)
- The circumstances in which the application will be refused

Many terms used by the Rules are defined by the Rules themselves, or within the definitions at Rule 6.

Top Tip

No two categories follow the same pattern. It is important to read the Immigration Rules carefully and look for what is NOT in the Immigration Rules as much as what IS in them.

For example:

The student category contains no provision relating to a grant of ILR, so a migrant who is in the UK as a student cannot apply for ILR under the student category

The Rules in Appendix FM for adult dependent relatives are all expressed by reference to entry clearance applications, so there is no route under the Rules for an application for leave to remain in that capacity (i.e. there is no possibility, within the Rules, of switching into this category)

The Temporary Worker (T5) categories make no reference to English language requirements: so an Applicant does not have to satisfy any such requirements.

2.1 Immigration history and subject access requests

When you first take on a case, it is imperative to obtain a proper immigration history of the individual. Some people may have a perfect record of their dealings with the Home Office, or, if they have received a refusal of an application, it may be that they can confirm that the Home Office has perfectly summarised their history. However, there may be cases where there is more to their history than is apparent from existing documents.

You can fill the gap: via a 'subject access request', and for any case with a significant procedural history, it will be advisable for an appellant's representative to obtain this.

Subject access requests can be made via an online form on the page which also contains the procedural requirements here https://www.gov.uk/government/publications/requests-for-personal-data-uk-visas-and-immigration/request-personal-information-held-by-uk-visas-and-immigration and can be made at the basic, specific or detailed level. All types are free.

There is a right of complaint to the Information Commissioner if the material is not provided in time, or is thought incomplete, and then onwards to the Information Tribunal. There is some guidance on disclosure on the Home Office website.

Sch 2, Pt 1, para 4 of the Data Protection Act 2018 contains the controversial 'immigration control' exemption under which the HO can refuse to provide information. How this plays out in practice remains to be seen. ILPA updates should be consulted regarding this issue.

Top Tip

Before starting to work out a client's future options, you should be able to produce a comprehensive immigration history in a form equivalent to this:

'Mr …………… is a citizen of ……… born. He obtained an entry clearance granted on ,,,,,,,,,,,. and was granted leave to enter on ………… as a ……….. His leave was subsequently extended in that capacity until ………… [and subsequently in the same or other categories]. He made an application for further leave to remain as a ………….. on ……….. and that was refused on ………..'

This will, in any case, constitute the "instructions" section of your initial advice letter, addressing the client directly ("you instructed me that…" "you told me that…").

Without such details of a person's history, you are simply not in a position to comprehensively and accurately advise them of their present status and future options.

2.1.1 Transitional provisions

When changes are made to the Immigration Rules, transitional provisions often accompany them. They will usually state that applications submitted before the date of a rules change will be considered under the rules in place before the change. In effect, in the time period following a change, there will be two or more sets of rules running side by side, covering similar purposes, but applicable to different migrants.

Usefully, there are archived versions of the Immigration Rules as they stood at various dates in the past on the GOV.UK website (see the 'Archive: Immigration Rules' link on the Immigration Rules page).

Top Tip

Beware – the transitional provisions are *seldom* in the Rules. Usually they are found in the Statement of Changes that introduces the new Rules. All statements of changes dating back to 1994 are accessible here: https://www.gov.uk/government/collections/immigration-rules-statement-of-changes

When looking, for example, at statement of changes HC 1043, search via ctrl +F for the heading "Implementation". There you will find the list of dates when changes came into force, and a statement that the changes apply only to those applications made from the date of the change.

2.1.2 Closed immigration routes

Over the years, many categories within the Immigration Rules have been closed to new applicants. These include Tier 2 (General) which was the main work route. At 9 am on 1 December 2020, Appendix Skilled Worker took the place of all Tier 2 (General) provisions in Part 6A of the rules, which were deleted, although applications made before this time and date were still to be decided under the rules in place beforehand (and which remain accessible via the archive page https://www.gov.uk/government/collections/archive-immigration-rules).

All existing Tier 2 General migrants are now to extend their leave under Appendix Skilled Worker. The same is the case for Tier 4 students who will now extend their leave under Appendix Student, instead, as all Tier 4 rules in Part 6A have been deleted.

However, some routes are closed more gradually, allowing migrants to complete their route to settlement within their original category. This is done by, first, deleting the entry clearance rules under the category, then eventually the leave to remain category and lastly the ILR category, as was done in relation to Tier 1 (General).

2.2 Common requirements of the Immigration Rules

Many different immigration categories include similar provisions, and rather than repeat the information it is more convenient to deal with them in one place.

Rule 39B lays out the general requirements as to 'specified' documents (i.e. specified in the Immigration Rules) that must be provided in support of an application. Where specified, supporting documentation must meet the requirements of the rules both in respect of form and content. A 'nearly' document just won't do!

A specified document must be verifiable, and so must include the contact details of the person or organisation creating the document.

These days original documents generally need not be supplied. This means copies or scanned copies can now be provided instead (they are uploaded online as part of the application process). If there are doubts about whether a document is genuine, verification rules will apply.

Where not in English or Welsh, a document must be accompanied by a full translation which includes the translator's credentials, the date and the translator's signature, and confirms that it is an accurate translation.

2.2.1 Evidential flexibility/ 'Documents not submitted with applications'

Where a document is not available, a full explanation should be provided in a covering letter. The necessary document should be provided as soon as possible, and before a decision is made on the application.

Sending documents late is never ideal: it runs the risk that an application is decided without regard to the late documents, because the Home Office struggles to link correspondence. There is no obligation on the decision maker to await the arrival of late documents.

Where a critical document is not supplied by the time the decision is made, the application is likely to fail.

The phenomenon of missing documents and documents being submitted in the wrong format has led to the development of the concept of **'evidential flexibility'**, as the Home Office have acknowledged that there can be unfairness where a document is submitted in the wrong format, simply due to innocent error by an applicant. Over time this has taken different forms: at one time it existed simply as a Home Office policy. Later it entered the Rules, which now make some limited provision for:

- in the old-style Points Based System cases under Part 6A (the remaining rules being applicable to existing Tier 1 Entrepreneurs, and Tier 1 Investors), for missing or wrongly formatted documents (via rule 245AA(b)) (a rule that gives some leeway, but which rules out the exercise of discretion for a missing *specified document*), and
- in Appendix FM cases, for missing or wrongly formatted documents including specified documents (via paragraph D(b) of Appendix FM-SE) (quite a generous rule).

There is no *general* requirement that the Home Office contact an applicant where documents are in the wrong form or missing. So individuals applying outside the PBS or Appendix FM are especially vulnerable. But the HO should do so in the specific circumstances outlined in these Rules.

Missing/imperfect documents and the Points Based System

The HO may contact the applicant or his representative in writing, and request the correct documents in the following circumstances (r245AA(b):

- specified evidence is missing from the documents; or
- a document is in the wrong format (for example, if a letter is not on letterhead paper as specified); or
- a document does not contain all of the specified information;

There is then a discretion:

- To seek further documents beyond those submitted with the application
- The discretion only arises where there is some imperfection in the specified documents supplied: ***not where a class of specified document is missing altogether***
- To be exercised where a document is in ***the wrong format*** e.g. not on letterhead paper, or ***does not contain all of the relevant information***
- There is a fast turnaround for the information to be provided 'The requested documents must be received at the address specified in the request within 10 working days of the date of the request' (r245AA(b))
- The discretion need not be exercised where it is anticipated that the issue is not material because the application will fail for another reason – arguably, this cannot simply be another imperfect sequence/document related reason, as there is no limit on the documents that might be sought, but would have to relate to the general refusal reasons or some other fundamental inability to meet the Rules
- Where the missing information can be found in other documents with the application, or online, there is a discretion to overlook its absence, and grant the application exceptionally

Missing/imperfect documents and Family life applications

The other discretion is for Appendix FM applications. It is found at paragraph D(b) of Appendix FM-SE. It is more generous than the PBS version.

- It provides for the same discretion as to the provision of documents in the wrong format and for a document that does not contain all the specified information
- It also provides for an application to be granted where there is missing information but that information can be found elsewhere in the application or from the website of the issuing organisation or its regulatory body.
- And it provides for the lifting of a requirement to provide a specified document where there is a valid reason not to provide it: for example because it is not issued in a particular country or has been permanently lost (D(e))
- Finally, the time scale is less strict: 'The material requested must be received at the address specified in the request within a reasonable timescale specified in the request'.

Example

Jahan's entrepreneur extension application is refused because the independent lawyer's letter confirming the availability of third party support omits the name of the legal representative who wrote it. This is a case where document has been provided but not all of the specified information has been provided therein: accordingly discretion can be exercised under Rule 245AA(b)(iv)

Johnson's entrepreneur application is refused because a letter from his bank does not show that it is regulated by the Financial Conduct Authority and the Prudential Regulation Authority. Discretion can be exercised here, without even seeking further information from Johnson, if the website of the bank contains the relevant information: Rule 245AA(d).

2.2.3 Maintenance

Entry, leave to remain and settlement are usually contingent on a person being able to adequately maintain and accommodate themselves and any dependants without recourse to public funds. It is now enshrined in statute, at s117B(3) of NIAA 2002 which emphasises that the public interest, from an economic well-being perspective, is best served by admitting people who are financially independent.

This principle is put into effect across the Rules by a series of maintenance requirements, and by a condition placed on most grants of leave denying the holder recourse to public funds (which they would in any case be unable to claim due to welfare benefits law.

An equivalent rule is found in most categories, specifying the conditions of a grant including access to public funds.

There are also rules which permit a discretion to award access to public funds: see for example, within Appendix FM, GEN1.10, stating that where leave is granted under certain exemptions within the rules, that is 'subject to a condition of no recourse to public funds unless the decision-maker considers that the person should not be subject to such a condition'.

Where the principle applies, the rules differ as to precisely how the requirement is to be met. They will either

- stipulate that a person must be able to maintain and accommodate themselves adequately without recourse to public funds;
- provide, as under the Points Based System and the work- and study appendices, that an applicant must be able to demonstrate a fixed amount of savings in a prescribed form; or
- require, as for some applications under the family life categories of Appendix FM, a specified level of income and/or savings (unless the sponsor is in receipt of particular benefits).

This section looks at the requirements an applicant will need to meet in cases where the rule stipulates that they must be *able to maintain and accommodate themselves and any dependants adequately in the UK without recourse to public funds.*

This includes children applying to join or stay with their settled parent(s) in the UK (r287/298 in Part 8), and partners under Appendix FM where the settled partner is receiving one of the listed disability-related benefits (e.g. Rule rE-ECP.3.3)

Key principles on maintenance

- 'Public funds' are exhaustively defined
- There must be no additional recourse
- Income support provides an objective measure as to adequacy
- The adequacy requirement is not an excuse for inquiry into lifestyle
- Third party support is permitted in law, unless excluded by a specific rule (as it generally is now under the PBS and Appendix FM).

2.2.3.1 Meaning of public funds

Public funds are exhaustively listed in r6 of HC395 which contains a long list of forms of public funds. In a relevant case this list should be scrutinised with care.

The list is exhaustive in the sense that any benefit not included in the rule is not considered to be a public fund for the purposes of the immigration rules. As can be seen (by omission), there are some public funds, such as legal aid, education, contributory benefits such as contributory job seekers' allowance, and NHS care that are not included in the definition and are not therefore treated as public funds.

The UKVI Public Funds Guidance contains an extremely complex set of specific rules and exemptions which should always be checked when advising a client regarding their entitlements.

This is important because a person should not claim public funds or other services to which they are not legally entitled, to avoid problems with later immigration applications, for example:

- the general grounds for refusal in Part 9 of the Rules include provisions for refusal for breach of conditions: r9.8.1-9.8.2 (the rules used to address this possibility more expressly see eg r322(4) a 'failure by the person concerned to maintain or accommodate himself and any dependants without recourse to public funds'; or
- cancellation of permission under r9.8.8 - once permission has been curtailed, a person would face removal under s10 IAA 1999 as a person who requires leave but does not have it.

The fact that a public fund or service is wrongly granted to them will not protect the applicant if they were not entitled to it.

The expression 'recourse to public funds' is further defined within the Public Funds definition in r6 of HC395. In short

- entry is not prohibited where the sponsor is already claiming public funds but
- will be prohibited where the migrant relies on their sponsor's entitlement to increased or additional public funds as a result of their arrival in the UK.

It also enables the sponsor to use their pre-existing public funds to support the applicant

- as long as the level of support is still 'adequate' (see below).

This means that, for example, a sponsor already in receipt of disability living allowance can use those funds to support an applicant. This principle is recognised in Appendix FM where a partner or parent is in receipt of specified disability related benefits: thus, in an entry clearance case for a partner, as an alternative to meeting the strict financial requirements of holding certain levels of funds via admissible forms of evidence and savings, E-ECP.3.1 references an alternative route of showing adequate maintenance via E-ECP.3.3, which, if a relevant benefit is available, then poses the simple question as to whether adequate maintenance is available.

The definition prevents reliance on any future additional entitlement to child benefit or tax credit to establish the relevant financial requirements in an entry clearance application but 6B permits reliance on those sources of funds in extension or settlement applications.

2.2.3.2 Required level of income

Outside the Points Based System and the income/savings-based requirements in most parts of Appendix FM, the maintenance requirement is whether the available funds are 'adequate', which is defined at r 6:

> "Adequate" and "adequately" in relation to a maintenance and accommodation requirement means that, after income tax, national insurance contributions and housing costs have been deducted, there must be available to the person or family the level of income or funds that would be available to them if the person or family was in receipt of income support.

The latest and historic benefit levels can be checked on Rightsnet's website here.

The maintenance calculation formula is set out in guidance Family Migration: Appendix FM Section 1.7A – Adequate maintenance and accommodation :

> $A - B \geq C$ A minus B is greater than or equal to C.
>
> Where:
>
> A is the net income (after deduction of income tax and National Insurance contributions);
>
> B is housing costs (i.e. what needs to be spent on accommodation); and
>
> C is the amount of Income Support an equivalent British family of that size can receive.

When preparing an Appendix FM application, the specified evidence requirements for those who are relying on 'adequate maintenance' by way of benefits and/or earnings/savings are set out in paragraphs 12 and 12A of Appendix FM-SE. The requirements are rather lighter as to the volume of documents: there is a specific calculation as to how savings are to be treated at paragraph 12B, by which total cash savings are divided into the number of weeks for which leave would be granted if the application succeeded and then added to the other available income. Further guidance as to this is found in the above linked guidance 1.7A.

We deal with family migration and private life cases generally in Modules 5 and 6. However, for now, it is worth appreciating that where the reason the application fails is because of an inability to show the technical maintenance requirements of Appendix FM-SE, the application may still succeed under the 10 year route to settlement which requires that one of the exceptions be established (i.e. that there is a British citizen or seven-year resident child involved, or that there are insurmountable obstacles to family life abroad); whereas if an exception is not established, the application may still succeed if 'exceptional circumstances' under rrGEN3.1/GEN3.2 apply (see section 6.1.4 below).

Top Tip

In any immigration case where maintenance is in issue outside the strict requirements in Appendix A under the points-based system or Appendix FM, make sure that you make clear to the decision maker how it is that the level of income satisfies the Income Support level.

You can best do this by way of cross referencing from a witness statement, and/or via a table that shows the notional benefit entitlement.

Also explain

- any unusual patterns of income as shown by the bank statements provided
- discrepancies between earnings as suggested by pay slips and actual deposits into bank accounts
- any discrepancy between documents and the client's account of how they are paid and what their business activities actually care
- any other income from business interests or informal loans

2.2.3.3 Third party support

'Third party support' refers to support that is provided by an additional party, such as a parent, other relative or friend. This issue has been contentious, with the government long seeking to exclude such reliance.

An applicant under Appendix FM cannot normally rely on third party support except as allowed for in paragraph 1(b) of Appendix FM-SE. It permits third party support only by way of:

- Maintenance payments from a former partner
- Income from a dependent child now over 18 and remaining in the same household who is part of the Appendix FM financial requirements (i.e. because they were a minor when the application was originally granted, see E-ECP.3.2.(1)(a))
- A gift of cash savings, the source being declared, and now being held by the applicant, their partner, or an applicant child's parent, or in an adult dependent relative case, the sponsor or the applicant
- a maintenance grant or stipend associated with undergraduate or postgraduate study/research

It is only where 'exceptional circumstances' in GEN.3.1. of Appendix FM apply that the wider category of Third Party support in para 21A Appendix FM-SE becomes relevant (see Module 6).

The availability of third-party support depends on the particular terms of the rules. Under the visitor route, Appendix Visitor now makes express provision for third party support, at V4.3, from a legally resident person 'with a genuine professional or personal relationship' with the proposed visitor, where they 'can and will provide support to the visitor for the intended duration of their stay'.

Under the UK Ancestry route in Appendix UK Ancestry, such support is expressly permitted under rUKA 5.3.

Example

Azim has been studying in the UK with the support of an uncle. He has now married a British citizen and wishes to remain as a partner. Neither he nor his spouse have jobs, but Azim's uncle is happy to support them until they can manage on their own.

In this case, where the uncle already has a history of providing support, there is good reason to think that the support will be adequate and that the offer is well considered and genuine. However third party support is not allowed under the 5-year route to settlement in Appendix FM. So the only way for his uncle to help will be if a very significant sum of money is given to Azim by his uncle, by way of a gift. Azim will have to ask his uncle to give him £62,500 as a lump sum. If his uncle obliges, and Azim then holds this amount for six months before the application is made, it will be treated as his own savings rather than third party support (Appendix FM–SE 1(b)(iii)).

Were Azim applying as a visitor, say, or under the ancestry category, he could still rely on his uncle's support. Visitors are specifically permitted third party support (rV4.3 of Appendix Visitor). A UK ancestry applicant can show they meet the requirement to maintain and accommodate themselves and any dependents (in rUKA 5.1) via a credible offer of third-party support under rUKA 5.3.

2.2.3.4 Sponsors and undertakings

A maintenance undertaking is mandatory under the adult dependent relative category of Appendix FM, which states:

E-ECDR.3.2. If the applicant's sponsor is a British citizen or settled in the UK, the applicant must provide an undertaking signed by the sponsor confirming that the applicant will have no recourse to public funds, and that the sponsor will be responsible for their maintenance, accommodation and care, for a period of five years from the date the applicant enters the UK if they are granted indefinite leave to enter.

The undertaking will be legally enforceable, so that the DWP or Home Office can recoup any public funds subsequently claimed by a disobedient migrant (r35).

2.2.3.5 Joint sponsors

Previously under immigration rule 317, the old version of the adult dependent relative category, it was possible for joint sponsors (e.g. two siblings) to give undertakings.

The equivalent category under Appendix FM, for adult dependent relatives, though, does not appear to allow for joint sponsors directly. However, as the GEN.3.2 exception is always available under Appendix FM where any of the requirements are not met, although the exception has a very high threshold. Any such case should be referred to a suitably accredited adviser.

2.2.4 Adequate accommodation

Most categories of the Immigration Rules (but not the PBS) require that the applicant(s) and any family members they are joining in the UK have adequate accommodation available to them. The requirements for accommodation are found in Home Office Guidance: The guidance Family Migration: adequate maintenance and accommodation.

Key principles on accommodation:

- Third party provision is permitted
- Statutory overcrowding renders accommodation inadequate
- Adequacy can have a wider meaning

The Home Office does not object to with accommodation being provided by a third party.

Accommodation must be adequate for the person coming to the UK and for those already occupying the accommodation. For people seeking entry on a long-term basis there are three considerations to the question of whether accommodation is adequate.

Firstly, in family cases, the sponsor/applicant must 'own or exclusively occupy' the proposed accommodation. This is not quite as onerous as it sounds as the guidance states that:

> Accommodation can be shared with others. 'Occupy exclusively' is defined in paragraph 6 of the Immigration Rules and means that at least part of the accommodation must be for the exclusive use of the family.

Secondly, the proposed accommodation must not be overcrowded once the applicant arrives. Overcrowding is defined in paragraph 6 of the Immigration Rules by reference to the Housing Act 1985, the Housing (Scotland) Act 1987 or the Housing (Northern Ireland) Order 1988 (as appropriate). The test for whether a property will be overcrowded is based on the permitted number of persons in a room, and in the property as a whole.

The guidance states:

> A house is considered to be overcrowded if 2 persons aged 10 years or more of opposite sexes, who are not living together as husband and wife, must sleep in the same room.

The Act also details the maximum number of people allowed for a given number of rooms or a given room floor area.

Account is taken only of rooms with a floor area larger than 50 square feet and rooms of a type used either as a living room or bedroom.

Rooms such as kitchens or bathrooms are excluded.

Under the Housing Act, the number of people sleeping in accommodation must not exceed the following:

Rooms	Persons permitted
1	2
2	3
3	5
4	7.5
5	10

*	with an additional 2 persons for each room in excess of 5

For the purpose of the Act:

- a child under 1 does not count as a person
- a child aged 1 to10 years counts as only half a person

Top Tip

In a case where the availability of adequate accommodation is in issue, make sure that you prove adequacy by reference to the statutory requirements: i.e.

- obtain a report from a professional or independent agent (some Councils' Residential Services departments now provide property inspections for immigration purposes) or
- refer to documented floor space, if there is a tenancy agreement or other documents showing the size and number of rooms

Example

Raman is applying to bring his wife and two children (aged six months and 18 months) to the UK. Raman has a letter from his landlord confirming that he is happy for Raman's family to live in his one-bedroom property.

This letter is not enough to satisfy the Rules. You also need to prove the size of the accommodation (which may be shown by the lease) and how many other people are living there. There will be two adults living in the accommodation who can share a room as they are a couple, plus a child aged under one year (who is not counted for statutory overcrowding purposes) and a child aged under 10 years (counting as half a person). So there are 2½ people, hence only two rooms used as living spaces are required. So long as both the living room and the bedroom have a floor space of at least 50 square feet each and the living room is not also an open-plan kitchen (which may render it unsuitable as sleeping accommodation), the accommodation requirement is satisfied. If the living room is also an open-plan kitchen, a report from the local council is recommended to determine whether it can nevertheless be used as sleeping accommodation.

2.2.5 Reporting and other conditions

Under Rules 325-326 (which constitute Part 10 of the rules), any foreign national aged 16 or over from countries or territories listed in Appendix 2 to the Immigration Rules needs to register with the police (or, if in London, at the Overseas Visitors Registration Office), as do the stateless and those holding non-national travel documents (e.g. a Refugee Convention travel document), where they are given limited leave to enter the United Kingdom for longer than six months or given limited leave which takes them over six months from arrival.

Exempt from this requirement are seasonal agricultural workers, private servants in diplomatic households and overseas government employee, ministers of religion, persons granted leave as partners of a person settled in the United Kingdom, as parents of children at school or on the basis of exercising access rights to a child here, and those granted asylum. Exceptionally, the requirement can be imposed on any other foreign national where the Immigration Officer considers it necessary to ensure that he complies with the terms of the leave.

Where the Immigration Rules provide for them, conditions will be applied to a grant of limited leave which prevent or restrict the right to take employment, which require a student to study at a particular college, and which prohibit recourse to public funds. These conditions will be specified on the document granting leave (i.e. the visa or Biometric Residence Permit).

From September 2018, for example, BRPs in family settlement entry clearance cases which involved document scanning to Sheffield, were to be issued with a National Insurance Number printed on the back.

If the grant of leave is silent in respect of a particular issue (i.e. the right to take employment), there will be no prohibition in that regard. The Home Office can also impose reporting, residence and other conditions on foreign nationals who are granted limited leave to enter or remain in the UK but this is not common.

A breach of conditions may and often does lead to removal from the UK under s10(1)(a) of the Immigration Act 1999.

Where a condition of leave has been breached

- the UKVI can cancel that leave under provisions in rr9.23-9.32, leading to removal under the amended s10.
- The breach can also be the ground upon which a subsequent application for an extension (r9.8.3 in Part 9) or entry clearance (r9.8.1-2 read with 9.8.4 in Part 9)) is refused.

2.2.6 Knowledge of Language and Life in the UK; and English language requirements

Immigration routes generally contain an English language requirement.

- For example, the English language requirements for the old Points Based System Rules are set out in Appendix B, which now only applies to existing Tier 1 Entrepreneurs. Table 1 lists the level of ability required for each route. Then Table 2 and the notes to it explain the five ways in which the requirement may be satisfied
- For many of the categories introduced largely as Appendices from December 2020, the requirement is contained in Appendix English Language (the introduction lists all categories to which it applies).
- To give another example, the English language criteria for partner applications for an extension of leave under Appendix FM are found in E-LTRP.4.1

There are several ways of showing English language proficiency. These will be

- Nationality of a majority English language speaking country
- Having a degree taught in English
- Under Appendix English Language rEL 7.1 allows some categories to qualify via a UK GCSE or A-Level qualification in English (language or literature)
- Passing an English language test
- Having already shown English language proficiency on a previous immigration application

To obtain settlement (ILR) most applicants must demonstrate their knowledge of English language and life in the UK, or that they meet the narrow criteria for exemption.

Those applying for ILR in the refugee, humanitarian protection, bereaved spouses and domestic violence categories, and those with discretionary leave, do not have to meet this requirement (though they must do so if applying for naturalisation).

These requirements are laid out in Appendix KoLL to the Immigration Rules: applicants must pass the Life in the UK test, and separately evidence that they can speak and understand the English language at minimum B1 level of the Common European Framework of Reference for Languages (CEFR) (equivalent to an ESOL qualification at entry level 3). The KoLL guidance is entitled Knowledge of language and life in the UK

For the categories covered by Appendix English Language, the "knowledge of life in the UK" requirement is, instead, set out in Appendix KOL UK.

The Life in the UK Test requirement is met by sitting and passing an examination with multiple choice questions based on the book 'Life in the United Kingdom: A Guide for New Residents'. The ESOL route (i.e. passing an ESOL qualification taught with citizenship materials) is no longer available.

The official website for those booking and preparing to take the test is https://www.gov.uk/life-in-the-uk-test.

Some of those who are unable to pass either or both KoLL tests, despite their best efforts, may be able to rely on a reduced requirement after having spent 15 continuous years in the UK (as specified in paragraph 3.2 of Appendix KoLL of the Immigration Rules – note that this exemption is not reflected in the newer Appendix KOL UK or Appendix English Language). They will then need to pass an English language qualification at Level A2 of the CEFR. Nationals of the countries listed at paragraph 3.2(d) must take and pass the Life in the UK test, however long that takes. The specified documents that must be submitted with the ILR application are in Part 4 of Appendix KoLL.

Rule 39C in Part 1 allows the UKVI to interview applicants for settlement to satisfy the Secretary of State that the KoLL requirements are met. If the decision maker has reasonable cause to doubt (on examination or interview or on any other basis) that any document submitted, by an applicant for the purposes of satisfying the requirements of Appendix KoLL, was genuinely obtained, that document may be discounted for the purposes of the application.

A common problem for those sitting the HO's secure English Language Test is not having the appropriate ID, often because the HO holds it. There is guidance about the ID and other requirements for taking the test on page Prove your English language abilities with a secure English language test (SELT).

Medical exemption from KoLL requirements

Requests for medical exemptions are to be supported by a specified type of medical professional where the medical expert is not the primary treatment or care provider, and a template for the format of the request is provided. The stated intention is to assist medical professionals in making judgements as to whether they can support exemptions.

2.2.7 Tuberculosis tests

Under rule A39 in Part 1 under 'medical', any person applying to enter the UK for more than six months or as a fiancé(e) or proposed civil partner from (that is applying from) a country listed in Appendix T must present, at the time of application, a valid medical certificate issued by a medical practitioner approved by the Secretary of State for these purposes, as listed on the GOV.UK website linked from this page, confirming that they have undergone screening for active pulmonary tuberculosis and are free from the condition.

2.3 The general refusal grounds

In this part we firstly address definitions and commonly used terms, and explain the architecture of Part 9 of the Immigration Rules, which was replaced in its entirety on 1 December 2020, with a completely numbering structure. The old paragraphs ranged from A320 to 324 as the Immigration Rules used to be numbered consecutively. The new Part 9 paragraph numbers range from 9.1.1 to 9.32.1. When reading immigration histories, you will still come across the paragraph numbers from the old Part 9, thus we provide a diagram which summarises the many general refusal grounds, matches the old and new Immigration Rules and indicates broadly when decisions are discretionary or mandatory. Finally, we go through each kind of general refusal reason in detail.

2.3.1 Introduction to the general refusal grounds

Immigration applications can be refused because they fail to meet the requirements of the route in question (for example eligibility or English language requirements). Or because the decision maker believes there to be a more fundamental problem with the application. The latter scenario is what Part 9 of the Rules deals with. Common problems arising in this context include clients being refused:

- Due to inconsistencies between the income claimed on their HMRC tax returns and in their immigration extension applications (leading to refusals on 'good character' grounds)
- Because past English language test results have been cancelled because a provider (usually ETS) has declared the results invalid (leading to refusals for dishonestly obtaining documents to support an immigration application)

- Due to omitting to disclose relevant information in an application form

For many years this has been known as the "*general grounds for refusal*". We will continue to so label it. The new title for Part 9 is simply "*grounds for refusal*". Which has scope to confuse: because it does not differentiate between the grounds for refusal under individual immigration routes and the more generalised ones.

From 1 December 2020 these grounds have been radically revised, with both a new structure and a completely new paragraph numbering system.

Top Tip

It will always be necessary to consider Part 9 (or the suitability criteria, if applicable) when taking a client's instructions, if necessary by asking direct questions to your client, in respect of criminal convictions (in the UK or abroad), their UK immigration history, and litigation/NHS debts.

Here are some terms frequently used in the context of the general refusal reasons:

1. **"Conducive" refusals:** refusals which are on the grounds that exclusion/refusal is conducive to the public good. These refusals usually involve criminality.
2. **"Good character" or "non-conducive" refusals**: refusals which are essentially due to character and conduct, but which falls short of the refusal for the "*conducive to the public good*" regime to kick in
3. **Mandatory ban**: fixed periods for which time an application faces refusal.
   a. **Mandatory ban for criminality**: for example any criminal offending covering a custodial sentence exceeding 12 months, or which is deemed to involve persistent offending or serious harm (eg r9.4.1). Convictions can be in the UK or abroad (r6).
   b. **Mandatory ban for overstaying/dishonesty**: depending on the speed and manner of departure there are bans of various lengths (12 months for overstaying where one leaves voluntarily at one's own expense up to 10 years for deception in the present application (see the table at r9.8.7)
4. **Breaches of immigration laws**: there are two separate definitions given in r6 (the Interpretation provision of the Rules). Note that present breaches include a *breach of conditions*, whereas past breaches *only* involve *overstaying, deception* and *illegal entry*. However once we reach the rules addressing previous breaches of conditions aside from overstaying, we see that it is only those breaches of conditions which were subsequently condoned by a subsequent grant of leave which are left out of account (r9.8.3).
   c. **Breach of immigration laws**: where the person is an overstayer, illegal entrant, is in breach of a condition of their permission (eg a prohibition on employment or study), or used deception in relation to their most recent application for entry clearance or permission
   d. **Previously breached immigration laws**: if the person overstayed or used deception in relation to a previous application for entry clearance or permission
5. **Cancellation (including curtailment and adverse variations)**: Part 9 provides not only for the *refusal* of applications but also for their *cancellation* on suitability grounds. The reference to "*cancellation*" here covers also what was previously termed "*curtailment*": indeed the word "curtailment" does not appear in Part 9. The interpretation provisions of the Rules (r6) define cancellation to include curtailment and cancellation of entry clearance or permission. It also includes an "adverse" variation where a person's leave is shortened so that it ends sooner than it would otherwise have done. This is typically done where there has been some failure of sponsorship and the SSHD thinks it fair to give a short period in which the migrant may obtain an alternative sponsor.

2.3.2 Architecture of Part 9

Part 9 is split into five sections, as follows:

- Limitations on the application of Part 9
- Grounds for refusal, or cancellation of, entry clearance, permission to enter and permission to stay
- Additional grounds for refusal of entry, or cancellation of entry clearance or permission, on arrival in the UK (these often differentiate between mandatory refusal at the border for certain failures, and discretionary refusal where entry clearance has already been issued)
- Additional grounds for refusal, or cancellation, of permission to stay
- Additional grounds for cancellation of entry clearance, permission to enter and permission to stay which apply to specified routes

So to put that more simply, essentially the scheme is to

6. Explain which bits of Part 9 apply to which species of immigration application, and
7. Then to provide for a multitude of grounds that are generally applicable for most applications
8. Add to that multitude some "Additional grounds" which bite only in particular circumstances: on arrival in the UK, for in-country cases only, and finally a few which apply only to particular routes.

Some initial points:

9. The role of Part 9 is to set out how the following general powers are to be exercised in the individual case. The IA 1971 authorises the grant (and thus refusal) of leave, and s76 of the NIAA 2002 addresses revocation of ILR; the Immigration (Leave to Enter and Remain) Order 2000 and Sch 2 of the 1971 Act empower cancelling entry clearance or permission.
10. Individual routes (usually) cross reference to Part 9 via the heading Suitability requirements: see for example for seasonal workers (SAW 2.1) "The applicant must not fall for refusal under Part 9".
11. Some Rules have their own internal Suitability regime: see for example Appendix FM for partners, where we find Section S-EC: Suitability-entry clearance (and similar rules governing leave to remain too at Section S-LTR: Suitability leave to remain). Before December 2020 Appendix V for Visitors had its own internal regime: now it simply cross-references to Part 9. There seems to be some inconsistency in the approach to cross-referencing: Appendix FM does not refer to Part 9. However r9.1.1(a) explains that many of its provisions do apply to Appendix FM applications
12. Whilst Appendix FM does not impose a mandatory ban on return to the UK for breach of immigration conditions, r9.8.2 (contriving to frustrate the Immigration Rules) does apply to family applications made under Appendix FM. It is often the basis upon which entry clearance applications, particularly those made under the partner category, are refused, where the applicant has what is considered by the HO to be a very poor immigration history (see below)
13. Part 9 does not apply to an application for leave to remain on the grounds of private life under paragraph 276ADE(1): except for the proviso that applications may be refused where the application is made for a purpose not covered by the Rules (9.1.1(b), 9.13.1)
14. Part 9 does not apply to the post-Brexit EU routes: thus we can see that Appendix EU and Appendix EU (Family Permit), and Appendix S2 Healthcare Visitor and Appendix Service Providers from Switzerland are wholly excluded (9.1.1(d), (e), (j) and (k)): nor does it apply to Turkish businesspeople and workers under Appendix ECAA, except (in line with the general scheme of the Brexit era) where conduct post-dates the end of the transition period
15. Typically the rules are paired, the first proviso addressing the circumstances in which an application might be refused, the second the circumstances in which it might be cancelled

16. Refusals are sometimes mandatory ("must be refused" or "must be cancelled") or discretionary ("may be refused" or "may be cancelled"). As the introductory passages admit, decision making cannot solely be guided by the general refusal reasons: where fundamental rights are in play, it must also be compatible with the Refugee Convention or the ECHR (and it may well have to be proportionate to any interference with EU Treaty Rights acquired before Brexit). Of course, any such questions must be referred to an suitably accredited adviser.

Top Tip

When taking instructions on a case where the general refusal reasons may be relevant:

- Check which immigration route is in play: Appendix FM, Appendix V Visitor, etc, and then check para 9.1.1 for the extent to which Part 9 applies to the route
- Work out where your client is in the immigration system: at the entry clearance stage, at the port of entry, applying for permission to stay, and then work out which of the refusal reasons at sections 2-4 apply (section 2 always applies, section 3 applies only on arrival, section 4 only applies to permission to stay cases)
- Work out whether your client needs face up to any route-specific refusal reasons under section 5: these essentially bite on dependents, and on sponsored and endorsed migrants, ie workers and students, and those in the global/exceptional talent route

The old Part 9 was arranged primarily by the decision making stage which a case had reached. So its order was:

- Refusal of entry clearance/leave to enter
- Cancellation of leave to enter
- Refusal of leave to remain
- Curtailment of leave to remain

Within each of these sections the refusal reasons tended to be arranged firstly by setting out the mandatory refusal reasons, secondly by setting out the discretionary refusal reasons.

Part 9 from 1 December 2020 is arranged by subject matter. It is helpful, particularly when looking at Section 1 r9.1.1(a)-(k) (which contains long lists of cross-references setting out which sections apply to which immigration categories) to gain an overview of how the numbering structure works. HJT does not normally cross-reference past and present Immigration Rules, taking the view that it is best to master the current provisions than refer to old ones. However, given the extensive case law relating to the old general refusal reasons, and the familiarity of many practitioners with the old numbering, for the time being we will provide the previous versions for comparison.

THE GENERAL REFUSAL REASONS			
Refusal issue	**Modern Rule**	**Old equivalent**	**Mandatory or discretionary under the modern rules (re both refusal and cancellation)**
Grounds applying at every stage of the immigration process			
Exclusion or deportation order grounds	9.2.1-9.2.2	r320(2)(a), r320(6), r321(4), r322(1B)	Mandatory for refusal and cancellation
Conduct, character and associations (AKA "Non-conducive grounds") (*Balajigari* cases)	9.3.1-9.3.2	r320(19), r321(5), r322(5)	Mandatory for refusal and cancellation
Criminality	9.4.1-9.4.5	r320(2)(b)-(d), r320(18A-18B),	Mandatory for refusal and cancellation where custodial

		r322(1C), r322(5A), r323(v)	sentence over 12 months or for persistent offenders or for offences causing serious harm (9.4.1-9.4.2) Discretionary for custodial sentences under 12 months, non-custodial sentences and out-of-court disposals recorded on criminal record 9.4.4 (though mandatory 1-year ban for visitors: 9.4.4)
Exclusion from asylum or humanitarian protection grounds	9.5.1-9.5.2	r323(iv)	Discretionary for refusal and cancellation
Involvement in a sham marriage or sham civil partnership grounds	9.6.1-9.6.2	r320(7A), (7B(d))	Discretionary for refusal and cancellation
False representations, etc	9.7.1-9.7.4	r320(7A), (7B(d)), r321A(2), r321B(iii), r322(1A), r322(2A), r323(ia)	Mandatory for refusal and cancellation where the decision maker can prove deception "*is more likely than not*" Otherwise discretionary for refusal and cancellation
Previous breach of immigration laws grounds	9.8.1-9.8.2	r320(7B), r322(11)	Mandatory refusal where the breach is within the relevant time periods set out at 9.8.7 Discretionary refusal where the relevant time period has passed but the migrant "*has previously contrived in a significant way to frustrate the intention of the rules*"
Failure to provide required information, etc grounds	9.9.1-9.9.2	r320(8), r321(6), r322(9), r323(vi)	Discretionary refusal and cancellation
Admissibility to the Common Travel Area or other countries	9.10.1-9.10.2	r320(4)	Re CTA: mandatory for refusal at entry clearance and permission to enter stage Re other countries: discretionary at any decision making stage
Debt to the NHS	9.11.1	r320(22), r322(12)	Discretionary refusal
Unpaid litigation costs	9.12.1	r320(22), r322(13),	Discretionary refusal
Purpose not covered by the Immigration Rules	9.13.1	r320(1), r322(1)	Discretionary refusal
Additional Grounds available on entry to the UK			
No entry clearance	9.14.1	r320(5)	Mandatory refusal
Failure to produce recognised passport or travel document	9.15.1-9.15.3	r320(3), r320(5), r320(10)	Mandatory refusal re proving identity and nationality Discretionary refusal if issued by unrecognised territory/authority, or one not accepting UK passports, or not complying with international practice Discretionary cancellation in either scenario where entry clearance already held
Medical	9.16.1-9.16.2	r320(17), r321A(3),	Mandatory refusal where medical inspector advises admission undesirable

			Discretionary cancellation where entry clearance already held
Consent for a child to travel	9.17.1	r320(16), r322(11)	Discretionary refusal
Returning residents	9.18.1	r320(9)	Discretionary refusal
Customs breaches	9.19.1-9.19.2	No direct equivalent	Discretionary refusal or cancellation
Change of circumstances or purpose	9.20.1-9.20.2	r321A(1), r321B(iv)-(v)	Discretionary refusal or cancellation
Additional Grounds available for extension/switching applications			
Rough sleeping in the UK	9.21.1-9.21.2	No direct equivalent	Discretionary refusal or cancellation
Crew members	9.22.2	r324	Discretionary refusal
Additional Grounds available for specific routes			
Ceasing to meet requirement of the rules	9.23.1	r323(ii)	Discretionary cancellation
Dependents	9.24.1	r323(iii), (vi)	Discretionary cancellation
Withdrawal of sponsorship or endorsement	9.25.-19.25.2	r323A(a)(ii), r323B, r323C(d)	Discretionary cancellation
Student does not start course or ceases to study	9.26.1	r323A(a)(ii)	Discretionary cancellation
Worker does not start work or ceases their employment	9.27.1	r323A(a)(i)	Discretionary cancellation
Sponsor loses licence or transfers business	9.28.1	r323A(b)	Discretionary cancellation
Change of employer	9.29.1	r323AA	Discretionary cancellation
Absence from employment	9.30.1	r323A(a)	Discretionary cancellation
Change of job or lower salary rate	9.31.1-9.31.2	r323AA(g)	Discretionary cancellation
Endorsing body no longer approved	9.32.1	r323B, r323C	Discretionary cancellation

2.3.3 Limitations on the application of Part 9

The limitations are quite dense reading, and sadly there is no substitute for staring carefully at each numbered paragraph to determine whether it may be applicable to your client's circumstances. However note:

- The limitations are usually expressed as a double negative: ie "Part 9 does not apply … except …" (so the numbered references *do* apply)

- There are four routes which are completely exempt from Part 9: Appendix E (dependents of Tier 1 Entrepreneurs), Appendix EU (Family Permit), Appendix S2 Healthcare Visitor and Appendix Service Providers from Switzerland

- Other than those clear exclusions, although at first sight it can be rather bewildering, on analysis we see that the general refusal reasons apply with full force to most regular immigration applications: for example the various Appendices governing study and work, and the surviving work/economic routes in Part 5 and Part 6 and Part 6A: the exclusions are essentially for private and family life (including the human rights oriented route r159I for domestic workers who are the victim of slavery or human trafficking), asylum and post-Brexit EU cases

- Appendix FM has rather a lot of *individual inclusions* notwithstanding its *general exclusion* from Part 9. The full list of provisions of Part 9 which *do* apply to Appendix FM are listed in Module 6.
- Permission for individuals under Appendix FM can be *cancelled* where an exclusion or deportation order is made (presumably following the grant of permission) (r9.1.1 referencing r9.2.2)
- Appendix FM's individual inclusions must be read alongside Appendix FM's own Suitability regime (so for example a partner seeking leave to remain under Appendix FM faces a mandatory refusal for imprisonment over 4 years under Appendix FM's own provisions (S-LTR.1.3) and for causing serious harm or persistently offending such as to show a particular disregard for the law (S-LTR.1.5), and a 10-year mandatory ban for sentences from 1-4 years under S-LTR.1.4: but also faces possible *discretionary cancellation* for offending (r9.4.5, brought into play by r9.1.1(a))

2.3.4 General principles regarding the general refusal reasons

The burden of proof lies on the SSHD to establish a general refusal reason: see eg Shen [2014] UKUT 236 (IAC) §25.

The UKVI guidance is titled General grounds for refusal (immigration staff guidance)

2.3.5 The generally applicable grounds for refusal and cancellation

These grounds, found in Section 2 of Part 9, apply at *all stages* of the decision making process. From now on we will use the abbreviations EC (entry clearance), PTE (permission to enter) and PTS (permission to stay).

2.3.5.1 Exclusion or deportation order grounds (9.2.1-9.2.2)

An application for EC, PTE or PTS ***must*** be refused on SSHD's personal direction of exclusion (9.2.1(a)); or A is subject to an exclusion order (9.2.1(b)); or to a deportation order or decision to make one (9.2.1(c)).

EC or permission held ***must*** be cancelled on SSHD's personal direction for exclusion (9.2.2).

An *exclusion decision* is a decision made personally by the SSHD directing an individual's exclusion. An *exclusion order* is the equivalent made under the EEA Regs 2016.

If you encounter a client with one of these orders in their immigration history, you should refer the case to a suitable accredited adviser.

2.3.5.2 Non-conducive grounds: character, conduct and associations (9.3.1-9.3.2)

Applications for EC, PTE or PTS ***must*** be refused where A's presence is not conducive to the public good on grounds of conduct, character, associations or other reasons (including convictions falling below the threshold to attract the criminality grounds) (9.3.1).

EC or PTE/PTS ***must*** be cancelled where P's presence in the UK is not conducive to the public good (9.3.2).

The Guidance on the *General grounds for refusal* explains the various factors that warrant consideration of potential refusal under the character, conduct and associations provisions. Single non-custodial convictions are unlikely to suffice; but many other forms of conduct, from deliberate or reckless building up of debts, corruption, assisting the evasion of immigration control, employing illegal workers, and deceitful dealings with HM Government, might do so, A pending prosecution should lead to an application being put on hold.

There have been many 'good character' refusals under this Rules's predecessor (r322(5)).

Where you think that your client's conduct may bring these rules into play, or where they present with a current or previous refusal on this ground, you should always refer the case to a suitable qualified adviser, as extensive knowledge of case law as well as human rights appeals and judicial review procedures may be necessary to advise and assist correctly.

2.3.5.3 Criminality grounds (9.4.1-9.4.5)

These, and the following, grounds are set out repetitiously, so this table should help:

<table>
<tr><th colspan="2">Mandatory grounds for refusal or cancellation</th></tr>
<tr><td>9.4.1 An application for EC/PTE/PTS must be refused</td><td>9.4.2 EC/permission held must be cancelled</td></tr>
<tr><td colspan="2">Identical for 9.4.1 and 9.4.2:
(a) 12-month custodial (ie prison) sentence in the UK or elsewhere; or
(b) persistent offender with a particular disregard for the law; or
(c) having caused serious harm by offending.</td></tr>
<tr><td colspan="2">9.4.4 An application for EC or PTE for less than 6 months (including visitors) must be refused
(a) prison sentence under 12 months in the UK or elsewhere, which ended less than 1 year before application date; or
(b) non-custodial sentence or out-of-court disposal recorded on criminal record in the UK or elsewhere where conviction was less than 1 year before application date</td></tr>
<tr><th colspan="2">Discretionary grounds for refusal or cancellation</th></tr>
<tr><td>9.4.3 An application for EC/PTE/PTS may be refused (where 9.4.2. and 9.4.4. do not apply)</td><td>9.4.5 EC or permission held may be cancelled (where 9.4.2. does not apply)</td></tr>
<tr><td colspan="2">Identical for 9.4.3 and 9.4.5:
(a) prison sentence of under 12 months in the UK or elsewhere; or
(b) non-custodial sentence or out-of-court disposal recorded on criminal record in the UK or elsewhere</td></tr>
</table>

The Guidance *Grounds for refusal – Criminality* (Version 1.0; 1 December 2020) summarises the December 2020 changes, which introduce:

1. a single threshold for mandatory refusal on the basis of a custodial sentence of at least 12 months, replacing the previous three sentence-based thresholds
2. a mandatory ground for refusal at the border for those entering as visitors or for less than 6 months
3. a mandatory ground for refusal or cancellation on the grounds of serious harm, persistent offending or where it is conducive to the public good

Also of interest in the Guidance, which is directed at UKVI caseworkers:

- Many immigration routes require the provision of a criminal record certificate, which is how some criminal records will come to light (see MIL 7.6.5). All non-custodial sentences and out-of-court disposals (apart from spent cautions) must be declared on application forms (as they are exempt from the provisions of the Rehabilitation of Offenders Act 1974)
- As we address in section 11.1 and 11.7.6, conduct by EEA citizens and their family members arising after 31 December 2020 will attract the domestic 'conducive to the public good' regime. The distinction is already drawn under the Suitability provisions of Appendix EU for the EUSS

which provide for the domestic regime to apply to post-transitional period conduct. The benefit of the doubt should be given vis-á-vis conduct whose timing is uncertain

- Criminality leading to a sentence of imprisonment should be referred to Criminal Casework to consider deportation action
- Even where a sentence exceeds four years, "*you must always consider if there are any very compelling factors which amount to an exceptional reason why the application should be granted*"
- Where the conviction is for an offence not recognised in the UK (eg homosexuality or membership of a trade union), there should not a mandatory refusal; where the offence is one where there is a "*broad equivalent in the UK context*" then the overseas offence should be treated in line with the UK one
- Suspended sentences are treated as non-custodial/other out of court disposals unless they are 'activated'. Where they are activated, due to reoffending or a breach of their conditions, the decision maker should "*consider the original suspended sentence length, the circumstances that led to its activation, and the length of time in custody the person was required to serve following activation*"
- Where sentences are to be served concurrently, the decision making should be guided by the longest imposed; if sentences are consecutive, then by the combined length of all sentences
- Acquittals should wipe the slate clean, though the conduct in question may still be considered for a non-conducive (character and conduct) refusal
- Hospital orders are treated in line with imprisonment
- Non-custodial sentences and out-of-court disposals
- Include fines, and absolute and conditional discharges, detention and training orders, confiscation and forfeiture orders, and disqualifications from driving
- Fixed penalty notices: which will not normally warrant refusal unless unpaid or where a challenge to the notice has led to a criminal conviction
- Generally this kind of offence warrants discretionary consideration of refusal: relevant considerations will be whether the migrant already has permission or if this is their first application, whether their offending began shortly after their UK arrival, whether there is multiple offending such as to warrant a refusal on persistency grounds, the time passed and the length of any sentence, UK ties, and the offence's relevance to the permission sought
- Include a caution (simple or conditional), youth caution, warning or reprimand. Simple cautions do not need to be declared, and if declared, should be ignored
- Community resolutions and binding-overs are not convictions but should be considered in the context of persistent offending and/or non-conducive grounds
- Sometimes there will be a pending prosecution. Where the prosecution is for an offence attracting a sentence that might materially impact on a decision, decision maker should hold the case until the outcome of the court proceedings is known. Applications made at the border cannot reasonably be put on hold, and will need a decision on the available facts
- A definition is given for persistence, which is to be considered in the light of the number and frequency of offending, its pattern, seriousness, and any escalation, and whether any particular disregard of the law has been shown (ie whether the behaviour indicates "*a lack of willingness or capacity to adjust their conduct so that it remains within the law over a reasonable period of time*":

A persistent offender is considered to be a repeat offender who shows a pattern of offending over a period of time. This can mean a series of offences committed in a fairly short timeframe, or offences which escalate in seriousness over time, or a long history of minor offences for the same behaviour which demonstrate a clear disregard for the law

- Serious harm may involve one or more violent, drugs-related, racially motivated or sexual offences will qualify, and sentencing remarks and offender management reports should be considered. The definition given is:

> An offence that has caused 'serious harm' means an offence that has caused serious physical or psychological harm to a victim or victims, or that has contributed to a widespread problem that causes serious harm to a community or to society in general.

Mahmood [2020] EWCA Civ 717 explains how to assess whether an offence has caused "serious harm" for the purposes of deportation; The meaning of the term 'persistent offender' in r398(c), and in the definition of 'foreign criminal in s117D, NIAA 2002) was considered in Chege [2016] UKUT 187 (IAC): see our section on deportation at 13.4.2.1.

2.3.5.4 Exclusion from asylum or humanitarian protection grounds (9.5.1-9.5.2)

Discretionary ground	
9.5.1. An application for EC/PTE/PTS ***may*** be refused	**9.5.2** EC or PTE/PTS ***may*** be cancelled
Identical for 9.5.1 and 9.5.2: (a) where SSHD has at any time decided that the individual should be excluded from refugee status or HP under 339AA/339D (ie for war crimes, crimes against humanity, and acts contrary to UN purposes, for refugee status; for past criminality, including committing international crimes, including offending in the UK which represents a danger to the community or the UK's security and the situation where their flight to the UK was to avoid punishment for a crime for HP); that HP should be revoked under 339GB (essentially the same reasons as under 339D); or that a person granted refugee status is in fact a danger to the UK under 339AC (being a danger to the community or the UK's security); or (b) where SSHD decides the above provisions would apply *were* the individual to claim protection, or where their protection claim was finally determined without reference to them	

It can be seen that r9.5.2(b) authorises exclusion where a protection claim was finally determined "*without reference*" to exclusion. Cases such as TB (Jamaica) [2008] EWCA Civ 977 hold that the SSHD cannot necessarily raise exclusion following judicial proceedings where the matter might have been raised but the point was not taken.

2.3.5.5 Involvement in a sham marriage or sham civil partnership grounds (9.6.1-9.6.2)

Discretionary ground	
9.6.1. An application for EC/PTE/PTS ***may*** be refused	9.6.2 EC or permission held ***may*** be cancelled
Identical for 9.6.1 and 9.6.2: where the decision maker is satisfied that it is more likely than not, that the person is or was involved in a sham marriage or civil partnership	

A sham marriage is defined (circuitously, the Rules' interpretation clause at r6 tells us we should refer to s62(3) of IA 2014, which then passes us onto s24(5) of IAA 1999, which says):

> "(a) either, or both, of the parties to the marriage is not a relevant national,
> (b) there is no genuine relationship between the parties to the marriage, and(c) either, or both, of the parties to the marriage enter into the marriage for one or more of these purposes—
> (i) avoiding the effect of one or more provisions of United Kingdom immigration law or the immigration rules;
> (ii) enabling a party to the marriage to obtain a right conferred by that law or those rules to reside in the United Kingdom."

The Guidance explains that involvement may go beyond being a party to a sham: it may include acting as a false witness or guest at the wedding, or introducing the parties, knowingly of the sham element.

We discuss sham marriage in the context of EEA cases at 11.5.4. Giri [2015] EWCA Civ 784 mentioned above at 9.3.4 shows that the HO must be able to point to cogent evidence to establish her case on balance of probabilities.

2.3.5.6 Providing false representations, documents, information, and material non-disclosure (9.7.1-9.7.4)

<table>
<tr><th colspan="2">Discretionary grounds</th></tr>
<tr><td>9.7.1 An application for EC/PTE/PTS may be refused</td><td>9.7.3 EC or permission held may be cancelled</td></tr>
<tr><td colspan="2">Identical for 9.7.1 and 9.7.3: if, in relation to the relevant application or in order to obtain supporting documents for this from SSHD or a third party
(a) false representations were made or false information/documents submitted (whether or not to the person's knowledge, and whether or not relevant to the application); or
(b) relevant facts were not disclosed</td></tr>
<tr><td colspan="2">9.7.4 Section 3C leave may be cancelled where the decision maker can prove it is more likely than not P used deception in the application for PTS</td></tr>
<tr><th colspan="2">Mandatory ground</th></tr>
<tr><td colspan="2">9.7.2 An application for EC/PTE/PTS must be refused where the decision maker can prove it is more likely than not that the individual used deception in the application</td></tr>
</table>

Further notes/Information

If you encounter any client with a current or former refusal on these grounds, you should refer the case to a suitable accredited adviser, as case law principles moderate these grounds quite significantly from case to case and advising on this is not within OISC 1 remit.

Top Tips

NON-DISCLOSURE OF CONVICTIONS

Refusal for dishonesty often follows where a previous conviction has not been disclosed. Do bear in mind that in these cases there can be a double reason to refuse:

- the fact of the conviction
- dishonesty in withholding the fact of the conviction, which is itself a false representation

Application forms make it very clear indeed that any relevant convictions should be disclosed. Nevertheless, as we have seen above, a credible innocent mistake may be forgiven, as it will not exhibit the relevant dishonesty required by the case law.

It will be readily appreciated that the more sophisticated the migrant and their application, and the more glaring the omitted criminality, the more difficult it will be to maintain a case of innocent error: it is important to critically interrogate the instructions you are given regarding the surrounding circumstances and the state of mind of the applicant to ensure that the case is put in the best light.

2.3.5.8 Previous breach of immigration laws grounds (mandatory bans) (9.8.1-9.8.4)

Past breaches of immigration laws are dealt with by a refusal regime based on periods for which there will be a mandatory ban on returning to the UK. The refusal provisions (9.8.1-9.8.2) are linked to a series of exclusion periods set out in the table at 9.8.7.

At the entry clearance and permission to enter stage, an application for EC/PTE:

- *must* be refused if A has previously breached immigration laws and the application was made within the relevant re-entry ban period in 9.8.7 (9.8.1(a)&(b))

- *may* be refused if A has previously breached immigration laws, the application was made outside the relevant re-entry ban period but A has previously contrived, in a significant way, to frustrate the intention of the rules or there are aggravating circumstances like failure to cooperate with redocumentation or enforcement processes (such as absconding or failing to report), or using a false identity (9.8.2(a)-(c)).
- So we can see that there is mandatory refusal for applications made *within* the ban periods, and discretionary refusal for applications *after* the ban has expired, essentially based on the existence of an *aggravated* breach

At the permission to stay stage, an application for PTS:

- *may* be refused where P previously failed to comply with conditions of permission, unless permission has previously been granted in knowledge of the previous breach (9.8.3)

Breach of immigration laws and overstaying disregards

A "*breach of immigration laws*" for these purposes (9.8.4(a)-(d))

- Applies only to conduct committed whilst an adult
- Includes overstaying, a breach of conditions which was not condoned by a subsequent grant of leave, being an illegal entrant, or using deception in relation to an application (whether successfully or not)
    - The Rules at r6 define overstaying as remaining beyond your last permission granted, including any statutory extension of leave under s3C/s3D IA 1971.
    - Overstaying will be disregarded where the person left the UK voluntarily and not at the SSHD's expense (9.8.5(a)-(c)):
- For up to 90 days where the overstaying began before 6 April 2017; or
- For up to 30 days where the overstaying began on or after 6 April 2017; or
- Where r39E applies
    - Overstaying will be disregarded where this arose from a refusal or cancellation decision which was later withdrawn, quashed or reconsidered by direction of a court or tribunal, so long as that legal challenge was lodged within 3 months of the decision (9.8.6)

Re-entry bans

Re-entry bans apply as follows, depending on the conduct of the person concerned (9.8.7(a)-(f)):

- 12 months if they left voluntarily at their own expense
- 2 years if they left voluntarily at public expense, *within* 6 months of the later event: being given notice of liability to removal, *or* of no longer having a pending appeal/admin review, whichever is later
- 5 years if they left voluntarily at public expense, *more than* 6 months after the later event of being given notice of liability to removal, or of no longer having a pending appeal or AR
- 5 years if they left or were removed from the UK as a condition of a caution under s22 Criminal Justice Act 2003 (unless any prohibition to return remains extant)
- 10 years if they were deported or removed at public expense
- 10 years if they used deception in an EC application (including a visit visa)

The "public expense" removal provisions at 9.8.7(b)-(c) are triggered by ***notice of liability to removal***. This is defined in the interpretation clause to the Rules at r6:

> a notice given that a person is or will be liable for removal under section 10 of the Immigration and Asylum Act 1999, and for notices that pre-date the Immigration Act 2014 coming into force,

refers to a decision to remove in accordance with section 10 of the Immigration and Asylum Act 1999, a decision to remove an illegal entrant by way of directions under paragraphs 8 to 10 of Schedule 2 to the Immigration Act 1971, or a decision to remove in accordance with section 47 of the Immigration, Asylum and Nationality Act 2006

Beyond the refusal provisions, permission (including s3C leave) ***may*** be cancelled where a person has failed to comply with conditions of their permission (9.8.8). The Cancellation Guidance explains that

> *the breach must be of sufficient gravity to warrant such action. You must not cancel leave when the breach is so minor that it would mean cancellation would be disproportionate.*

Previous HO guidance has pointed to other exceptions which it is not so easy to find in the current policies:

- Where the applicant has been accepted by UKVI as a victim of trafficking (RFL5.4)
- Where the applicant was in the UK illegally on or after 17 March 2008 and left the UK voluntarily (i.e. without being removed) before 1 October 2008 (RFL5.4)

Contriving to frustrate

The concept of contriving to frustrate the Rules (previously r320(11), now r9.8.2) was at one time explained in the Entry Clearance Guidance which listed the forms of 'service and support' which the Rules targets: various kinds of benefits, tax credits, gaining employment and accessing goods or services. Aggravating circumstances are specified: e.g. absconding, not complying with reporting conditions, recourse to NHS treatment to which one is not entitled, using false identities, involvement in sham marriages and vexatious attempts to avoid removal.

In Azerkane [2020] ECHR 380 the ECtHR reiterated its view that bans on re-entry were likely to be disproportionate where of unlimited duration; whereas a finite ban on return made it more likely that a decision was proportionate.

Many overstayers depart the UK rather than pursue lengthy legal proceedings here in order to try and return via the entry clearance route, so putting their immigration history into a better light. There is a danger that over-reliance on this Rule could undermine the public policy to encourage such departures. The UT made this point in PS India [2010] UKUT 440 (IAC), explaining that the HO should be careful when refusing applications from abroad from former overstayers to avoid discouraging compliance with the entry clearance route.

2.3.5.9 Failure to provide required information, etc (9.9.1-9.9.2)

An application for EC/PTE/PTS ***may*** be refused (9.9.1), and EC or permission held ***may*** be cancelled (9.9.2), where A fails without reasonable excuse to comply with a reasonable requirement to be interviewed, provide information or biometrics, undergo a medical test or provide a medical report.

NB: the failure to provide biometrics, for application refusals, can be in relation to biometrics requested otherwise than in relation to the application (9.9.1(c)).

Guidance document Suitability: failure to provide required information, attend interview caseworker guidance was first published on 1 December 2020 and has since been updated.

2.3.5.10 Admissibility to the Common Travel Area or other countries (9.10.1-9.10.2)

An application for EC/PTE/PTS ***may*** be refused if A is seeking to enter the UK with a view to travelling to another part of the CTA but does not satisfy the decision maker that they will be admitted there (9.10.1).

An application for EC/PTE/PTS ***may*** be refused if A fails to satisfy the decision maker that they are admissible to another country following their UK stay (9.10.2).

2.3.5.11 Debt to the NHS (9.11.1)

An application for EC/PTE/PTS ***may*** be refused where the HO has been notified of an outstanding NHS debt of at least £500.

There is bespoke guidance on this subject: *Suitability: Debt to the NHS* (Version 2.0; 22 December 2020). Where your instructions show that your client has at any time since April 2015 used secondary NHS care to which they were not entitled free of charge, you should pass the case to a suitable accredited adviser, as Home Office discretion will come into play and may need to be argued in your client's next application.

2.3.5.12 Unpaid litigation costs grounds (9.12.1)

An application for EC/PTE/PTS ***may*** be refused where there has been a failure to pay litigation costs awarded to the HO. Litigation costs are likely to arise in judicial review proceedings and civil claims (eg for false imprisonment following a person's release from detention): if unsuccessful in a JR the claimant is usually required to pay the SSHD's legal costs. If a claim succeeds, then usually they are not required to pay costs. Claims often settle with an agreement to reconsider a decision, which may or may not include an offer to pay the other side's legal costs. The Order concluding the JR proceedings, from the UT or Administrative Court, will include any costs order.

The Guidance *Suitability: unpaid litigation costs* (Version 4.0; 22 December 2020) contains further information as to how the information is to be obtained. It does say that where a plan is in place to pay an outstanding debt by instalments, the debt should be ignored. However, if litigation debt may be an issue, as arising from your client's immigration history (past JRs not covered by legal aid should be a red flag) you should refer the case to a suitable accredited adviser, as Home Office discretion will come into play and may need to be argued in the application.

2.3.5.13 Purpose not covered by the Immigration Rules grounds (9.13.1)

An application for EC/PTE/PTS ***may*** be refused where PTE/PTR is sought for a purpose not covered by the Immigration Rules.

2.3.6 Additional grounds available at the UK border

These grounds comprise section 3 of Part 9, headed "Additional grounds for refusal of entry, or cancellation of entry clearance or permission, on arrival in the UK".

2.3.6.1 Lack of prior entry clearance (9.14.1)

PTE ***must*** be refused where entry clearance is required but the passenger is required to hold entry clearance but does not have it.

2.3.6.2 Failure to produce recognised passport or travel document grounds (9.15.1-9.15.3)

PTE ***must*** be refused if the passenger does not produce a passport or other travel document which satisfies the decision maker of their nationality and identity. Stateless persons or refugees may provide a travel document issued by another country than that of their nationality (9.15.1).

PTE ***may*** be refused if the passenger produces a passport which (9.15.2):

- Was issued by a territorial entity or authority not recognised as a state or dealt with as such by the UK government (9.15.2(a)) (the Guidance lists passports from the Republic of China

(Nationalist China – Taiwan), Somalia, Iraq (S-, M- and N- series passports), and South African temporary passports, and documents from Yemen (Royalist authorities) and Turkish Republic of Northern Cyprus)

- Was issued by a territorial entity or authority which does not accept UK passports for immigration purposes (9.15.2(b)); or
- Does not comply with international passport practice (9.15.2(c)).

EC or permission held ***may*** be cancelled where they fail, on arrival, to produce a passport or travel document meeting 9.15.1 or 9.15.2.

"Passport" is defined in r6 of the Rules, as a document which:

> (a) is issued by or on behalf of the government of any country recognised by the UK, or dealt with as a government by the UK, and which complies with international passport practice; and
> (b) shows both the identity and nationality of the holder; and
> (c) gives the holder the right to enter the country of the government which issued the document; and
> (d) is authentic and not unofficially altered or tampered with; and
> (e) is not damaged in a way that compromises the integrity of the document; and
> (f) is used by the rightful holder; and
> (g) has not expired.

2.3.6.3 Medical inspector's advice (9.16.1-9.16.2)

PTE ***must*** be refused if granting entry would be against the advice of a medical inspector, unless strong compassionate grounds justify admission (9.16.1).

EC or permission held ***may*** be cancelled if granting entry would be against the advice of a medical inspector (9.16.2).

2.3.6.4 Consent for a child to travel (9.16.1-9.16.2)

PTE ***may*** be refused to a child if travelling without a parent or guardian where the relevant adult fails to provide written consent on request.

2.3.6.4 Returning residents (9.18.1)

A person seeking entry as a returning resident ***may*** be refused PTE if they do not meet the requirements of r18, or that they do not seek entry for settlement. We address this area in detail in MIL at 4.1.3.

2.3.6.5 Customs breaches grounds (9.19.1-9.19.2)

PTE ***may*** be refused (9.19.1), and EC or permission held ***may*** be cancelled (9.19.2), for a customs breach, irrespective of whether criminal prosecution is pursued. In cancellation cases the Guidance suggests having regard to the non-conducive (character and conduct refusal grounds too).

This is defined by r6 as a breach of any provision of the Customs and Excise Acts or any other breach relating to an assigned matter (ie any matter where the Customs Commissioners or HMRC have a power or duty which the SSHD may exercise at the border).

The Guidance *Grounds for Refusal – Customs breaches* (Version 1.0; 1 December 2020) explains that these breaches may involve prohibited or restricted goods, or goods which infringe intellectual property rights or may fail to declare goods which exceed their duty-free allowances. They can include, but are not limited to the following:

- possession of prohibited substances, including Class C drugs, even if for personal use

- possession of prohibited items such as offensive weapons, obscene material, certain products of animal origin (POAO)
- non-declaration of duty-payable goods
- possession of large quantities of goods such as alcohol and tobacco products beyond what could reasonably be classed as for personal use or gifts
- driving a vehicle which has been adapted to conceal goods

Decision makers should consider whether it is proportionate to refuse entry. Therefore, if this issue is relevant in your client's case, it should be referred to a suitable accredited adviser.

2.3.6.6 Change of circumstances or purpose grounds (9.20.1-9.20.2)

EC or permission held ***may*** be cancelled if there has been a sufficiently significant change in circumstances since EC or permission was granted (9.20.1). The example given in the Guidance *General grounds for refusal – Considering entry at UK port* (section 3, v29.0; 11 January 2018) is a person coming to work in the UK but the job offer being withdrawn.

EC/PTE ***may*** be cancelled on P's arrival if their purpose in entering the UK is different from that specified in their EC (9.20.3). This may arise from answers at interview or inferences may be drawn from a baggage search.

2.3.7 General refusal grounds for permission to stay cases only

These are found in section 4 of Part 9, titled Additional grounds for refusal, or cancellation, of permission to stay.

2.3.7.1 Rough sleeping in the UK (9.21.1-9.21.2)

PTS or any other permission held by P ***may*** be cancelled where the decision maker is satisfied that P has been sleeping rough in the UK. This new rule is legally contentious and if you receive an enquiry from someone threatened with cancellation, the case should be referred to a suitable accredited adviser, as there are case law arguments to be made as to why the rule should not be applied, or discretion should be exercised in an individual case.

2.3.7.2 Crew members (9.22.1)

The members of a ship or aircraft's crew are normally expected to depart at the end of their stay. However, PTS ***may*** be refused unless it is being granted to fulfil the purpose for which P had PTE.

2.3.8 Route specific cancellation powers

These are found in section 5 of Part 9, titled Additional grounds for cancellation of entry clearance, permission to enter and permission to stay which apply to specified routes

2.3.8.1 Ceasing to meet requirement of the rules (9.23.1)

EC or permission held ***may*** be cancelled if the migrant ceases to meet the requirements of the rule under which it was granted.

2.3.8.2 Dependent grounds (9.24.1)

EC or permission held as a dependent ***may*** be cancelled if the principal's permission is cancelled.

2.3.8.3 Withdrawal of sponsorship or endorsement grounds (9.25.1-9.25.2)

EC or permission held ***may*** be cancelled where sponsorship of endorsement is withdrawn. This possibility is relevant to those migrants who must have sponsors or endorsing bodies: Students; Child Student; Skilled Worker; Intra-Company Transfer; Intra-Company Graduate Trainee; Representative of an Overseas Business; T2 Minister of Religion; T2 Sportsperson T5 (Temporary Worker); Start-up; Innovator; or Global Talent (9.25.1).

Permission held by a Student ***may*** be cancelled where sponsorship is withdrawn due to a failure to attain Level B2 in speaking, listening, reading and writing English following a pre-sessional course (9.25.2).

The Skilled Worker guidance explains that if the applicant's sponsor loses its licence while the application is under consideration, the SSHD has a duty to inform the applicant promptly. This is consistent with the case law on fairness, particularly Pathan.

2.3.8.4 Student does not start course or ceases to study (9.26.1)

EC or permission held by a Student or Child Student ***may*** be cancelled if

i) they do not start, or cease, to study
ii) if the course start date is delayed by over 28 days or
iii) if they or their sponsor confirm that the course will cease before the CAS end date (9.26.1(a)-(d)).

The Guidance indicates that cancellation of permission for early course finishes should be to the new end of the course plus any additional period of wrap-up that was originally given.

2.3.8.5 Worker does not start work or ceases their employment (9.27.1)

EC or permission held by a Skilled Worker, person on the Intra-Company routes, Representative of an Overseas Business, T2 Minister of Religion, T2 Sportsperson or T5 (Temporary Worker) ***may*** be cancelled if

(a) they do not start, or cease, to work for their sponsor
(b) the CoS start date for the job is delayed by over 28 days; or
(c) they or their sponsor confirm that the work has ceased or will cease before the CoS end date

The Guidance indicates that cancellation of permission to 60 days will be appropriate in these cases absent an aggravating factor.

2.3.8.6 Sponsor loses licence or transfers business (9.28.1)

EC or permission held by a Student, Child Student, Skilled Worker, person on the Intra-Company Routes, T2 Minister of Religion, T2 Sportsperson, or Tier 5 (Temporary Worker) ***may*** be cancelled if:

(a) Their sponsor has no licence; or
(b) The business is transferred to another business, institution or organisation which fails to apply for a sponsor license within 28 days of the transfer, or which is refused a licence, or the licence granted would not allow that business to issue a CoS/CAS to the migrant.

2.3.8.7 Change of employer (9.29.1)

Permission held by a Skilled Worker, person on the Intra-Company routes, T2 Minister of Religion, T2 Sportsperson, or T5 (Temporary Worker) ***may*** be cancelled for changing employer unless:

- They are a Government Authorised Exchange or Seasonal Worker and the change is authorised by the sponsor (9.29.1(a))
- The new employer sponsors them or the change is covered by TUPE Regulations (9.29.1(b))
- They are a T2 Sportsperson or a T5 (Temporary Worker): Creative or Sporting Worker and they are sponsored by a sports club and are being temporarily loaned to another club, to return to their sponsor; and such loans are specifically permitted by the relevant sports governing body; and the sponsor has made arrangements to continue to meet sponsor duties (9.21.1(c)(i)-(v))

Absence from employment (9.30.1)

Permission held by a Skilled Worker, Intra-Company, Representative of an Overseas Business, T2 Minister of Religion, T2 Sportsperson or T5 (Temporary Worker) ***may*** be cancelled if the individual is absent from work without pay or has their pay reduced for more than 4 weeks per calendar year, unless the absence is due to:

- Maternity, paternity or parental leave; statutory adoption leave;
- sick leave,
- assisting with a national or international humanitarian or environmental crisis if agreed by the sponsor; or
- taking part in lawful strike action (9.30.1(a)-(e)).

2.3.8.9 Change of job or lower salary rate (9.31.1-9.31.3)

Permission held by a Skilled Worker, Intra-Company, Representative of an Overseas Business, T2 Minister of Religion or T5 (Temporary Worker) ***may*** be cancelled in certain circumstances.:

1. Where the worker has changed jobs or receives a lower salary rate (so a salary rise is not caught, though the change must still be notified to the SSHD unless relating only to an annual increment or a temporary salary reduction permitted under the Sponsor guidance)
2. Where a job loses its shortage occupation classification
3. Where the job changes sufficiently that its SOC code changes (so a change in role within the same SOC code is fine) or
4. A lower salary is received such that the going rate is no longer met, unless an exception applies. The exceptions are for:

    - A participant in a graduate training programme covering multiple roles who is changing SOC code within (or at the end of) that programme whose sponsor notifies the SSHD of the change of job and salary is protected from this (r9.31.2)
    - Salary drops due to permitted absences (r9.31.1)
    - For persons on the ICT route whose reduction is whilst they are abroad
    - For Skilled Workers who would nevertheless meet the 70 point requirement even after the change (r9.31.3).

2.3.8.10 Endorsing body no longer approved (9.32.1)

EC or permission held as a Start-up, Innovator or Global Talent ***may*** be refused if their endorsing body ceases to be approved for endorsing migrants on the route on which P was endorsed.

Casework Tip

CONSIDERING A GENERAL REFUSAL CASE

When confronted by a possible general refusal scenario, bear in mind:

Which general refusal reasons apply to the immigration route in question (r9.1.1)

(a)Are the refusals mandatory ("*must be refused*") or discretionary ("*may be refused*")?

(b)Are there any definitions in r6 or Part 9 that you should consider when determining whether the general refusal reason may bite in your particular case?

2.3.9 Cancellation of entry clearance/permission to enter or stay

Part 9 now includes cancellation within each of the paragraphs addressing particular scenarios. You can see whether a cancellation power is available by looking at the structure of each of the refusal grounds. Typically the 2nd paragraph of each ground addresses cancellation. Section 5 of Part 9 is wholly focussed on cancellation powers - all the scenarios covered there involve some material change of circumstances. As already noted, the term "cancellation" now generally replaces "curtailment", though the latter is still used in Appendix EU.

There is specific guidance *Cancellation of entry clearance and permission* (Version 1.0; 22 December 2020). If you receive an enquiry from someone whose leave has been cancelled, you would not be permitted to assist them with challenging such a decision and you should refer the case to a suitable accredited adviser.

2.3.10 Remedies regarding the general refusal reasons

Appeals under the 'relevant provisions' of the NIAA 2002

The general refusal reasons often feature in appeals (see generally Part 14 of MIL). Of course, unless there is a refusal of a human rights or asylum claim, there will be no right of appeal: the only remedies will be administrative review or judicial review. Both appeals and judicial review are outside the OISC 1 remit, thus either type of case must be referred to a suitable accredited adviser.

Administrative review

The Administrative Review guidance explains that:

> Administrative review is available both if the alleged error could have made a difference to the original decision or could have an unfair impact on the applicant's future applications, for example because they may now be refused on general grounds.

So, a refused migrant may wish to use administrative review to clear their name of allegations of misconduct relevant to the general refusal reasons even though they may recognise that their application is doomed to fail for other reasons. Although only some of the general refusal reasons are mentioned as case working errors at Appendix AR AR.2.11(a), any general refusal can be challenged given AR2.11(c):

> Where the original decision maker otherwise applied the Immigration Rules incorrectly.

It may be that litigation is required to determine the extent to which administrative review will reconsider the exercise of discretion in relation to the general refusal reasons. See generally Part 14 of MIL for a detailed discussion of administrative review.

Where there is no human rights or asylum refusal, and administrative review fails, then consideration will need to be given to judicial review (again see Part 14 of MIL).

Further notes/Information

Where a refused application involves a human rights claim, there may be a right of appeal. There is no direct avenue in these appeals to review the adverse exercise of discretion. Appeals are just about whether an immigration decision is outweighed by private and family life. However, the general refusal issues will be relevant in assessing the public interest side of the balance once a private and family life case reaches the stage at which proportionality is assessed. Presumably a mandatory refusal reason will carry more weight than a discretionary one.

2.4 Policies, Concessions and Operational Guidance

Knowledge of policies and concessions is an important part of an immigration caseworker's arsenal. Many concessions from the past have now been withdrawn or incorporated into the Rules (for example, there was once a 'seven years' child concession' which was, for non-British citizen children, rather similar to what is now found in section 117B(vi) of the NIAA 2002, and in Rule 276ADE and the Appendix FM exception at Ex.1).

There are different kinds of guidance.

- There are 'concessions' which effectively create alternative residence routes outside the Immigration Rules altogether (e.g. the carers policy) – we deal with these in Module 4.
- There is guidance that explains how particular Immigration Rules or the EEA Regulations will be operated and interpreted in practice; there is an ever-growing set of guidance of this kind, indeed now virtually every part of the Rules has its own associated guidance. For example, UKVI guidance Family life (as a partner or parent), private life and exceptional circumstances is where one would find definitions of concepts within the Immigration Rules such as 'insurmountable obstacles'; we deal with this guidance alongside the Rules in question in the following Modules.
- There is guidance that explains the procedures and processes by which an application will make its way through the system (for example, there is a detailed explanation of the way in which applications from the destitute will be deal with in the fee waiver guidance which is at time of writing located in Other cross-cutting guidance
- There is guidance that has special force because it is *statutory guidance*: it is issued to explain the approach that will be taken to implementing a particular statutory duty. An example is Every Child Matters – Change for Children which contains very important material explaining how section 55 of the Borders, Citizenship and Immigration Act 2009 (which creates a duty to safeguard and promote the welfare of children in immigration cases) should be approached.
- There is guidance which summarises particular immigration routes and processes: this is essentially a guide for the use of unrepresented migrants (for example there is an overview of the student visa requirements and process).

The majority of policies and concessions can be located in one or more of the collections below, which comprise sets of instructions to Home Office caseworkers, Immigration Officers and Entry Clearance Officers – now found on the GOV.UK website under the title, Operational Guidance. These collections are broken down as follows:

- **Asylum policy –** previously called the 'Asylum Policy Instructions' and the 'Asylum Process Guidance': guidance to Home Office staff dealing with asylum cases. Covers screening and routing, asylum support, children, detention and reporting, decision making, country information, appeals, and voluntary departures.
- **Immigration Staff Guidance**: guidance mainly for Home Office caseworkers making decisions on non-asylum in-country applications, though often an overlap with the ECG and Modernised Guidance (see below). Includes many current policies and concessions, sometimes in the annexes, on a wide range of issues connected with immigration applications. Examples of guidance collections contained here are:
    - **Family of people settled or coming to settle:** this is essentially the body of guidance on family migration

- **EEA, Swiss nationals and EC association agreements** (formerly European Casework Instructions (ECI)): guidance for EEA nationals and their family members including guidance on free movement rights and the EU Settlement Scheme as well as frontier workers
- **Nationality Guidance** – formerly Nationality Instructions (NIs): for nationality applications
- **Working in the UK**: this contains guidance on all work categories
- **Studying**: this contains guidance on all study categories
- **Other cross-cutting guidance:** contains guidance on topics such as administrative review, s3C leave, fee waivers, knowledge of language and life in the UK, public funds and calculating continuous leave for ILR

- **Entry Clearance Guidance (ECG)**: these comprise instructions to ECOs on how to interpret the Immigration Rules and assess applications. Much of the guidance to ECOs has now been put into the Immigration Staff Guidance collection, particularly where it overlaps with the HO policies on similar applications made from within the UK.
- **Enforcement** section of 'operational guidance – formerly Enforcement Guidance and Instructions (EIG): formerly known as the Operation Enforcement Manual, these are instructions to Immigration Officers carrying out removals and other enforcement action. The sections on bail and detention are useful. The chapters of the manual were re-numbered, rendering references to specific chapters in case law obsolete.

These are very large documents and are frequently altered, so there is little point in keeping a hard copy: indeed, it is positively dangerous to presume that the same policy matrix is in place when you next make an application as when you last acted for someone in that situation.

It is not easy to find exactly where the individual Guidance documents exist within the operational guidance section of the GOV.UK website, or even to know that they exist at all. Sometimes, they do not exist within a collection, so are impossible to locate from within the website itself. It may be easier to do an internet search for them – using the search term 'UKVI guidance + subject matter'.

You may want to create a library within your firm of particularly useful policies when you cite them in your casework (they can be saved onto a hard-drive as PDF files) – they may alter or sometimes disappear before your client's application is finally decided. You may be able to find a policy prevailing at a particular time, if you can recall or ascertain its location within the structure of the historic Home Office website, in the snapshots provided by the UK Government Web Archive which show the contents of the Home Office website at particular times. You can subscribe (here) to a daily HO email service which informs you when guidance has been updated.

2.4.1 The relationship between rules and guidance

Always remember that guidance is neither law nor rule. Where it is inconsistent with the Rules, the Rules take priority. An advisor who relies on guidance which is patently different to the Rules *may* be cruising for a bruising encounter with the courts or Tribunals. This is particularly the case where the guidance simply summarises a particular part of the rules for convenience. It may be a different matter where a passage of guidance clearly and deliberately sets out a departure from the Rules. Nevertheless, the Immigration Rules are the complete legal code that applies to all applications, and for advisers it is the rules that need to be considered first and foremost. The guidance, though sometimes useful to help explain what the rules mean, is not always accurate, up to date or comprehensive.

The case of Alvi [2012] UKSC 33 decided that any requirement on the basis of which an application can be refused must be in the rules. It could not be merely contained in the guidance. Shortly after this decision, several Appendices to the Immigration Rules were added which moved such requirements from guidance to the rules.

If you want to rely on a particular policy you must establish its existence at the relevant time. Old policies may be no longer in force. A useful current policy may not have been effective at the critical past date of decision in your client's case. Beware:

Policies can appear and disappear without notice.

Top Tip

As we have seen above, when identifying an immigration route under the Rules, there are always several places to look:

The Immigration Rule that is in force at the time you are planning an application (or as at the date of decision when considering appeals and other remedies).

Any definition of a word or concept within the Rules may be found in the general definitions in Rule 6, or in the introductory part of the relevant category.

Any Home Office policy – this may usefully explain or interpret the intended operation of the rule, and may additionally provide some leeway outside the rule's strict confines – you may find these in the Operational Guidance, this Manual, or on the Refugee Legal Group, or on the ILPA website

2.5 Statutory duty to safeguard children

As well as the rules and policies set out in the previous units, there is one very important statutory duty which runs across the whole of immigration control, and which aims to ensure that the best interests of the child are always kept at the centre of decision making.

This has been introduced to bring the HO into line with the UK's commitments under the UN Convention on the Rights of the Child (more about which can be read in Module 5 in the section on private life and children under Rule 276ADE(1)(iv)).

Section 55 of the Borders, Citizenship and Immigration Act 2009 introduced an obligation to make arrangements to ensure that immigration functions are discharged with regards to the need to safeguard and promote the welfare of children who are in the United Kingdom. In so doing the Act aligns the duty imposed with that imposed on public authorities under the Children Act 2004, s.11(2).

The duty applies to the Home Office and also to those performing immigration functions, broadly defined. It only applies to children present in the UK. However, this is not to say that child welfare considerations are irrelevant to decision making in entry clearance cases.

By section 55(3), a person exercising any of the specified functions must, in so exercising them, have regard to any guidance given to the person by the Secretary of State for the purpose specified in BCIA 2009, s 55(1). The statutory guidance Every Child Matters: Change for Children was issued in November 2009. It explains that the section 55 duty includes:

- ensuring that children are growing up in circumstances consistent with the provision of safe and effective care; and undertaking that role so as to enable those children to have optimum life chances and to enter adulthood successfully;
- having regard to their 'physical, intellectual, emotional, social and behavioural development' and their 'optimum life chances'; and their 'physical, emotional and educational needs' and 'the likely effect on [them] of any change in [their] circumstances'

None of this means that the rights of children are a trump card, however. Although the misdemeanours of parents should not be held against their children, the realities of the parents' immigration status must be given appropriate weight in decision making.

Where children are affected by enforcement action (e.g. detention and removal), either directly or indirectly, the Office of the Children's Champion offers advice to UKVI decision-makers on the implications for the children's welfare, to enable an informed decision to be made giving due weight to their best interests. As far as the Home Office is concerned, neither the advice nor the best interests of the children need be determinative of the outcome of the case: but they must make a child's best interests a primary consideration.

Module 3: Visitors

3.1 Introduction to Visitors

Until 30 November 2020, all the rules on visitors were contained in Appendix V. Then as part of the effort to simplify the immigration rules they split up into the following separate appendices:

- Appendix V: Visitor
- Appendix Visitor: Permitted Activities (previously contained in Appendices 3, 4 and 5 of Appendix V)
- Appendix Visitor: Visa national list (previously appearing as Appendix 2 to Appendix V. NB: some countries have been renamed but the old names still appear)
- Appendix Visitor: Permit Free Festival List (previously appearing as Visitors Appendix 5. Permit Free Festivals contained in Appendix V)
- Appendix Visitor: Transit Without Visa Scheme (previously at rr V7.6-9 in Appendix V)

Changes between Appendix V and Appendix V: Visitor are

The requirement for marriage/CP visitors, even from non-visa states, to hold prior entry clearance is disapplied to Swiss nationals from 1 January 2021

- Study up to 6 months is permitted under the standard route.
- Voluntary work no longer needs to be incidental to the visit but can be main reason (but is limited to 30 days – see PA3).
- Students aged 16 or over enrolled in courses overseas may receive research tuition in the UK
- Provision for academic visitors in exchange arrangements has been widened beyond those conducting research while on sabbatical (V15.3)
- Drivers on international routes can now collect as well as deliver goods and passengers in and out of the UK (PA 9)
- An addition of alternative means to prove identity and nationality, beyond a passport, has been made for EEA and Swiss nationals who may use their national ID cards.
- Whereas the pre- 1 December 2020 Appendix V contained its own suitability provisions, there now appears a mere cross-reference to the new **Part 9** and the requirement for those applying for PTS (permission to stay) not to be in breach of immigration laws (unless r39E applies) or on immigration bail (see V3.1&2). Please refer to Module 2 for section 2.3 on grounds for refusal.

3.2 Appendix V: Visitor

The introduction outlines the four types of visitor as being

- Standard visitors who wish to undertake permitted activities
- Marriage/civil partnership visitors, seeking to tie the knot or give notice to do so
- Permitted Paid Engagement visitors, experts in their field coming for paid work for up to one month
- Transit visitors, entering the UK for up to 48 hours en route to another country outside the CTA (unless the Transit Without Visa Scheme Appendix applies)

It reminds applicants that:

- They can only work if expressly allowed by Appendix Permitted Activities.

- The maximum length of stay for each category is set out at V17.2 and in Appendix Visitors: Permitted Activities.
- Multiple entry visit visas allow for staying in the UK for normally no more than 6 months at a time.

The Legal Framework

- Appendix V: Visitor
- Appendix Visitor: Permitted Activities
- Appendix Visitor: Visa national list
- Appendix Visitor: Permit Free Festival List
- Appendix Visitor: Transit Without Visa Scheme
- The Home Office guidance: Visit guidance, Considering human rights claims in visit applications, Transit guidance
- Guidance for applicants: marriage, permitted paid engagement, standard visitor visas, transit and ADS Agreement visits, Visiting the UK: guide to supporting documents

Home Office policy/guidance used to provide substantially more detail than now, and some of the older guidance may have useful things to say. Whilst it may no longer reflect Home Office policy, it will be hard for the Home Office to argue that older policy on substantially the same rules is no longer applicable.

Some principles:

- It is not possible to switch into a visit visa
- Visa nationals require visit visas
- For nationals of Oman, Qatar, UAE and Kuwait, visa-free visits for up to six months are enabled via the Electronic Visa Waiver (EVW) scheme, which allows visa presentation at the border in electronic form (and a level of discretion regarding punctuation discrepancies with passports).
- A six-month visit visa costs £95
- Non-visa nationals may simply travel to the UK and then seek leave to enter as a visitor at the port of entry, unless seeking to visit for more than six months or visiting for the purposes of marriage of civil partnership, or of giving notice of such , but…
- Non-visa nationals *may* apply for a visa
- Each visitor in a group must fully satisfy the rules
- A visa will be valid, unless single or dual entry, for multiple uses during its lifetime (thus the term 'multiple entry' visa): it will usually be issued for six months. Where the person has built up a good immigration history, the HO may grant a long-term visit visa for two, five or 10 years, but which cannot be used for any single visit for more than six months. On each entry under a long-term visa, the person will be treated as having been granted leave to enter for six months (under the Leave to Enter or Remain Order 2000).
- A different fee is payable according to the duration sought (2 years – £361, 5 years – £655, 10 years – £822). In a move to attract Chinese tourists to the UK, all standard visit visas issued in China will be valid for two years (but for no extra fee).

Non-visa nationals – when should they apply for a visit visa?

It will be sensible for a non-visa nationals to consider applying for a visa if there is a risk they might be refused leave to enter on arriving in the UK without one. Thousands of individuals are refused entry to the UK each year. A visa application, whether granted or refused, can save the cost and frustration of travelling to the UK only to be held for several hours in the airport before being sent back home.

Some will be refused at port for providing inadequate or inconsistent information; failing to convince the HO that they will leave the UK at the end of their visit, or not work here; or a lack of documentation addressing these issues. Where it can be predicted that a Border Force official may have such concerns, the visitor should be prepared to deal with them. Having advised a client of any potential weaknesses and how they might be addressed, ultimately it will be for the applicant to decide whether to apply for a visa or not.

V 1.1-4 Entry requirements for visitors

Visitors require prior EC under V1.1. (and will otherwise be refused entry under V1.2) where the visitor is:

- A visa national as listed in Appendix Visitor: Visa national list, unless one of the exceptions in that Appendix applies or they are eligible under Appendix Visitor: Transit Without Visa Scheme
- Of any nationality (except Swiss) and applying in the marriage/CP visitor category
- Seeking to enter for over 6 months

V1.3 provides that the following can apply for permission to enter at the border:

- Non-visa nationals (unless non-Swiss nationals coming to marry/enter into a CP or coming for more than 6 months)
- Visa nationals covered by an exception in the visa nationals appendix or entitled to transit without a visa.

Child visitors holding EC may be refused entry unless they travel with the person identified in their EC or hold EC stating they are unaccompanied. They may still be granted entry if adequate arrangements for travel reception and care have been made and their parent or legal guardian has provided consent (V1.4 read with V5.1&2)

V 2.1-6 Validity requirements for entry clearance or permission to stay as a visitor

V2.1-2 requires applications to be made:

- From outside the UK online on the specified form "Apply for a UK visit visa" (the old paper form is still here for reference) or,
- If applying in country to extend a visit visa Application to extend stay in the UK: FLR(IR)

Further validity requirements are that:

- The fee is paid and biometrics – as well as a passport or other document establishing nationality and identity - are provided (V2.3)
- EC applications are made to the relevant post abroad and PTS (permission to stay) applications are made by a person in the UK with a standard or marriage/CP visa (V2.4&5)

Where these requirements are not met, applications *may* be rejected and not considered (V2.6).

V 3.1-2 Suitability requirements for all visitors

These are

- not to fall for refusal under Part 9;
- be in breach of immigration laws unless r39E applies; or
- be on immigration bail (V3.1&2).

The suitability provisions which were contained in Appendix V before 1 December 2020 have been scrapped.

The provisions in the 1 December 2020 version of Part 9 (renamed Grounds for Refusal) which apply *specifically* to visitors (although the rest of Part 9 applies to visitors too where appropriate) are as follows:

- 9.4.4(a) EC applications ***must*** be refused where the applicant has been sentenced to 12 months of imprisonment anywhere, if they apply within 12 months of the end of the sentence.

- 9.4.4(b) EC applications ***must*** also be refused where the applicant was convicted of a criminal offence anywhere and received a non-custodial sentence or out-of-court disposal recorded on their criminal record, if the application is made within 12 months of that conviction

The 10-year re-entry ban for deception in previous applications in Part 9 r9.8.7(f) is now limited to entry clearance applications, expressly including visitor applications, as was previously the case in Appendix V's Suitability requirements at V 3.10(f)).

Other refusal or cancellation reasons under Part 9 also apply, and you should consult Module 2, section 2.3 Grounds for Refusal for further information.

V 4.1 (a)-(j) Eligibility requirements for visitors

All but transit visitors must meet the requirements in V4.2-6, plus other requirements for those applying: as a minor (V5.1&2); under the Approved Destination Status Agreement (V6.1); to receive private medical treatment (V7.1-3); as an organ donor (V8.1-4); to study as a visitor (V9.1&2); as an academic seeking EC for 12 months (V10.1); to receive work related training (V11.1-3); to marry/form a CP (V12.1&2); to undertake permitted paid engagements (V13.1-3) or if applying in-country for PTS (V15.1-5).

V 4.2-3 Genuine visitor requirement

The decision maker must be satisfied that the applicant will leave at the end of their visit and not live in the UK for extended periods or make the UK their main home through frequent or successive visits; that they will not undertake prohibited activities (V4.4-6); and that they have sufficient funds to cover all reasonable costs of their visit. "Reasonable costs" expressly include the cost of the return or onward journey, costs relating to dependants and planned activities (eg private medical treatment). Only funds held in financial institutions which meet FIN2.1 in Appendix Finance are taken into account (V4.2).

A third party who has a genuine professional or personal relationship with the visitor can provide sufficient funds for travel, maintenance and accommodation so long as this covers the duration of the visit and the third party is not in breach of immigration law at the time of decision or UK entry by the visitor (V4.3).

One of the most common reasons to come here is to visit family. The visit rules do not specify particular requirements for this class of visit. In Ahsrif 01/TH/3465, the Tribunal pointed out that:

> The whole point of a family visit is that the existence of family ties will normally furnish the reason for the visit, since it is hardly surprising that members of a family separated by many thousands of miles may from time to time wish to see each other.

Relevant factors in relation to intention include:

- The purpose or purposes of the visit (see Appendix Visitor: Permitted activities below)
- Immigration history: previous compliance with immigration laws is an excellent indicator of intention to leave – both regarding visits to the UK and elsewhere ('especially the USA, Canada, Australia, New Zealand, Ireland, Schengen countries or Switzerland' says the guidance). Where there have been previous breaches, evidence will need to be provided of a clear change in circumstances to allay the obvious concern.
- The immigration history and status of the sponsor, friend or relative that the person is visiting, or of such whom the Home Office know to be in the UK, even where there is no stated intention to visit them
- Family links with own country, such as spouse, children, parents or relatives for whom the visitor is the usual carer
- Other links, such as a job to return to or studies to complete

- Levels of income (it may be more difficult to suggest someone has a temptation to overstay if they earn an above average income in their own country, and whereby doing so they would be exchanging that lifestyle for becoming an overstayer without the right to work). Watch out for the evidence supplied as to the availability of funds, because if bank statements do not dovetail with claimed earnings, the decision maker may be left doubtful as to whether they are being told the whole story.
- Absence or otherwise of links in the UK – this could cut both ways, as having a sponsor is helpful, and having someone to visit provides a permitted purpose for the visit. On the other hand, if the family here has shown a 'pattern of immigration', some ECOs will suspect that, like them, the applicant will never leave. A failure to reveal the presence of a family member will be thought suspicious, and may give rise to an allegation of deception.
- Whether a respectable applicant will seriously wish to exchange their life in the country of origin for what would effectively amount to being an outlaw in the United Kingdom, unable to work or study lawfully
- Whether documentary evidence can be verified
- Inconsistent information, e.g. discrepancies in the information provided by an applicant and statements made by their sponsor – the Home Office may contact sponsors to discuss the prospective visit, or on the visitor arriving in the UK
- A search of the applicant's baggage

Additionally, the Home Office Visit guidance raises the following factors as relevant to the assessment of the applicant's personal circumstances:

> the duration of previous visits and whether this was significantly longer than they originally stated on their visa application or on arrival – if this is the case, you should not automatically presume that the visitor is not genuine, but this may be a reason to question the applicant's overall intentions

The guidance does acknowledge that a person might 'extend their stay to do different permitted activities' from those they intended on entry. A person's intentions can change, but where they do, it will usually be sensible to explain to the Home Office why the visit was longer than expected.

Example

Don Juan applies for a visa to visit the UK, explaining that he is coming as a tourist to see the sights for a period of two weeks. He provides an outline and costed itinerary for his trip, evidence that he has the means to fund it, and a letter from his employer confirming that he is entitled to leave for two weeks. His application is successful and he is granted a visa for six months.

Shortly after arriving in the UK, he has a romance with a man he meets at a party, and cannot drag himself back home until six weeks have passed and the affair has run out of steam.

Having assessed his genuine intention to visit for a two-week holiday, the Home Office will be understandably miffed that he stayed for much longer. Next time he applies for a visit visa, they may suspect that that he lied to them about his intentions, his finances and his employment. He will need to explain why he stayed longer than intended, and how he was able to do so, given that the evidence he relied on in his earlier application all pointed towards a two-week holiday.

Another relevant factor is:

> whether, on the balance of probabilities, the information and the reasons for the visit or for extending their stay provided by the applicant are credible and correspond to their personal, family, social and economic background

This is self-explanatory. Where, on the facts of the case, this may be in issue, it may be sensible for the applicant to submit a detailed letter or statement explaining the purpose of the visit in detail, identifying any possible concerns, and rebutting them.

Example

Khadija, from Bangladesh, is in relatively low paid employment in her country, and her trip to the UK to see a friend is going to cost her six months of her normal salary. The Home Office may suspect that she has other intentions (e.g. to work in the UK and/or overstay).

Khadija explains in a letter that she has been saving many years for this holiday, and provides evidence of a savings account into which she has deposited small sums over a long period of time. She also explains that she grew up with her friend, that they are particularly close, and her friend has family commitments in the UK which prevent her travelling to Bangladesh. She can also confirm that she fully understands the implications of breaching the immigration laws and does not want to prejudice any future visits by doing so. Her friend can also write a letter confirming the importance of their relationship and the difficulties she has in travelling to Bangladesh.

Frequent and successive visits

Para V4.2(b) states that the person 'will not live in the UK for extended periods through frequent or successive visits, or make the UK their main home'. This provision was initially added to the Rules following the Tribunal's decision in Sawmynaden [2012] UKUT 161 (IAC).

Mrs Sawmynaden was a retired widower with two daughters and six siblings in the UK. The HO refused her application for a five-year visit visa because her intention to visit the UK to spend time with her family would have made a total of 14½ out of the last 18 months spent in the UK. The refusal stated that:

Given that you have been spending long periods of time in the UK over the last few years, this raises doubts as to your true intentions. Given all of the above and considering your application as a whole, I am not satisfied that you are genuinely seeking entry as a visitor for a limited period as stated by you, not exceeding six months and that you intend to leave the UK at the end of the period of the visit as stated by you (as required [under the old visit rules] by Paragraph 41 (i) and (ii) of the Immigration Rules.

The Tribunal allowed the appeal, laying out important principles on visits to family in the UK:

(i) There is no restriction on the number of visits a person may make to the UK, nor any requirement that a specified time must elapse between successive visits.
(ii) The periods of time spent in the United Kingdom and the country of residence will always be important.
(iii) Both the expressed purpose of the visit and details of how time visiting in the past has been spent are material, together with the length of time that has elapsed since previous visits. There is nothing objectionable about a grandparent helping with childcare or an adult child helping with an elder's care needs.
(iv) The links that the appellant retains with her country of residence (including the presence of other family there) will be a material consideration.
(v) The Tribunal is required to ascertain what is the reality of the arrangement entered into between the appellant and the host in the United Kingdom. Is the reality that the appellant is resident in the United Kingdom and intends to be for the foreseeable future?
(vi) The issue may be approached by considering whether the reality is that the appellant is now no more than a visitor to her country of residence as the purpose of the return home is confined to using his or her presence there solely as the means of gaining re-admission to the United Kingdom.
(vii) This does not preclude the appellant from remaining in the country of residence for the least amount of time sufficient to maintain her status as a genuine visitor.
(viii) Family emergencies, whilst likely to result in a longer visit than the established pattern, should not be held against an applicant without adequate supporting evidence to that effect. Thus, the pregnancy of a daughter or daughter-in-law or the aftermath of the birth might explain a more-protracted stay (within the 6-month duration of a single permitted visit); so, too, a serious medical condition.

(ix)There may be comparisons with the person who owns homes in two different countries. Is he resident in both or a visitor to one of them?

Although the current rules might make it a little easier to refuse an application in Mrs Sawmynaden's circumstances, Home Office guidance is *not unhelpful*.

You should look at:

- the purpose of the visit and intended length of stay stated
- the number of visits made over the past 12 months, including the length of stay on each occasion, the time elapsed since the last visit, and if this amounts to the individual spending more time in the UK than in their home country
- the purpose of return trips to the visitor's home country or trips out of the CTA and if these are used only to seek re-entry to the UK
- the links they have with their home country or ordinary country of residence – consider especially any long term commitments and where the applicant is registered for tax purposes
- evidence the UK is their main place of residence, for example
- if they have registered with a general practitioner (GP)
- send their children to UK schools
- the history of previous applications, for example if the visitor has previously been refused under the family rules and subsequently wants to enter as a visitor you must assess if they are using the visitor route to avoid the rules in place for family migrants joining British or settled persons in the UK

There is no specified maximum period which an individual can spend in the UK in any period such as '6 months in 12 months' (as long as each visit does not exceed the maximum period for that visit, normally 6 months). However, if it is clear from an applicant's's travel history that they are seeking to remain in the UK for extended periods or making the UK their home you should refuse their application.

So, it is not clear that an application such as Mrs Sawmyaden's would necessarily fail under these principles. It will be important that where applicants are making frequent and lengthy visits to the UK, they are well prepared for a robust interview on entry, on each occasion, and ready with evidence of their settled lives elsewhere.

It will be important to explain clearly why a client is not intending to make the UK their home and give reasons why the applicant's intentions are for the purpose only to visit. It is important to explain all the reasons the person will leave at the end of the visit.

Example

Mr Patel is a widow from Gujarat in India. He is recently retired from his job as a senior civil servant in the Ministry of Agriculture. He has two married sons, five grandchildren and four brothers and sister who live in various parts of the UK. He wants to apply for a five-year visit visa so that he can spend time with each of his family members in the UK. This is his retirement present to himself.

Since his retirement he has started to develop his own piece of family land that he inherited from his father. Two more sisters and one brother live near the family land and are going to help him.

Some points that could be explained in his application are:

-The links Mr Patel retains with his home, including what he intends doing there in the future and the presence of his family members there and his relationship with them.

-The expressed purpose of the visit and his relationship with those he is visiting.

-The periods of time he intends to spend both in the UK and at home although there is no restriction on the number of visits a person may make to the UK nor any requirement that a specified time has to elapse between each visit.

It will be important to describe his ties with his own country and why he will be motivated to leave the UK at the end of any visit.

It will be important that where applicants are making frequent and lengthy visits to the UK, they are well prepared for a robust interview on entry, on each occasion, and ready with evidence of their settled lives elsewhere.

Maintenance and accommodation

An applicant must have access to sufficient resources to maintain and accommodate themselves adequately for the whole of their planned visit to the UK. The Guidance points out that there is no set level of funds required for an applicant to show this. The Home Office will expect enough information to be provided with the application to be able to assess the likely cost of the visit.

An applicant will need to provide very good and consistent evidence of their existing resources, including resources that they will continue to receive at home during their visit, and those available from any sponsor. The Home Office assessment will take account of any ongoing financial commitments the applicant has in their country of residence such as rent/mortgage payments and any dependants who they support financially, including those who are not travelling with them.

Where the majority of these funds have not been held in their account for long, the Home Office will need evidence of the origin of the money. Any funds that are not explained and evidenced will be treated as suspect.

Note also the additional requirements where the funds are being provided by a third party (V4.3).

V 4.4-6 V 4.4-6 Prohibited activities and payment requirements for visitors

The visitor must not intend to

- Work in the UK unless allowed under Appendices Permitted Activities, Permit Free Festivals or the Permitted Paid Engagements in V13.3. Working includes: taking employment or otherwise doing work for an organisation or business; establishing or running a business as a self-employed person; work placements or internships; or direct selling to the public, or providing goods and services (V4.4(a)). Permitted activities must not amount to employment or filling-/providing short-term cover for, a role in a UK based organisation. Where the visitor is paid and employed outside the UK they must remain so (V4.5)
- Receive payment from a UK source for activities in the UK apart from:
- reasonable travel or subsistence expenses, including fees for board meeting attendance by a director
- international drivers undertaking activities permitted under PA 9.2
- prize money
- billing UK clients for time in the UK where the visitor's overseas employer has contracted to provide services to a UK company with the majority of such work being done overseas. The payment must be less than the visitor's salary
- salary payments by a multinational company made for administrative reasons from the UK
- for paid performances as an artist, entertainer or musician at a festival listed in the relevant Appendix
- for permitted paid engagements (V4.6).
- Study unless under Appendix Visitor: Permitted Activities (V4.4(b))
- Access medical treatment unless they meet the requirements to receive private medical treatment or donate an organ (V4.4(c))
- Marry/enter a CP unless they meet the marriage/CP visit requirements (V4.4(d))

It will be difficult to evidence that a person is not going to do something that is prohibited. The Home Office will suspect that those who are not well placed in their own country may think they can benefit from illegal employment in the UK. Such an applicant may want to address this potential concern directly in their statement. Similarly, a visitor coming to see a girlfriend or boyfriend may want to confirm they have no intention of marrying whilst they are here (unless of course they are applying for a marriage visit visa).

Top Tip

There are many applicants who will find it difficult to succeed in an application for a standard visit visa, particularly those who are from developing countries or who are not high net-worth individuals. The quality of the application will be fundamental to the prospects of success. Applicants should consider providing:

- detailed itinerary and costing for the trip
- a statement from the applicant explaining the purpose of the visit in detail, and any relevant background to the decision to come to the UK to visit. Why the UK? Why now?
- evidence how they will spend their time here (e.g. invitations from family members, or research into the sights they intend to visit)
- evidence of a settled life to return to at the end of the visit – work, employment, family responsibilities etc. Explain, with evidence, how the visit can happen, given those reasons to return – e.g. a letter from an employer confirming the person has been given leave for the relevant period, if necessary explaining how their absence will be dealt with, a letter from the college confirming the student will be on vacation at the relevant time, or evidence of alternative temporary arrangements for the care of dependants. Where there is no obvious incentive to return, the statement will need to be even more compelling. The object will be to persuade the Home Office that the person has a good life back home
- where the person has family here, this will often be seen as a negative factor. Explain their immigration history, and why, unlike them, the person has no wish to settle in the UK. Where the family have a poor immigration history, explain how the person is different
- evidence of funds
- if the cost of the visit may be considered to be disproportionate in light of the person's overall resources, the reasons for the visit will need to be clearly laid out. A person may well be willing to spend more on a visit to a close family member or friend than merely to see the sights
- their provenance (is the source of funds clear) and their accessibility. Unidentified deposits in bank accounts must be avoided. Approach evidencing the funds as you might do for an application under Appendix FM, ensuring that all the evidence is consistent (or provide an explanation if it is not)
- more evidence rather than less. If the applicant is working, payslips and bank statements, and letters from the employer (on headed notepaper) should be provided. If not, and in any case, other evidence of income from property or land, business accounts, tax returns etc. should be provided. If the applicant is studying, then plenty of evidence of that, and their progress in their studies, and an explanation as to how they can afford the time and funds for the trip
- evidence of accommodation
- evidence of previous compliance with immigration controls in the UK or elsewhere
- a clear statement addressing any facts which might be seen as potential weaknesses, previous reasons for refusal, and the applicant's intention to leave the UK at the end of their visit and not to work in the UK during it. Home Office decision makers are trained to identify potential weaknesses, so address them head on. A surfeit of honesty can be disarming

Also:

- make sure the application form is completed fully and accurately and the information on it is internally consistent and consistent with any other information the Home Office may have on the applicant (e.g. from previous applications, or from applications by family members)
- make sure documentary evidence is verifiable, and presume it will be verified
- remember that friends and relatives here may be contacted by the Home Office to confirm their understanding of any relevant facts (e.g. the length and purpose of the visit) so ensure family is informed of the importance of remembering the relevant details mentioned in the application

- present the documentation in a way that is easy for the Home Office to access and understand. Provide good quality translations where necessary. Explain and cross refer to the documentation in a covering letter.

V 5.1-2 V 5.1-2 Additional eligibility requirements for child visitors

- Arrangements for travel, reception and care in the UK must be adequate (V5.1)
- If no parent or guardian who is based in the child's home country or country of residence, travels with the child, they must consent to the child's travel, reception and care in the UK. This consent may be requested in writing (V5.2).

V 6.1 Additional eligibility requirement for visitors under the Approved Destination Status Agreement

To be eligible, an applicant must be a Chinese national and intend to enter, travel within the UK, and leave the UK as part of a tourist group.

V 7.1-3 Additional eligibility requirements for visitors coming to the UK to receive private medical treatment

- The medical inspector must be satisfied that, if the applicant has a communicable disease, they are not a danger to public health (V7.1)
- Private medical treatment must have been arranged before travel to the UK. A letter from the treating doctor or consultant must be provided. It must mention the condition requiring treatment or consultation; where this is to take place; and an estimate of cost and (finite) duration (V7.2)
- Applications for 11 months' EC must, further, be supported by evidence from the doctor or consultant that the treatment is likely to take between 6 and 11 months and a tuberculosis test certificate if their country of residence in listed in Appendix T (V7.3).

V 8.1-4 Additional eligibility requirements for visitors coming to the UK to donate an organ

Under this category, the extra requirements are to genuinely intend to donate an organ or be assessed as a potential organ donor for an identified recipient who may be a relative or with whom they have a close personal relationship (V8.1). The applicant must show that the recipient either is lawfully present in the UK or will be at the time of the transplant (V8.4).

The applicant must show written confirmation of medical tests showing they are a donor match to the recipient, or that they are undergoing further tests to be assessed as such (V8.2). In addition, a letter dated within 3 months of the intended UK arrival date is required. This must be from either the lead nurse or coordinator of the UK NHS Trust's Living Donor Kidney Transplant team or a UK consultant either registered with the NHS or appearing in the Specialist Register of the GMC (V8.3).

V 9.1-2 Additional eligibility requirements for visitors coming to the UK to study for up to six months

Where relevant to the subject, and unless exempt, the applicant must, before commencing their course, satisfy Appendix ATAS (V9.1).

If an applicant studies abroad and seeks to visit the UK for research or learning about research at a UK institution, their overseas course provides must confirm the relevant of this to their course and that the applicant will not be employed at the UK institution. The overseas institution must, strangely, also confirm the applicant will not work as a sponsored researcher under Appendix Tier 5 (Temporary Worker) Government Authorised Exchange Scheme Worker (V9.2).

V 10.1 Additional eligibility requirements for academics seeking to come to the UK for more than 6 months

To be eligible for 12 months' EC, an academic must be highly qualified in their field of expertise in which they currently work at an academic or higher education institution overseas (V10.1(b)&(c)).

They must intend to do one or the permitted activities in PA11.2 (Science and Academia), which are to: take part in a formal exchange; carry out research while on sabbatical; or research, teach or engage in clinical practice as an eminent senior doctor or dentist, so long as this does not amount to filling a permanent post (V10.1(a)).

If their country is listed in Appendix T, they must provide at tuberculosis test certificate (V10.1(d)).

V 11.1-3 Additional eligibility requirements for visitors coming to the UK for work related training

Written confirmation is required for

- Clinical attachment or dental observer posts, in the form of the offer and confirmation they have not previously undertaken this activity (V11.1)
- PLAB tests, from the GMC (V11.2)
- Objective Structured Clinical Examinations, from the Nursing and Midwifery Council (V11.3)

V 12.1-2 Additional eligibility requirement for visitors coming to UK for purpose of marriage or civil partnership

The applicant must

- be aged 18 or over at the date of application (V12.1); and
- intend to give notice of marriage or civil partnership, or to marry/form a CP (which is not a sham) during the time applied for – unless they are a "relevant national" as defined in s62 of the Immigration Act 2014 (V12.2) NB: before the end of 2020 this definition includes both EEA and Swiss nationals, thereafter only Swiss nationals.

V 13.1-3 Additional eligibility requirement for visitors coming to UK for Permitted Paid Engagements

Visitors in this category must be 18 or over on application date and must intend to undertake a PPE, having arranged this before travelling to the UK and declared these in their application. They must be evidenced by a formal invitation and related to the visitor's expertise and occupation (V13.1&2).

PPEs are listed in V13.3 as:

- An academic highly qualified within their field of expertise, coming to examine students or participate in chair selection panels, having been invited by a higher education- or research institution or an arts organisation as part of that institution or its quality assurance process
- An expert coming to lecture in their subject area, invited by a higher education or research or arts organisation, without this filling a teaching position.
- An overseas designated pilot examiner coming to assess pilots against aviation regulatory requirements of other countries, if an approved training organisation regulated by the UK Civil Aviation Authority
- A qualified lawyer coming to provide court or tribunal advocacy or other form of dispute resolution or legal proceeding if invited by a client
- A professional artist, entertainer or musician coming for an activity directly related to their profession if invited by a creative (arts or entertainment) organisation, agent or broadcaster
- A professional sportsperson coming for an activity directly related to their profession if invited by a sports organisation agent or broadcaster.

V 14.1-2 Eligibility requirement for visitors coming to UK to transit

Unless the applicant is eligible to apply to apply for entry at the border under the transit without a visa scheme, via nationals must hold EC as a standard, marriage/CP or transit visitor (V14.1).

To be eligible for EC or PTE (permission to enter) as a transit visitor, applicants must be genuinely transiting to a country outside the CTA (to which they are assured entry) within 48 hours of entry to the UK. They must not claim public funds or medical treatment, work or study (V14.2).

V 15.1-5 Additional eligibility requirements for permission to stay as a visitor [i.e. extension applications]

For PTS, an applicant must be in the UK as a visitor (V15.1). Those in the UK for private medical treatment must prove that they have met the cost of treatment so far and provide a letter from their doctor or consultant detailing the medical condition requiring further treatment (V15.2).

Academics seeking to extend their permission to stay must intend to do one or more of the activities in PA11.2 (Science and Academia); still be working in their field of expertise in which they are highly qualified and in which they worked at an academic or higher education institution prior to their visit (V15.3).

PLAB visitors seeking to resit their test must have confirmation of this in writing from the GMC (V15.4).

Those undertaking unpaid clinical attachment or dental observed posts must have passed the PLAB test (V15.5)

V 16.1 Decision

If all suitability and eligibility requirements are met, the application will be granted. If not it will be refused.

V 17.1-3 Period and conditions of grant for visitors

Visa holders must not access public funds, work (unless permitted by the PPEs in V13.3 or by appendices Permitted Activities, Permit Free Festivals) or study (unless permitted by PA2 and PA17.1-3).

The table at V17.2 sets out the maximum lengths of stay for each category, which is then elaborated upon at V17.3:

- Standard and marriage/CP visitors: 6 months
- Chinese tourists on the ADSA: 30 days
- PPE: 1 month
- Private medical treatment: 11 months (may extend for another 6 months after that for the same purpose)
- Academic visitors, their child or partner: 12 months (if undertaking one or more of the activities in PA11.2 (Science and Academia))
- Standard visitors may be granted PTS to make up no more than 12 months in total (including the period of EC); and may be granted PTS for up to 6 months to re-sit the PLAB test
- Standard visitors who have passed the PLAB test may be granted PTS to undertake an unpaid clinical attachment for up to a total period of 18 months (inc EC and first extension)
- Transit visitors: 48 hours
  Transit without a visa: until 23.59 the day after arrival

3.3 Appendix Visitor: Permitted Activities (paragraphs PA1-PA18)

This separate Appendix sets out a summary table at PA 1 of permitted activities, and a roadmap of which provisions to refer to (further below) for each category:

- Standard: all permitted activities in this appendix (only Chinese ADSA visitors are restricted to tourism)
- Marriage/CP: marry or form a civil partnership, or give notice of this. They may also do all permitted activities in this appendix, other than study as set out in PA17.1-3.
- PPE visitors may do the permitted paid engagements in Appendix V: Visitor at V13.3. and all permitted activities in this appendix other than study as described in PA 17.1-3.and transit as described in PA 18.
- Transit visitor: transit the UK as described in PA 18.

The remaining appendix is ordered by headings according to subject matter, and provides as follows, for each. It is essential to put forward, and adequately evidence, one or more of the permitted activities when applying. If the Home Office accept the application is being made for a genuine purpose, that should go some way to allaying any concerns there may be as to the possibility of overstaying or working illegally.

1. Tourism and Leisure: includes visiting friends and family, going on holiday, taking part in educational exchanges or visits with a state or private school and attend recreational courses (not English courses) for up to 30 days (PA 2)
2. Volunteering: up to 30 days for a charity registered with the Charity Commission for E&W or NI or the Office of the Scottish Charity Regulator (PA 3)
3. General Business Activities: attending meetings, conferences, seminars and interviews; giving talks or speeches on a non-profit basis, negotiating and signing deals and contracts, attending trade fairs for promotion (not sales), visiting and inspecting sites, gathering information on behalf of overseas employers; briefings on UK based customers' requirements where the work is to be done outside the UK (PA 4)
4. Intra-corporate Activities: employees of overseas businesses may advise, consult, troubleshoot, train and share skills and knowledge on a specific internal project with UK employees of the same corporate group, but not directly with clients. Regulatory or financial auditing may be carried out by an internal auditor visiting from an overseas branch of the same group of companies (PA 5&6)
5. Manufacture and supply of goods to the UK: a visiting employee of an overseas manufacturer with a purchase- supply or lease contract with a UK company can install, dismantle, repair, service or advise on- equipment or computer software or hardware (PA 7)
6. Clients of UK export companies: a seconded employee of an overseas company which is a client of an UK export business can oversee the requirement for goods and services, so long as the two companies are not in the same group. Multiple visits covering the duration of the contract may be allowed exceptionally (PA 8)
7. Overseas roles requiring specific activities in the UK (PA 9)
   - Translators, interpreters, PAs and bodyguards employed overseas by an overseas businessperson may provide the relevant support to that person in the UK. PAs and bodyguards must not provide personal care or domestic work for that person in the UK
   - Tour group couriers contracted to an overseas company may enter and depart with a tour group organised by that company.
   - Journalists, correspondents, producers or cameramen may gather information for an overseas publication, programme or film
   - Archaeologists may participate in one-off excavations
   - Market researchers and analysts may conduct market research or analysis

- Overseas academic professors may accompany students on study abroad programmes and provide a small amount of teaching that does not amount to filling a permanent teaching role at the host institution (PA 9.1)
- Drivers may deliver or collect goods or passengers on a genuine international route and undertake cabotake operations. Drivers must be employed or contracted to an operator registered in a country outside the UK or be a self-employed operator and driver based outside the UK. The operator must hold an International Operators Licence or be operating on an own account basis" (PA 9.2.The definitions of cabotage operations, International Operator Licence and Own Account have been added to the definitions in r6 (Introduction to the immigration rules).
- Work-related training (PA 10)
- Medical, dental or nursing graduates may undertake unpaid clinical attachments or dental observer posts which involve no treatment of patients, or conduct independent research. They must provide the offer letter and confirmation they have not undertaken this activity before (PA 10.1 (a) read with V 11.1).
- They may take the PLAB test with written confirmation from the GMC (PA 10.1(b) read with V 11.2); and the OSCE with written confirmation from the Nursing and Midwifery Council ((PA 10.1(b) read with V 11.3).
- Overseas employees may receive training from an UK company (which is not available overseas), on work practices and techniques, which the recipients require for their overseas employment.
- Corporate trainers contracted by the same international corporate group to which a UK company belongs can provide a short series of training to that company's employees

8. Science and academia (PA 11)
   - Scientists and researchers may gather information and facts for a project relating to their overseas employment. They can also share knowledge or advise on an international UK-led project, so long as this does not amount to research in the UK (PA 11.1).
   - Academics may take part in formal exchanges with UK counterparts (including doctors) and undertake research for their own purposes while on sabbatical. Eminent senior doctors or dentists may participate in research, teaching or clinical practice but not thereby fill a permanent teaching post. (PA 11.2).
9. Legal: expert witnesses can give evidence in court, and other witnesses may attend a hearing if summoned. Overseas lawyers may advise UK clients on international litigation or – transactions (PA 12.1&2).
10. Religion: religious workers may preach or do pastoral work (PA 13).
11. Creative
    - Artists, entertainers and musicians may perform individually or as a group; participate in competitions and auditions; make personal appearances and participate in promotions, or in cultural events or festivals listed in Appendix Visitor: Permit Free Festival List (PA 14.1)
    - Personal, technical or production staff of the above may support the activities in PA 14.1 or in V 13.3 (activities directly related to their profession if invited by a creative (arts or entertainment) organisation, agent or broadcaster) (PA 14.2 read with V13.3)
    - Actors, producers, directors or technicians employed overseas as part of a film crew may participate in shooting a film programme or other media content financed and produced overseas (PA 14.3)
12. Sports
    - Sports persons may participate in tournaments or events individually or as a team; make personal appearances and participate in promotion; participate in trials (not in front of paying audiences); and participate in unpaid short periods of training. Amateurs may join amateur teams or clubs to gain experience (PA 15.1).
    - Personal or technical staff of the above, or sports officials may attend the same event and support the above activities or those in V13.3(f) (activity directly related to profession if invited

by a sports organisation agent or broadcaster). Personal or technical staff must be employed by the sports person overseas. (PA 15.2 read with V13.3(f)).

13. Medical treatment and organ donation (PA 16): this provision contains nothing but a cross reference to Appendix V: Visitor (Eligibility requirements for visitors coming to the UK to receive private medical treatment (V7.1-3) and to donate an organ (V8.1-4) (see above).
14. Study as a Visitor (PA 17)
    - Study of up to 6 months at an accredited institution is permitted so long as the requirements in Appendix ATAS, if applicable, are met (PA 17.1 read with V9.1)
    - Research or receiving research tuition at a UK institution is permitted to those aged 16 or over enrolled abroad on a degree (or higher) course, so long as the ATAS requirement, if applicable, is met, and their overseas course provider confirms the relevance of the research or research tuition to their course. The overseas provider must also confirm that the applicant will not be employed at the UK institution, and that the applicant will not work as a sponsored researcher under Appendix Tier 5 (Temporary Worker) Government Authorised Exchange Scheme Worker (PA 17.2 read with V9.1&2).
    - Medical, Veterinary or Dentistry students aged 16 or over and enrolled in a degree course or higher abroad may study electives in the UK relevant to their course which are unpaid and involve no treatment of patients. They must meet the ATAs requirement where relevant (PA 17.3 read with V9.1)
15. Transit (PA 18): this provision contains nothing but a cross reference to Appendix V: Visitor (Eligibility requirements for visitors coming to UK to transit V14.1&2)

3.4 Appendix Visitor; Transit Without Visa Scheme (paragraphs TWOV1-TWOV5)

This appendix sets out at TWOV 1 that, to be granted PTE (permission to ender, the new LTE), all TWOV 2 requirements must be met, plus one of the requirements in TWOV 3.

TWOV 2 requires that the person must

16. Have arrived and will depart by air
17. Ge genuinely transiting via a reasonable route
18. Not access public funds or medical treatment, work or study in the UK
19. Genuinely intend to leave before midnight the day after arrival day
20. Be assured entry to their destination country and all countries to be transited on the way there

TWOV 3 requires that the person must also be doing only one of the following:

- Be travelling to or from Australia, Canada, NZ or the USA and have a valid visa for the relevant country or entered that country with a valid visa within the last 6 months (TWOV3(a)&(b) – these do not apply to Syrian nationals holding a US B1 or B1 category visa)
- Hold one of the range of specific residence permits set out at TWOV 3 (c)-(k)

Any of the visas and residence permits in TWOV3 must not be in electronic format only (TWOV5).

The transit guidance under "DATV [Direct Airside Transit Visitor]: permission to enter" states that In exceptional circumstances, for example where a passenger's flight has been cancelled, it may be necessary to allow the passenger to enter the UK landside and in such cases you should consider granting leave outside the rules (LOTR) in line with the Border Force guidance on LOTR.

3.5 Refusals and remedies

Approximately 300,000 visit visa applications are refused each year (of a total of 2.2 million, so about 15%).

There is no right to appeal against the refusal of a visit visa, nor a right to seek administrative review (except for cancellation on arrival, see above), so the remedies will be to apply again, or seek judicial review.

An appeal may be available if the visit visa is treated as a human rights claim, but this will be rare. Basically this will only arise where the application is based on a very strong family relationship, such as visiting a close family members, or a partner or child in the UK.

The UK authorities clearly think that those refused a visit visa should find it quicker and cheaper to apply again than to bring a legal challenge against the decision. This may be true, if the Home Office's reasons for refusal can be fully addressed by providing relevant further information and better supporting evidence. However, where a person has been refused on the grounds of genuineness, it will be difficult to persuade the decision maker to take a different view.

As to whether to apply again or not, the adviser must consider whether the person can make a materially stronger application. If so, it is better to make that application.

- A judicial review is more likely to succeed where all potential areas of concern have been addressed in detail and the Home Office refusal is, consequently, on weak ground.
- The test on judicial review will be whether a reasonable decision maker would have refused in the same circumstances. The Judge will not make their own mind up on the issue. They will just ask whether the decision is irrational. Where one or more of the reasons for refusal potentially hold water, the judicial review is likely to fail.

Module 4: Ancestry and Returning Residents

4.1 Appendix UK Ancestry

This route is for the grandchildren of British citizens who emigrated from the UK in times past. The children, born outside the UK, of such emigrants will usually have been born British, and will be free of immigration control, but *their* children born outside the UK will not have been born British. In some circumstances those second-generation children born outside the UK may register as British citizens (under ss3(3) or 3(5) of the BNA 1981), but if they cannot they may be able to come to the UK and settle under the relatively benign requirements of the UK ancestry route.

One of the main attractions of the ancestry visa is that it leads to settlement after five years. In addition, there are no restrictions on employment and the Immigration Staff Guidance on UK ancestry suggests that examination of the applicant's ability to maintain themself is relatively limited, providing they can do so by some means that include some sort of employment. It is not strictly necessary to show employment when applying for extensions, although it would certainly be helpful to be able to be able to do so. As no access to public funds is permitted before settlement, most individuals on this route will be in work or self-employment in any case.

A list of Commonwealth countries is repeatedly linked to in the Ancestry guidance, this guidance was withdrawn and has been recently significantly amended and is now available. Some confusion reigns over the membership of Zimbabwe. Zimbabwe left the Commonwealth in 2003, does not appear on the Commonwealth's own list, but has not been deleted from schedule 3 to the British Nationality Act 1981.

Appendix UK Ancestry

The introduction to Appendix UK Ancestry, in force since 1 December 2020, outlines the route as intended for Commonwealth citizens aged 17 of over, whose grandparent was born in the UK, the Channel Islands or the Isle of Man, seeking to live and work in the UK. Dependent partners and children can apply under this route, which also leads to settlement.

The appendix is structured as follows:

- Validity requirements for UK Ancestry
- Suitability requirements for UK Ancestry
- Eligibility requirements for UK Ancestry
- Decision on an application for UK Ancestry
- Settlement on the UK Ancestry route
- Decision on an application for settlement on the UK Ancestry route
- Dependants of a person with UK Ancestry

Certain provisions are duplicated identically at the EC, PTS and ILR stages for main applicants and dependants, and thus are not listed below. They are that:

- For any application to be valid, the fee and IHS must be paid and biometrics as well as a passport/acceptable travel document must be provided
- Prior EC is required in all cases before arrival in the UK
- To be valid, PTS applications by the main applicant require prior entry clearance in this category
- Applications not meeting all validity requirements *may* be rejected and not considered
- The Suitability requirement is not to fall for refusal under Part 9 and if applying for PTS not to be in breach of immigration laws. Where r39E applies, that period of overstaying is disregarded.
- The Eligibility requirements include a TB test certificate where required under Appendix T
- Suitability and Eligibility requirements must be met or the application *will* be refused
- Upon EC/PTS grant, the following are permitted: work, including self-employment, voluntary work and study subject to the ATAS requirement in Appendix ATAS

- Conditions on grants of EC/PTS include no access to public funds and registration with the police if required by Part 10
- Administrative review is available on refusal

Set out below are only the remaining requirements

Validity requirements for UK Ancestry (main applicant)

- Use of the right online form – EC: UK Ancestry, Right of Abode or Returning Residents visa; PTS: Application to extend stay in the UK: FLR(IR) (UKA 1.1)
- A is a Commonwealth citizen who if applying for EC must be 17 or over at date of planned arrival (UKA 1.3 & UKA 1.4)

Eligibility requirements for UK Ancestry

- A must have a grandparent born in the UK or Islands (UKA 4.1)
- A must be able to maintain and accommodate A and dependants without recourse to public funds (UKA 5.1); funds are to be shown in accordance with Appendix Finance (UKA 5.2). Credible promises of third-party support from family or friends may be taken into account (UKA 5.3)
- A must be able to work and intend to seek and take employment in the UK (UK 6.1)
- If A is under 18 their parent or legal guardian must consent in writing (UKA 7.1) which confirms support for the application, A's living arrangements in the UK and their travel and reception arrangements (UKA 7.2)

Decision on an application for UK Ancestry

Grants will be for 5 years (UKA 9.1)

Settlement on the UK Ancestry route (main applicant)

- Validity: this requirement mandates use of online form SET(O)(UKA 10.1) A must still be a Commonwealth citizen at the time of application (UKA 10.3).
- Eligibility: A must still meet the maintenance and ability to work requirements (UKA 12.1)
- Qualifying period: 5 years in the UK with permission on this route (UKA 13.1)
- Continuous residence: A must meet Appendix Continuous Residence (UKA 14.1)
- English: speaking and listening skills at B1 unless exempt (UKA 15.1) in accordance with Appendix English Language (UKA 15.2)
- KoLL: A must meet the requirements in Appendix KOL UK (UKA 16.1)

Dependants of a person with UK Ancestry

Dependants were previously covered under Part 5, but specific provisions now appear in this Appendix.

Validity: use of the correct online form "Join or accompany a family member" on the "Find and apply for other visas from outside the UK" form; for PTS Form FLR(IR) (UKA 18.1); Applicants for PTS must not have been a Visitor, Short-term Student, Parent of a Child Student, Seasonal Worker, Domestic Worker in a Private Household; or have hat LOTR (UKA 18.3).

Relationship requirements for partners

- A must either have permission on the UK Ancestry route; or be applying at the same time as their sponsor (S) who is being granted permission; or applying for PTS where their sponsor is settled (or British after becoming settled on the Ancestry route) (UKA 21.1).

- Unless married/in a civil partnership, 2 years' cohabitation is required, any previous relationship has permanently broken down and A and S are not so closely related that they would not be allowed to marry or form a civil partnership in the UK (UKA 21.2).
- The relationship must be genuine and subsisting (UKA 21.3) and A and S must intend to live together throughout A's stay in the UK.

Relationship requirements for children

- A must be the child of a person (P) who has permission on the UK Ancestry route; or who is applying at the same time (and is granted permission); or who is settled or British after settling on this route (UKA 22.1).
- A's parents must both be applying at the same time as A or be in the UK with non-visitor leave unless the parent with Ancestry leave is the sole surviving parent or has sole responsibility for A; or there are serious and compelling reasons to grant A permission to come or stay with the parent with Ancestry permission (22.2).
- Care requirement: suitable arrangements for care and accommodation which comply with UK law must be in place (UKA 23.1)
- Age requirement: A must be under 18 unless last granted permission as a dependent child (UKA 24.1); if aged 16 or over they must not be leading an independent life (UKA 24.2).

Financial requirement for partners and children: Adequate maintenance and accommodation for A, their sponsor and any other dependents without recourse to public funds (UKA 25.1). Funds must be shown as specified in Appendix Finance (UKA 25.2) and credible promises of third party support may be taken into account (UKA 25.3).

Conditions: A will be granted permission in line with S unless S has settled or become British, in which case A will be granted 30 months' permission to stay (UKA 27.1&2).

Settlement for dependants

- Validity: application on online form Set(O) (UKA 28.1); A must be present in the UK on application date (UKA 28.2).A's last grant of leave must not have been as a Visitor, Short-term Student, Parent of a Child Student, Seasonal Worker, Domestic Worker in a Private Household; or have hat LOTR (UKA 28.3).
- Eligibility for settlement – partners and children: A's sponsor must at the same time be granted Ancestry settlement or they must already have settled on this route or have naturalised after settling on this route (UKA 30.1).The relationship and financial requirements are identical to those at the EC/PTS stage.
- English and KoLL: A must show speaking and listening skills at B1 unless exempt (UKA 34.1) in accordance with Appendix English Language (UKA 34.2). A must meet the requirements in Appendix KOL UK (UKA 35.1).

Evidence

As there is no specified evidence under this category, evidence of ancestry must be provided that is compelling. That should include, when relying on blood relationships, the full birth certificates of the applicant, the relevant parent, and the grandparent, as well as marriage certificates where the applicant or direct ascendant relative has changed their names on marriage. An ability and intention to work can be proven by way of evidence of qualifications, current and previous work experience, CVs, job applications or offers in the UK, and, where there is a disability or illness, additional medical information confirming an ability to work.

4.1.3 Returning residents – r18-20 in Part 1

If a person with ILR leaves the UK, they may resume their residence in the UK without the need for entry clearance if (r18) they:

(i) had indefinite leave to enter/remain when they last left the UK

(ii) have not been away for more than 2 years

(iii) did not receive assistance towards the cost of leaving

(iv) now seek admission to continue their settled life in the UK

A person who *has* been away for more than two years but who can demonstrate that they have strong ties to the UK and intends to make it their permanent home may be granted indefinite leave to enter upon application for entry clearance. Note that ILR granted under Appendix EU ('settled status') lapses after five, not two years – see further Module 8).

Rule 19A provides exceptions from r18(ii) and (iii) (the absence limit of two years and the reference to assistance in leaving) for those ILR holders who were absent while accompanying their partner who is

1. a member of HM Forces serving overseas; or
2. a British citizen or is settled in the UK and
   (i) a permanent member of HM Diplomatic Service;
   (ii) a comparable United Kingdom based permanent staff member of the British Council;
   (iii) a permanent staff member of the Department for International Development; or
   (iv) a permanent Home Office employee.

The old guidance at Chapter 1, Section 3, Annexe K of the IDIs (archived on 23 June 2016 but still available here), were quite generous in their interpretation of this rule:

1. FACTORS TO BE CONSIDERED IN CASES WHERE PARAGRAPH 19 OF HC 395 MAY APPLY

The factors that should be considered in assessing whether a person comes within Paragraph 19 are set out below:

- the length of his original residence here;
- the time the applicant has been outside the United Kingdom;
- the reason for the delay beyond the 2 years – was it through his own wish or no fault of his own? Could he reasonably have been expected to return within 2 years?
- why did he go abroad when he did and what were his intentions?
- the nature of his family ties here – how close are they, and to what extent has he maintained them in his absence?
- whether he has a home in the United Kingdom and, if admitted, would resume his residency.

The longer a person has remained outside the United Kingdom over 2 years, the more difficult it will be for him to qualify for admission under the discretion contained in Paragraph 19.

2. Other circumstances to be considered

Other more specific circumstances which might apply in favour of an individual are:

- travel and service abroad with a particular employer prior to returning with him;
- service abroad for the United Kingdom Government, as an employee of a quasi/government body, a British company or a United Nations organisation;
- employment abroad in the public service of a friendly country by a person who could not reasonably be expected to settle in that country permanently;
- a prolonged period of study abroad by a person who wished to rejoin his family here at the end of his studies;
- prolonged medical treatment abroad of a kind not available here;
- whether the person contacted a post abroad within 2 years to express his future intention to return to the United Kingdom.

Nevertheless, the person's leave automatically lapses by operation of law upon remaining outside the UK for more than two years, and they will be required to apply for entry clearance before being able to return.

Where a person who has not applied for an entry clearance to return is refused leave to enter as a returning resident at the port, the Immigration Officer would, in the past, usually grant a period of six months leave to enter as a visitor. There is no provision to appeal against that decision, and an application will have to be made outside the rules for the reinstatement of ILR. That being said though, a decision to grant leave to enter for six months may be unlawful if the Immigration Officer has failed to consider whether or not it is appropriate to grant entry as a returning resident.

9th July 2012 - Appendix FM

Module 5: Long Residence and Private Life

Further notes/information

Because this route is the one under which many claims with a human rights dimension will be argued and determined, it is the most appropriate chapter for us to deal with the approach to the assessment of Article 8 ECHR outside the Immigration Rules **(thus Chapter 10, on human rights generally, focuses on rights beyond private and family life)** so what follows is our central reference point for the consideration of Article 8. **NB If a case involves a human rights dimension this must be referred on to a suitable accredited advisor.**

5.1 Introduction

The long residence and private life provisions begin at r276A. When conducting casework, they should be read alongside:

1. Modernised Guidance: Other immigration categories: Long residence; and
2. Modernised Guidance: Family of people settled or coming to settle Family life (as a partner or parent) and private life

As usual, for the purposes of the OISC level 1 course, we cite or summarise particularly important passages of Guidance within the course.

The UKVI category outline for long residence may be helpful but may not always be accurate (it also does not have the status of law or policy, and neither do the guidance notes which come with application forms).

Until 9 July 2012, there were two routes to settlement on the grounds of long residence for persons of good character whose residence would not offend the public interest:

- 10 years continuous and lawful residence, or
- 14 years of continuous residence (whether lawful, unlawful or a combination of the two).

The 14-year category is now closed (except for people granted an extension of stay on this basis following an application made prior to 9 July 2012, who will be able to apply for ILR once the requirements of the old rule are fully met: 276A2).

Since 9 July 2012, the 14 year rule has been replaced for post July 2012 applicants by the provisions of the 'private life' category at rule 276ADE(1) (see below): i.e. it shifts from being a '14 year rule' to being a '20 year rule' (for those who are not the special cases heralded below).

Thus, now there is only one direct route to *settlement* on long residence grounds for persons of good character whose residence would not offend the public interest, under rule 276B, which requires:

- 10 years continuous and lawful residence

However there are some other avenues under Rule 276ADE. The Rule, despite its obscure title, is in fact one of the most cited rules, because it is available to overstayers without UK family for people who have been resident here for significant periods. . Leave granted under this route results in *30-month grants of limited leave* on a *10-year settlement route*. You will see that these are 'long residence' routes to a greater or lesser extent, though the length of residence is far less for the young and for those who cannot integrate abroad. These require:

- 20 years unlawful residence for those who are not children or young people who have lived half their lives here, or who are unable to show there are very significant obstacles to their integration in the country of return
- 7 years' residence for a child who can show their departure would be unreasonable
- residence of half their life for a young person aged under 25
- any period of residence for a person who can show there are very significant obstacles to their integration in the country of return

5.2 The 10 year rule

5.2.1 Continuous lawful residence

Under the 10 year rule (276A to 276D), the leave must be continuous and lawful. The terms 'continuous residence' and 'lawful residence' are defined in rule 276A(a) and (b) respectively:

Continuous residence is residence for an unbroken period, and it not broken by absence of up to 6 months or less at any one time, so long as the applicant had leave to enter or remain on leaving and returning, but is broken if they

- are removed, deported or depart following a refusal of leave
- leave evidencing a clear intention not to return or where there is no reasonable expectation of lawful return
- are convicted and sentenced to a custodial non-suspended sentence
- are abroad for more than 18 months during the relevant period

Lawful residence is that:

- with leave to enter or remain, or where one is exempt from immigration control
- with temporary admission (or immigration bail) where leave is subsequently granted (e.g. where the application which led to a grant of temporary admission subsequently succeeds, as with an asylum claim made at the port of entry)

Note that under 276A(a), absence from the UK for a period of six months or less does not break a person's continuous residence, provided that the applicant in question has existing limited leave to enter or remain upon their departure and return – there is no requirement that they must have the same form of leave on return as on departure – so they might return abroad with student leave and return as a Tier 2 migrant (subject to the other provisions in 276A(a)).

The guidance goes further than the customary condoning of 28 days overstaying (or 14 days on or after 24 November 2016 if r39E applies) which we often find in the rules relating to the circumstances of the applicant at the date of application. It makes it clear that historic gaps of up to 28 days will also be ignored.

However, overstaying at the time of an application for ILR under the Long Residence provisions can only be condoned in accordance with r39E (normally only 14 days are allowed and only where there were circumstances outside the applicant or adviser's control). The case of Hoque [2020] EWCA Civ 1357 sets out how the provisions are to be applied.

Example

Walter is from Kenya. He entered the UK on 1 December 2004. He has entry clearance as a student valid until June 2007. On 24 July 2007, he leaves the country. He returns to the UK on 22 August 2007 with entry clearance granted on 25 July 2007.

His continuity of residence is broken – he did not have 'existing limited leave to enter or remain upon … departure and return' under rule 276A(a), and given that he overstayed for more than 28 days before leaving the country, 276B(v) does not assist him.

Harvey is from the USA. He enters the UK on 1 December 2002 and is granted leave to remain until 1 May 2004 as a student. He left the UK on 27 April 2004 and returns on 26 September 2004, with a new entry clearance operating as leave to enter, again as a student.

His continuity of residence is not broken – he has 'existing limited leave to enter or remain upon … departure and return' and he was not absent for more than six months.

The *long residence* guidance is very useful. It shows:

- There is a discretion to ignore a break in residence exceeding 28 days (i.e. a discretion *outside* the rule that is more generous than the rule itself). It is available where
    - The applicant has acted lawfully throughout their stay and has always sought to obey the rules.

   - There are 'exceptional reasons why a single application was made more than 28 days out of time' (e.g. postal strike, Home Office error, hospitalization, unexpected or unforeseeable causes including unavoidable circumstances)
- Once an applicant has built up a period of 10 years continuous lawful residence, there is no limit on the length of time afterwards when they can apply. This means they could leave the UK, re-enter and apply for settlement based on a 10 year period of continuous lawful residence they built up in the past. This is subject to the provision that the applicant must not be in the UK in breach of immigration laws at the date of application, except for any period of overstaying 14 days or less allowed by r39E.
- Time spent in the Republic of Ireland, Channel Islands or the Isle of Man does not count as residence in the UK for the purposes of long residence even though they form part of the common travel area.
- Time spent in the UK with a right to reside under the EEA regulations will be treated as lawful residence (by way of an exercise of discretion), although whether residence with derivative rights can be included is still in the process of being clarified.

Time spent awaiting an appeal hearing can count towards long residence – where the 10 years of residence has accrued during a period of continuing leave under s3C or 3D of the 1971 Act, an application can be submitted to the Home Office to vary the existing application or where there is a right of appeal to the Tribunal under s120 of the NIA 2002 as applicable.

Caseworker Tip

-When presenting the evidence in a long residence application, make it easy for the decision maker and everyone else who ever reads the paperwork by providing a table of the evidence, showing the date that each piece of evidence covers, and using a witness statement to introduce the documents (e.g. 'from 2002 – 2003 I lived at this address and I worked nearby' (reference tenancy agreement and pay slips), and explain why there may be periods that are not covered (e.g. 'unfortunately when I lost my job I also lost my accommodation soon afterwards, and I became homeless').

-When arguing long residence cases outside the Rules by reference to private life, compliance with the Rules and guidance set out by the Home Office may still be important – so the fact that the Rules condone short breaks in leave or excess periods abroad for compassionate or humanitarian reasons may justify an appeal succeeding by reference to Article 8 ECHR.

Example

Vallerie is subject to immigration control. She has lived in the UK for just over 10 years, via various grants of leave to remain as a student. She wishes to apply for indefinite leave to remain under the long residence route: she still has leave as a Tier 4 student. However, she has accumulated excess absence abroad as she was away for seven months in a single year.

This excess absence disqualifies her from succeeding under the Rule, but the Home Office guidance states that 'it may be appropriate to exercise discretion over excess absences in compelling or compassionate circumstances, for example where the applicant was prevented from returning to the UK through unavoidable circumstances'.

So it will be important to investigate the justification for the delay in her return. If she has a good explanation relating to circumstances beyond her control and can show she returned to the UK as soon as she was reasonably able, then discretion might be exercised outside the Rules.

Alternatively, depending on how much leave to remain she has presently, she could postpone her application, and calculate whether the excess absence in question will drop out of the calculation if she can time her application such that it is split over two consecutive years.

5.2.2 Other considerations: character, conduct and the public interest

Having met the 10-year requirement, the Home Office will then consider whether:

(i) having regard to the public interest there are no reasons why it would be undesirable for him to be given indefinite leave to remain on the ground of long residence, taking into account his:

- (a) age; and
- (b) strength of connections in the United Kingdom; and
- (c) personal history, including character, conduct, associations and employment record; and
- (d) domestic circumstances; and
- (e) compassionate circumstances; and
- (f) any representations received on the person's behalf;

These factors enable the Home Office to exercise discretion not to grant leave, though it is not common for an application to be refused on these bases. Where, due to criminality, the application falls foul of rule 9.4.1-9.4.5 in Part 9, limited leave can be granted until the relevant time period has elapsed.

For a grant of indefinite leave, the applicant will also have to meet the knowledge of English language and life in the UK requirement in Appendix KoLL (see Module 2). If they have not yet done so, or settlement is delayed by the 'suitability' requirements of paragraphs S-ILR.1.5. or S-ILR.1.6. in Appendix FM, they will be granted a further 30 months.

Applications under the 10-year long residence category are made on forms FLR(LR) and SET(LR).

Top Tip

What can you suggest to a client who is nearly but not quite at the 10-year point of continuous lawful residence in the UK? An application under the 10-year rule cannot be made more than 28 days before the qualifying period is met. However, so long as they arguably satisfy the requirements of a different category, they can apply for an extension of stay under that category. If they then reach the 10 year point before that application is decided, and meet the KoLL requirements, they can then apply to vary that application: i.e. submit a new application under the 10-year rule which will replace the earlier undecided application. They will have reached the 10-year point whilst their leave is extended under s3C of the 1971 Act but that is no problem. Their leave has been lawful and continuous: they are entitled to vary their application so long as it has not yet been decided.

If they reach the 10 year point *after* the extension application is refused, their leave will be extended under section 3C of the IA 1971 whilst an appeal or administrative review can be brought or is pending.

5.3 Private life under the rules

The OISC 1 guidance on competence states as follows:

Level 1 adviser's client must as soon as possible, be referred on to an adviser who is authorised at a higher Level in cases involving detailed representations and follow-up correspondence such as:

- applications for Leave to Remain on the grounds of 20 years' residence in the UK
- applications for Further Leave to Remain on the basis of Family or Private Life under the 10 year route [...]
- applications in which human rights grounds should be raised

Thus all the information provided in this section is merely intended to assist you in spotting and referring these cases.

Further notes/information

The concept of 'private life' comes from Article 8 of the European Convention on Human Rights, the 'right to respect for one's private and family life, his home and his correspondence'. It has become government policy from July 2012 to seek to define private life for Immigration Rule purposes, rather than leaving it to the case law from the domestic courts and the European Court of Human Rights.

Indeed, the Home Office are generally disinterested in pre-July 2012 rulings.

The private life category of the Immigration Rules, at Rule 276ADE(1), allows a person to apply to regularise their stay in the UK on private life grounds, essentially long residence, where some or all of that residence has not been lawful.

Rule 276ADE(1) defines a person who will be entitled to a grant of leave to remain on private life grounds as one who:

(iii) has lived continuously in the UK for at least 20 years (discounting any period of imprisonment); or

(iv) is under the age of 18 years and has lived continuously in the UK for at least 7 years (discounting any period of imprisonment) and it would not be reasonable to expect the applicant to leave the UK; or

(v) is aged 18 years or above and under 25 years and has spent at least half of his life living continuously in the UK (discounting any period of imprisonment); or

(vi) subject to sub-paragraph (2), is aged 18 years or above, has lived continuously in the UK for less than 20 years (discounting any period of imprisonment) but there would be very significant obstacles to the applicant's integration into the country to which he would have to go if required to leave the UK.

These points arise:

the reference at 276ADE(1)(vi) to sub-paragraph 2 is irrelevant in most cases, as it only applies to asylum seekers facing removal to a third country responsible for considering their claim under the Dublin Regulation, and bars them from this route.

The route is subject to 'suitability' requirements (276ADE(1)(i), cross-referencing to those in Appendix FM at Section S-LTR of the partner category: we deal with these below). The only rule in Part 9 (Grounds for Refusal) that applies to private life applications is r9.13.1 which provides for discretionary refusal where an application is made for a purpose not covered by the Rules (this refers presumably to free standing Art 8 claims which do not refer to the private life provisions).

Whereas a child has to show *reasonableness plus seven years' residence*, a young person who has lived here for half their life *does not have to show reasonableness at all*. So an applicant who has lived here for ten years would have a watertight case under the rule on their 18th birthday, whereas the day before they would have had to satisfy the more subjective test of reasonableness too, although they would have had a very strong case indeed on that limb

periods of imprisonment will be deducted from the total period of residence (i.e. rather than requiring the applicant to start the clock from scratch following release)

for those familiar with the now closed 14-year unlawful residence category, note that there is nothing that 'stops the clock' running following the service of an enforcement notice telling someone to leave the country under 276ADE(1): the moment of clock-stopping is 'the date of application', in the opening words of 276ADE itself. This may mean that a child who lacked the relevant residence at the date of application, but acquires it by the date of hearing, may need to argue their seven years' residence wholly outside the Rules (where it will be relevant because of s117B(6) NIAA 2002)

276ADE(vi) is the sub-rule under which all applicants are residually assessed if they lack the qualities of 20-year residence or youth for sub-rules (iii)-(v): you will see many references to it in your caseload once you read refusal letters. The need for '*very significant obstacles*' to integration raises particular obstacles for individuals of high calibre. Whatever their ties abroad, they are likely to be seen as individuals well equipped to make their way in the world.

Obvious there may be an explanation why assertions are unsubstantiated and private life must be assessed in the round, not compartmentalised. The evidential requirements for proving length of residence under 276ADE(iii) are set high. It is expected that applicants will be able to provide independent evidence of each 12-month period they have lived in the UK plus travel documents covering the whole period, unless a very good explanation has been provided as to why they cannot. A large envelope will be required.

NB If a case involves a human rights dimension this must be referred on to a suitable accredited advisor. All Private Life applications inevitably involve at least an assessment of the applicability of relevant human rights law, which is why the OISC 1 competence guidance categorically exempts Private Life applications from OISC 1 competence. All cases must be referred to a suitable accredited adviser.

Further notes/information

5.3.1 Suitability Rule

The first consideration will be whether an application would fall to be refused under the 'suitability' requirements in paragraphs S-LTR 1.2 to S-LTR 4.5 in the 'Family life with a partner' category of Appendix FM (see Module 6).

5.3.2 Rule 276ADE(1)(iv) – Children and when it is reasonable to expect them to leave the UK

This requirement appears both in the private life rules for children (276ADE(1)(iv)), and in the Exception (paragraph EX1) which applies to partners and parents under Appendix FM who have children who are British citizens or have lived in the UK for seven years or more (see Module 6).

One preliminary point to emphasise is that the test is one of reasonableness: obviously that is very different to a test based on 'insurmountable obstacles' or 'exceptional circumstances', thresholds cited elsewhere in the Rules. Indeed the Family life (as a partner or parent), private life and exceptional circumstances (on the analogous provision in Appendix FM at EX.1.(b)) itself recognises that insurmountable obstacles represents 'a different and more stringent assessment'.

Nevertheless, the test is one of seven years' residence *plus* reasonableness: so the mere fact of seven years' residence is not sufficient on its own, albeit that it does represent something of a presumption as to a certain level of ties having developed.

In the world of immigration law, there is a hierarchy of children:

(a) British citizen children are the best protected: because the rights flowing from nationality must be taken into account

(b) 7-year resident non British citizen children are next best protected: because they have the benefit of the "reasonableness" test

(c) All children have some protection: because their best interests must be assessed

Principles relevant in all cases involving children

Before we say more about the proper approach to the cases of qualifying children, it is useful to set out the principles that apply generally.

There are three dominant considerations in these cases, which overlap:

- Section 55 of the Borders, Citizenship and Immigration Act 2009 and the general duty to ensure that immigration functions safeguard and promote child welfare (see Chapter 2 for an introduction to s55). Section 55 is the means by which UK law recognises the relevance of the UNCRC to immigration cases. Which leads us onto

- The UK's obligations enshrined in the UN Convention on the Rights of the Child (UNCRC). Perhaps the most important part of the UNCRC is Article 3.

- The notion of a child having sufficient connections outside the family unit as to have established a private life in their own right. Article 8(1) of the UNCRC expressly proclaims that 'States Parties undertake to respect the right of the child to preserve his or her identity'.

The Family life (as a partner or parent), private life and exceptional circumstances has changed over time, but essentially makes these points. Absent other factors, the reason why a period of substantial residence as a child may become a weighty consideration in the balance of competing considerations is that in the course of such time roots are put down, personal identities are developed, friendships are formed and links are made with the community outside the family unit. The degree to which these elements of private life are forged and therefore the weight to be given to the passage of time will depend upon the facts in each case. Significant weight must be given to such a period of continuous residence. The longer the child has resided in the UK, and the older the age at which they have done so, the more the balance will begin to shift towards their departure being unreasonable. At one time the Home Office Guidance stated that 'strong' or 'powerful' reasons were required to justify a child's departure, and the case law upheld that Guidance as setting the appropriate threshold.

The Home Office Guidance over time has identified various relevant considerations. One might think that not all of these sit well with the need to identify 'strong reasons' for uprooting a seven-year resident child:

- whether removal would give rise to a significant risk to a child's health

- the natural expectation that children will reside with their parents, which is generally in their best interests, and that it will normally be reasonable, where parents have no right to reside here, to expect them to follow their parents abroad

- the extent of wider family ties in the UK, where a child depends on, or requires support from wider family members

- whether the child is likely to be able to (re)integrate readily into life in another country, relevant factors include whether: the parents have that nationality; they have resided there; there are social and cultural ties remaining; the child is able to speak, read and write the language or is likely to be able to learn within a reasonable time.

The provisions of s117B of the NIAA 2002 should not trump the best interests of any children affected by an immigration decision: indeed, s71 of the IA 2014 stresses that nothing in the 2014 Act is intended to diminish the child safeguarding duty under s 55 BCIA 2009.

5.3.2.1 British Citizen Children

Nationality is particularly important, because a national of a country is entitled to enjoy its protection and support, socially, culturally and medically, and to benefit from educational opportunities owed to citizens.

When you are working on an application which involves children, make sure you carefully follow up every possible avenue of enquiry. Think about anything that shows that any relevant children have an independent life outside of the family unit with which they face removal.

Remember that the case law had held that you have a real advantage if a child has been here for more than seven years at a time of their life when they are integrating socially beyond the family unit (i.e. seven years' residence from starting primary school/reception classes is weightier than seven years' residence that includes a period as a baby)

-the younger the child, the more work you need to do to show integration outside the family.
-at any age, interrupting a critical moment of life or study during formative years is likely to be very important.
-family life with extended family members will often be important for the children

Relevant evidence will be:
-independent assessments from teachers
-reports from social workers or other child-centred professionals
-letters from family friends talking about relationships with other children
-letters from figures in the community speaking of the child's involvement with sports clubs, youth groups or the church

-print outs of health records from a doctor's surgery are perhaps the least impressive of the possible documents, but may be better than nothing. It is best practice to be sparing in the provision of reports which are largely repetitive, for example just selecting recent ones together with occasional past reports that give a flavour of the child's progress generally.

5.3.3 Rule 276ADE(1)(vi) – Very significant obstacles to integration

Rule 276ADE(1)(vi) requires that 'there would be very significant obstacles to the applicant's integration into the country to which he would have to go if required to leave the UK'. This formulation replaced an earlier version which required the claimant to have 'no ties' to the other country.

The 'very significant obstacles to integration' test

The significant obstacles test is future looking. Preparing a case on this basis will focus on the problems the applicant will face in returning to their country of origin. Indeed, this is a significant difference between the approach to a private life case within the rules and outside them: the rules focus heavily on the prospects of integration abroad, whereas Article 8 looks first to the strength of connections here.

Relevant considerations in assessing the prospects of integration abroad are identified Family life (as a partner or parent), private life and exceptional circumstances:

-The possibility of (re-)integrating in one's own country is to be assumed, the burden of proof being on the applicant to show otherwise.

-Claims must be substantiated by *independent and verifiable documentary evidence* – unsubstantiated assertions will not count for much.

-A *very significant obstacle* is one that would seriously inhibit integration and/or cause very serious hardship.

-Routine problems such as learning a new language or finding employment are not enough.

The guidance then sets out the HO's specific approach to the following factors: cultural background; length of time spent in the country of return; family, friends and social network; faith, political or sexual orientation of sexual identity.

What follows on from this is a list of arguments as to why the following 'common claims' on their own do not necessarily constitute 'very significant obstacles': absence of family or friends in the destination country; applicant never having lived there (or only for a brief period); inability to speak the local language; absence of employment prospects.

Relevant factors appearing in the guidance as showing that there are no very significant obstacles are:

-living amongst the diaspora here

-family connections abroad (including ones which could potentially be strengthened in the future) which may be shown by the family or friends visiting, perhaps sponsored by the applicant or their extended family

-the presence of family, friends or social networks organisations abroad that could assist them in integrating

Examples of common Rule 276ADE cases and their merits

1 Hossain is a citizen of Pakistan aged 26. He has been present in the UK for five years as a student. His sponsor has lost their licence and although the Home Office has given him 60 days to find a new one, he has not managed to do so. Accordingly, his application for further leave as a student has been rejected. He is not sure what to do next.

Hossain can make an application under the private life route, but given his age and length of residence in the UK the only route open to him will be 276ADE(vi). As a person who has studied in the UK and who may well have been funded through those studies by family in Pakistan, it is very hard to see that he will be able to sustain a case based on facing very significant obstacles to integration in his country of origin.

2 Mitsuda is a citizen of Japan aged 23. Her father was an international businessman who separated from her mother when Mitsuda was very young. She and her mother went to live in New Zealand and various other countries before she came to study in the UK aged 18 as a student whilst her mother remained abroad. Her studies have now come to an end and she is considering applying to remain in the UK on a longer-term basis. She does not speak Japanese and has no friends in Japan: her mother now lives in Canada.

Mitsuda's application under 276ADE(vi) might succeed. Absent close family or language skills she may be able to establish very significant obstacles to integration. However the challenge she will face is that she has qualifications and the Home Office may take the view that she is essentially an independent young person who can make her way as well in Japan as in the UK. A judge on appeal might be more sympathetic.

3 Fawaz is a citizen of Bangladesh aged 69. Her husband died some years ago. She came to visit her sons in the UK and remained here after her visit visa expired because she was taken ill. She did not return following her recovery and now several years have passed. The rest of her children have relocated to other parts of the world.

Fawaz may be able to persuade a decision maker that she lacks the social capital to integrate back in Bangladesh.

4 Farid is a citizen of Afghanistan. He came to the UK as an unaccompanied minor aged 8. He is now aged 17½ having been repeatedly granted discretionary leave to remain once he came to the attention of the authorities, having been looked after by his older brother for a few years after he arrived here. His leave to remain is just about to expire.

At the present time Farid would need to show that his return to Afghanistan would be unreasonable given that he is still aged under 18. However if he made the application after attaining the age of 18, because he would have lived in the UK for more than half his life and so would not have to show that departure was unreasonable.

All of these cases must be referred on to a suitable accredited advisor, as they all constitute application under the private life 10-year route to settlement (see OISC guidance).

Relevant factors that might be relevant to establishing very significant obstacles will include (these are derived from casework experience beyond the Home Office policy):

- The age they came to the UK. The more experience they have had of living in the country to which they would return or be removed, particularly as an adult, the weaker their case will be.
- The extent to which they will be able to find work and accommodation in that country. In some countries, it is hard to find work without the practical support of family or social connections, even to the extent of setting oneself up as a roadside trader. Expert or other evidence may be useful here in establishing the relevant cultural norms. Bear in mind the extent of any funds that might be expected for their support from family and friends in the UK, or available to them under the Home Office's voluntary return arrangements.
- Their health (though as a cumulative factor amongst others, otherwise the N v UK line of authority, ruling out non-removal on health grounds unless a person is near death or similar, will be cited against the client).
- Their sex or sexuality, or any other factor which might lead them to being exploited or oppressed, particularly where young or psychologically vulnerable.
- The extent to which their country is in a state of upheaval (e.g. by reason of war or environmental disaster).

Module 6: Family Life under Appendix FM

6.1 Family Life under Appendix FM

Subject to the transitional provisions (see below), applications made to join or remain with settled family members in the UK are made under Appendix FM to the Immigration Rules. When brought into force on 9 July 2012, these rules represented a huge shake up to the system of family migration into the UK.

We will explain here the rules under Appendix FM. and, where necessary, the 'old' rules (in brief, which are in Part 8 of the Rules) for those applying under the transitional provisions.

Appendix FM deals with four categories of family migration, providing a route to enter and remain in the UK for those with family life as;

A partner
- including those whose relationships have ended due to domestic violence or bereavement

A parent
- of a child in the UK

A child
- of a partner or parent

An adult dependent relative

In all categories, applicants will always need to meet 'suitability' and some 'eligibility' requirements.

The suitability requirements largely mirror the grounds for refusal in Part 9 of the Immigration Rules, i.e. grounds for refusal relating to criminality, deception and owing money to the NHS, but there are some material differences.

The eligibility requirements relate to one or more of the following criteria;

- **Relationship**
  - Always mandatory. Sponsor must be
  - a British citizen; or
  - settled or in the UK; or
  - in the UK with limited leave:
  - under rEU3 of Appendix EU (i.e. pre-settled status as a person in the UK since before the transition period) or
  - as a worker or business person under Appendix ECAA Extension of Stay
- **Financial**
  - Minimum Income Requirements for partner and child categories
  - Adequate Maintenance for parents and others
  - Adequate accommodation
  - No financial requirements where EX1 applies
- **English language**
  - Basic English for partners and parents
  - No English requirement where EX1 applies
- **Immigration status**
  - Switching in-country
  - Except for fiancees and adult dependent relatives

- Few immigration status requirements where EX1 applies

As laid out in paragraph section GEN 1.1 of Appendix FM (below), Appendix FM was drafted with a view to incorporating family life considerations into the rules. The rules were also designed to incorporate the government's duty to give safeguard and promote the welfare of children in the UK (i.e. the 'best interests of the child' principle). And at the same time, take account of the public interest considerations implicit in Article 8(2) ECHR: respecting private and family life, protecting public safety, health and morals, the economy, and the rights and freedoms of others, and preventing disorder and crime,

As with the private life category, where the Appendix FM requirements are not met, the government's intention is that family life applications should be allowed only where removal from the UK would be unjustifiably harsh. However there is an important structural difference between private life and the family life rules. The private life routes do not claim to cater for all scenarios. Thus leaving room for consideration outside the Rules, by the yardstick of unjustifiable harshness. Whereas for all cases considered under Appendix FM, GEN.3.2 provides that cases should receive a residual consideration within the Rules: even where some requirement of Appendix FM is not met. Thus for family life cases generally there is a 3-stage consideration:

- Consider the case under the relevant sub-route within Appendix FM: partner, parent, adult dependent relative etc
- If it fails, conduct a residual consideration applying the test of "unjustifiably harsh" circumstances under rGEN.3.2

The third stage, as we will see, exists in the partner and parent 'in-country' routes, which insert an intermediate stage between (1) and (2): ie where the person is in breach of Immigration Rules, or fails to meet the financial or English language requirements, their application may still succeed if it would be unreasonable for a qualifying child to leave the UK or where there are insurmountable obstacles to a couple's relocation abroad, under rEX1.

NB: any case which does not meet *all* of the basic, 5-year route requirements (relationship, finance, English, immigration status, suitability) must be referred toa suitable accredited adviser.

6.1.1 Navigating Appendix FM

Navigating Appendix FM is never easy. The individual paragraphs of Appendix FM are referenced by a complex lettering scheme that is not in alphabetic order (provoking Underhill LJ in Singh [2015] EWCA Civ 74 to say that 'I do not doubt that some subtle intelligence is at work, but the system is quite opaque to the uninitiated and adds to the difficulty of finding one's way around').

The sections are, however, helpfully grouped under the following drop-down index here:

- General
- Exceptional circumstances
- Family life with a partner
- Section EX: Exception to certain eligibility requirements for leave to remain as a partner or parent
- Bereaved partner
- Victim of domestic violence
- Family life as a child of a person with limited leave as a partner or parent
- Family life as a parent of a child in the UK
- Adult dependant relative
- Deportation and removal

To give a rough idea of how the lettering system in the main body of the Appendix works, the table below provides a brief glossary:

Letters at the start – type of rule	Letters in the middle – type of leave	Letters at the end – category
S = Suitability E = Eligibility D = Decision	EC = Entry Clearance LTR = Leave to Remain ILR = Indefinite Leave to Remain	P = Partner BP = Bereaved Partner DV = Victim of Domestic Violence C = Child (of a person with ltd leave) PT = Parent (of a child in the UK) DR = Dependent Relative
NB: The Suitability provisions applicable to all categories are those in the Partner category		

6.1.2 Operational guidance

Broadly, guidance on Appendix FM can be found in the Immigration Staff Guidance 'Family of people settled or coming to settle'. This collection now contains the following:

- Family migration: adequate maintenance and accommodation
- Adopted children and children coming to the UK for adoption caseworker guidance
- Chapter 08: appendix FM family members (immigration staff guidance)guidance on specific requirements under Appendix FM such as the English language and financial requirements
- English Language requirement: family members
- Family life (as a partner or parent), private life and exceptional circumstances
- Partners, divorce and dissolution
- Victims of domestic violence

The IDIs Chapter 08: family members. This contains

- the transitional provisions for persons granted leave under the pre-July 2012 family migration routes are at rules A277 to A280 of Part 8 of the Immigration Rules (these cases being rare now)
- other guidance pertaining to these

Further notes/information
Some parts of these policy documents deal in more detail with **application of paras EX.1 and EX.2** guidance on domestic violence applications and adopted children **These must be referred on to a suitable accredited advisor**

6.1.3 Section GEN

Appendix FM begins with Section GEN: General. This section provides definitions of terms used elsewhere in Appendix FM, and includes an important procedural provision at GEN.1.9. as to the circumstances in which the family life rules will be applied. We lay out here the most important paragraphs of Section GEN.

- GEN.1.2. defines the relationships considered under the 'family life as a partner' category (spouses, civil partners, fiancé(e)s/proposed civil partners, and those in a relationship akin to marriage who have been cohabiting for two years).
- GEN.1.3. allows applicants living outside the UK with their British citizen or settled partner or child to seek entry clearance to accompany them to the UK – normally a sponsor must be physically 'present' in the UK. Those with LTR under Appendices EU or ECAA Extension of stay, however, must be in the UK. Both these sponsor categories are defined
- GEN.1.4. defines references to the word "specified" as referring to the critically important 'specified evidence' regime found in Appendix FM–SE.
- GEN.1.6. lists the majority-English speaking countries whose nationals will automatically meet the English language requirement in the partner and parent categories.
- GEN.1.8. incorporates into Appendix FM the provisions in Part 8 of the rules relating to polygamous marriages and the children thereof.
- GEN.1.9. outlines the circumstances in which there will be no need to make a valid application (i.e. fee-paid and using the right form) in order to access consideration of one's case under the family life provisions in Appendix FM.
- GEN.1.10 confirms that where leave is granted under 'exceptional circumstances' in GEN.3.1.(2) or GEN.3.2.(3) (see below), the grants of leave will be subject to a condition of no recourse to public funds unless the decision maker considers, with reference to paragraph GEN.1.11A, that the applicant should not be subject to such a condition. The grant of leave will be as per these categories:
    - D-ECP.1.2. (grant of 33 months entry clearance as a partner with 'exceptional circumstances' on the 10-year route)
    - D-LTRP.1.2. (grant of 30 months leave to remain as a partner with EX. 1&2 or 'exceptional circumstances' on the 10-year route)
    - D-ECC.1.1 (child entry clearance duration in line with parent)
    - D-LTRC.1.1 (child LTR in line with parent, settlement via para 298)
    - D-ECPT.1.2. (grant of 33 months entry clearance as a parent with EX.1 or 'exceptional circumstances' on the 10-year route)
    - D-LTRPT.1.2. (grant of 30 months leave to remain as a parent with EX.1 or 'exceptional circumstances' on the 10-year route)

NB: any reference to leave outside the Rules in these paragraphs was deleted on 10 August 2017. Which is of course consistent with the objective of all family life cases being considered within the general framework of Appendix FM, either via the criteria of each route, or where some requirement cannot be met, via the EX1 or GEN.3.2 dispensations.

- GEN.1.11. allows the HO to apply conditions as it considers appropriate in a particular case – that is even if the Rules applying to that particular type of leave do not specify that such a condition should be applied
- GEN.1.11A provides that leave listed in GEN.1.10. will normally be granted subject to a condition of no recourse to public unless the applicant has provided satisfactory evidence that (a) they are destitute as defined in section 95 of the Immigration and Asylum Act 1999, or (b) there are particularly compelling reasons relating to the welfare of a child of a parent in receipt of a very low income.
- GEN.1.15. provides that where a person applies for ILR, but is granted only limited leave, they must pay the immigration health charge (which they would have had to pay if they had applied for limited leave).
- GEN.1.16. Where an application or claim raising Article 8 is considered under Appendix FM and EX.1. applies, the requirements of paragraphs RLTRP.1.1(c) and R-LTRPT.1.1.(c) are not met. In other words, the conditions for the five-year route to settlement for parents and partners will not be met in these circumstances and any grant will be on the 10-year route.

6.1.4 Exceptional circumstances

There are special provisions for individuals who cannot fully meet the financial requirements, or who cannot meet some other requirements of Appendix FM but can show that refusing their application would be unjustifiably harsh having regard to their private and family life We deal with these provisions later in this Module. It's hard to understand who is a special case until you understand who the routine cases are under Appendix FM. Of course, this kind of work falls beyond the scope of OISC level 1. So for this course you just need to be aware of the general situations which fall into the different kinds of exceptional cases.

6.1.5 Suitability and the applicable grounds for refusal

Those applying under either Part 8 or Appendix FM categories (and Private Life, which is in Part 7) must not fall foul of the the 'suitability' provisions. They apply regardless of the date the application was made, and are located in sections S-EC, S-LTR and S-ILR under the Appendix FM partner category (though they are located within the partner category, they are cross-referenced from the Private Life rules and all the family categories, so they apply across the board).

Appendix FM applications are, since 11pm on 31 December 2020, subject to the following grounds for refusal in Part 9 of the rules:

(a) EC or permission held ***must*** be cancelled on SSHD's personal direction of exclusion (9.3.2) or where presence is not conducive (9.3.3)
(b) EC or permission ***may*** be cancelled for a prison sentence of less than 12 months or non-custodial sentence or out of court disposal (9.4.5)
(c) EC or PTS ***may*** be cancelled for false representations etc or failure to disclose information (9.7.3) (for PTS applications only – see more detailed provision below and in the rules)
(d) EC or permission held ***may*** be cancelled, where A fails without reasonable excuse to comply with a reasonable requirement to be interviewed, provide information or biometrics, undergo a medical test or provide a medical report (9.9.2)
(e) Mandatory and discretionary grounds re: failure to produce a recognised passport (see details for 9.15.1-3 in section 2.3 Part 9 grounds for refusal in Module 2)
(f) EC or permission held ***may*** be cancelled if granting entry would be against the advice of a medical inspector (9.16.2)
(g) EC or permission held ***may*** be cancelled, for a customs breach, irrespective of whether criminal prosecution is pursued (9.19.2)
(h) EC or permission held ***may*** be cancelled if there has been a sufficiently significant change in circumstances since EC or permission was granted (9.20.1)
(i) EC or permission held ***may*** be cancelled if they cease to meet the requirements of the rule under which it was granted. (9.23.1)
(j) EC or permission held by P as a dependent ***may*** be cancelled if the person on whom P is a dependent has, or has had, their permission cancelled. (9.24.1)
(k) An application for EC/PTE ***may*** be refused for previous breaches of immigration laws where an application is made outside the re-entry ban period (9.8.2(a)&(c) – refer to the detail below and in the Rules)

Thus, most of the grounds for refusal which are applicable to Appendix FM applications are discretionary (as indicated by the word "may" rather than "must").

Whilst Appendix FM does not impose a mandatory ban on return to the UK for breach of immigration conditions, r9.8.2 (contriving to frustrate the Immigration Rules) does apply to family applications made under Appendix FM. It is often the basis upon which entry clearance applications, particularly those made under the partner category, are refused, where the applicant has what is considered by the HO to be a very poor immigration history.

When advising potential Appendix FM applicants, any potential issues under the applicable grounds for refusal must be explored, as well as any under the Suitability grounds.

As with the general grounds, the suitability provisions can be mandatory or discretionary, and they are found only in the partner route but apply to all Appendix FM categories as well as Private Life.

All sections in this book dealing with 'suitability', e.g. 5.3.1, are now consolidated into this part.

6.1.5.1 'Suitability' at the entry clearance stage

The suitability requirements for entry clearance are mandatory for

- being subject of a deportation order (S-EC.1.3)
- where SSHD personally directs that exclusion is conducive to the public good (S-EC.1.2)
- exclusion is for the public good owing to:
    - conviction and imprisonment for either: at least four years (S-EC.1.4(a)); at least 12 months to less than four years (where sentence ended within 10 years before application)(b); up to 12 months (where sentence ended within five years before application) (S-EC.1.4)(c)
    - other convictions with non-custodial sentences, or for reasons of, including, character or associations making entry to the UK undesirable (S-EC.1.5)
- noncompliance, without reasonable excuse, with a requirement to attend an interview; provide information or physical data; or undergo a medical examination or provide a medical report (S-EC.1.6)
- where medical reasons make admission to the UK undesirable (S-EC1.7)
- having left or been removed from the UK within five years before decision, as a condition of a caution under s22 of the Criminal Justice Act 2003 (S-EC.1.8)
- SSHD considers the applicant's parent/partner poses a risk to the applicant for reasons of being a registered but non-compliant sex offender (S-EC.1.9) *NB: this is relevant to parent, partner and child applications under Appendix FM*

The suitability requirements for entry clearance are discretionary for

- provision of false information, statements or documents by anyone in connection with the application, including false information given to anyone else to obtain a supporting document, or failure to disclose important facts in relation to the application, even where the applicant was unaware (S-EC.2.2)
- failure to provide, where requested or required, a maintenance undertaking (S-EC.2.4)
- having received, within a year before application, a non-custodial sentence or other out of court settlement which appears on the criminal record, or SSHD views offending as having caused serious harm, or views the applicant as a persistent offender with a particular disregard for the law (S-EC.2.5)
- failure to pay litigation costs awarded to the Home Office (S-EC.3.1 – see Immigration Staff Guidance on Litigation Debt) or outstanding overseas NHS charges of at least £500 (S-EC.3.2)

Analysing the entry clearance Suitability Rules we see that:

- There is no mandatory ban for historic dishonesty unless it is thought to fall within S-EC.1.5, i.e. 'conduct ... character ... or other reasons'.
- On 6 April 2016, the HO introduced a new breed of suitability criteria, whereby leave *may* be refused ie where there is no presumption of refusal.
- These rules are sometimes based on a simple factual finding (e.g. an extant deportation order under S-EC.1.3) and sometimes on a judgement which will have to be made following the evaluation of relevant evidence e.g. that there was no 'reasonable excuse' for non-compliance with information gathering efforts (S-EC.1.6).

- In old-style appeals under the saved provisions of NIAA 2002, the factual findings and the consequent judgements as well as the exercise of the discretion in S-EC.2.1.-2.5. were matters on which an Immigration Judge could make up their own mind.
- In modern appeals on 'human rights' grounds only, the relevance of the general refusal- and suitability reasons is indirect. They are a factor counting in favour of the public interest against the rights of the individual. The FTTcan depart from whatever evaluations were made by the Home Office if it finds that there are strong private and family life interests with which the interference is disproportionate.
- Where criminality is involved, the Appendix FM guidance refers to Criminality: Article 8 ECHR cases in 'criminality and detention (Immigration Staff Guidance). Art 8 representations in any case involving criminality should always address paras 398-399 in Part 13.

6.1.5.2 'Suitability' at the leave to remain stage

The suitability requirements for applications for leave to remain are similar to those on entry clearance, but not identical. The mandatory grounds for refusal on the basis of criminality and past deception are certainly tougher for in-country applicants.

Additionally:

- A person *may* be refused on suitability grounds for the previous use of deception (S-LTR.4.2-4.3.). That provision does not apply in respect of entry clearance, though if a person who is likely to be caught by that provision decides to make the application from outside the UK, they may well get caught by r9.8.7.
- A person *will* be refused if their presence is not conducive to the public good because the Secretary of State has excluded them from protection,or would have done so if they had applied for it (S-LTR.1.8.)
- Advisers will need to address any issues in the person's immigration history which might lead to the application being refused for the previous use of deception (allegations of which may not have been raised by the Home Office when that previous application was refused). A subject access request (see Chapter 2 at 2.1.1) might help anticipate problems which can then be addressed in the application, on the presumption that the Home Office will spot any inconsistencies in information provided in support of the application and previous applications, potentially going back many years.
- The exact wording of the Rule against any criminal offending is always important. For example section 38(2) of the UK Borders Act 2007 addressing Interpretation sets out that 'the reference to a person who is sentenced to a period of imprisonment of at least 12 months— (a) does not include a reference to a person who receives a suspended sentence (unless a court subsequently orders that the sentence or any part of it (of whatever length) is to take effect).' The r6 definitions of "custodial sentence" and "period of imprisonment" appliy this definition to the Rules generally.
- It is necessary to be realistic in assessing the public interest –ZH (Bangladesh) [2009] EWCA Civ 8 held that illegal working is not sufficient to exclude a person from the benefits of the then-extant 14-year 'unlawful residence' rule. See also Aissaoui [2008] EWCA Civ 37.

The suitability requirements for leave to remain are divided into 3 kinds: automatic refusals, cases where the misdemeanour brings a presumption of refusal, and pure discretionary cases. The mandatory ones ('will be refused' S-LTR.1.1) are

- being subject of a deportation order (S-LTR.1.2)
- applicant's presence not being conducive to the public good (disregarding any legal or practical reasons militating against removal – S-LTR.3.1), owing to:
  - having a conviction and prison sentence of between 12 months and under 4 years, unless 10 years have passed from the end of the sentence
  - having a conviction and prison sentence of 4 years or more
  - offending which has caused serious harm or its persistence shows particular disregard for the law (S-LTR.1.5); other convictions or conduct, character, associations or other reasons making their presence undesirable (S-LTR.1.6);

- having been excluded from refugee status or HP; or disentitled to protection from non-refoulement (for reasonable grounds to view them as a danger to security, or due to conviction for a particularly serious crime); or where SSDH would have thus decided had an asylum claim been made in which those issues were addressed (S-LTR.1.8)
- noncompliance, without reasonable excuse, with a requirement to attend an interview; provide information or physical data; or undergo a medical examination or provide a medical report (S-LTR.1.7)

One set of suitability requirements for leave to remain are discretionary, albeit with a presumption of refusal ('will normally be refused' – S-LTR.2.1) for

- providing false information, statements or documents, by anyone, regardless whether to the applicant's knowledge, including false information given to anyone else to obtain a supporting document, or failure to disclose material facts, in relation to the application (S-LTR.2.2)
- failure to provide, where requested or required, a maintenance undertaking (S-LTR.2.4) or comply with a marriage investigation as notified under s50(7)(b) of the 2014 Act (S-LTR.2.5)

Another set of suitability requirements for leave to remain are discretionary without any such presumption('may be refused' – S-LTR.4.1) for

- having made false statements or failed to disclose material facts in any previous Home Office application for entry clearance, leave to enter or remain or a variation of leave, or in a human rights claim; or for a document to support such a claim/for [EEA] residence documentation; regardless of whether the application succeeded (S-LTR.4.2/4.3)
- failure to pay litigation costs awarded to the Home Office (S-LTR.4.4) or outstanding overseas NHS charges of at least £500 (S-LTR.4.5)

6.1.5.3 'Suitability' at the indefinite leave to remain stage

The suitability requirements for indefinite leave to remain are mandatory ('will be refused' S-ILR.1.1) for

- being subject of a deportation order (S-ILR.1.2)
- applicant's presence not being conducive to the public good (disregarding any legal or practical reasons militating against removal – S-ILR.3.1), owing to:
    - having a conviction and prison sentence of at least four years (S-ILR.1.3); of at least 12 months to less than 4 years (end of sentence less than 15 years ago) (S.1.4);
    - prison sentence of less than 12 months (end of sentence less than seven years ago) (S-ILR.1.5); conviction for or admission of an offence, with a non-custodial sentence or out of court settlement entered on criminal record (within two years of date of decision) (S-ILR.1.6) *NB: where one of these two grounds is or would be the sole ground for refusal of ILR, further leave can be applied for or granted until the relevant barring period has passed. This is true for all Appendix FM categories (see generally the second 'Decision' paragraph under ILR for each category) – as well as for ILR following 10 years' leave in the Private Life category under para 276ADE (see para 276DG).*
    - offending which has caused serious harm or its persistence shows particular disregard for the law (S-ILR.1.7); other convictions or conduct, character, associations or other reasons making their continued presence undesirable (S-ILR.1.8)

- having been excluded from refugee status or HP; or disentitled to protection from non-refoulement (for reasonable grounds to view them as a danger to security, or due to conviction for a particularly serious crime); or where SSDH would have thus decided had an asylum claim been made in which those issues were addressed (S-ILR.1.10)
- noncompliance, without reasonable excuse, with a requirement to attend an interview; provide information or physical data; or undergo a medical examination or provide a medical report (S-ILR.1.9)

The suitability requirements for indefinite leave to remain are discretionary ('will normally be refused' – S-ILR.2.1) for

- provision of false information, statements or documents, by anyone, regardless whether to the applicant's knowledge, including false information given to anyone else to obtain a supporting document, or failure to disclose material facts, in relation to the application (S-ILR.2.2)
- failure to provide, where requested or required, a maintenance undertaking (S-ILR.2.4)

The suitability requirements for indefinite leave to remain are discretionary ('may be refused' – S-ILR.4.1) for

- having made false statements or failed to disclose material facts in any previous HO application for entry clearance, leave to enter or remain/-vary leave, or in a human rights claim; or for a supporting (or EEA residence) document; regardless of whether the application succeeded (S-ILR.4.2 & 3)
- failure to pay litigation costs awarded to the Home Office (S-ILR.4.4) or outstanding overseas NHS charges of at least £500 (S-ILR.4.5)

6.1.6 Making a Family Life Application

Fiancé(e)s/proposed civil partners (unless they are also unmarried partners as defined in GEN.1.2.) and adult dependent relatives can only apply from overseas. Other applications can be made from overseas or from within the UK. For basic information on entry clearance see this UKVI page.

Applications for leave to remain should be made on form FLR(M), for partners who meet all the requirements of the rules, or otherwise on form FLR(FP) for any (including 5-year route) parents, those relying on the Exception (i.e. para EX.1.), or those relying on GEN.3.2.

The usual provision condoning 14 days of overstaying under r39E is referenced within Appendix FM. There is additionally a policy to permit late applications after this period which 'could include delays resulting from unexpected or unforeseeable circumstances such as' serious illness, postal or travel delays and an inability to provide essential documents for exceptional and unavoidable circumstances beyond the applicant's control including Home Office fault or delay, or theft, fire and flood – any of these excuses must be backed by evidence.

A valid application will not be required when a human rights claim is made in the following circumstances (GEN.1.9.) (all human rights claims are outside OISC 1 competence so must be referred):

- as part of an asylum claim, or as part of a further submission in person after an asylum claim has been refused;
- where a migrant is in immigration detention. A migrant in immigration detention or their representative must submit any application or claim raising Article 8 to a prison officer, a prisoner custody officer, a detainee custody officer or a member of Home Office staff at the migrant's place of detention; or
- in an appeal (subject to the consent of the Secretary of State where applicable)

6.1.7 Appendix FM-SE

Appendix FM-SE contains many substantive and complex requirements in addition to those in Appendix FM. These apply largely, but not wholly, in respect of the financial requirements. These include (but are not limited to):

- The decision-maker will only consider documents that have been submitted with the application unless they have contacted the applicant under the evidential flexibility rule at paragraph D(b).
- Where a specified document is missing or in the wrong format or does not contain all the specified information, the decision maker should contact the applicant and give them a few

days to provide the correct document unless the application also falls to be refused on other grounds.

- For those relying on income from salaried employment, they will be able to use their gross annual salary at its current level from their current employment only where they have been employed with the same employer for a minimum of six months, and only where they have been paid at that level for that six month period (i.e. the level of gross annual salary will be taken as being the lowest income of that six month period). If this provision is not met, the sponsor will need to rely on their actual earnings over the previous 12 months.
- Where the British citizen is living outside the UK with their partner, they will both need to meet the financial requirement in respect of income earned abroad, and have a source of income available to them when they return to the UK (see e.g. paragraph 4).
- Under Appendix FM-SE, an application cannot rely on third party support, other than for maintenance payments, income from a dependent child of age 18 or over who remains part of the household, gifts of cash savings held for at least six months, and a maintenance grant for studies (paragraph 1(b)).
- Appendix FM-SE requires a great deal of specified evidence to be provided of the partners and applicants income, in its various forms, and savings. As an example, for those relying on income from salaried employment, they must provide wage-slips, bank statements and a letter from the employer (answering five specified questions) for the six month or 12 month period. Additionally, the Home Office reserves the right to request P60s and a contract of employment. For those relying wholly or partly on self-employed or other forms of income, completely different but even more onerous requirements apply.
- Detailed provisions as to the form that documents must take are laid out in paragraph 1. An application can be refused, for example, if the employer's letter is not on company-headed paper and signed by a senior manager.
- The specified documents evidencing income and savings are provided for in paragraphs 2 to 11. Where the sponsor is relying on certain benefits under E-ECP3.3, only paragraphs 12 and 12A apply.
- On the basis of the specified evidence provided under paragraphs 2 to 11, the income will then be calculated in accordance with paragraphs 13-20A. Paragraph 21 removes benefit and tax credit payments and any other source of income not specified elsewhere from the gross annual income calculation.

Even where the applicant meets the financial requirements, many will find it very difficult to provide all the specified evidence. Unless paragraph D(e) applies, their application stands to be refused if they do not.

In addition to the financial requirements, Appendix FM-SE specifies the evidence required to prove the marriage or civil partnership, that the English Language requirement is met, and for all the key requirements of the adult dependent relative category.

Top Tip

If you are seeking to evidence the available income in a category such an Appendix FM where the requirements are rigorous, don't just leave it to the decision maker or judge to try and fathom out the meaning of a bundle for themselves.

Specify:

(a) what the requirement is and
(b) how it is met

- Explain the level of income you have to show under Appendix FM
- Explain the form of income which you are relying on to satisfy that requirement
- Reference and set out the relevant sub-rule which governs the acceptable evidence under Appendix FM-SE
- Cross reference the witness statement or representations to the pages of the evidence bundle that demonstrate that the requirement is satisfied

For example, if relying partially on rent, explain that the evidential requirement is at para 10 of Appendix FM-SE and that you have satisfied it thus:

'Please find enclosed –

- proof of ownership by way of mortgage statement (page …)
- 12 months of bank statements with the rent receipts marked (pages … to …)
- A rental agreement between my client and his lodger .... dated .... and covering the whole of this 12 month period (page …)'

6.1.8 Sponsors with LTR under Appendices EU and ECAA (EEA/Swiss or Turkish sponsors)

Sponsors with leave to remain under

(a) rEU3 of Appendix EU (pre-settled status holders who were resident continuously before the end of transition – GEN.1.3(d)), and
(b) under Appendix ECAA Extension of stay
were added, at the end of the transition period (see section 11.1) to the list of persons who can sponsor an applicant under Appendix FM.

Their inclusion could prevent long separations between, for example, new spouses or civil partners abroad, and their sponsors, pending the sponsor's attainment of settled status (in the entry clearance context), or a long period during which the applicant would need to acquire leave on alternative immigration routes to remain with their UK based partner in the UK.

Before advising a client to apply under Appendix FM with a presettled status sponsor, any potential EUSS application which could be made instead, must be explored, given the extremely high cost and level of inconvenience involved in the Appendix FM settlement route, compared with the EUSS route (see section 11.7).

It is important to remember that pre-settled status holders can continue to sponsor family members under the EU Settlement Scheme, in the capacity of a "Relevant EEA Citizen". The precondition for EUSS sponsorship is that the family relationship existed before 11pm on 31 December 2020. To children born or adopted thereafter to/by the pre-settled status holder, this precondition does not apply, although children must apply 3 months after birth or adoption if born on or after 1 April 2021.

Spouses and civil partners who entered the marriage or civil partnership after the end of the transition period can also, still be sponsored under the EUSS scheme if they can prove that their relationship with the sponsor was already durable by that date. Remember that 2 years' cohabitation and even a relationship of 2 years' duration are not strict requirements under Appendix EU or the EUSS guidance. Please refer to the durable partner sections in Module 11 for further information.

A few other clarifications:

- LTR holders under both appendices can sponsor **Partners**, including fiances, for entry clearance (E-ECP.2.1(d)&(e)) or leave to remain (E-LTRP.1.2(d)&(e) and consequently those applicant's children under the category "**Family life as a child of a person with limited leave as a partner or parent**" (i.e. as the child of the applicant partner of the sponsor).
- The bereaved partner (**BPILR**) and domestic abuse (**DVILR**) settlement categories are only open to pre-settled status holders under Appendix EU, not LTR holders under Appendix ECAA.
- Pre-settled status holders who are children can, additionally, technically "sponsor" their parent in the "**Parent of a Child in the UK**" category for EC (E-ECP|T.2.2(c)) and LTR (E-LTRPT.2.2.(c)).
- However, settlement for such a parent is excluded until the child becomes settled (E-ILRPT(1A)&(1B)). This should not be a problem as the child will have already begun their 5-

year route to settlement under Appendix EU when their parent applies to commence their own (at least) 5-year route to settlement under Appendix FM.

- Further to the parent category, a pre-settled status holder can also be the "other parent (E-ECPT.2.3(b)(i) & E-LTRPT.2.3(a)&(b)).
- For purposes of **Paragraph: Exception** (EX1(a)) (see section 6.2.5 below), the child, who cannot be reasonably expected to leave the UK (and on the basis of a parental relationship with whom the applicant makes use of that paragraph to be excused from meeting certain Appendix FM requirements), can, as before, only be a British citizen or a child who has lived in the UK for 7 years. Therefore, a 10-year route parent application wil generally not be possible in reliance on the relationship with a pre-settled status child (unless the child can be deemed to have resided in the UK for 7 years but is not yet eligible for settled status because of an excessive absence, breaking their continuous residence under Appendix EU).
- However, under EX1(b), a partner with whom the applicant has a relationship, the continuation of which abroad would face insurmountable obstacles, *can* be a LTR holder under either Appendix EU or Appendix ECAA.
- **Adult depentend relatives** can be sponsored by pre-settled status holders for entry clearance (E-ECDR.2.3(b)(iv)). ILR on the ADR route requires that a pre-settled status holding sponsor, for the applicant to be eligible for ILR, to have at least made a valid application for ILR by the time their adult dependent relative applies to settled (E-ILRDR.1.3.(b)), which reflects the position of ADRs of refugees or HP holders of LTR, who are covered by the same subparagraph.

Given the remaining EUSS options for many family members this sponsorship category is likely to become more heavily used a little further down the line, and should technically finish not too long after 30 June 2026, when most of the last pre-setted status holders should have attained settled status (depending on how many manage to apply for- and be granted EUPSS after the end of the grace period (which ends on 30 June 2021).

6.2 Family life as a partner under Appendix FM

This category provides for entry clearance, leave to remain and indefinite leave to remain for partners, defined at GEN.1.2. as:

(i) the applicant's spouse;
(ii) the applicant's civil partner;
(iii) the applicant's fiancé(e) or proposed civil partner; or
(iv) a person who has been living together with the applicant in a relationship akin to a marriage or civil partnership for at least two years prior to the date of application, unless a different meaning of partner applies elsewhere in this Appendix.

Note that for partners who are neither married not in a civil partnership, two solid years of cohabitation must be shown.

In addition to the suitability criteria, there are relationship, financial, English language and immigration status requirements. Where 'Section EX: Exception' applies, the applicant will not need to meet the financial, English language or most of the immigration status requirements. This difference is what allows the immigration community to talk of the 'five-year' and '10-year' routes to settlement – because someone who qualifies only under the more limited requirements that operate when the EX exception is established will be granted leave, but under the longer settlement route. From 10 August 2017, there will be, presumably rare, grants on the 10-year route where even EX1 is not met but applications succeed after consideration under the 'exceptional circumstances' two-stage procedure in GEN.3.1. and GEN.3.2. (see above).

It is important to realise that many relationships between partners may fall outside Appendix FM altogether. These cases will be considered under GEN.3.2s, and, on appeal, with the section 117 (NIAA 2002) guidance in mind. For example:

- A couple where the migrant has been excluded for suitability reasons
- A couple who have not cohabited for two years (because of the GEN definition of partner)
- A couple where the sponsor is not a British citizen, settled or holder of refugee/HP leave, or a holder of LTR under EU3 of Appendix EU, or under Appendix ECAA Extension of Stay (E-LTRP.1.2)
- A couple where either is aged under 18 at the date of application
- A couple where the applicant is present as a visitor or with other leave, save for that of fiancé or in recognition of extant family proceedings, granted for six months or less (E-LTRP.2.1)

The possibility of cases falling through the gaps in the Ex.1 exception is shown by Sabir [2014] UKUT 63 (IAC), where the Tribunal says that the exception (at Rule EX.1) is not 'free standing', making it clear that one must be suitable to apply under Appendix FM to benefit from the exception.

As we saw above, GEN.3.2 now provides for a residual consideration of cases under Appendix FM even though one of the key criteria under Appendix FM is not met, or the case falls foul of the General Refusal reasons. So the historic strictness of the eligibility hurdle has been removed for post-August 2017 cases. GEN.3.2 apparently authorises consideration of an application where those involved do not meet the 'partner' requirements, for example for a couple who lack two years' cohabitation. Of course, in such a case, the relevant wider 'exceptional circumstances' necessary meet the GEN.3.2 threshold would have to be met. GEN.3.2 applies to all applications considered under Appendix FM (except bereaved partner and domestic violence provisions – see GEN.3.2(4)).

- Family Policy Family life (as a partner or parent), private life and exceptional circumstances, sets out its definitions of "exceptional circumstances, "exceptional", "unjustifiably harsh consequences" and a "relevant child

The policy states that the changes of 10 August 2017 restructured Appendix FM such that it now provides a complete framework for our Article 8 decision-making in cases decided under it.It also contains a very length and detailed list of 'relevant factors' to be weighed against the public interest, the first of which is the best interests of the child, factors under which are in turn set out in the policy..

As you can see, there are a series of questions arising in an Appendix FM case. We summarised these at the start of this Module: but now we set them out in a bit more detail. Firstly, taking the example of the in-country partner:

(a) Does the case succeed under the Rules i.e. have the Suitability, Eligibility, Immigration and Financial Requirements been satisfied, in which case the appeal succeeds under the Immigration Rules without regard to the Exception at Ex.1. ***If not, OISCc 1 advisers must refer the case to a suitable accredited adviser. The below is provided as further information.***
(b) If not (a) for the sole reason a partner applicant fails to meet the Financial requirement, can 'Exceptional Circumstances' para GEN.3.1. be applied for the applicant to benefit from the wider list of financial sources and evidence in para 21A Appendix FM-SE
(c) If para 21A of App FM-SE cannot be satisfied, or if the Immigration or English requirements are not met, is the Exception within the Rules at Ex.1&2 in play
(d) If not (a), (b) or (c), can 'Exceptional Circumstances' para GEN3.2. be applied. Does nevertheless Article 8 ECHR, taking into account whether there are particularly compelling or exceptional circumstances present leading to unjustifiably harsh consequences, render the immigration decision disproportionate.

The Leave Outside the Rules policy remains available here but any Article 8 representations should be made with reference to the Appendix FM framework.

6.2.1 Relationship

The applicant's partner must be:

- a British citizen in the UK, subject to paragraph GEN.1.3.(c); or

- present and settled in the UK, subject to paragraph GEN.1.3.(b); or
- in the UK with refugee leave or with humanitarian protection; or
- in the UK with LTR under rEU3 Appendix EU; or
- in the UK with LTR under Appendix ECAA Extension of Stay.

The reference to GEN.1.3. (see Section GEN above) concerns British citizen and settled partners living outside the UK and returning to the UK with the applicant. The partners will be treated as being in the UK for the purposes of the application.

Additionally:

- The applicant and partner must be aged 18 or over at the date of application.
- The applicant and their partner must not be within the prohibited degree of relationship.
- The applicant and their partner must have met in person.
- The relationship between the applicant and their partner must be genuine and subsisting.
- If the applicant and partner are married or in a civil partnership it must be a valid marriage or civil partnership, as specified.
- If the applicant is a fiancé(e) or proposed civil partner they must be seeking entry to the UK to enable their marriage or civil partnership to take place.
- Any previous relationship of the applicant or their partner must have broken down permanently (unless polygamous, via the reference to r278(i)).
- The applicant and partner must intend to live together permanently in the UK.

Categories of partner

'Pre-flight' partners of refugees and those with humanitarian protection continue to be dealt with under the family reunion provisions in Part 11 of the Rules. Sub-paragraph (c) above relates only to whose relationship (as defined in GEN.1.2.) was formed after the partner left their country of nationality.

Fiancé(e)s and proposed civil partners must apply for entry clearance (E-ECP.2.8., E-LTRP.1.12). They must be seeking entry to the UK to enable their marriage or civil partnership to take place,, within six months of arriving here. They cannot apply for leave in this Appendix FM category from within the UK.

Example

Algernon, a US citizen, is in the UK on student leave. He falls in love with Algerina, a British citizen. They swear lifelong loyalty to one another and become engaged. They do not wish to marry for at least a year in order to explain things to their families. Algernon wants to know whether he can remain in the UK with Algerina on a long-term basis.

As things stand, there is a difficulty. Fiancés can only enter the Appendix FM routes by seeking entry clearance (E-LTRP.1.12). If the couple marry within the currency of his leave, then of course there would be no difficulty in seeking leave to remain. Algernon should steel himself for a trip abroad to seek entry clearance to return here, and they would then have to time his return and their marriage arrangements such as to secure the wedding within that period of fiancé leave.

Present and settled

The meaning of 'present and settled' and 'settled in the United Kingdom' is set out in Rule 6 of the Immigration Rules and in essence means possession of ILR or the right of abode combined with physical presence in the UK. An EEA national or non-EEA family member with a permanent right of residence in the UK must be considered as present and settled until the end of the grace period on 30 June 2021.

Validity of marriage

The parties to a marriage or civil partnership will need to show that they are legally married according to the laws of the country in which the marriage took place (although see below for polygamous marriages), or that they have contracted a legal civil partnership in a country in which such partnerships are recognised. These countries are listed at Schedule 20 of the Civil Partnership Act 2004. At the time of writing this numbered some 75 jurisdictions (see: the IDIs at Chapter 8, section 2, Annex H for the list as it was in January 2013).

The rule that marriages will be recognised if legally contracted in the country in which they take place is a long standing rule of international private law. For authority see Berthiaume v. Dastous [1930] AC 79 and Rule 67 of *Dicey* 14th edition. This means that even quite unusual marriage arrangements, such as marriages by proxy where one or both participants are in the UK whilst the marriage is formalised in their country of origin, must be recognised (CB Brazil [2008] UKAIT 00080). For a while the UT ruled that proxy marriages in EU law had to be recognised in the EEA Sponsor's (EEA) country of nationality: this misapprehension was corrected in Awuku [2017] EWCA Civ 178.

Where there are complications in evidencing the legality of the marriage, an option would be for the person to come to the UK as a fiancé(e), and then register the marriage once here.

The requirement that the marriage is legal will in some cases mean that relevant formal divorce papers or other evidence of a divorce that was effective in the country in which it took place will need to be produced. The complex issue of domicile may also arise in some spouse cases.

In addition, the applicant must demonstrate that they have an intention to live permanently with the other (defined as below, in Rule 6 of the Interpretation section of the Introduction to the Immigration Rules) and, if married or in a civil partnership, that the marriage is genuine and subsisting.

'Intention to live permanently with the other' or 'intend to live together permanently' means an intention to live together, evidenced by a clear commitment from both parties that they will live together permanently in the UK immediately following the outcome of the application in question or as soon as circumstances permit thereafter. However, where an application is made under Appendix Armed Forces the words 'in the UK' in this definition do not apply.

Genuine and 'Subsisting' Relationships and Marriages; and having met

The relationship has to be **genuine**: i.e. it must not be a sham.

Also it has to be **subsisting**: i.e. there must still be a genuine ongoing relationship between the couple.

Nevertheless, these two requirements are not intended to be equivalent to the old 'primary purpose' rule. That infamous provision for many years required applicants to prove a negative: namely that the application was not being made for the *primary purpose* of gaining entry to the UK, irrespective of whether the couple actually did intend to live together afterwards.

Example

Khalid is a British citizen. He is married to Ambreen, to whom he is introduced by his family, in Pakistan, her country of origin. They married around five years ago. An application for Ambreen to join him in the UK is made.

This application may well be heading for refusal given the delay since the marriage. An ECO may well think that even if the marriage *was* pursuant to a genuine relationship, that things have cooled between the couple. A strong evidence-backed case should be put to explain the reasons for the passage of time.

Relevant evidence might be:

- Concrete evidence of the relationship's duration and any period of cohabitation (bearing in mind relevant cultural factors, which might rule out cohabitation) including shared financial responsibilities (i.e. both names appearing on utility and other bills)

- Proof of family life: visiting each other's families, and having made practical arrangements for life together here).

Remember: the fruitier the immigration history, the more likely it is that there will be suspicions. There are no specified evidence requirements in the partner rules for proving that the relationship requirements are met. So it is a matter of collecting the best available evidence that the relationship is legally valid, genuine and subsisting. Interviews and home visits by the UKVI are not unusual, and nor indeed are immigration officials turning up as unwanted guests at marriages in the UK and whisking one party into detention. Investigating potentially sham marriages is a priority for the UKVI.

The couple **must have met** at the time of the application. This allows for arranged marriages, where the couple do not meet until the day of the wedding, but it may exclude some marriages that would be legal in the country in which they take place, such as marriages in absentia, by telephone or by proxy, unless the couple have met by the time of the application.

Applicants and their partners should submit:

- evidence of registered relationships (e.g. birth, divorce and marriage certificates), with translations where necessary
- statements from both parties giving some history to the relationship and intentions for the future
- evidence of cohabitation
- photos and other evidence of any ceremony, and time spent together (but not DVDs or video cassettes)
- phone records – with itemised billing where possible, but phone cards if that is all there is (see *Goudey* above)
- other evidence of contact (e.g. emails, social media, cards, plane tickets)

Whilst there is no longer a requirement to seek permission from the Secretary of State to get married in the UK, registrars already have powers to notify the Home Office of suspicious marriages. The provisions of the Immigration Act 2014, operational in April 2015, extend the length of time needed to give notice of marriage from 15 to 28 days, and will require registrars to notify the Home Office of all marriages involving a non-EEA party who is not settled in the UK. The immigration authorities will then have the power to delay marriages for up to 70 days whilst they investigate the immigration status of the parties, the genuineness of the marriage, and to take enforcement action where appropriate. Read more on these provisions in Immigration Bill Factsheet 12.

Top Tip

In any case where the genuineness of the relationship is disputed, always check the documents provided to show cohabitation carefully:

- Has any permission that is required for co-occupancy been obtained?
- Are there any potential inconsistencies between the contents of the documents and the relationship history?

Issues such as these need to be explained carefully by detailed witness statements

Getting married in the UK

There is no requirement for migrants planning to marry in the UK to seek the permission of the Home Office to do so. The Certificate of Approval scheme, introduced AITCA 2004, and designed to introduce such a requirement, was abolished on 9 May 2011. The scheme was held to be unlawful by the House of Lords in 2008 in the case of Baiai [2009] 1 AC 287. After several modifications it was finally abandoned.

One part of the original scheme does remain, which is the requirement to give notice to marry or register the civil partnership at a 'designated office'. All registration offices in Scotland and Northern Ireland are designated offices, as are 76 offices in England and Wales. Both parties will need proof of their name, age and nationality, but there is no prescribed way of evidencing these.

When this regime was introduced, the HO estimated that 35,000 marriages per year would need to be referred to themselves for potential investigation and that 6,000 marriages would then be actively investigated. Molina [2017] EWHC 1730 (Admin) explain the difference between a **sham marriage** and **a marriage of convenience**: the former involves a marriage where there is no genuine relationship between the parties, whereas the latter connotes one contracted to secure an immigration advantage, whether or not there is a genuine bond between the participants.

A new referral scheme was introduced on 2 March 2015, contained in part 4 of the Immigration Act 2014. Under it, any proposed marriages or civil partnerships in the UK from which a non-EEA national could benefit in immigration terms can be referred to the Home Office. and to be investigated under an extended notice period of 70 days. Now, notice of all marriages in England and Wales must be given at least 28 days in advance of the marriage taking place, replacing the previous notice period of 15 days.

If the Home Office decides not to investigate then the Home Office should inform the registrar and the marriage can proceed after the conclusion of the normal 28-day notice period. If the Home Office does decide to investigate further, then the notice period is extended to 70 days to allow time for investigation and for enforcement action to be taken.

The Home Office may prevent the marriage taking place where the parties fail to co-operate with the investigation.

Examples of risk factors which may identify the marriage as being at high risk of being a sham include: (*Sham Marriages and Civil Partnerships Background Information And Proposed Referral And Investigation Scheme*, Home Office November 2013)

- Is of a nationality at high risk of involvement in a sham, on the basis of objective information and intelligence about sham cases.
- Holds a visa in a category linked by objective information and intelligence to sham cases.
- Has no immigration status or holds leave which is due to expire shortly.
- Has had an application to remain in the UK refused.
- Has previously sponsored another spouse or partner to enter or remain in the UK.
- Is or has been the subject of a credible section 24/24A report, which explains for example how the couple could not communicate in a common language and did not know basic information about each other.

Polygamy, prohibited relationships and age

Under the immigration rules the spouse in a polygamous marriage is not permitted to enter or remain in the UK on the basis of the marriage if there is another person living who is the spouse of the sponsor and who at any time since their marriage has been in the UK or has been granted a certificate of entitlement (see rule 278). This does not mean that polygamous marriages are not recognised or lawful in the UK, but rather that only one spouse from such a marriage may enter the UK.

'Prohibited degree of relationship' is defined in rule 6 as having the same meaning as in the Marriage Act 1949, the Marriage (Prohibited Degrees of Relationship) Act 1986 and the Civil Partnership Act 2004 and the list is set out at pg 7-8 of the Family Policy: Partners, divorce and dissolution.

The justification put forward by the Home Office at the time of the change was that it would help to prevent forced marriages. The Supreme Court found that the rule change was not a lawful way of deterring or preventing forced marriages. The actual effect, at least in some cases, was to force the young British spouse to live abroad until aged 21, away from home, friends and family.

6.2.2 English language requirement

Applicants in the partner category must submit with their application proof that they meet the English language requirement. The precise evidence is specified in Appendix FM-SE (at paragraphs 27 to 32).

Guidance English language requirement: family members under Part 8, Appendix FM and Appendix Armed Forces was updated on 15 July 2020 to include reference to COVID-19 concessions applicable to those unable to take a test for reasons of the pandemic.

Previously, the English language requirement applied to an initial application for leave in this category, but not for the extension that the partner will apply for after 30 months. That changed for those whose initial period of leave expires from 1 May 2017. They will need to show a higher level of English when applying for their extension.

The English language requirement can be met in four ways:

- by being a national of a specified majority English speaking country listed in GEN.1.6.
- by having passed an approved English language speaking and listening test at minimum level A1 (or A2, as the case may be) of the Common European Framework of Reference for Languages (CEFR) with a provider approved by the Secretary of State (as specified in Appendix O)
- have an academic qualification which is either a Bachelor's or Master's degree or PhD awarded by an educational establishment in the UK; or, if awarded by an educational establishment outside the UK, is deemed by UK NARIC to meet or exceed the recognised standard of a Bachelor's or Master's degree or PhD in the UK, and UK NARIC has confirmed that the degree was taught or researched in English to level A1 (or A2) CEFR or above.
- by exemption

Exempt from the requirement are:

- those aged 65 or over at the date of application
- those who have a physical or mental condition that would prevent them from meeting the requirement
- where there are exceptional compassionate circumstances that would prevent the applicant from meeting the requirement.

The concession relating to long term residents of countries where there is no approved test centre in that country was withdrawn on 24 July 2014 for applications made on or after that date (or for some countries on or after 14 August 2014). Where an applicant is unable to take the test, the Guidance states that they must demonstrate, as a result of exceptional circumstances they are unable to learn English before coming to the UK or it is not practicable or reasonable for them to travel to another country to take an approved English language test. Provide evidence of previous efforts to access learning materials or to travel overseas and the obstacles to doing so. The guidance states that

> This must include evidence provided by an independent source (e.g. an appropriately qualified medical practitioner) or capable of being verified by the decision maker.
>
> Examples of situations in which, subject to the necessary supporting evidence, the decision maker might conclude that there were exceptional circumstances, might include where the applicant:

- is a long-term resident of a country in international or internal armed conflict, or where there is or has been a humanitarian disaster, including in light of the infrastructure affected.
- has been hospitalised for several months immediately prior to the date of application.
- is the full-time carer of a disabled child also applying to come to the UK.
- is a long-term resident of a country with no approved A1 test provision and it is not practicable or reasonable for the applicant to travel to another country to take such a test.

- is a long-term resident of a country in which the applicant faces very severe practical or logistical difficulties, which cannot reasonably be overcome, in accessing the learning resources required to acquire English language speaking and listening skills at CEFR level A1.

  Lack of or limited literacy or education will not in itself be accepted as exceptional circumstances.

Paragraphs 32A-32D of Appendix FM-SE deal with the aftermath of the recent scandal, when some approved test providers were found to be selling test certificates to thousands of migrants who, it is alleged, did not actually sit the test. Applicants previously relying on dodgy certificates can be required to provide new test certificates. See further Module 2 at 2.3.3.

These Rules provide that:

- Where the decision maker has reasonable cause to doubt that an English language certificate was genuinely obtained, or has received information that the test provider withdrew the test result, they *may* discount the test certificate and require a new one to be provided.
- Where the test result is invalid for other reasons yet was previously accepted as part of the evidence supporting a successful application for leave, then it *will* be accepted as valid.

6.2.3 Financial requirement

For applications made under the transitional provisions (i.e. under the old Rules), the applicant will need to show adequate maintenance and accommodation without recourse to public funds (as defined in Rule 6). Applicants under Appendix FM will need to meet the very onerous income threshold (in addition to having adequate accommodation) unless the partner is in receipt of specified disability- related benefits.

Note that, after JCWI and others campaigned for the suspension of the requirement given the impact of COVID-19, both relevant guidance documents (Family Migration: Appendix FM Section 1.7A – Adequate maintenance and accommodation and Family Migration: Appendix FM Section 1.7 Appendix Armed Forces Financial requirement were amended to include the following COVID concessions, in both sections at the very end of the document: :

- A temporary loss of employment income between 1 March 2020 and 1 January 2021 due to COVID-19 is disregarded so long as [the financial requirement] was met in the preceding 6 months
- Those who are furloughed are deemed to receive 100% of their income
- A temporary loss of annual income due to COVID-19 between 1 March 2020 and 1 January 2021 will generally be disregarded for self-employment income
- Evidential flexibility is to be applied where the applicant cannot obtain evidence for reasons related to COVID-19

This clearly falls short of an outright suspension of the financial requirements, and the concession cut off date of 31 August 2020 will have harsh consequences for many families. Further changes and updates will be captured on an ongoing basis in our special online module COVID 19 – Immigration Law, Policy and Procedure which is available via your subscription.

The basic idea is this:

- The couple must show proscribed funds via income and savings (dependent on the number of children who have no long-term right to be in the UK)
- Only having regard to certain kinds of income
- Though if the sponsor is on certain kinds of benefit, the requirements are relaxed, so that the only question is whether *in fact* the applicant can be maintained and accommodated without recourse to public funds

There are similar provisions governing entry clearance and extension applications, though as always there a few differences. Remember, all the requirements have to be shown via specified evidence. We always advise course delegates to read the course text alongside the Rules themselves. But here it is especially important to do so.

We will first look at applications for entry clearance under the Partner category:

E-ECP.3.1. The applicant must provide specified evidence, from the sources listed in paragraph E-ECP.3.2., of-

(a) a specified gross annual income of at least-

- (i) £18,600;
- (ii) an additional £3,800 for the first child; and
- (iii) an additional £2,400 for each additional child

For now we can refer to this sum as the **target income**.

Children receive a particular definition for these purposes (E-ECP.3.1):

- They must be dependent children (i.e. part of the present application or already in the UK with leave) aged under 18 (or have been of such an age when they entered the route); and
- They must not be British citizens, or have ILR, or have EEA residence rights

The target income has to be met via funds from any and all of four income sources (E-ECP.3.2). Namely:

- The sponsor's income from employment/self-employment, including from earnings overseas where the sponsor is returning to the UK with the applicant
- Pension income from both applicant and Sponsor
- Maternity allowance or bereavement benefit, or payments due to Armed Forces service
- Other income

Then E-ECP.3.1(b) provides that if there isn't enough money to make the target income, you can plug the gap with savings. You need a set sum of savings, plus two and a half times the difference between the target income and your actual income. The set sum is £16,000. So if the target income was £18,600 and the available income was £16,000, then the difference would be £2,600. So you would multiply that by 2.5 (£6,500) and add that to the £16k, giving a necessary savings sum to plug the gap of £22,500.

Then there is the let-off for people on benefits: E-ECP.3.3. This lists a series of benefits, for example disability living, attendance and carer's allowances. Where the sponsor is receiving one of these,

> the applicant must provide evidence that their partner is able to maintain and accommodate themselves, the applicant and any dependants adequately in the UK without recourse to public funds.

So that's maintenance done. Then we have the requirements for accommodation: E-ECP.3.4. Here the requirement is essentially that

- There is adequate accommodation without recourse to public funds
- Which is not overcrowded or otherwise contravenes public health
 not only the family unit applying, but any other residents)

You must consider the financial requirements in Appendix FM alongside requirements in Appendix FM-SE.

Detailed guidance on the financial requirements is in the guidance at An is in receipt of one of the benefits listed in E-ECP.3.3/E-LTRP. 3.3, the g accommodation is in Annex FM 1.7a.

For a useful summary of the 'accommodation' requirement, relevant wish to refer to the entry clearance guidance MAA.

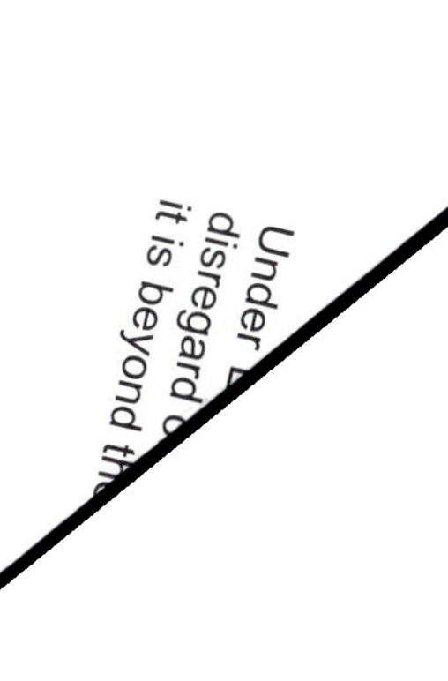

18,600 x 2.5 + 16,000 = 62,500

Appendix FM-SE sets out the evidentiary requirements necessary to meet the financial requirement, please refer back to section 6.1.7 above which lists these.

There are some differences between the income requirements for in-country applications as opposed to entry clearance ones:

- For entry clearance applications, it is only the sponsor's income from employment which is relevant (i.e. the applicant's current income or income from future employment is ignored). Where the application is made in-country, the applicant's income from lawful employment and self-employment can count toward meeting the income threshold E-LTRP.3.2(b).
- For in-country cases, there are some additional funds that can be factored into meeting the Target Income: E-LTRP.3.2(f)-(g). Namely the lawful earnings, maternity allowance and bereavement benefit, and other specified income, and savings, of a dependent child aged over 18.

Some other points to note:

- The minimum income threshold survived challenge in the courts (though the judges made it clear that some flexibility was essential as to how the target income was met): so we have to live with its strictures.
- As we mentioned earlier, there is a discretion available to decision makers to relax the strict requirements of the Rules (GEN.3.1) to allow alternative or additional sources of income to be taken into account where a refusal is possible on grounds of failing to meet the financial requirement. A decision maker has to relax the criteria where failing to do so could result in unjustifiably harsh consequences for the applicant/partner/any affected child. The basic idea is that other sources of funds, such as credible and verifiable third party support and earnings from genuine job offers can be included.

The GEN.3.1 requirements are beyond the scope of OISC level 1: you should refer cases like this onwards.

6.2.4 Immigration status

The immigration status requirements for applying for leave to remain (i.e. from within the UK) as a partner are:

E-LTRP.2.1. The applicant must not be in the UK-

- as a visitor;
- with valid leave granted for a period of 6 months or less, unless that leave is as a fiancé(e) or proposed civil partner, or was granted pending the outcome of family court or divorce proceedings

E-LTRP.2.2. The applicant must not be in the UK-

1. on immigration bail, unless
   - SSHD is satisfied they arrived over 6 months prior to application and paragraph EX.1. applies; and
   - Paragraph EX.1 applies; or
2. in breach of immigration laws (except that, where paragraph 39E of these Rules applies, any current period of overstaying will be disregarded), unless paragraph EX.1. applies

[illegible] E-LTRP.2.2.(b), for those applying before 24 November 2016, there was the more generous [illegible] of 28 days. This has now been replaced by r39E, limiting overstaying to 14 days, only where [illegible] control of the applicant or their adviser.

Oddly, an illegal entrant or overstayer can rely on EX.1. to make an application under the rules in this category, but a visitor or person granted leave for six months or less cannot. Applicants in this position must use their judgement when deciding whether to apply outside the Rules while they have that leave, or overstay before doing so. Of course this is one of the many gaps in the Rule where GEN.3.2 can come to one's aid: but as always the threshold is whether refusal would be 'unjustifiably harsh' so one would need a really good excuse for evading the implication that visitors should be returning abroad to seek entry clearance.

On 22 July 2020, the guidance Family life (as a partner or parent), private life and exceptional circumstances was first updated in relation to COVID concessions. This formalises, albeit in vague terms, some of these concessions relating to immigration status such as the exercise of discretion in relation to: absences from the UK, overstaying, remaining abroad while LTR lapsed or having been a visitor, where these circumstances were caused by the pandemic, such as on grounds of travel restrictions. Please refer to our special module COVID 19 – Immigration Law, Policy and Procedure for further detail on these and other concessions and temporary policies.

Examples

Olatunde is present in the UK as a student with leave for another three months. He has met the love of his life and wants to marry her. He asks you if he will have to leave the country in order to make an entry clearance application.

He does not have to depart. So long as he marries his partner reasonably soon, he will be entitled to apply to switch his status from student to partner. This is clear from the Immigration Status requirements at E-LTRP2.1-2.2: he is not present as a visitor or otherwise with less than six months' leave, and he is not present in breach of immigration laws and he is not on immigration bail.

Emanuel is from Malaysia; her partner David is a British citizen. They formed a relationship in recent years whilst he worked in Malaysia. He has now returned to the UK for a lengthy period of contract work. They are planning to make an application for her to join him on a spouse visa in the future. In the meantime he will visit her several times a year, whilst she will make one lengthy visit a year here. She enters the United Kingdom as a visitor together with their young daughter, Hannah. Hannah is taken ill whilst here and they wish to make a partner application under Appendix FM.

Emanuel's leave as a visitor would, previously, have ruled out an Appendix FM application as the bar to 'switching' from that category pervades both five- and 10-year settlement routes. This is an example of a case where 'an application for ... leave to ... remain ... does not otherwise meet the requirements of this Appendix or Part 9 of the Rules' and so we have to look at GEN.3.2.

Please remember that this case thereby falls outside your OISC 1 remit and must be referred on to a suitable accredited adviser. The following information is provided just for background.

Emmanuel and David would have to argue that the 'Exceptional Circumstances' in para GEN.3.2. apply but, even if they succeed in doing so, they would still need to deal with the possible suspicion that the visit application had been a vehicle for making an otherwise impermissible in-country application all along. The health of a British citizen child will clearly be a very important factor. This would be treated as a 'primary consideration' (GEN.3.3.(1)) if they succeed in having the application considered under para GEN.3.2. Depending on all the circumstances it may still be preferable to return abroad and apply for entry clearance, to avoid the delay, cost and stress of possible refusal and subsequent lengthy appeal proceedings, so long as their lifestyle and patterns of earnings are such that their income/savings can meet the financial evidence requirements.

6.2.5 Section EX: Exceptions to certain eligibility requirements for leave to remain as a partner or parent:

NB This is not level 1 work and should be referred on to a suitable accredited advisor

Where paragraph EX.1 applies, an application for leave to remain under the Appendix FM 'partner' or 'parent' categories will only have to meet the 'suitability', 'relationship' and part of the 'immigration status' requirements. This arrangement is created by para R-LTRP.1 which at (c) and (d) creates two routes within Appendix FM. The first is the five year settlement route; the second is the 10 year settlement route. First R-LTRP.1 splits applicants under these routes into two groups, those that can meet all the requirements and those who can't. And then D-LTRP.1.1 provides for a five year route to settlement for the first group, and D-LTRP.1.2 provides for a 10 year route for the others.

The 10 year route does not include all of the regular Appendix FM requirements: you can see this from the fact that it only includes the partner route provisions for Suitability, and then the Eligibility criteria up to E-LTRP.2.2. And in fact E-LTRP.2.2 is not a knock-out: because as we are about to see, overstayers and illegal entrants can qualify for the route if they meet the EX. Exception.

Which requirements drop out of the equation on the 10 year route? All those from E-LTRP.2.2 onwards. Essentially the bar on presence in breach of the immigration laws, and the financial and English language and requirements.

The structure of the Ex Exception is as follows.

Ex.1

- There are two kinds of exception
- For partners without qualifying children: they must show 'insurmountable obstacles' to life together abroad and
- For qualifying children – i.e. 7-year resident or British citizen children, if expecting the child's departure abroad would be unreasonable

Then EX.2 explains that the 'insurmountable obstacles' test is a high one: very significant difficulties which could not be overcome or would entail very serious hardship.

Note that EX.1 does not apply to entry clearance applications. So those applicants must always meet every requirement of the Rules. An application for entry clearance that does not meet all the requirements of the Rules will be considered under the 'Exceptional Circumstances' proviso at paras GEN.3.1. and GEN.3.2: such applications can succeed where there is strong private and family life in play and refusal would result in unjustifiably harsh consequences.

Migrants whose cases are granted by reference to the Ex. Exception receive 30 months grants of leave within the rules but on a 10 year route to settlement.

6.2.6 Decision

Spouses, civil partners and unmarried partners will be granted (see Section D-LTRP):

- 33 months leave to enter or
- 30 months leave remain
- on a 60 month route to settlement or
- on a 120 month route if relying on EX.1

Fiancées and proposed civil partners will be granted six months leave to enter.

In all cases, including those of a fiancée or proposed civil partner granted six months leave to enter who has now registered their relationship, further leave to remain will usually be granted for 30 months at a time until the migrant becomes entitled to ILR.

Where the applicant has extant leave at the date of decision, the remaining period of that extant leave up to a maximum of 28 days will be added to the period of limited leave to remain granted under that paragraph (which may therefore exceed 30 months).

A person granted 30 months leave on the 120 month route will, if they meet all the requirements of the rules for their next extension application (i.e. they no longer have to rely on EX.1), be able to switch into the 60 month route at any point without having to wait for their current grant to come to an end, but any time spent on the 120 month route will not count towards the 60 month requirement. This will reduce their route to settlement from 120 months to 90 months.

Example

Elijah is present in the UK under Tier 2 General, unfortunately his sponsor employer loses their licence to employ migrants and Elijah's leave is curtailed. Elijah cannot find another suitable Tier 2 sponsor and his leave runs out. He would have left the UK but he has met Mary, a British citizen; they hope to live together in the UK permanently. Mary has a rare medical condition that can only be treated in the UK, as her consultant confirms.

Elijah is an overstayer. So he cannot qualify under the five year route to settlement as he cannot meet the full requirements for partners: he is present in breach of immigration laws. However he has a very strong case to meet the EX. exception: Mary's medical condition surely represents insurmountable obstacles to life abroad for them. So he should receive a grant of leave. It will be on the 10 year route.

When his leave comes up for renewal towards the end of the first 30 months, he will no longer be an overstayer. So he can switch to the five year route so long as he meets the financial and English language requirements.

Conditions of leave

The essential conditions are:

- No recourse to public funds on the 60 month route
- No recourse to public funds on the 120 month route unless the Secretary of State considers that the person should not be subject to such a condition' (see D-LTRP.1.2.)

You may sometimes come across people granted leave under the old rules that were in force until July 2012. Under that system, a spouse, civil partner or unmarried partner would have been granted 27 months leave to enter, or 24 months leave to remain, with no recourse to public funds. Those still in the UK with limited leave under the old rules, can apply for ILR after 24 months in the UK.

6.2.7 Indefinite leave to remain

Whether applying for ILR under the partner category in Appendix FM or under the old rules, substantially the same relationship and financial requirements apply as for leave to enter and remain.

The couple will need to show their relationship is subsisting and that they continue to intend to live together permanently in the UK. The financial requirement under Appendix FM is slightly different though in that it does not require the applicant to divide their saving by 2.5. All savings over £16,000 can be used to meet the income threshold where it partners cannot meet it from their income alone.

For those applying under Appendix FM, essentially the same grounds apply but are instead found in the 'suitability' provisions (S-ILR). From 6 April 2018 the relevant ILR eligibility paras of Appendix FM make it clear that ILR after five years is only available where both grants of leave were on the five-year route (i.e. in both applications the HO accepted that all requirements were satisfied).

Example

Jim married his partner and was granted leave under Appendix FM five years ago, all the requirements of the five year route being satisfied. His leave was extended under the five year route after 30 months. They have three British citizen children. He accepted a caution for criminal damage one year ago.

Jim will run into S-ILR.1.6. His application will face refusal because he has received an out-of-court disposal recorded on his criminal record within the past 24 months. If he nevertheless applies for ILR (and of course he needs to take some action to stay lawful at the end of his second 30 month grant of leave) then he will be granted 30 months further leave: D-ILRP.1.2 which expressly caters for S-ILR.1.6 refusals.

From 6 April 2018 the relevant ILR eligibility paras of Appendix FM make it clear that ILR after five years is only available where both grants of leave were on the five-year route (i.e. in both applications the HO accepted that all requirements were satisfied).

Applicants for settlement under the age of 65 must meet the knowledge of English language and life in the UK (KoLL) requirements under Appendix KoLL unless exceptions apply: see section on Settlement.

Where the KoLL requirements are not yet met, or the application for ILR must be delayed due to the criminality provisions, the applicant will be able to apply for further limited leave.

6.3 Bereaved partners and domestic abuse

Normally, if a marriage or partnership has ended during the probationary period (the term traditionally given to the period of limited leave prior to settlement being granted), the foreign national is expected to leave the UK unless they can qualify under another category (e.g. as the parent of a child in the UK). However, in the following two circumstances partners will be able to apply for ILR notwithstanding the end of the relationship. These provisions are essentially the same under the old and new rules.

They initially applied only to partners of British citizens and those with ILR but, under a belated rule change, from 10 January 2019, they will now apply also to partners of refugees.

These categories do not have any exceptional route within the rule, unlike the parent and partner routes under Appendix FM. So if the claim fails under the rules, consideration would have to move straight to a further assessment based on whether there are compelling circumstances justifying departure from the rules, in the light of the five stage Razgar analysis discussed in Chapter 5 at section 5.4.1 and taking account of relevant factors in assessing proportionality as set out in Chapter 5 and above. It might, for example, be relevant that the individual in question has severed ties abroad and come to this country in the expectation of settling here. However, if their former partner is there only meaningful link with this country, then it is difficult to see such cases getting off the ground.

These applications will not necessarily be deemed to be human rights claims such that their refusal generates a right of appeal: they do not benefit from the Home Office policy of designating most Appendix FM applications as such automatically (see e.g. Appendix AR (AR3.2(c)(viii)). So a distinct case will have to be put, on Article 8 grounds (presuming there to be no asylum claim), to have a chance of accessing the appeal system.

NB Level 1 covers work relating to bereaved partners with straightforward cases. Work relating to domestic abuse or bereaved partners who are also overstayers must be referred on to a suitable accredited advisor.

6.3.1 Bereaved spouses or partners

Bereaved partners will be entitled to apply for indefinite leave to remain if the partner they joined in the UK died during the period of partner leave if the relationship was genuine, permanent and subsisting, at the time of the bereavement (E-BPILR.1.1-E-BPILR.1.4). Applications will subject to the suitability provisions (via the cross reference to the Suitability requirements of the Partner route for ILR), but not the Knowledge of Life and Language in the UK requirement (as there is no reference to Appendix KoLL).

The applicant may apply even though they are an overstayer (E-BPILR.1.2).

Examples

Dominica obtained entry clearance as the partner of a British citizen, Raphael exactly two years ago. They subsequently cohabited and had a baby son. Raphael was killed in a car accident a few weeks ago. Dominica wants advice on her position.

Dominica was granted leave as a partner of a British citizen who has died, and clearly the relationship was genuine, subsisting and permanent given the facts we have been provided with. So the eligibility requirements of E-BPILR.1.1-1.4 are met; and there are no facts present here to pose a problem under the suitability requirements.

This is a straightforward case within the scope of OISC level 1: Dominica is very unlikely to be an overstayer given that the normal grant of entry clearance as a partner would be 33 months, i.e. more than the 24 months which have elapsed since she obtained entry clearance.

Andrea obtained entry clearance as the partner of David. David passed away four years ago. Andrea wants to know if she can make an application under the Rules. She has been unable to face up to any personal administration since his death and has let her visa expire.

Andrea can make an application. E-BPILR.1.2. requires that the 'last grant of limited leave' was as a partner or bereaved partner. So there is no requirement for current leave. You need to check that their relationship was still subsisting on a permanent basis at the time of his death E-BPILR.1.4.

Andrea mentions that she has a recent minor criminal conviction and asks if this will affect her chances of settlement.

You will need to look into this carefully: minor convictions may well postpone access to indefinite leave to remain because of the Suitability criteria for settlement: however D-BPILR.1.2. permits a grant of limited leave for 30 months.

This is a more complicated scenario that we are including for a bit of signposting practice: the overstayer component means it should be referred onwards.

6.3.2 Victims of domestic abuse

Partners under Appendix FM who are victims of domestic abuse (formerly termed 'domestic violence' or DV: indeed this Appendix FM route still retains the DV prefix) may be granted ILR where the marriage or relationship breaks down permanently whilst they hold limited leave as a result of domestic abuse (DVILR).

The guidance is titled Victims of domestic violence.

The key criteria for the route are:

(a) Having entered the UK as the *partner* (but not fiancé(e)) of a British citizen, person with ILR or person with refugee leave (E-DVILR.1.2.)
(b) Having done so under Appendix FM or r352A (the latter for refugee spouses) (E-DVILR.1.2.)
(c) Having remained in the Appendix FM partner route if there was a subsequent grant of leave (E-DVILR.1.2(a)) or received a special grant of leave to access public funding because the SSHD recognised that that was appropriate given the need to give the applicant the chance to apply to enter the route (E-DVILR.1.2(b))
(d) The relationship breaking down permanently, due to domestic abuse, during the last period of leave (E-DVILR.1.3)

Two other things worthy of note that are not apparent from DVILR itself:

(e) Domestic abuse is widely defined in order to tally with the modern recognition of the various forms that abuse may take: so the *Victims of Domestic violence* Guidance explains that domestic abuse is essentially an incident/pattern of incidents of controlling, coercive or threatening behaviour, violence or abuse between those aged 16 or over who are, or have been, intimate partners or family members regardless of gender or sexuality, and may be psychological, physical, sexual, financial or emotional.

(f) The SSHD is rather strict about the kinds of evidence required, see the *Victims of Domestic violence* Guidance which contains a Table of evidence which is classified as Conclusive (e.g. police cautions), Strong (e.g. where a member of a Multi-agency risk assessment conference has confirmed the claim; and various family court orders), Moderate (GP reports, and reports of police attendances) and Weak (any uncorroborated evidence from the applicant, family and friends, or from professionals who are just repeating the applicant's word).

There is no requirement to have current leave at the date of applying for ILR, so long as the relationship broke down due to domestic abuse whilst the person had leave. This is realistic: victims may have long overstayed by the time they are able to make the application.

Public funding is available for these applications for those who cannot afford to pay for advice and representation. Applications are made on form SET(DV). The normal fee for settlement applications is payable, but a fee waiver is available for those who can show they are destitute.

The suitability provisions in S-ILR apply (see 6.2.7 on Suitability at the ILR stage for Partners, above). Where a person is unable to meet the requirements for ILR because of the sanctions in S-ILR.1.5. or S-ILR.1.6, which delay settlement for those with convictions, the person will be granted 30 months leave rather than ILR. In that case, the DV Rules do not provide for any condition to be placed on the grant of limited leave, so the person should be allowed recourse to public funds (subject to the HO's discretion under paragraph GEN.1.11.). That person will then be able to apply for ILR when the sanction period is over.

There are no financial or English language or Life in the UK requirements to meet in this category.

Example

Olivia enters the UK with entry clearance to join Donald here. She was assaulted by him several times in the course of their relationship and fled the family home. What extra information do you need to determine whether she would have a viable domestic violence application?

Clearly she has the starting point for an application. Note she does not need extant leave. However she does need to have entered the UK with leave as a partner D-DVILR.1.2., and the language above is vague on that.

Then D-DVILR.1.3. requires that

- an applicant provides evidence of the domestic abuse, and

- that the relationship broke down as a result of abuse.

So Olivia needs to gather up some evidence that confirms that domestic abuse was responsible for the relationship breaking down.

Destitution domestic violence concession (DDVC)

This concession allows prospective applicants for ILR under the domestic violence rule, who are destitute, to apply for three months of discretionary leave to allow them to claim benefits and secure temporary accommodation whilst they make and await a decision on the domestic violence application.

Details of the concession and an application form are at: https://www.gov.uk/government/publications/application-for-benefits-for-visa-holder-domestic-violence – there is also a briefing in the House of Commons Library. A person granted DDV leave will not have to pay a fee when applying for ILR under the rules.

The application is very straightforward, can be emailed to the HO, and will be decided in a few days. Having been granted DL in this capacity, the person will then be expected to make their ILR application within the three-month period following the grant (in which case they will remain entitled to recourse to public funds due to s3C of the 1971 Act, see Chapter 1).

In FA (Sudan) [2018] EWHC 3475 (Admin) the Court emphasised that an applicant had to have entered the UK via the appropriate immigration route under the Rules to qualify for such an application.

Note that this work is permitted to be undertaken by OISC 1 advisers who are aware of the DVILR requirements. Even while you assist with the DDVC, is vital to *immediately* start the referral process to a suitable accredited adviser for the full DVILR application as 3 months are a short time for that person to gather sufficient evidence for what is a difficult application to make.

6.4 Parent of a child in the UK (Appendix FM section EC-PT onwards)

The Appendix FM category, 'family life as a parent of a child in the UK' is, according to the guidance Family Policy Family life (as a partner or parent), private life and exceptional circumstances :

> The parent route is not for couples who are in a genuine and subsisting partner relationship. An applicant cannot meet the parent route if they are or will be eligible to apply under the partner route, including where for example the definition of partner cannot be met, or other eligibility criteria for access to a 5-year route are not met. Applicants in this position must apply or will only be considered (where they are not required to make a valid application), under the partner route, or under the private life route.

For entry clearance applications, the applicant must have:

- sole parental responsibility for the child
- direct access (in person) to the child, as agreed with the parent or carer with whom the child normally lives or as ordered by a court in the UK- in addition in such cases:
  o the parent or carer with whom the child normally lives must be a British citizen in the UK or settled in the UK, or in the UK as a pre-settled status holder under rEU3 of Appendix EU, and not the partner of the applicant
  o the applicant must not be eligible to apply for entry clearance as a partner under Appendix FM

For leave to remain applications where the applicant is in the UK, the following requirements must be satisfied:

- the applicant has sole parental responsibility for the child
- the child normally lives with the applicant and not their other parent (who is a British citizen or settled in the UK, or in the UK as a pre-settled status holder under rEU3 of Appendix EU), and the applicant must not be eligible to apply for leave to remain as a partner under Appendix FM
- the parent or carer with whom the child normally lives must be a British Citizen or settled in the UK

In all cases, the applicant must provide evidence that they are taking, and intend to continue to take, an active role in the child's upbringing

This route is not for parents of children when the parents remain in an enduring cohabiting relationship. If they do so, and neither have leave, they will need to make an application outside the Rules on Article 8 grounds (or, as discussed above where we address Exceptional circumstances, perhaps inside the Rules relying on GEN.3.2).

Additionally, the applicant must be either the primary carer of the child, or exercising access rights.

Examples

Esmerelda, a Peruvian national, is in an occasional relationship with Peter, a US citizen settled in the UK. They have a child, Benjamin, aged eight. Peter and Esmerelda are going through a rocky patch in their relationship. Benjamin lives with Peter in the UK.

The gateway requirement for the entry clearance route is E-ECPT.2.3 which demands that the applicant either has sole parental responsibility for the child, or that the child normally lives with a person settled in the UK (or a British citizen) who is 'not the partner of the applicant'. This application will probably founder on that latter requirement, as their relationship is extant, albeit it in difficulties.

Errol is the former partner of Jacinta, a British citizen. Their relationship irrevocably broke down around two years ago and Errol returned to his country of origin, Jamaica. There have not been any family law proceedings between them yet. Their son Ricardo lives with Jacinta; she has stopped Errol seeing him ever since. However Errol is very eager to resume contact with Ricardo.

Unlike in the last scenario, there is no longer a problem with E-ECPT.2.3 as Ricardo lives with a parent who is 'not the partner of the applicant'. But E-ECPT.2.4 poses a real obstacle: Errol clearly does not have agreed access to Ricardo, nor does he have court-ordered access. He either needs to persuade Jacinta to change her stance, or initiate family proceedings.

6.4.1 Relationship requirements

'A parent' is defined under paragraph 6 of the Immigration Rules:

'a parent' includes:

- the stepfather of a child whose father is dead and the reference to stepfather includes a relationship arising through civil partnership;
- the stepmother of a child whose mother is dead and the reference to stepmother includes a relationship arising through civil partnership; and
- the father as well as the mother of an illegitimate child where he is proved to be the father;
- an adoptive parent, where a child was adopted in accordance with a decision taken by the competent administrative authority or court in a country whose adoption orders are recognised by the United Kingdom or where a child is the subject of a de facto adoption in accordance with the requirements of paragraph 309A of these Rules (except that an adopted child or a child who is the subject of a de facto adoption may not make an application for leave to enter or remain in order to accompany, join or remain with an adoptive parent under paragraphs 297-303);
- in the case of a child born in the United Kingdom who is not a British citizen, a person to whom there has been a genuine transfer of parental responsibility on the ground of the original parent(s)' inability to care for the child.

Parenting roles, relationships and sole parental responsibility

A parent applying to exercise access rights to a child must be *'taking* [in the present tense] *an active role in the child's upbringing'*. This requirement is designed to prevent a parent who has not previously taken an active role from applying under the rule in order to begin doing so. A parent who has yet to take an active role for whatever reason, even if it is because they are outside the U.K, but now genuinely wants to do so, will have to make an application outside the rules.

The concept of *'sole parental responsibility'* is not defined in the rules. In the 5 year route guidance it is used interchangeably with the term *'sole responsibility'*. The guidance defines *'sole responsibility'* thus:

> Sole responsibility means that one parent has abdicated or abandoned parental responsibility and the remaining parent is instead exercising sole control in setting and providing the day to day direction for the child's welfare.

The Guidance indicates that the SSHD may interview the applicant or contact the other parent to investigate the question of 'sole responsibility'.

'Parental responsibility' is a legal concept and a central part of the regime for parents as set out in the Children Act 1989. In normal circumstances both parents will have parental responsibility from the child's birth if both appear on the birth certificate. There is no suggestion though that that Act is a reference point for assessing the parental roles under the Immigration Rules.

The Tribunal has recognised that '*taking an active role in a child's upbringing*' does not require regular face to face access. That sensible approach is essential in order to make sure that the entry clearance route remains meaningful. The '*active role*' can be demonstrated either by taking a role in a child's daily care or by participating in significant decisions in the child's life. There are various kinds of court order arising from family proceedings that may provide for a degree of contact that falls short of having '*an active role*'.

6.4.2 Entry clearance as a parent

For applications for entry clearance as a parent, the relevant child must be under 18 at the date of application, a British citizen or settled in the UK, and living in the UK (or if the child is a British citizen, it must be one who is coming to the UK to live or have contact with the applicant). Relevant criteria:

- The parent must have sole parental responsibility, or access rights to the child, and provide evidence that they are taking and intend to continue to take an active role in the child's upbringing (E-ECPT.2.3-2.4.)
- Financial requirements: are whether maintenance and accommodation can be provided 'adequately' (E-ECPT.3.1-3.2 – see Chapter 2 addressing maintenance for a discussion of how these kinds of requirement are to be established)
- English language requirements as discussed above for the partner route E-ECPT.4.1-4.2)
- The generic suitability criteria at Section S-EC: Suitability–entry clearance are cross referenced in as a requirement

6.4.3 Leave to remain as a parent

Most of the requirements for entry clearance are repeated under the leave to remain route. The differences are that

- There are immigration status requirements consistent with the general scheme of Appendix FM – there is a bar on visitors and individuals granted less than six months leave unless the grant was due to family law proceedings

- There is provision for accessing the exceptional route (EX.1), as with partners, where a child has lived in the UK for seven years leading up to the application (E-LTRP.2(d))

The maintenance and accommodation requirements need not be met where that exceptional route is satisfied (E-LTRPT.4.1.-4.2)

6.4.3.1 Three-route structure – all requirements met for 5 year ILR route, EX1 exception or GEN.3.2met for 10 year ILR route

For applications for leave to remain, we see the same three-route structure as for partners. Again, this section is only provided for your information, but any case not falling within all the basic requirements must be referred onwards:

- If all the requirements of the route are satisfied (i.e. financial and English language requirements as above; the eligibility requirements are once again sole parental responsibility, or access rights to the child, where they are taking and intend to continue to take an active role in the child's upbringing), then there is a five-year route to settlement under R-LTRPT.1.1.(c) and D-LTRPT.1.1, via two consecutive 30-month grants of limited leave.
- If some of the relevant requirements are not satisfied, then there is a 10-year route to settlement where paragraph EX1 applies, i.e. where there is a ***seven-year resident or British citizen child whose relocation abroad would not be reasonable*** (we have discussed the relevant

considerations in detail in Module 5 *276ADE(1)(iv) – Children and when it is reasonable to expect them to leave the UK*). The requirements that are lifted are those for adequate maintenance and accommodation without recourse to public funds, relevant English language proficiency, and immigration status – see R-LTRPT.1.1.(d) and D-LTRPT.1.2.

- Where even any of the more limited requirements, which must be met with EX1, are not satisfied, the applicant may wish to attempt to rely on the relevant 'Exceptional Circumstances' paragraph, inserted in Appendix FM as GEN.3.2 in August 2017. Where satisfied, leave *must* be granted, and this will be on the 10-year route to settlement. The threshold is high: GEN.3.2. requires satisfactory evidence of:

> ...exceptional circumstances which would render refusal of entry clearance, or leave to enter or remain, a breach of Article 8 of the European Convention on Human Rights, because such refusal would result in unjustifiably harsh consequences for the applicant, their partner, a relevant child or another family member whose Article 8 rights it is evident from that information would be affected by a decision to refuse the application.

Example

Above we saw two scenarios where the applicants would struggle to meet the requirements of the Parent route: Esmerelda (because she was still in a relationship with her children's father) and Errol (because his former partner blocked access to the child).

Neither of them will get any help from the EX.1 exception, because that relaxes some of the Rules' requirements, but not the all-important *Eligibility* requirements involving *Relationship*.

However under the GEN.3.2 provision they may be able to make an application on the basis that there would be *unjustifiably harsh consequences* for the '*applicant, their partner, a relevant child*'.

6.4.3.2 Ineligibility for this route

As under the partner route, it is possible to be ineligible for the parent route whatsoever: for example it is not available to

- those here as visitors (any length of visitor leave) and others who hold less than six months leave unless it was granted specifically pending the outcome of family/divorce proceedings (E-LTRPT.3.1. being a requirement of R-LTRPT.1.1(d)(ii)). This part of the immigration status requirement, unlike that regarding overstayers and those on immigration bail, cannot be circumvented by application of EX1
- those who are eligible to apply for leave under the Appendix FM partner route (see paras E-ECPT 2.3 (b)(iii) and E-LTRPT 2.3 (b)(iii))
- as usual under Appendix FM, the generic suitability criteria at Section S-LTR: Suitability leave to remain are cross referenced in as a requirement.

6.4.3.3 *Zambrano* parents

A parent who succeeds in establishing a right to reside under the CJEU judgement in Ruiz Zambrano (implemented at Reg 16(5) of the EEA Regs 2016 and now also under Appendix EU) will also usually be entitled to a grant of leave under the parent category (because satisfying the criteria of sole carer is likely to satisfy both the EEA and parent routes, as the relevant child/children would be at risk of having to leave the European Union if their sole carer's residence here was in jeopardy).

The guidance at Appendix FM Section 1.0b of the IDIs used to state that a parent application that falls to be refused under the criminality provisions in Appendix FM should then be passed to the European Casework section if the circumstances give rise to a right to reside for the parent.

This guidance was replaced with Immigration Staff Guidance: Family of people settled or coming to settle Appendix FM 1.0b: family life (as a partner or parent) and private life: 10-year routes, which in turn was replaced by Family Policy Family life (as a partner or parent), private life and exceptional circumstances neither of which made any mention of alternative consideration under Zambrano.

Applications for Zambrano carers remain open under the EUSS Scheme until the end of the grace period on 30 June 2021. **Zambrano cases are outside OISC 1 competency and must be referred onward**

Example

Tara is a US citizen and is the former partner of Ben, a British citizen. They have a child, Lucy, aged six, a British citizen; Tara is Lucy's primary carer. Ben sees her only very occasionally and has developed alcohol dependency in recent years. Tara has overstayed her leave and has no possibility of remaining under the Immigration Rules.

Lucy is a British citizen and thus an EU national. Accordingly if her primary carer was forced to depart the UK for the USA (i.e. to a destination outside the EU) she would lose the benefit of her EU citizenship. Although *Zambrano* applications can be refused where there is another UK-resident parent who could care for the child, it is difficult to see that Ben could be expected to do so.

6.4.4 Other requirements

The 'suitability' requirements always need to be met. Unless Section EX: Exception applies, the same immigration status and English language requirements apply as for the Partner category. That includes the additional English language requirement for those whose first grant of leave under this category expires from 1 May 2017 (E-LTRPT.5.1.A). The financial requirement is for the applicant to adequately maintain and accommodate themselves and any dependants in the UK without recourse to public funds and not the far higher minimum income requirement in the Partner and Child categories of Appendix FM.

6.4.5 Grants of leave

As with the Partner category, successful applicants will be granted 33 months on entry clearance or 30 months leave to remain, to begin a 60-month route to settlement, or 120 months where EX1 has been applied at any stage. There will be a condition prohibiting recourse to public funds unless they can show they are destitute.

A parent may though fail to complete the route if the relevant child reaches maturity before settlement has been granted. The Statement of Intent states in this regard that:

> On the 10-year family route, the limited leave period of 30 months will not be shortened if a child in whose best interests the migrant is to remain in the UK will turn 18 before that leave period expires. But, to continue on or complete the route, the migrant parent or carer will have to satisfy the UK Border Agency at the next application stage that, where the child has turned 18, there continues to be a reason why it would breach Article 8 for the migrant parent/carer to be removed from the UK.

For extensions beyond their youngest child's 18th birthday, they will need to show the child remains dependent on them. This presents a daunting prospect for any parent who is first granted leave under this rule when their child is over eight years old: early signs of independence may bar the child's straightforward access to ILR

From 6 April 2018 the relevant ILR eligibility paras of Appendix FM make it clear that ILR after five years is only available where both grants of leave were on the five-year route (i.e. in both applications the HO accepted that all requirements were satisfied).

6.5 Children of people with limited leave as partners and parents

This Appendix FM category (Section EC-C and Section R-LTRC for entry clearance and leave to remain respectively) is for a child whose parent has or is being granted limited leave as a partner or parent under Appendix FM. Children applying together with their parent can be added to the parent's application.

Children whose parent or parents are settled or applying for settlement in the UK will apply under the rules in Part 8.

As with other provisions for children in the Immigration Rules, the child must be under 18 at the date of their first application in this category, but not when making subsequent applications. This means that a child who reaches 18 before they are entitled to a further extension of leave or settlement will still be treated as if they are under 18 when the subsequent application is considered. For all children though, regardless of age, whether on initial application or at any stage before they are settled, they must not be married or in a civil partnership, must not have formed an independent family unit and must not be leading an independent life (as defined in paragraph 6).

For entry clearance, the child must be coming to the UK with or to join a parent, who has limited leave as a partner or parent. Where that parent is not the partner of the child's other parent, the parent must have sole responsibility for the child, or there must be serious and compelling family or other considerations which make exclusion of the child undesirable. We consider the definitions of 'sole responsibility' and 'exclusion undesirable' below in the section *Children of settled parents*.

For applications for leave to remain, there is no immigration status requirement, so the child can be here irregularly. The financial requirement is the same as the Partner and Parent categories, depending on the parent's leave. If granted under the partner category, the minimum income requirement applies; if as a parent, the lower 'adequate maintenance'. It will be the parent's income and savings that is relevant, not the child's. There will be no financial requirement to meet where the parent is on the 120-month route to settlement. Leave will be granted in line with the non-settled parent.

The child's application for ILR at the end of the parent's five- or 10-year route will be made under rule 298 at the same time as the parent's application (see section *Children of settled parents*).

6.6 Children of settled parent(s)

This category remains under Part 8 of the Immigration Rules, paragraphs 296 to 300, and is unaffected by Appendix FM.

Under Rule 6 the definition of a 'parent' is deemed to include:

- stepfather of a child whose father is dead
- stepmother of a child whose mother is dead
- father or mother of an illegitimate child (providing he can prove paternity)
- an adoptive parent where the child was adopted in accordance with a decision taken by the competent court or administrative authority in a country whose adoption orders are recognised in the UK

Position of the parents

- All remaining parents in or coming to UK
- OR sole responsibility
- OR exclusion undesirable

Position of the child

- Under 18
- Not living independent life

Under paragraph 296, where a parent is party to a polygamous marriage, and that parent would be refused under paragraphs 278 or 278A, their children may be refused too (even where they would otherwise meet the requirements of paragraph 297). This provision has been considered by the Tribunal in the case of SG (child of polygamous marriage) Nepal [2012] UKUT 00265(IAC).

For entry clearance, the child must be seeking to join or accompany a parent who is present and settled in the UK in the following circumstances:

- both parents are present and settled or being admitted for settlement or
- one parent present and settled and the other being admitted for settlement or
- one parent present and settled or being admitted for settlement who can show that they have had sole responsibility for the child's upbringing or
- one parent is present and settled in the United Kingdom or being admitted on the same occasion for settlement and the other parent is dead or
- a parent or another relative present and settled or being admitted for settlement where there are serious and compelling family or other considerations which made the exclusion of the child undesirable and where there are suitable arrangements made for the child's care

Under options 1, 2, and 4, the application will be relatively straightforward. In addition to proving that both parents are settled in the UK, or that one parent is dead, the applicant will need to show they are not leading an independent life (as defined in paragraph 6 of the Immigration Rules, and below), and that they can be maintained and accommodated adequately without recourse to public funds.

It is in respect of options 3 and 5 that complications can arise. It can be seen that there are additional requirements that apply where one of the parents resides outside the UK with no intention of joining the child in the UK, or where the child is seeking to join a relative who is not a parent. In such cases, the UK-based parent or relative will have to show a very good reason why the child should be allowed to settle in the UK rather than continue their life in the country in which they are living. These reasons, (i.e. 'sole responsibility' and 'exclusion undesirable') are examined in more detail below.

Prior entry clearance is required where the child is seeking indefinite leave to enter. A child may also apply for ILR from within the UK.

6.6.1 In-country applications

Under rule 298, a child who is under 18 at the date of application can apply for indefinite leave to remain if they have or have had limited leave in any category. A child who is here as a visitor, for example, can apply from within the UK to settle in the UK if both parents are settled, or one is settled and the other is dead, or the parent here has sole responsibility, or a parent or relative is settled and exclusion of the child is undesirable.

If the child is over 18 at the date of application, they must have previously been granted limited leave as a child in a category leading to settlement, and must still not be leading an independent life.

6.6.2 Not leading an independent life

The definition in Rule 6 is as follows:

"Must not be leading an independent life" or **"is not leading an independent life"** means that the person:

(a) does not have a partner; and

(b) is living with their parent (except where they are at boarding school, college or university as part of their full-time education); and

(c) is not in full-time employment (unless aged 18 or over); and

(d) is wholly or mainly dependent upon their parent for financial support (unless aged 18 or over); and

(e) is wholly or mainly dependent upon their parent for emotional support.

Where under these rules a relative other than a parent may act as the sponsor or carer of the person, references in this definition to "parent" shall be read as applying to that other relative.

6.6.3 Sole responsibility

In order to show that the sponsoring parent in the UK has sole responsibility for the child, notwithstanding that they live in different countries, they will need to show that they have been, so far as is possible at arm's length, exercising the normal role played by a caring parent. It is acceptable that the child's day to day care is delegated to another person in the child's own country but evidence that ultimate control rests with the sponsoring parent is required.

The IDIs (chapter 8, Section 5A Annex M) elaborate on the meaning of sole responsibility and state that the following factors are to be used as guidance on how to assess it:

- the period for which the parent in the United Kingdom has been separated from the child;
- what the arrangements were for the care of the child before that parent migrated to this country;
- who has been entrusted with day to day care and control of the child since the sponsoring parent migrated here;
- who provides, and in what proportion, the financial support for the child's care and upbringing;
- who takes the important decisions about the child's upbringing, such as where and with whom the child lives, the choice of school, religious practice etc;
- the degree of contact that has been maintained between the child and the parent claiming 'sole responsibility';
- what part in the child's care and upbringing is played by the parent not in the United Kingdom and his relatives.

The IDIs also say that sole responsibility should have been exercised for a substantial period of time: however in Nmaju v ECO [2000] EWCA Civ 505, the court took a different view, saying that 'Time cannot on its own be a conclusive factor'.

Important decisions in case law on this point worth noting

The tribunal case of *TD Yemen* [2006] UKAIT 00049 includes a useful summary of the relevant case law on this issue and holds that the test is whether the parent has continuing control and direction over the child's upbringing, including making all the important decisions in the child's life. The case also notes that where the child's non-UK resident parent took any role in the child's upbringing it would have to be clearly established that they had abdicated any responsibility for the child and helped out only under the Sponsor's direction.

Example

Fatima, from Egypt, entered the UK as a work permit holder and has worked as a nurse for over five years. She now has ILR. She is sponsoring her husband and child to come to the UK. This will be a straightforward application on both counts.

However, if Fatima was applying for only the child to come to the UK to join her, it would be a far more problematic application if the father remains involved in the child's life. She would have to demonstrate sole responsibility (i.e. that the father did not financially support or take any important decisions in the child's life) or that the exclusion of the child would be undesirable.

If there is no father involved, and the child has been looked after by Fatima's family in Egypt whilst she has been in the UK, Fatima will still need to show that she meets the sole responsibility requirement, that is that she has directed the child's upbringing and has not fully delegated that direction to her family.

In either scenario, if the child's well-being was threatened, however, then she might have a viable case under the 'serious and compelling circumstances' limb of the rule that we address next.

Top Tip

Factors to look out for in a sole responsibility case are:

- Letters from school(s) in the country where the child lives confirming that they have dealt with the sponsoring parent
- Travel by the sponsoring parent to the country where the child lives
- Records of financial arrangements by which the sponsor pays for education and other needs
- A lack of contact with the other living parent and an explanation of the reasons for this, and the location of that parent if known
- Detailed evidence regarding what steps have been taken to provide educational, social, behavioural, and religious guidance
- Whether the child(ren) is/are old enough to usefully provide a witness statement

6.6.4 Serious and compelling family or other considerations making exclusion undesirable

There is no particular definition of what may constitute serious and compelling circumstances. Clearly it could cover the scenario where the child faces real problems abroad, as where recent care arrangements have broken down. the phrase 'family or other circumstances' suggests that real benefit to the child *or* to the sponsoring parent/s or other relative could be a valid consideration in interpreting this part of the rule.

However, in Hardward v SSHD (00/TH/01522) 12 July 2000, the Tribunal suggested, after reviewing the case law that the key factors are:

- willingness and ability of the overseas adult to care for the child
- poor living conditions – but not necessarily intolerable
- greater vulnerability of small children.

Article 8 and 'best interests' principles will usually now play an important role in showing the test is met. **Therefore, this type of case should be referred onwards.**

Important decision in case law on this point worth noting

In the case of Mundeba, the Upper Tribunal adopts a more inclusive approach to the 'exclusion undesirable' test than has traditionally been the case, reading into it at least some of the more child-centred modern considerations one would expect in this day and age. Still, though, the test seems to require something more than best interests. Note though that Mundeba concerned an application for a boy to join his settled adult sister in the UK. A relationship between a parent and child will be seen as generally more compelling, including emotional factors relating to the sponsoring parent.

Top Tip

Look out for:

- Emotional ties going beyond the normal situation where a family has chosen to live apart
- Original separation due to reasons beyond the family's control
- Motivation for travel here other than the standard of living
- Explanation of why extant care arrangements are no longer available

Explanation of why extant care arrangements are no longer available

Example

Azadeh is an Iranian citizen and the mother of Bahar, her 14-year old child from an earlier relationship as a youth. Azadeh came to the UK as a spouse some years ago and has ILR. Bahar has been living with her aunt, Azadeh's sister, who looks after her; Azadeh has taken a 'hands off' approach in recent years. However the aunt has recently developed significant health problems which are making it much more difficult to care for Bahar, particularly as the latter needs a firmer hand now she is a teenager.

From these facts, there would be no possibility of a 'sole responsibility' case succeeding as Azadeh has not exercised sufficient control over Bahar's upbringing. However there is clearly the beginnings of a case on 'serious and compelling reasons' grounds under r297(i)(f). One would need to obtain further evidence to confirm that suitable arrangements were in place for Bahar's care in the UK, and that adequate accommodation and maintenance are available

6.7 Adult dependent relatives

This Appendix FM category, 'Adult dependent relative' (ADR), replaced the Part 8 (Rule 317) provisions for 'Other family members' for applications made on or after 9 July 2012. In very narrow circumstances, it provides the opportunity for an adult British citizen, settled person, refugee or person with humanitarian protection to sponsor a parent, grandparent, sibling or child over 18 to settle in the UK. Its predecessor, Rule 317, already involved a high threshold: In Joseph [1988] Imm AR 329 the High Court made it clear that the word 'most' which qualified the requirement for exceptional compassionate circumstances was not 'surplusage' and added 'significantly to the other words which appear in the rule'.

JCWI's report on the ADR category, 'Harsh, Unjust, Unnecessary', published in July 2014, records that for the first year of its operation, only 34 settlement visas were issued (even then often only after appeal) and states that:

> It is almost impossible to succeed in this visa category. Fit and healthy parents and grandparents cannot even apply. The All-Party Parliamentary Group on Migration (APPG) has stated that this visa category has 'in effect been closed'.

Applications under this category can only be made from outside the UK (as shown by the fact that there are simply no sub-routes headed 'leave to remain').

Guidance on this category is in the IDIs at Module 8, Annex FM 6.0.

6.7.1 Relationship and threshold requirements

The key requirements of the route are

- A relationship between applicant and sponsor: parent, grandparent, brother/sister, son/daughter: and all must be over 18 (E-ECDR.2.1)
- Parents and grandparents must not be in a subsisting relationship with another person – *unless* that person is applying alongside them (E-ECDR.2.2)
- The sponsor must be aged over 18
- And the sponsor must be present and settled in the UK, or have been granted international protection (E-ECDR.2.3)
- A requirement for *long-term personal care* to perform *everyday* tasks due to *age, illness, or disability* (E-ECDR.2.4)
- Which cannot be met via help from the sponsor because it is *wholly unavailable* (whether from family members or otherwise) or *unaffordable* (E-ECDR.2.5)

Just to drum home some points arising from this:

- Not just any relative can apply. There is no express requirement that the applicant is living alone, but if they are not, it will be all the more difficult for them to meet the threshold requirement at E-ECDR.2.5.
- Additionally, E-ECDR2.2 excludes parents and grandparents who are in a subsisting relationship with a person who is not also the sponsor's parent or grandparent, though it should be remembered that a parent can include a step-parent where the biological parent is dead (see Rule 6 definition).

Examples

Amanjit is married to Amrit. They are both British citizens, and work as doctors with the NHS. Their family lives in India. They want to bring Amanjit's younger brother Sarbjit, aged 25, to the UK as Sarbjit has always looked up to her; she helped him with his schoolwork.

Clearly these facts will get nowhere near the threshold. An adult brother can qualify: but they must establish major care needs which are unmet abroad.

Amanjit and Amrit give up on that project. They now wish to bring Darshan and Avni, Amanjit's parents, to the UK. The couple are very old.

Darshan and Avni are eligible to enter the route in terms of relationship, as 'If the applicant is the sponsor's parent … they must not be in a subsisting relationship with a partner unless that partner is also the sponsor's parent … and is applying for entry clearance at the same time as the applicant': E-ECDR.2.2. So a parent who is applying alongside the other parent can qualify. Of course, the question of high level care needs still needs examination

6.7.2 Meeting the 'threshold' requirement

An indication of the difficulty of meeting this requirement is given in the examples provided in the Guidance:

Example

A person (aged 85) lives alone in Afghanistan. With the onset of age he has developed very poor eyesight, which means that he has had a series of falls, one of which resulted in a hip replacement. His only son lives in the UK and sends money to enable his father to pay for a carer to visit each day to help him wash and dress, and to cook meals for him. This would not meet the criteria because the sponsor is able to arrange the required level of care in Afghanistan.

Evidential requirements are specified in Appendix FM-SE as below;

- The relationship must be proved by birth or adoption certificates, or other documentary evidence (para 33)
- Evidence of care needs must be proved by independent medical evidence from a doctor or other health professional (para 34)
- Evidence of inability to meet care needs abroad must be proved by evidence from a central or local health authority, a local authority, or a doctor or other health professional (para 35)
- If care was formerly provided by private care arrangements, evidence of this, and why they have ceased (para 36)
- If care can no longer be afforded, payment records and an explanation of the change of circumstances (para 37)

Immigration Rules 36-39 give the ECO the power to refer the applicant for medical examination and to require that this be undertaken by a doctor or other health professional on a list approved by the British Embassy or High Commission.

Example

Reverting to the family of Amanjit and Amrit we talked out above. No application was made whilst both parents were alive. Unfortunately Avni passes away, leaving Darshan a widower. His physical care needs significantly worsen and he starts to have falls around the house, leaving him with injuries of varying severity. The family all chip in to contribute towards a carer for him. However, the carers prove unreliable and Darshan has stopped trusting them. Now Amanjit and Amrit are becoming desperate, and come back to you.

Now we start to see the real challenge that the route presents. Darshan may well have a case that, '*as a result of age, illness or disability [he] requires long-term personal care to perform everyday tasks*': E-ECDR.2.4. And the specified evidence provisions in Appendix FM-SE para 34 demand that this be provided by independent evidence: i.e. 'from a doctor or other health professional'

But E-ECDR.2.5 demands that he '*must be unable, even with the practical and financial help of the sponsor, to obtain the required level of care*'. So the rule looks at the potential help which might come from other sources, including the sponsor. First it looks at whether the care is available from any source abroad whatsoever; secondly it expressly looks at whether the available care is '*affordable*'.

Given that here the sponsors presumably earn significant sums, they will be unlikely to be able to show that arrangements in India are unaffordable. So they must show that the '*required level of care*' is not available (even though *some* care might be *affordable*). This will require demonstrating both that other alternative care from family and extended family is not available, and also that there are no national or local authority care arrangements that are accessible: the specified evidence provisions in Appendix FM-SE para 35 require that this comes from independent sources, i.e. medical professionals, central or local health authorities, or a local (presumably non-health) authority. So there is a lot of work ahead to get the application off the ground.

6.7.3 Financial requirement

There is a generalised requirement for adequate maintenance and accommodation (though not via the thresholds and calculations that are necessary for the partner route) (E-ECDR.3.1); sponsors without international protection (British citizens and those settled here) must provide an undertaking of responsibility for maintenance, accommodation and care for five years (E-ECDR.3.2). The sponsor's undertaking will be legally binding (r35). The forms of relevant evidence are specified:

> In addition, in all cases the applicant must provide evidence from the sponsor that the sponsor can provide the maintenance, accommodation and care required, in the form of any or all of the following:
>
> - Bank statements covering the last six months;
> - Other evidence of income – such as pay slips, income from savings, shares, bonds – covering the last six months;

- Relevant information on outgoings, e.g. Council Tax, utilities, etc, and on support for anyone else who is dependent on the sponsor;
- A copy of a mortgage or tenancy agreement showing ownership or occupancy of a property; and
- Planned care arrangements for the applicant in the UK (which can involve other family members in the UK) and the cost of these (which must be met by the sponsor, without undertakings of third party support).

'Care' is not defined in the Immigration Rules. It remains open to question therefore whether a successful applicant will be entitled to free NHS treatment. They are unlikely to be excluded under NHS regulations, or under the 'no recourse to public funds' provision, but the government could decide that the NHS is nevertheless entitled to be reimbursed for the cost of any such treatment by the person signing the undertaking.

6.7.4 Decision

Successful applicants sponsored by a British citizen or settled person will be given indefinite leave to enter. They will have no recourse to public funds for the length of the sponsor's undertaking (i.e. five years from the date of entry).

Those sponsored by a relative with limited leave as a refugee or person with humanitarian protection will be granted leave in line, and can apply for ILR at the same time as the sponsor. The sponsor will not need to provide an undertaking on entry, but the applicant will have no recourse to public funds as a condition of entry. The five-year sponsorship undertaking will have to be signed by the sponsor at the ILR stage.

Top Tip

Relevant factors in a dependant relative case are likely to be:

- Medical evidence demonstrating that a high level of care required
- Evidence showing this cannot reasonably be provided outside of the family unit e.g. psychological issues, or issues of trust and/or dignity
- Evidence showing there is no publicly funded system of care for the elderly
- Evidence showing there is no culture of privately funded care, and that experience or research shows that those individuals who might be employed as carers are not capable of addressing issues of emotional and psychological need

Bear in in mind the possibility of obtaining evidence from an independent expert on the care facilities in the country of origin

Remember that these cases may be run in the alternative under Article 8 ECHR. Look for:

- Evidence that family life is established (visits, other forms of communication)
- That separation was for reasons other than pure choice, or that circumstances have changed since any real choice was exercised
- Support of the dependent relative without any danger of recourse to public funds
- Realistic care arrangements amongst a loving family in this country contrasted with isolation abroad, bearing in mind that the European Court said in Pretty v United Kingdom (2002) 35 EHRR 1 at [65] that 'The very essence of the Convention is respect for human dignity and human freedom.'

Module 7: Introduction to the Points Based System (PBS)

This Module represents an introduction to one of the most complicated and convoluted aspects of the immigration system – the Points Based System ('PBS'). Much of the work is very specialist. However, recent reforms have simplified the structure of the PBS, making it more approachable. Our strategy to introduce you to the PBS will be to first outline the structure common to PBS routes. We then address each route in some more detail, giving you enough detail to ensure a solid foundation that will enable you to work with the PBS. Throughout, we give practical examples to help you understand how the Rules work in practice.

We do not aim to capture every detail and nuance of the PBS routes. When it comes to putting your knowledge from this course into practice, therefore, it is important that you refer to the Rules themselves. This Module should give you the confidence and ability to do so without getting lost in the morass of provisions and Guidance.

Overview

The Points Based System divides the categories of visa available into Appendices. Some of these stand alone, while others are grouped under the labels 'T1', 'T2' and 'T5'. The letter 'T' here refers to the Tiers into which the PBS used to be divided. You may still see reference to these Tiers when dealing with, for example, permission to stay applications from those who entered the UK before the PBS was reformed in late 2020.

In the modern rules, the 'T' labels are purely classificatory. They indicate that routes sharing a label deal with a similar theme. For example, the T5 routes are all short-term work visas. But there is limited substantive overlap. To carry on the example, it is not necessary to read one T5 route to understand another.

There are two significant routes which have not been modernised and simplified: Investors and Entrepreneurs. The latter is a legacy route, remaining live only for migrants already within the route; the former is still available to new applicants, though the SSHD presumably has plans to update it in line with other routes. Entrepreneurs must show they meet the English language and financial requirements by reference to the "old" PBS Appendices Appendix B and Appendix C; both Investors and Entrepreneurs can be joined by family members via the bespoke PBS dependents route found in Part 8 of the Rules; and their ILR applications are governed by r245AAA which defines the way in which '*continuous period … lawfully in the UK*' is measured.

Investor, business development and talent visas

Appendix Global Talent
Appendix Start-up
Appendix Innovator
Tier 1 (Investor) visa – discontinued

Further notes/information

The old Entrepreneur Visa (Tier 1) has been replaced by the Innovator visa and Start-up visa. However, if someone already has a Tier 1 Entrepreneur visa they can still apply to settle in the UK if they qualify until 5th April 2025. They can apply to extend the existing Entrepreneur visa until 5th April 2023. They can apply for family members to join them.

Skilled workers – Long Term Work

Appendix Skilled Worker
Appendix Intra-Company Routes
Appendix T2 Minister of Religion
Appendix T2 Sportsperson

Students

Appendix Student
Appendix Child Student
Appendix Short-term Student
Appendix Parent of a Child Student

Short-term work visas

T5 temporary workers divided into:

- Seasonal workers
- Creative or sporting workers
- Religious workers
- Charity workers
- International agreement workers
- Government authorised exchange workers

Each T5 temporary worker route is contained in its own Appendix.

There is also:

- Appendix T5 (Temporary Worker) Youth Mobility Scheme
- Appendix Service Providers from Switzerland

Appendix Representative of an Overseas Business

This route pre-dates the PBS and is commonly known as the sole representative route. It permits individuals to move to the UK to represent their company here.

7.1 The Rules and the Guidance

As we emphasise throughout our training on the Immigration Rules, it is essential to read the Rules carefully and critically against your client's circumstances. Under the PBS this is even more important, because there is so little discretion within the system.

The Guidance

Most PBS routes are accompanied by Caseworker Guidance. Though aimed at Home Office staff, these documents are also of use to the practitioner. They explain the Home Office's understanding of the Rules, paraphrasing and adding detail. This paraphrasing may be useful where the Rules themselves are unclear.

The Guidance also contains extra pieces of information: there may be hints on how the Home Office think about a particular kind of scenario, e.g. via practical examples. Or the procedures which will be applied to a particular stage in the process, or express policy criteria for exercising discretion outside the Rules, may be set out.

The Guidance sometimes sets out additional information as to how a particular requirement is to be satisfied. However, there was a landmark Supreme Court judgement that held that all mandatory requirements relevant to a grant of leave, including evidential requirements, must be listed in the Immigration Rules: this decision led to the Home Office putting virtually every requirement into the Rules.

It is therefore now very rare to find a strict requirement to satisfy the core requirements for entry clearance or leave to remain in Guidance that does not derive directly from the Rules. However, additions made by the latter to our overall understanding of the Points Based System are still useful to the practitioner. For example, the English language sections of some of the published Guidance gives a detailed explanation of the testing procedures that is not found in the Rules themselves. Frequently, the Guidance elaborates usefully on requirements stated only briefly in the Rules. For example, the requirement that an applicant for a Student visa is a "genuine student" receives no further explanation in the Rules; whereas the Guidance explains how the Home Office will assess "genuineness", and the sorts of factors and evidence caseworkers will take into account.

It can be tempting to use the Guidance as a substitute for the Rules. However, this is bad practice. You should always read both, alert to the fact that the Rules are the bottom line.

If there is some lack of clarity, then you can always quote the Guidance at the Home Office if it suits your application: but whilst this may often work (and if it fails *might* lead to a successful if time-consuming legal challenge), the Home Office would usually be entitled to reply 'The Rules are the Rules. Our Guidance aims to help. But you should go by the Rules.'

As well as the detailed Guidance, there are also brief summaries of each route on the gov.uk website, giving a brief overview of the key criteria and means of joining the route: for example this is the one on Innovators.

7.1.1 The scheme of the Rules

Each PBS route is contained in its own Appendix. For example, the rules on Students are contained in Appendix Student; the rules on Innovators in Appendix T1 Innovator. Each Appendix is largely self-contained and follows roughly the same scheme:

- First, there are validity requirements. These are normally formal, for example mandating the payment of the correct fee. An application which fails to meet these requirements will be invalid and will not be considered. Switching criteria are also found here.
- Second are suitability requirements. These are general requirements of suitability for a grant of permission to enter or stay in the UK. For example, not being present in the UK in breach of immigration rules at the time of the application. Most PBS routes refer to Part 9: grounds for refusal, a separate section of the Rules where the "general" refusal reasons based on immigration history, dishonesty, criminality and other generic issues are addressed.
- Third are eligibility requirements. These are the core requirements of a particular route which must be satisfied for an applicant to be granted permission. Many PBS routes require applicants to score a specified number of 'points' to be eligible for permission. Financial and English language requirements normally come under this heading. Usually there is a distinct set of requirements for 'Entry' mandating prior entry clearance before travelling where applying out-of-country and requiring proof of being free from TB. There may be distinct requirements for permission to stay and entry clearance applications.
- Fourth, the Appendix will state the period and conditions of grant. These explain what an applicant can expect if their application is successful. There are commonly restrictions on work and study, and a prohibition against accessing public funds.
- Fifth, there will be an explanation of whether, and under what conditions, dependents may join the migrant.

Each Appendix must be read with four other sections of the Rules:

- Appendix English Language. Each PBS Appendix specifies what level of English language an applicant must show to be eligible for permission under that route. Appendix English Language explains the permissible ways for applicants to prove that English language ability; for example acceptable tests.
- Appendix Finance. As with English language, this Appendix shows how applicants can demonstrate the funds required by any given PBS route.
- Part 9: general grounds for refusal.
- Rule 6.2. This contains general definitions applicable to the entirety of the Rules.

Some Appendices also refer to other parts of the Rules. For instance, governing bodies for T2 Sportsperson applications are found at Appendix M. These will always be referred to by the route in question. And the Appendices Shortage Occupation List and Skilled Occupations set out eligible jobs for sponsored workers.

Lastly, there are general requirements which apply to all applicants under the Rules. For example, applicants from certain countries are required to undergo screening for tuberculosis; the precise requirements are in Appendix T: tuberculosis screening. As these are not specific to PBS applications we do not discuss them in any detail in this Module.

Top Tip

Once you reach the point of determining which route your client is interested in pursuing, there is a distinct methodology to be followed:

- Find the Appendix in question (e.g. Appendix T2 Sportsperson)

- Make sure you have reviewed the latest version of the Guidance for the route in question

- Remember, the ultimate question is what the Rules say

- The Guidance may help with interpreting the Rules, and especially with applying them, but it is the Rules which really matter.

7.2 General requirements – validity and suitability

Validity and suitability requirements are largely common across PBS routes.

To be valid, in general:

- The application must be made on the correct form. The forms are online, accessible through gov.uk. Each PBS Appendix states the requisite form.
- The application fee and Immigration Health Charge must be paid.
- Biometrics must be provided.
- The applicant must establish their nationality and identity by providing a passport or other travel document.
- If the route requires sponsorship, the applicant must have a certificate of sponsorship.
- The applicant must meet the route's age requirement.
- The application must comply with switching criteria. Most PBS routes are generally permissive, but prohibit switching from
    - Visitor
    - Short-term Student
    - Parent of a Child Student
    - Seasonal Worker
    - Domestic Worker in a Private Household
    - Outside the Immigration Rules.

If an application does not meet these criteria it will be invalid. This can be significant as it may cause the applicant to inadvertently become an overstayer.

For suitability:

- None of the general grounds refusal in Part 9 may apply.
- The applicant must not be in the UK in breach of immigration law (subject to the exception in r39E – see section 1.5.4) or on immigration bail.

7.3 Investor, business development and talent visas

7.3.1 Innovator visa

The Innovator visa has largely replaced the old Entrepreneur visa which was closed to new applicants on 29 March 2019. The requirements are found in Appendix Innovator.

The route is essentially for a person who wants to set up or run a business in the UK. However, it is far less flexible than the old Entrepreneur route. Previously any kind of enterprise could be relied on to support an application and the HO would assess its viability as a business. Now the assessment is carried out by an endorsing body, and the bodies in question tend to be high-tech business incubators or similarly specialist entities. Many restrict endorsements to individuals who they already have an established relationship with.

Investment Funds

A person must have at least £50,000 in investment funds to apply for an Innovator visa to set up a new business.

The funding can come from any source.

There is no need for any investment funds if the business is already established and has been endorsed for an earlier visa.

They can form a team with other Innovator applicants, but cannot share the same investment funds.

If the endorsing body confirms that the funds are available to the applicant, then no further evidence is required. However, if some or all of the funds are not confirmed as available by that body, then the funding provider has to write a signed declaration explaining how they know the applicant, the sum being provided, and confirming that the funds have not been promised to anyone else.

Example

Jose has a strong endorsement to support his application to enter the Innovator route. His endorsing body is providing £40,000 of the required funds.

Jose will need to provide the additional £10,000 from other sources. If his endorser is happy to verify the availability of those funds, then he needs only to provide their endorsement letter confirming this. But if they are unable or unwilling to do so, he will have to provide the various additional kinds of evidence identified at paragraphs INN 8.4-7.

Financial requirement

Applicants for permission to stay who have already been in the UK for at least 12 months do not need to show maintenance funds.

All other applicants need to prove that they have enough personal savings to be self supporting. They will have to show they had at least £1,270 in their bank account for 28 consecutive days before applying for the visa.

Additional funds are necessary for each dependent. The amount depends on the type of dependent and can be held by either the main applicant or the dependent. No additional funds are necessary if the dependent has been in the UK for 12 months with permission. The amounts are:

- £285 for a dependant partner

- £315 for the first dependant child
- £200 for each additional child.

You cannot rely on the same funds for maintenance as you are using to demonstrate available investment funds. Nor can you use money earned while working in the UK illegally.

Knowledge of English

Most people will need to show their knowledge of the English language before they apply.

This can be achieved by passing an approved English language test with at least CEFR level B2 in reading, writing, speaking and listening or having an academic qualification that was taught in English and is recognised by UK ENIC as being equivalent to a UK Bachelor's degree, Master's degree or PhD.

There is no need to prove knowledge of English if a person has already proved it to be level B2 or above in an earlier successful application.

Exceptions from this rule apply to nationals of specified countries listed here https://www.gov.uk/innovator-visa/knowledge-of-english

Age requirement

A person must be over 18 years old to apply for this route.

Endorsement by an approved body

Before the application is made the business or business idea has to be assessed and endorsed by an approved body. The approved body will provide an endorsement letter if it is assessed that the business is viable. The endorsement letter must confirm both of the following:

(a) The applicant's business venture meets **all** of the requirements in the table below:

Innovation	**Viability**	**Scalability**
The applicant has a genuine, original business plan that meets new or existing market needs and/or creates a competitive advantage.	The business plan is realistic and achievable based on the applicant's available resources. The applicant has the necessary skills, knowledge, experience and market awareness to successfully run the business.	There is evidence of structured planning and of potential for job creation and growth into national and international markets.

(b) The endorsing body is satisfied that:

- the applicant made at least a significant contribution to the business plan
- the applicant will have a day-to-day role in carrying out the business plan.

For established businesses which have been endorsed for an earlier visa under Appendix Innovator, Appendix Start-up, or the Tier 1 (Graduate Entrepreneur) route, the endorsing body must confirm that:

- The 'new business' requirements immediately above continue to be met

- The business is active, trading and sustainable, and the applicant has made progress against their business plan

- The business is registered with Companies House, with the applicant listed as a director or member.

A list of the approved bodies can be found on gov.uk here. The page gives a brief description of the types of business each body will consider endorsing.

> **Example**
>
> Marvin wants to set up a business consultancy as some college friends of his successfully did so relying on investment funds from relatives under the old Entrepreneur route.
>
> Marvin may struggle to find an Endorsing body that is willing to back this enterprise as sufficiently innovative.

Settlement

Settlement will be available after 3 years. Strict criteria apply. For details of the criteria see paragraphs INN 16.1-22.2 in Appendix Innovator.

In particular, the endorsing body must provide a letter confirming:

- The applicant has shown "significant achievements" judged against their business plan;

- The business appears to be sustainable for at least the following 12 months;

- The applicant has played an active key role in the day-to-day management and development of the business; and

- The business meets at least **two** out of the of the following **seven** requirements:

    - A minimum of £50,000 has been invested into the business with the aim of furthering the objectives in the business plan;
    - In the last three years the number of customers has at least doubled and currently the number is higher than the mean number of customers for UK businesses offering comparable services or main products;
    - The business has engaged in 'significant research and development activity' and applied for intellectual property protection in the UK;
    - The minimum annual gross revenue of the business has reached £1 million in the last full year covered by its accounts;
    - The minimum annual gross revenue of the business has reached £500,000 in the last full year covered by its accounts. Of the £500,000, at least £100,000 must be generated from overseas exports;
    - Generation of the equivalent of a minimum of 10 full time jobs for resident workers;
    - Generation of the equivalent of a minimum of five full time jobs for resident workers with an average gross annual salary of £25,000.

> **Example**
>
> Elton successfully obtained an Innovator visa for three years for his business providing niche IT support services and is now approaching the first opportunity to apply for settlement. His business has made

good progress, £50,000 having been invested in it, and it now employs three staff full time; turnover may reach £500,000 for the next tax year.

From what we see here, there is probably not enough for an ILR application. Two of the seven criteria must be met. As he completed the requisite investment, Elton only needs to meet one other requirement, but he cannot meet the staffing requirements, and the fact he has aspirations to make £500k turnover soon indicates that he will not have done in the last accounting year.

One would need to check whether he has increased his customer base from the opening period such as to make a credible case for having 'doubled' his customers or beaten the sector average (as worded, the Rule seems to compare one to the average business, not the average start-up!). One can see an argument for not taking on too many customers when first getting the business going, in order to support an argument that the customer base has subsequently 'doubled'. One should also see whether he has conducted significant research and development such as to be able to tenably apply for intellectual property protection.

If Elton cannot muster a positive case for two of the seven criteria, he should apply for limited permission to stay instead of settlement.

Documents that must be provided

- The Endorsement letter from the approved body that has assessed the business or business idea.
- A current passport or other valid travel ID. This must have a blank page for the visa.
- Evidence the financial maintenance requirement is met.
- Proof that the English language requirement is met.
- Evidence of the investment funds (if setting up a new business).
- Tuberculosis test results if the applicant is from a country where they have to take the test.
- Certified translations of any documents that are not in English or Welsh

7.3.2 Start-up visa

The Start-up visa largely replaces the old Graduate Entrepreneur visa. The requirements are found in Appendix Start-up.

The Start-up visa requirements largely mirror those of the Innovator visa with the exception of the need for investment funds.

There is an identical requirement to show that the applicant has enough personal savings of £1,270, unless they are applying for permission to stay and have already been in the UK for 12 months with permission. The age requirement is at least 18 years old and there is the same requirement to demonstrate knowledge of the English language to B2 level. See above at Innovator visa for details.

Endorsement by an approved body

The endorsement letter must confirm that the applicant's business venture meets the same essential requirements as to innovation, viability and scalability as for Innovators, but:

- Regarding viability, the applicant may still be *actively developing* their business skills etc.
- The endorsement letter must confirm that:
  - the applicant will spend the majority of their working time in the UK on developing their business venture;
  - the applicant is either the sole founder of the business or an instrumental member of its founding team; and
  - the applicant created their own business plan.

Applicants may not have previously set up a business in the UK, unless they did so while in the UK with permission on the Start-up route, as a Tier 1 (Graduate Entrepreneur), or a Student on the doctorate extension scheme.

A list of the approved bodies for Start up can be found on gov.uk here.

Settlement

The maximum leave granted is two years, and the route does not lead to settlement.

However, the Innovator route (see section 7.3.1) does lead to settlement, and those in the Start-up category can switch to that route.

Existing or recent Graduate Entrepreneurs can switch into the new category if they have not yet had the maximum two grants under the Graduate Entrepreneur route.

7.3.3 Global Talent visa

This route is for exceptionally talented individuals wishing to work in the UK within their chosen field of excellence: they will either already be recognised world leaders or have been identified as showing exceptional promise such as they are likely to become such. As the Guidance puts it, the route is

> for talented and promising individuals in the fields of science, engineering, medicine, humanities, digital technology and arts and culture (including film and television, fashion design and architecture) wishing to work in the UK.

The application has two stages, which the Guidance styles as Stage 1 and Stage 2 applications:

- Stage 1 is an application for endorsement
- Stage 2 is an application for permission to enter or stay once endorsement has been granted.

It is possible to apply for both stages at the same time, though the Stage 2 application will not be considered until endorsement is granted. It would be sensible to apply in this way if, for example, you are in the UK with permission and must make a new application to avoid becoming an overstayer.

The criteria for endorsement are found in Appendix Global Talent. There are various classes of application, for example, those under the sciences (endorsed by bodies including the Royal Society), the Arts (Arts Council England), and the IT sector (Tech Nation). This gov.uk page links to documents identifying the relevant endorsing bodies.

The Home Office caseworker guidance is fairly sparse on Stage 1 endorsement. More useful guidance may be found by going to the website of the relevant endorsing body. For instance, Arts Council England offers guidance here.

You can apply under *Exceptional Talent* or under *Exceptional Promise*. The former is the route for the established talents, the latter being for the up-and-coming.

To give an example, under the fashion design industry route, an 'Exceptional Talent' applicant must establish that they are a leader in their field, confirmed by having won an international award for excellence, showing significant media recognition of their work across countries, internationally significant catwalk shows, or extensive distribution or sales of their collections. Whereas an 'Exceptional Promise' applicant needs to show international medica recognition of their work across countries, sponsorship from the British Fashion Council or a related body, an order placed by a luxury retailer, or recognition by leading industry players.

Examples regarding Appendix L and Royal Society, etc.

Shirley is a US national with a PhD working in the UK for Cancer Research UK pursuing cutting edge medical research, presently with leave as a Skilled Worker, whilst she pursues her research fellowship.

She qualifies under the Science, engineering, humanities and medicine fields endorsement route (GTE 8.1): because simply holding such a position is sufficient. Of course she still has to make the 'immigration' part of the application to the Home Office.

David is a US national working as an Associate Professor in continental philosophy at the London School of Economics.

David may qualify under GTE 8.2(b): because this is *potentially* an eligible academic position at a UK Higher Education Institute. However this applies only if the stringent requirements for the recruitment process (GTE 8.6) were satisfied, which include an external consultation with an expert outside the establishment, at least three academics interviewing him, and at least two references.

Example regarding Arts Council England

Dmitri is a musician. He has a significant following online and sold records in his country of origin in his youth, around a decade ago. He has given several concerts in the UK which have been written up favourably in the national music press here.

Dmitri has some potential for meeting the 'exceptional promise' requirements under the arts and culture route: for example, he can cite the UK music press reviews as recent media recognition of his work so long as they were published in the last five years (GTE 3.4(a)), and can provide evidence of performances recognised in his field (GTE 3.4(c)). As to the latter, Dmitri must show that these performances demonstrate a "developing international presence", i.e. that he has been "regularly booked as part of professional artistic programmes" (Arts Council England Guidance).

There is no English language requirement within the route until the settlement stage is reached.

Applicants may apply for entry clearance from locations other than their home country, i.e. from entry clearance posts where they are situated at the time of the application, provided that the post in question has been designated as appropriate for this route, and they are living *there* lawfully (r28A(b)).

Settlement applications are possible after:

- Three years continuous lawful residence if endorsed by the Royal Society, British Academy, Royal Academy of Engineering or UKRI, or under the exceptional talent criteria by Arts Council England or Tech Nation; or
- Five years continuous lawful residence if endorsed under the exceptional promise criteria by Arts Council England or Tech Nation.

It is possible to aggregate some other kinds of PBS leave to make up the relevant period, so long as the last grant of leave was under Exceptional Talent/Promise (GTE 11.3).

7.3.4 Investor visa (Tier 1)

The general purpose of this route is to allow generous immigration consequences for people with a high net worth who make a substantial financial investment in the UK. The requirements are found in part 6A of the Rules paragraphs 245E-245EF and Appendix A paragraphs 54 to 65-SD

They enjoy certain benefits seldom available to other migrants; for example, there is no English language requirement in this route, the rationale being that they will not need to work in order to support themselves (though there is still an English language requirement for settlement as an Investor). The financial firepower they need to evidence in order to be granted a visa is such that there are no separate maintenance requirements; it is simply presumed that they will be able to look after themselves given their overall wealth. From 6 November 2014 the criteria changed: previously only £1m of investment funds were required of which only £750,000 had to be held in stocks, shares and bonds, whereas since then £2m of solid investment has been required. Significantly bigger investments may give speedier access to settlement.

The key requirements are in the Tables in Appendix A: Table 7 addresses modern applications for entering the route, Table 8A concentrates on extension applications, and Table 9A deals with ILR (8B and 9B address investors who entered under the pre-November 2014 Rules). Appendix A then gives further details as to how those criteria are to be satisfied:

- A56-A57 give further details of the timing of entry into the route and which Table subsequently applies
- A59 gives details of opening a UK bank account
- A60 addresses currency conversion
- A61-A61-SD detail the requirements for establishing ownership of the investment funds including those from one's partner
- A63 addresses the investment date
- A65 deals with qualifying investments

The requirements have been tightened up over time because of fears that the route had encouraged some applicants with dubious sources of funds. Now particular attention will be given to whether (r245EB(e)):

- The applicant was, or is, not in control of the money or the investment decision, or at liberty to make the decision
- Any of the money was transferred internationally by means which are unlawful in the relevant country
- Any of the money was acquired via conduct which is unlawful in the uk
- Whether the money was made available to the applicant by a third party not of good character

A person must have at least £2,000,000 investment funds to apply for a Tier 1 (Investor) visa. Those funds must have been held for the previous two years. If they have not been held for two years, then documents showing the origin of the funds must be provided.

Example
Jermaine, a US citizen, wants to make an investment having just received a significant inheritance of several million. He has held the money for a week, but wants to enter the Tier 1 Investor route as soon as possible.

Jermaine must hurdle the requirement to have held the money in Table 7 (i.e. £2 million) for two years (A-64). A person who has not held the funds for two years in a bank account or within investments backed up by portfolio report from an investment manager or other admissible evidence needs to provide the further specified evidence in A64A-SD: inheritances are dealt with expressly therein at (vii)-(viii).

Other eligibility requirements are that the person must:

- be 18 or over to apply for this visa
- be able to prove that the money belongs to them or their husband, wife, unmarried or same-sex partner
- have opened an account at a UK regulated bank to use for the funds

The funds must be:

- held in one or more regulated financial institutions i.e. regulated by the Financial Conduct Authority (FCA)
- free to spend ('disposable') in the UK
- the bank will have to confirm checks for money-laundering have been carried out

The money can be in the UK or overseas when the application is made.

Investment from the applicant's own money

If the person is using their own money to invest, they should be able to show:

- how much money they have and where it's being held
- where the money came from if they have had the money for less than two years, for example it was inherited from a relative
- that the money can be transferred to the UK and converted to sterling (if it's not already in the UK)

Investment from a partner's money

If the person is using a partner's money they will need to provide:

- a certificate of marriage or civil partnership, or in the case of unmarried or same-sex relationships, proof that you are in a long-term relationship (at least two years)
- a statement from your partner confirming that they will allow you to control the funds in the UK
- a letter from a legal adviser stating that the declaration is valid

Example

Liu Wei wishes to enter the investment route. He has funds of £1 million. His long-term girlfriend Li Min has funds of £1 million. She is willing to support his investment plans.

Liu may rely on the funds of his unmarried partner which count as 'money of his own'. However their relationship must be extant at the date of application and they must have cohabited for two years for her to meet the definition. There will then be a further tranche of 'specified documents' to be provided, as set out in A61-SD, proving the relationship, the fact of cohabitation, and a declaration confirming Liu has beneficial ownership of the money such that he can freely dispose of it for himself, and the validity of that declaration must be backed up by a lawyer's letter.

There are various restrictions on the forms of eligible investment, the objective is to secure investment in the stocks and shares of actively trading UK companies. One cannot invest in property or in companies making their money from activities including property investment. Government bonds have been taken off the list of eligible investments. Also:

- Intermediary vehicles must be FCA regulated and the final investment destination and method of transfer must be disclosed.
- Strong evidence is required that companies are actively trading in the UK. They must: be registered with Companies House, and with HMRC for tax and PAYE; have a business bank account showing regular trading or goods or services; and they must have at least two employees who are based in the UK, and who are not also directors.
- The 'price of investments' means the price the applicant paid for the investment, rather than the face value of the investment, as face value is not of itself evidence of money invested.
- The investment supporting the application must not have been made more than 12 months before the application date (Table 8A).

Example

Crassus plans to use the investor route to enter the UK. He has slightly over £2 million of investments in UK shares in companies trading in the energy business. He wants to rely on this investment (which he manages himself) for his application.

You should check whether he has made the investment in the last 12 months; otherwise it is ineligible. So long as that requirement is satisfied, then the investments may be relied upon. As he self-manages his investment, he will need to provide evidence himself of the investment via share documents showing the value of the shares, the date of purchase and the owner.

There are transitional arrangements under which the restrictions on investing in government funds pre-29 March 2019 do not apply to those already on the route. The previous rules continue until 5 April 2023 for extensions and 5 April 2025 for settlement.

For details of supporting documents that will be needed see https://www.gov.uk/tier-1-investor/documents-you-must-provide

Extension of leave as an investor

The main controls on extending leave relate to the need to have made the investment and the source of funds (Table 8A).

- The investment has to be made within three months of entry to the UK (or from the date entry clearance was granted if there is no clear evidence of the entry date.
- Delays in investment can be condoned only if there are *exceptionally compelling reasons* for the delay beyond the applicant's control
- The investment must have been maintained throughout the period of leave
- There can be retrospective auditing of the source of the funds (r245EB(e))

Example

Croesus has invested £2.2 million in shares in active trading UK companies. He accordingly scores points for £2 million of qualifying investments.

Croesus may pay up to £200,000 in fees, transaction costs and tax out of the investment funds. He has already invested sums including a significant surplus before the sums in question became due. However, he would not be entitled to run a bare £2 million fund and then top it up subsequently with further sums in order to compensate for monies paid out for those purposes.

Indefinite leave to remain as an investor

Investors are eligible for ILR after two, three or five years, depending on whether they invested £2m, £5m or £10m. They have to satisfy the same requirements for continuous lawful residence as do other PBS migrants (see Appendix Continuous Residence). The requirement to have been absent for no more than 180 days annually can be challenging for the globally mobile.

Example

Midas plans to enter the UK as an investor relying on £2 million. He does not expect to increase his investment significantly during his time here.

If his application succeeds, Midas will be granted entry clearance for three years and four months. He will then have to apply for leave to remain, which should be granted for two years. Once he has achieved five years of relevant continuous residence (he may include time after the grant of entry clearance but before arriving in the UK as part of that period, although of course it will be counted towards the maximum 180 days abroad), he can apply for settlement.

7.3.5 Tier 1 Entrepreneur extension and settlement rules

7.3.5.1 Extension of a Tier 1 Entrepreneur visa

Although the Entrepreneur route is now closed to new applicants, existing Tier 1 Entrepreneurs can apply to extend their visa until 5 April 2023 (or 6 July 2025 if they ever had leave as a Graduate Entrepreneur). The requirements are found in Table 5 of Appendix A and r245DD.

- They must be registered as a director or as self-employed no more than six months after the date they were given permission to stay in the UK under a Tier 1 (Entrepreneur) visa.
- They will have to prove they have been self-employed, a member of a partnership or working as a director of a business three months before they apply.
- They must have created at least two full time jobs that have existed for at least 12 months during their last grant of leave, and this has to be evidenced via very strict requirements, including that payments to workers have been made via HMRC's Pay As You Earn requirements (this requires that printouts of Real Time Full Payment Submissions are provided).
- They must provide a business plan and establish that they only work for their entrepreneurial business: and their business cannot simply involve contracts of service for other businesses such as to amount to 'disguised' employment
- They must show they can support themselves.
- They must have invested into one or more UK businesses either £200,000 in cash or £50,000 in cash, the amount depends on the level of funds the initial application was based on. At the time the route closed, Graduate entrepreneurs were allowed to make applications based on the lower sum.
- They should include any dependants who are on the current visa in the application to extend - including children who have turned 18 during the stay in the UK.
- They must apply online.

See https://www.gov.uk/tier-1-entrepreneur/extend-your-visa

> **Example**
>
> Ayan is coming to an end of his initial grant of leave as an Entrepreneur. He comes to see you in the office. He has employed three full-time staff members throughout his period of leave but he is worried about whether his bookkeeper kept adequate records: they seem to have simply kept a paper record of salary and tax deducted at source.
>
> This sounds problematic. It seems that the substantive requirements for an extension of leave based on job creation have been met (i.e. there have been more than two full-time employees for more than a year during the last grant of leave). However it does not seem that the technical requirements can be met: because Ayan lacks 'printouts of Real Time Full Payment Submissions showing that the applicant complied with Pay As You Earn (PAYE) reporting requirements to HM Revenue & Customs' (Appendix A 50(a)).

7.3.5.2 Settlement after a Tier 1 Entrepreneur visa

Tier 1 Entrepreneurs can apply to settle in the UK. They must make their applications before

- 6 April 2025 when the route will finally close for ILR purposes
- 6 July 2027 for applicants who spent time under the Graduate Entrepreneur route.

The requirements are found in Table 6 of Appendix A and r245DF.

An applicant must have been living continuously in the UK

- for three years if they have created 10 new full-time jobs or generated £5 million in a three-year period
- for five years if they do not meet those requirements for the accelerated route

The essential criteria are:

- They can demonstrate that the required investment into a UK business was completed
- That they registered with HMRC as self-employed or with Companies house as a Director within six months of entering the UK or within six months of their last grant of leave, and that that registration took place more than three months before the ILR application
- That they created two full time jobs which lasted for at least 12 months of the applicant's last period of leave
- The application can still be tested for the genuineness of the underlying investment and the associated business, and applicants must demonstrate that they intend to continue with the business.

As usual they are subject to the continuous residence requirement. Thus they cannot have been outside the UK for more than 180 days in any 12 months during that time.

Applicants aged between 18 and 64 must also pass the Life in the UK Test and meet the English language requirements.

The general refusal reasons apply, so as always it is important to check for any relevant misconduct or criminal convictions before making the application.

They must apply online. See https://www.gov.uk/settle-in-the-uk/y/you-have-a-work-visa/tier-1-entrepreneur-visa

Example

Emmanuel is present as a Tier 1 Entrepreneur having previously been granted an extension of leave in this route. He has been present in the UK for six years under the Entrepreneur route, having missed out on the opportunity to apply for settlement sooner because of a break in his continuous residence early on during his first period of leave in this route. He comes to see you with a view to making a settlement application now: he was last given an extension of leave 10 months ago, running until 14 months from now. He has now achieved five years on the trot without breaking his continuous residence.

Emmanuel still faces a problem with a settlement application. He has to show that he created or maintained two jobs in the last extension of leave that lasted for 12 months. However, given that his present grant of leave has not yet endured for 12 months, he does not satisfy the requirement that 'the jobs must have existed for at least 12 months during the most recent grant of leave. Luckily for him, so long as he keeps those employees working for him, he has plenty of leave to remain within which to make good the missing two months.

7.4 Skilled Workers

The Skilled Worker routes allow employers to recruit skilled employees from outside the United Kingdom to fill a particular post. Some lawyers concentrate on these kinds of applications, because of the high volume of applications required by large employers. Many other lawyers never come across one. For this reason we give a general overview of the basic ideas before we zone in more closely on some aspects of the routes.

There are four sub-categories:

- **Appendix Skilled Worker** – for those with offers of skilled work, including shortage occupations
- **Appendix Intra-Company Routes** – for existing employees of multinationals who need to be transferred to the UK for training purposes or to undertake skilled work: the overseas employer must be linked to the UK branch by common ownership or control. There are two sub-categories:

- **Intra-Company Transfer**: for postings up to five years, for individuals who have been working for the firm for at least 12 months. Postings may be longer for high earners.
- **Graduate Trainee**: for recent graduate recruits being transferred to the UK for training as part of a structured graduate training programme with clearly defined progression towards a managerial or specialist role within the organisation for a maximum period of 12 months.

- **Appendix T2 Minister of Religion** – for a Minister of Religion undertaking preaching and pastoral work, Missionary, or Member of a Religious Order, taking up employment or a post/role within their faith community.
- **Appendix T2 Sportsperson** – for elite sportspersons or coaches whose employment will make a significant contribution to the development of their sport at the highest level in the UK.

Overview of the skilled worker and T2 routes

Central concepts are the **Certificate of Sponsorship** (CoS) and the **CoS Checking System** (CoSCS). The former is the means by which the Sponsor records all relevant criteria for the job in question; the latter is the central record maintained by the Home Office on which these are registered. The CoS has a unique reference number, and contains information about the job in question and the applicant's personal details (see e.g. paragraph SW 5.1 in Appendix Skilled Worker, or SP 5.4 Appendix T2 Sportsperson). A multiple entry CoS may be issued for a person who travels significantly (*Guidance for Sponsors Part 2* S7.23-28). The Sponsor has duties (see the *Guidance for Sponsors Part 3*) including the requirement to report not turning up for work on the first day, unreasonable absence (e.g. beyond 10 days), significant changes of employment circumstances and information suggesting an employee is breaching the terms of their leave.

It is not the physical CoS which lies at the system's heart, because applications are checked against the CoSCS, which you will see many references to in the Rules. So if relevant information is missing from the electronic version, or were the existence of the hard copy not to be verifiable in the Home Office sponsor system virtual world, a paper hard copy would be useless.

The general policy of these routes is that migration should not displace settled workers who could fill the work role in question. To achieve this, there was previously a limitation on the permissible number of Skilled Worker (then 'Tier 2') applicants. However, this limit was removed in 2020. Now, the policy is achieved by focusing on skilled occupations. There is also genuineness testing, aimed at ensuring the migrant is the right fit for the role.

The routes require entry clearance to be obtained before travelling for those applying from abroad, Students must leap various hurdles, such as obtaining the consent of their educational Sponsor, if backed by a government or international scholarship agency.

Previously, there was a prohibition for those who own more than 10% of the shares of the Sponsor business. This has now been abolished, raising the possibility of an entrepreneur seeking to sponsor themselves as an employee.

SKILLED WORKERS AND T2 ROUTES: LEGAL FRAMEWORK			
UKVI overview links	**Appendix**	**Caseworker Guidance**	**Sponsor Guidance**
Intra-Company Transfer	Appendix Intra-Company Routes	Intra-Company Routes	Compiled here. This links to both the general sponsor guidance and the route-
Skilled Worker	Appendix Skilled Worker	Skilled Worker	
T2 Sportsperson	Appendix T2 Sportsperson	T2 Sportsperson	

T2 Minister of Religion	Appendix T2 Minister of Religion	T2 Minister of Religion	specific guidance.

7.4.1 Appendix Skilled Worker 

Appendix Skilled Worker enables UK employers to recruit workers to work in the UK in a specific job. The job must come under an eligible occupation code listed in Appendix Skilled Occupations.

The minimum age for applicants is 18.

Additionally:

- the certificate of sponsorship reference number must be used within three months of issue, and the application for entry clearance must be made no more than three months before the commencement of employment
- the applicant must not have previously applied for leave using the same certificate of sponsorship reference number
- the sponsor must be A-rated, unless exceptions apply

Then the CoS has to hurdle some more barriers: the Sponsor must not be hiring the worker out to a third party for routine contract work, and applicants must survive a genuineness audit. The job must not be a "sham", or created primarily to support the applicant's immigration to the UK. The applicant will not be granted leave if the sponsor does not have a genuine need for the job. The Guidance indicates that decision makers may need to revert to the sponsor before finally determining an application where there are initial concerns on these grounds.

Example

Mithras applies for leave as a Marketing Director for one-branch outfit Harry's Hair Salon having been assigned a CoS with the appropriate salary.

Marketing Directors come under occupation code 1132 and are listed in Table 1 of Appendix Skilled Occupations. Their entry in Table 1 confirms that Marketing Directors are eligible for ICT and ICGT.

However, the Home Office would be entitled to question whether a small firm really needs a full–time person in this role. A very thorough business case would need to be established.

7.4.1.1 Points

Applicants must make up a total of 70 points. 50 points come from mandatory requirements:

- Sponsorship (20 points)
- Job at appropriate skill level (20 points)
- English language (10 points)

The remaining 20 points must come by satisfying one of the tradeable points routes. Each tradeable points route requires that the applicant's salary is at or above whichever is higher of:

- A mandatory minimum salary; or
- A specified percentage of the 'going rate' for the relevant occupation code.

The salary requirement varies depending on the type of job and the applicant's labour history. Requirements are lower for:

- Applicants with a relevant PhD
- Shortage occupations
- New entrants to the labour market

- Health and education occupations listed in Table 2 of Appendix Skilled Occupations

Some routes carry additional requirements set out in SW 8.1-14.5. The table at paragraph SW 4.2 points you to these.

The going rates are found in Appendix Skilled Occupations. They assume a working week of 39 hours. The rate will be adjusted to the number of hours an applicant will be working, as stated by their sponsor. For example, the going rate for driving instructors is £22,800 per year. If an applicant were to work 41-hour weeks as a driving instructor, the rate would be adjusted to (£22,800 x 41) ÷ 39 = £23,969 per year. Some occupation codes (e.g. healthcare-related jobs) assume a different number of hours. For example, the going-rate for pharmacists assumes a 37.5-hour week. Full details are in Tables 2 and 3 of Appendix Skilled Occupations.

An applicant's salary is their guaranteed basic gross-pay. It does not include other pay or benefits, such as over-time pay, bonuses, or in-kind benefits. In relation to the mandatory minimum salary (but *not* the percentage of the going rate requirement), only salary for the first 48 hours a week counts.

Example

Marjorie applies for permission to stay in the UK as the manager of a wine bar. She will be working 39 hours a week. Turning to Appendix Skilled Occupations, she will see this comes under occupation code 1224, "Publicans and managers of licensed premises".

This is not a shortage occupation (Appendix Shortage Occupation List), nor is it eligible for PhD points. If Marjorie falls into one of the various sub-categories of new entrants to the labour market she can rely on the option E tradeable points route. This requires a salary exceeding both £20,480 per year and 70% of the going rate for occupation code 1224.

Otherwise Marjorie must rely on option A. This requires a salary exceeding £25,600 per year and 100% of the going rate for occupation code 1224. The going rate is £21,800. Aisha's application will therefore only succeed if her salary will exceed £25,600 per year.

7.4.1.2 Financial requirement

Unless they are applying for permission to stay and have been in the UK with leave for 12 months, the applicant must have either

- Funds of at least £1,270; or
- A maintenance undertaking from their sponsor.

7.4.1.3 English language skills

10 points will be awarded for knowledge of English at or above level B1 of the CEFR.

The migrant will need to show competence in the English language by:

- passing a specified test at the appropriate level;
- coming from a majority English speaking country; or
- having been awarded a degree taught in English

7.4.1.4 Appropriate skill level

The appropriate occupation code will be selected by the applicant's sponsor. This must be an eligible occupation code as listed in Appendix Skilled Occupations.

In addition, the decision maker must not have reason to believe that the sponsor chose a less appropriate occupation code because the most appropriate code:

- is not eligible under the Skilled Worker route
- has a higher going rate than the proposed salary

- is not a shortage occupation
- is not eligible for PhD points.

The decision-maker will consider whether there is a genuine need for the job, whether the applicant has the skills and experience to do the job, and the sponsor's history of compliance with immigration law.

7.4.1.5 Switching

The rules for switching are the same as for other PBS routes. Switching is permitted unless the applicant was last granted leave as a Visitor, Short-term Student, Parent of a Child Student, Seasonal Worker, Domestic Worker in a Private Household, or outside the Immigration Rules.

7.4.1.6 Period and conditions of leave, and curtailment

Entry or permission will be granted until 14 days after the end date stated on the certificate of sponsorship. The maximum end date is 5 years after the start date.

The migrant must work in the employment for which they have been sponsored, but can also take supplementary employment and do voluntary work. 'Supplementary employment' is narrowly defined in paragraph 6 of the Immigration Rules.

Home Office guidance provides for a sponsored worker to be given a limited opportunity to find a new Sponsor if their existing one loses their licence. Thus, their leave is normally curtailed when their Sponsor loses their licence, to 60 days where there is a greater period than that left on their visa.

7.4.1.7 Settlement

Skilled Workers can settle in the UK after 5 years of continuous lawful residence, providing their employer still holds a sponsor licence and still requires the applicant for the employment in question for the foreseeable future. Time spent in the UK under the Global Talent, Innovator, T2, and Representative of an Overseas Business routes, and under the old Tier 1 route, can be aggregated with the time spent under Tier 2.

The Sponsor must back the application by certifying that they are still needed in the role and will be for the foreseeable future, and confirming that their salary meets the minimum requirements and will continue to do so (and this may be audited subsequently).

There is a minimum salary requirement (dependent on the type of occupation and previous leave, either £25,600 or £20,480, or the going rate, whichever is higher). The requirements are at paragraph SW 24.3.

Salary will be checked against the last 12 months of PAYE records. If they do not show the necessary salary, for example because the sponsor intends a forthcoming pay increase, the Home Office caseworker may request further information from the sponsor. The sponsor should explain if the applicant is not being paid the appropriate rate due to maternity, paternity or adoption leave, sick leave, or legal industrial action.

The applicant must meet the knowledge of life and language in the UK requirements and must not have committed any overstaying beyond that which the Home Office condones (i.e. the 14 days permitted under Rule 39E).

7.4.2 Tier 2 (Ministers of Religion)

B2

Contained in Appendix T2 Minister of Religion, this category is intended for ministers of religion undertaking preaching and pastoral work, missionaries or members of religious orders. Those applying under the minister of religion category need to:

- be qualified to do the job in question;

- intend to base themselves in the United Kingdom;
- intend to comply with the conditions of permission to stay and leave the United Kingdom when their leave expires.
- show that they genuinely intend to undertake, and are capable of undertaking, the role for which they have been employed.

They must provide a CoS confirming that these requirements are met, and that they will be employed mainly for preaching and pastoral duties (unless in a senior position), with pay and conditions in line with the equivalent for settled workers. If the planned functions are at a lower level than leading the congregation, it may be more appropriate to consider the T5 Religious Workers route.

The maintenance requirement is £1,270, subject to the ordinary exception for those who have been in the UK for 12 months with permission. The English language requirement is a minimum of Level B2.

Leave is granted for whichever is shorter of the period of employment stated on the applicant's Certificate of Sponsorship plus 14 days, or 3 years and 1 month.

Applicants may settle in the UK after 5 years if they meet the same requirements as for Skilled Workers except that there is no specific salary requirement other than pay being equal to other settled workers in the same role. Their Sponsor must confirm they are still needed for the role.

7.4.3 T2 Sportsperson 

Contained in Appendix T2 Sportsperson, this category is for sportspersons who are internationally established at the highest level; and will make a significant contribution to the development of their sport at the highest level in the United Kingdom.

Sportspersons must be endorsed by their Governing Body. Governing bodies for various sports are listed at Appendix M of the rules. The Governing Body must provide a letter confirming this endorsement, and that the applicant is internationally established at the highest level and will make a significant contribution to the sport's development at the highest level in the UK. The applicant must also have a Certificate of Sponsorship from an approved sponsor.

Separately from this endorsement, T2 sportsperson applicants require a valid certificate of sponsorship from an approved sponsor. The sponsor must show that the potential employee:

- is qualified to do the job in question;
- intends to base themselves in the United Kingdom;
- has been endorsed by the governing body for his/her sport (listed in Appendix M). The endorsement must confirm that the player or coach is internationally established at the highest level and their employment will make a significant contribution to the development of his sport at the highest level in the UK;
- will comply with the conditions of their permission to stay and leave the United Kingdom when their leave expires.

Funds of £1,270 are required subject to the ordinary exception for those who have been living in the UK for 12 months with permission, and basic English at level A1.

7.4.4 Intra-Company Routes

The Intra Company Routes allow multi-national employers to offer non-UK resident workers a role in a UK branch of the organisation.

Requirements are broadly similar to Skilled Worker, featuring the usual restrictions on the validity of a CoS, and then constraints on points scoring. The occupation must be listed in Appendix Skilled Occupations as eligible for Intra-Company Transfer and Graduate Transfer.

7.4.4.1 Certificates of Sponsorship

The company needs to be on the list of licensed sponsors to be able to sponsor one of their employees to come to the UK to live and work. The list is found here.

The sponsor is responsible for checking that the employee can do the job they are hiring them for and that it qualifies them for a visa. They will then issue a CoS.

7.4.4.2 Types of Intra-company Transfer visa

There are 2 types of Intra-company Transfer visa.

Long-term Staff

This visa is for those transferring into a role that requires them to have had previous experience working for the company.

They will need to have worked for the company for more than 12 months, unless their salary will be £73,900 or more a year to work in the UK.

Graduate Trainee

This visa is for transfers into graduate trainee programmes for specialist roles. The employee will need to be a recent graduate with at least three months' experience with the employer overseas.

They must show that they are on a structured graduate training programme, with clearly defined progression towards a managerial or specialist role, and that their Sponsor has assigned no more than 20 CoSs for the financial year.

7.4.4.3 Appropriate salary

There is a minimum salary of £41,500 for Intra-Company Transfer and £23,000 for Graduate Transfer. Some occupations have higher minimum salaries found by referring to the "going rate" stated in Appendix Skilled Occupations.

7.4.4.4 Personal savings

Applicants who have been in the UK for 12 months with permission do not need to show funds. Other applicants must show funds of £1,270, or receive a maintenance undertaking from their employer. The sponsor must confirm this undertaking on the certificate of sponsorship.

7.4.4.5 Period of permission

Permission will be granted for a maximum of 5 years for Long-Term Staff, and 1 year for Graduate Trainees. This is subject to a maximum overall time period which can be spent on the route:

- High earners (i.e. earning £73,900 or more) may not be granted cumulative periods of permission totalling more than 9 years in any 10-year period;

All other applicants are subject to a limit of 5 years from cumulative periods of permission in any 6-year period.

7.5 Students

There are three routes for student applicants:

- Appendix Student. This is the general student route. It allows applicants aged 16 or over to come to the UK to study at a licenced student sponsor.
- Appendix Child Student. This route enables children aged 4 to 17 to study at an independent school in the UK which has sponsor status.
- Appendix Short-term Student (English language). This allows applicants aged 16 or over to study a short-term English language course at an accredited institution. The course must be between 6 and 11 months.

An applicant who wishes to study a course shorter than 6 months may instead apply under Appendix Visitor.

The prospective student route that used to exist under Part 3 of the Immigration Rules is now closed.

Student immigration has been something of a battleground in recent years. As the largest group of migrants from outside the EEA, students have been at the centre of the government's policy to reduce net migration into the UK. Hundreds of colleges, including publicly funded universities, previously granted sponsor licences to recruit overseas students have seen their sponsor licences revoked for failure to comply with the requirements of the scheme. Sponsors have been made wholly responsible for ensuring those they sponsor comply with the Rules, and will lose their licence if more than 10% of their sponsored students are refused leave by the Home Office.

Students must show their intention to study in the UK is genuine. Additionally, Appendix Student provides for maximum time limits to study in the UK, reducing the chance of the route leading to settlement under the 10 year long residence rule.

Appendix Student requires applicants to gain 70 points. Applicants are awarded 50 points for 'study requirements' relating to the course studied and sponsoring arrangements. The remaining 20 points are gained by meeting the financial and English language requirements.

POINTS BASED SYSTEM STUDENT ROUTES LEGAL FRAMEWORK			
UKVI overview links	**Appendix**	**Caseworker Guidance**	**Sponsor Guidance**
Student Visa	Appendix Student	Student and Child Student Version 2.0	On gov.uk here
Child Study Visa	Child Student		
Short-term Study Visa	Appendix Short-term Student (English Language)	Short-term Student (English Language) Version 1.0	N/A (no sponsorship)

7.5.1 Requirement to have a sponsor

Before a student can apply to come to the UK to study under Appendix Student or Child Student, they must be sponsored. The sponsor will be the education provider in the UK that has accepted the student for a course of study. The education provider must have a Home Office sponsor licence. They will issue sponsored students with a CAS; essentially a reference number from the Sponsor Management System.

The Home Office states that sponsorship plays two main roles in the application process:

- It provides an assurance that the education provider is confident that the student is capable of doing the particular course of study; and
- It involves a pledge from the sponsoring education provider that it will accept responsibility for the student whilst they in the UK.

The register of student sponsors is here.

7.5.2 Licensing of sponsors

All education providers need a Home Office sponsor licence if they want to recruit foreign students. To get a licence, education providers need to show they are inspected or audited or hold valid accreditation with one of the Home Office approved accreditation bodies.

All sponsors must apply for a Basic Compliance Assessment within 12 months of being granted their licence. On passing, they will be upgraded from probationary sponsor status to student sponsor status. Sponsors who do not apply for or are refused HTS status will have their licence revoked, and will not be able to sponsor further students.

To comply with the licence requirements, sponsors must:

- Keep a copy of all their foreign students' passports and biometric residence permits;
- Keep each student's contact details and update them as necessary;
- Report to the Home Office any unauthorised student absences including a student who;
  - Fails to enrol with them by no later than 10 working days after the end of their prescribed enrolment period;
  - Misses 10 consecutive expected contacts. For students in schools, Further Education (FE) and English Language Colleges this will normally be where the student has missed two weeks of a course. In the Higher Education (HE) sector, where daily registers are not kept the Home Office will accept this reporting where the student has missed 10 expected interactions (e.g. Tutorials, submission of coursework etc);
  - Stops attending either because they have withdrawn from the course or because the student has said they are leaving, within 10 working days of this being confirmed;
  - Defers their studies after their arrival in the UK. In such cases the student's permission to be in the UK will cease to be valid as they will no longer be actively studying. The sponsor will need to notify the Home Office of the deferral and advise the student to leave the UK. When the student is ready to resume their studies they will need to make a fresh visa application.
- Report to the Home Office any students who discontinue their studies (including any deferrals of study);
- Report to the Home Office any significant changes in students' circumstances, (e.g. if the duration of a course of study shortens);
- Maintain any appropriate accreditation;
- Offer only those courses to international students which comply with the Home Office conditions;
- Comply with applicable PBS rules and the law; and
- Co-operate with the Home Office as to the sponsorship requirements generally.

Course drop out rates or visa refusals exceeding 10% of the sponsor's students will raise concerns about the sponsor's recruitment processes and their overall suitability as a sponsor. An investigation by the SSHD may ensue, leading to suspension or revocation of HTS status or the licence itself.

7.5.3 Appendix Student

This is the category under which most applications for the purpose of study in the UK are made.

7.5.3.1 Eligibility

When the student applies for their entry clearance or an extension, they will need a valid CAS from a licensed sponsor.

If applying for entry clearance, the student must also provide evidence of meeting the financial requirement. Applicants for permission to stay only need to provide financial evidence if they have been in the UK for less than 12 months.

The English language requirements are found at rule ST 13.1-4. Appendix English Language explains that it is for the sponsor to assess that the English language requirements are met when issuing the CAS. A failure by the sponsor to properly do so could render the CAS invalid.

The student may also need to satisfy the Home Office as to their English language proficiency and that they are a genuine student. Applicants may be interviewed for this purpose. Failure to attend an interview without a reasonable explanation is a discretionary ground of refusal (r9.9.1(a) and r 9.9.2(a)) Part 9 of the Immigration Rules).

If refused a visa, or leave to remain, applicants can apply for administrative review of the decision under Appendix AR of the Immigration Rules. Applicants will not usually be able to rely on evidence not submitted with their application. It is therefore important to get the application right first time.

Visas are granted for the full duration of the course, and a little bit extra.

There are a number of general requirements and restrictions under Appendix Student. These relate to:

- Age
- Security clearance (in the sense that some studies that could be used for nefarious purposes must get special clearance)
- Level of study
- Maximum time limits for studying in the UK
- Particular requirements for postgraduate doctors or dentists on a recognised Foundation Programme
- Sponsorship by a Government or international scholarship agency
- The Entry Clearance Officer must be satisfied that the applicant is a genuine student

Many additional requirements relate to the validity of the CAS. We look at these under the 'CAS' section further down.

Applicants will be expected to provide specified evidence of the qualifications they relied on when applying to the education provider for sponsorship, so that they can be verified by the UKVI.

7.5.3.2 Low risk countries

However, students from specified countries considered low risk will receive light-touch scrutiny and will not have to produce documentary evidence to support their application unless requested to do so. Students of low risk countries can still be interviewed to test their genuineness.

The list of low risk nationalities, at paragraph ST 22.1 of Appendix Student, to holders of which (including dual nationals) these different documentary requirements apply so long as they apply in their country of residence or for LTR in the UK, are as follows:

Australia · Austria · Bahrain · Barbados · Belgium · Botswana · Brazil · Brunei · Bulgaria · Cambodia · Canada · Chile · China · Croatia · Republic of Cyprus · The Dominican Republic · Estonia · Finland · France · Germany · Greece · Hungary · Iceland · Indonesia · Ireland · Italy · Japan · Kazakhstan · Kuwait · Latvia · Liechtenstein · Lithuania · Luxembourg · Malaysia · Malta · Mauritius · Mexico · Netherlands · New Zealand · Norway · Oman · Peru · Poland · Portugal · Qatar · Romania · Serbia · Singapore · Slovakia · Slovenia · South Korea · Spain · Sweden · Switzerland · Thailand · Tunisia · United Arab Emirates · United States of America.

Also benefiting from this light-touch scrutiny are holders of British National (Overseas) passports, or passports issued by Hong Kong SAR, Macau SAR, or Taiwan.

7.5.3.3 Age restrictions

The applicant must be at least 16 years old. If under 18, the applicant must have the support and consent of their parent(s).

7.5.3.4 Security clearance

Where the applicant wishes to undertake a course in a discipline listed in Appendix ATAS to the Immigration Rules, they will need a valid Academic Technology Approval Scheme (ATAS) clearance certificate from the Counter-Proliferation Department of the Foreign and Commonwealth Office. Appendix 6 includes courses involving various sciences, maths and engineering which might provide the necessary skills for would-be terrorists (and vets).

7.5.3.5 Maximum length of stay as a student

If the course is below degree level, the grant of leave the applicant is seeking must not lead to the applicant having spent more than two years in the UK as a Student migrant since the age of 18 studying courses that did not consist of degree level study. Degree level study is defined in paragraph 6 as;

'A course which leads to a recognised United Kingdom degree at bachelor's level or above, or an equivalent qualification at level 6 or above of the revised National Qualifications Framework, or levels 9 or above of the Scottish Credit and Qualifications Framework'.

There is also a 5-year time limit for those studying at degree level. This provision was designed to make it more difficult for a student to meet the requirements of the 10-year long lawful residence rule, the 'holy grail'. Exceptions to the 5-year rule include (ST 19.4):

- Professional qualifications in architecture, medicine, dentistry, law, veterinary studies and music.

The 5-year limit previously also applied to studies above degree level. These studies are now not subject to any maximum length of stay.

Examples

Huang is present as a Student. He wants to apply for leave to remain for a further course. He has so far studied for four and a half years at undergraduate level in classical civilisation, and now wishes to study for a law conversion course.

Although in general a student may not spend more than five years in the UK studying at undergraduate level, Huang is permitted to do so for a law conversion course.

Aiman is a citizen of Malaysia present as a Student. He wants to apply for further leave to remain for 12 months in order to study for a NCC Education Level 4 Diploma in Business. You look at his immigration history and see that he has spent 18 months in the UK achieving a Level 4 Certificate in Professional Marketing; he tells you he passed that course in 11 months of study.

As he has already been studying courses that are below degree level (you can use the Ofqual Register of Regulated Qualifications to assist with assessing qualification levels), he must watch out for the rule on 'below degree level' studies: he must not have spent more than two years in this immigration route studying courses at that level. The Rules make it very clear that it is the length of leave and not the length of study which matters. Accordingly it is clear that the new course would take him over the maximum permitted.

The complex provisions as to how the length of study is calculated for such cases are explained in the Caseworker Guidance starting at page 69. The measure is the period of leave granted rather than the actual period spent studying.

7.5.3.6 Genuine student provision

This provision applies both to applications for entry clearance and for in-country applicants. It allows for students to be interviewed by the decision maker in order that their English language skills can be tested, and to satisfy them that the applicant is a genuine student.

The ECO should interview the applicant in accordance with their policy as laid out in the Caseworker Guidance (pages 14-20). This basically says certain factors should be taken into account:

- All relevant evidence from both interview and application
- Immigration history and compliance in the UK and abroad (bearing in mind lengths of stay in other countries and their purpose)

- Education history and future study plans bearing in mind the time since they were last in education, whether they demonstrate *sufficient commitment* to the course, whether it represents academic progression
- Their research into, and knowledge of, the place and course of study, bearing in mind its relevance to their post-study plans
- The circumstances of any dependent and the impact that might have on the applicant's ability or motivation to study: particularly where the purpose of studies is said to be related to a benefit by way of education, employment or health for a dependent
- Their personal and financial circumstances bearing in mind any dependents in the UK and abroad, living costs in the UK and their ability to maintain themselves without working, how their funds for study have been acquired, the distance between their proposed accommodation and place of study
- Whether the application is to study at an institution that is under investigation or has been identified as of concern, or if the application is being managed by an agent as to whom there are *concerns*

The interview may be short and brutal. Some critics with experience of the system opine that the decision maker may well be looking for reasons to refuse the application and will take no prisoners. There are high expectations as to the precise reasons why *this* institution has been chosen as the place of study when compared to other similar seats of learning, and precisely why the component modules will advance the applicant's career path. Advisors should ensure their clients are adequately prepared for their interview. The ECO may review the website of their chosen sponsor: so the applicant may be well advised, for instance, to find out the opening times of their college's library before their interview! However, ECO questioning must be fair, both exploring all material issues fully and giving an opportunity to respond to concerns in the mind of the potential decision maker.

Example

Xan is a citizen of China. He plans to come to the UK as a Tier 4 student. He wants to know what to expect at the interview which has been scheduled following his application.

The ECO may expect detailed knowledge of the course of studies and an explanation of how it fits into the individual's career plans, and that the costs are realistic given the circumstances of the applicant and their family. Failure to attend an interview without a reasonable explanation is a discretionary ground of refusal (r9.9.1(a)). It is therefore key to advise clients of the potential for an interview at the earliest opportunity.

Furthermore, if refused, applicants have to apply for administrative review of the decision. Applicants will not usually be able to rely on evidence not submitted with their application. It is therefore important to get the application right first time.

7.5.3.7 The Certificate of Acceptance for Studies ('CAS')

All applicants under Appendix Student must hold a valid CAS. Paragraphs ST 1.2(d), ST 7.1-6 and ST 23.1 lay out the detailed requirements that need to be met for the CAS to be valid. These include requirements that:

- The CAS must have been issued by a licenced sponsor, and no more than six months before the application is made, and the offer must not have been withdrawn;
- If for entry clearance, the application is made no more than six months before the course start date; if for permission to stay the limit is three months;
- The CAS cannot have been used for a previous decided (i.e. valid) application;
- The CAS must contain mandatory information concerning the applicant and the course (e.g. the study address, the course fees, any work placements involved, how the applicant's English language skills were assessed);

- If not issued for studies, the CAS must be issued to a student union sabbatical officer or person on the doctorate extension scheme;
- The applicant must have met the English language requirements (see below);
- The CAS must be for a single course of study, or for a pre-sessional course followed by a degree;
- The CAS must state whether the course is full time or part-time.

The **CAS must be issued for a course which**;

- Leads to an 'approved qualification' (see below);
- Where the sponsor has student sponsor status (or Probationary Sponsor Status and applicant is under 18), the course in England & Wales or Northern Ireland is at RQF Level 3 or above, or in Scotland is at Level 6 SCQF or above; or
- Where the Sponsor has Probationary Sponsor status, the course in England & Wales; or Northern Ireland is at RQF Level 4 or above, or the course in Scotland is at SCQF Level 7 or above; or
- Where the course is an English language course, it is at minimum Level B2 CEFR; or
- If for a person studying at an overseas Higher Educational Institution, is a short term Study Abroad Programme at degree level recognised as equivalent to a UK degree by UK ENIC;
- Or the course must be a recognised Foundation Programme for postgraduate doctors or dentists; and
- For permission to stay applications, the course must represent genuine academic progress i.e. (i) be above the level of the previous course for which the applicant was granted leave as a Student, or (ii) involve further study at the same level, which the Sponsor (which must have a track record of compliance) confirms as complementing the previous course of study or the applicant's genuine career aspirations.
- Where the course is being delivered under a partnership between a higher education institution and a research institute, the course must be accredited at RQF level 7/Level 11 SCQF or higher.

Restrictions also apply to courses where there is a work placement involved.

Examples

Christopher plans to seek entry clearance for a course in Biology as a Student which starts in nine months' time. He wants to apply in good time to be confident of getting a place on the relevant course.

The CAS must not be issued more than six months before the application is made, and the entry clearance application must be made no more than six months before the course starts.

Christopher's application is made and succeeds. He arrives in the UK with his CAS. However, when the immigration officer checks the register of CASs online, he discovers that the CAS was cancelled because the offer has been withdrawn.

Christopher can be refused leave to enter because of a change of circumstances. Where the offer has been withdrawn, a key requirement will no longer be satisfied (ie the CAS is no longer valid). The situation would be the same if the institution's licence had been revoked.

Harpreet was granted entry clearance as a student to study tourism and hospitality at QCF/RQF level 4. He now wishes to extend his permission to remain to study Hospitality Management. When you look up the courses, you see that the new course is also at QCF/RQF level 4.

As he was previously granted leave as a student, he must show academic progression. Consecutive courses at the same level clearly do not necessarily demonstrate this. He does not benefit from one of the exceptions, e.g. resitting, PhD studies, loss of the Sponsor's licence, student sabbatical officer, etc. As no exception applies (ST 14.4), the requirements of ST 14.1-3 must be satisfied: so as this does not represent degree level studies, the course must be above the level of the previous course for which a CAS was issued. Harpreet must rethink.

There is one saving grace under Home Office policy for students whose sponsor's licence has been revoked whilst their application has been pending consideration. Sometimes the student will know of the revocation (e.g. because the college shuts down) but sometimes foreign students may only be a limited part of the institution's business (and a college may not shout about the loss of its licence!). So long as they have not been complicit in the misbehaviour that led to the college's loss of licence, students will normally have their existing leave curtailed such that they are left with 60 days remaining, or be given an extra 60 days within which to regularise their position.

Example

Orinoco is studying at Womble College. He has applied for further permission under Appendix Student. However, the College has its licence revoked before his application is decided. When the UKVI decision maker looks up the CAS, they will see that the College is no longer entitled to issue valid CASs. So the application is liable to be refused.

However, hopefully the policy to limit leave at this point to 60 days, providing the student is not suspected of involvement in the malpractices leading to revocation, will help. So the decision maker should remember this policy and give Orinoco the benefit of it. Orinoco will then be able to use this period to find another Sponsor, or find an alternative immigration application to make; otherwise he must leave the country.

The policy does not apply where the CAS if withdrawn or invalidated by the Sponsor, even if the migrant is not at fault.

An **approved qualification** is one that is (ST 9.1):

(1) validated by Royal Charter,

(2) awarded by a body that is on the list of recognised bodies produced by the Department for Business, Innovation and Skills,

(3) recognised by one or more recognised bodies through a formal articulation agreement with the awarding body,

(4) in England, Wales and Northern Ireland, on the Register of Regulated Qualifications (https://register.ofqual.gov.uk/) at Regulated Qualifications Framework (RQF) level 3 or above,

(5) in Scotland, accredited at Level 6 or above in the Scottish Credit and Qualifications Framework (SCQF) by the Scottish Qualifications Authority,

(6) an overseas qualification that UK NARIC assesses as valid and equivalent to Regulated Qualifications Framework (RQF) level 3 or above,

(7) covered by a formal legal agreement between a UK recognised body and another education provider or awarding body. An authorised signatory for institutional agreements within the UK recognised body must sign this. The agreement must confirm the UK recognised body's own independent assessment of the level of the student sponsor's or the awarding body's programme compared to the Regulated Qualifications Framework (RQF) or its equivalents. It must also state that the UK recognised body would admit any student who successfully completes the student sponsor's or the awarding body's named course onto a specific or a range of degree-level courses it offers, or

(8) an aviation licence, rating or certificate issued in accordance with EU legislation by the UK's Civil Aviation Authority.

7.5.3.8 English language

The English language requirements under Tier 4 are at paragraphs ST 13.1-4.

Applicants must show:

- English language at level B2 CEFR if studying at bachelor's degree level or above; or
- Level B1 CEFR if studying below degree level.

As with other PBS routes, detail on proving English language ability is contained in Appendix English Language:

- Nationality of (or successfully studying for an academic qualification at degree level plus taught in English) a majority English speaking country
- Obtaining an academic qualification at degree level plus in the UK
- Having passed an approved English language test at B1/B2 (for 'below degree level/degree level' studies)
- For colleges with a track record of compliance, confirmation in the CAS that the college has confirmed English language proficiency at B2.

Sponsors must confirm on the CAS that they have checked that English language requirements are met.

> **Examples**
>
> Ashfar plans to make an extension application within Appendix Student and has a Sponsor lined up; they have confirmed they will make him an offer as soon as he has the paperwork in order. He does not have a suitable English language test result yet, and is planning to sit a test soon.
>
> Ashfar should get on with getting the test result. The CAS will not be issued until he has satisfied the college of his English language proficiency. A delayed test result could prevent the CAS being issued, which could mean that he has to make an application for further leave to remain without a CAS in the hope that one reaches him to forward to the Home Office before his application is decided. There is no legal obligation on UKVI to await the document, however.
>
> Darshan wants to apply for entry clearance as a Student. He has evidence of English language proficiency as he has passed the relevant test with a provider listed on gov.uk here (EL 6.1) at level B1 across the board. He is nervous about speaking English under pressure, though, and seeks reassurance.
>
> Darshan can be invited for interview and asked to demonstrate his English language proficiency. He will not be expected to sit a formal English language test – the test is whether his English skills are at the level indicated in the CAS. Indeed, it is even possible to be interviewed at the port of entry after entry clearance has been issued.

7.5.3.9 Financial requirement

Students will be expected to show that they hold sufficient funds to cover the full costs of their course fees (or for the first academic year if the course is for a year or more) plus £1334 for maintenance if studying in London and £1023 for those studying outside London for each month of the course up to a maximum of nine months.

Study is considered to be in London if it takes place within Greater London (r6.2).

The funds must consist of one or more of:

- Cash in an account in the applicant's name (including a joint account);
- Cash in an account owned by the parents or legal guardians of the student where the relationship can be proven and permission to use the funds is demonstrated by specified evidence;
- For child students, cash in an account in their parent's name (with prescribed additional evidence such as a birth certificate and a letter from the parent);
- A loan in the applicant's name;
- Official financial or government sponsorship.

7.5.3.10 Length and conditions of leave

Leave will be granted for the duration of the course. The following table sets out the extra leave that is granted on top of this period:

Type of course	Period of entry clearance to be granted before the course starts	Period of entry clearance to be granted after the course ends
12 months or more	1 month	4 months
6 months or more but less than 12 months	1 month	2 months
Pre-sessional course of less than 6 months	1 month	1 month
Course of less than 6 months that is not a pre-sessional course	7 days	7 days
Postgraduate doctor or dentist	1 month	1 month

Those completing a PhD in the UK can apply for an additional 12 months leave under the doctorate extension scheme (see ST 18.1).

The no recourse to public funds condition will always be applied. Employment is forbidden except as follows:

- employment during term time of no more than 20 hours per week for those studying at degree level and above at a higher education provider with a track record of compliance
- employment during term time of no more than 10 hours per week for those studying below degree level (including Foundation degrees) at a higher education provider with a track record of compliance
- employment (of any duration) during vacations (for those permitted to work)
- employment as part of a course-related work placement which forms an assessed part of the applicant's course and provided that any period that the applicant spends on that placement does not exceed half of the total length of the course undertaken in the UK
- employment as a Student Union Sabbatical Officer, for up to 2 years, provided the post is elective and is at the institution which is the applicant's Sponsor – this is not permitted for Child Students
- employment as a postgraduate doctor or dentist on a recognised Foundation Programme

Additionally, a Student may not be self-employed, or employed as a Doctor in Training other than a vacancy on a recognised Foundation Programme, professional sportsperson (including a sports coach) or an entertainer, and must not fill a full-time vacancy other than a vacancy on a recognised Foundation Programme.

Example

Edna and Josephine have been granted leave as Students. Edna will be studying for a law degree at Bristol University. Josephine will be studying for a Level 5 foundation degree at Bolton University. Each wishes to know whether they can work in the UK and on what terms.

Edna is studying a degree level course at a higher education provider with a track record of compliance (the Student Sponsor Register states the sponsor and licence type) and so can work for up to 20 hours weekly in term-time (and longer outside term-time).

Josephine is pursuing a course that is below degree level (see the GOV.UK website What qualification levels mean) and so can work for no more than 10 hours per week (and longer outside term-time).

7.5.3.11 Extensions

To apply for an extension as a Student a person must have, or have last been granted, entry clearance, leave to enter or leave to remain in one of the following categories:

ST 4.3 requires that the applicant must be applying for leave to remain for the purpose of studies commencing no more than 28 days after the applicant's current permission (including 3C leave) expires. The application must also be no more than 3 months before the start date of the new course.

Where the gap between the leave running out and the new course is more than 28 days, the student is expected to return home and apply for entry clearance.

7.6 T5 Short Term Work visas

These routes compile and replace a range of schemes and programmes that formerly existed both inside and outside the immigration rules.

The routes are divided into various Appendices. It is helpful to first refer to the general T5 (Temporary Worker) Guidance before turning to the Rules.

Further notes/information

2 Temporary Workers

Seasonal Worker

Creative and sporting

Charity worker

Religious worker

Government authorised exchanges

International agreement

TIER 5 OF THE POINTS BASED SYSTEM LEGAL FRAMEWORK			
UKVI overview links	**Immigration Rules Appendices**	**Caseworker Guidance**	**Sponsor Guidance**
Tier 5 (Youth Mobility Scheme)	Appendix T5 (Temporary Worker) Youth Mobility Scheme	T5 (Youth Mobility Scheme) caseworker guidance	N/A

T5 Temporary Worker:			
(Creative and Sporting)	Creative or Sporting Worker	T5 Temporary Worker Guidance	All Sponsor Guidance is linked on gov.uk here
(Charity Worker)	Charity Worker		
(Religious Worker)	Religious Worker		
(Government Authorised Exchange)	Government Authorised Exchange		
(International Agreement)	International Agreement		
(Seasonal Worker)	Seasonal Worker		

7.6.1 T5 (Temporary worker)

These routes are for certain types of temporary worker. For which reason they are obviously not generally routes which can lead to settlement.

7.6.1.1 Creative and sporting category

This category is for migrants who want to come to the United Kingdom to work as sports people for up to 12 months, or to perform as entertainers or creative artists for up to 24 months. The requirements are then sub-divided into sporting and creative requirements.

Sporting

This subcategory is aimed at sportspeople who are internationally established at the highest level in their sport and/or whose employment will make a significant contribution to the development and operation of that particular sport in the United Kingdom and for coaches who must be suitably qualified to fulfil the role in question. The sponsor must have an endorsement from the appropriate governing body under Appendix M confirming that these requirements are met.

Sporting sponsors must be a sporting body, sports club, events organiser or other organiser operating, or intending to operate, in the sporting sector. An agent cannot be a sponsor under T5 sporting subcategory. The prospective sponsor must submit an endorsement from the Home Office recognised governing body for the sport. A governing body is one that is recognised by one of the home country sports councils (for example Sport England). A list of the approved governing bodies is at Appendix M to the Immigration Rules.

Migrants holding leave as a T5 sportsperson may switch into the T2 Sportsperson route when seeking permission to stay, provided they meet the requirements for that route.

Creative

In order to gain a licence as a sponsor of creative workers and their entourage, the prospective sponsor must be operating, or intend to operate, in the creative sector.

Examples include a national body, event organiser, producer, venue, agent or other similar organisation. Where applicable, the prospective sponsor must prior to issuing each certificate of sponsorship commit to having applied the Home Office codes of practice for taking into account the needs of the resident labour market in that field. The codes of practice will operate in three specific areas: dance, theatre, and film & television.

7.6.1.2 Charity worker category

Migrants coming to work temporarily in the United Kingdom as charity workers should only be undertaking voluntary activity and not paid employment. The migrant should intend to carry out fieldwork directly related to the purpose of the sponsoring organisation. They must not fill a permanent position.

Migrants entering the United Kingdom under the charity workers subcategory will be given a maximum of 12 months' permission to stay. Their dependants will be allowed to work if they are accompanying or joining them in the United Kingdom.

7.6.1.3 Religious worker category

The religious worker category is for people coming to the United Kingdom to work temporarily. Religious workers can:

- undertake preaching, pastoral work and non-pastoral work;
- work in the United Kingdom in the same capacity as they are working in an overseas organisation (although their duties in the United Kingdom may be different); or
- work in a religious order with a community which involves a permanent commitment, such as a monastery or convent. The work in a religious order must be in the order itself or be outside work directed by the order. A migrant can apply if he or she is a novice whose training means taking part in the daily community life of the order.

The work must not fall under the role of a T2 Minister of Religion. The applicant therefore cannot lead a congregation.

The work of a member of a religious order must be within the order itself, or outside work directed by the order. Teachers working in schools not maintained by their order must apply as a teacher under Appendix Skilled Worker. Novices whose training consists of taking part in the daily community life of their order may apply under this category, but anyone studying for a qualification, on a formal full-time course of study or training in an academic institution not maintained by the order should apply as a student under Appendix Student. People who are not members of a religious order, but who are working or studying within such a community, are not eligible to apply under this category and must satisfy the requirements of the relevant work or study category.

Migrants entering the United Kingdom under this category will be given a maximum of 24 months' permission to stay. Their dependants will be allowed to work if accompanying or joining them in the United Kingdom.

Sponsors wishing to apply for a licence under this category must be a bona fide religious institution (defined in detail in the Religious Worker Sponsor Guidance), i.e.

- A registered charity (or exceptionally, explaining why not)
- A faith-based community with a common system of beliefs (in something transcendental, metaphysical or ultimate) and practices
- Which does not discriminate on gender, nationality or ethnicity grounds, does not act contrary to the public interest, and does not encourage breach of UK laws

7.6.1.4 Government authorised exchange category

A list of approved government authorised exchanged schemes is at Appendix N to the Immigration Rules.

The government authorised exchange category is for people coming to the United Kingdom through approved schemes that aim to share knowledge, experience and best practice. This category must not be used to fill job vacancies or to bring unskilled labour to the United Kingdom.

Migrants entering the United Kingdom under the government authorised exchange category will be given a maximum of 12 or 24 months' permission to stay, depending on the scheme. Their dependants are allowed to work if they are accompanying or joining them in the United Kingdom.

Usually there will have to be an overarching body to administer an exchange scheme under this category. This overarching body will be the sponsor and must apply for a licence. The scheme and the overarching body must have the support of a United Kingdom government department or one of its executive agencies. The overarching body will assign certificates of sponsorship to migrants who meet the requirements of the scheme. A full list of sponsors can be found here. Sponsors must be A-rated to issue a CAS for a government authorised exchange worker.

Appendix Student graduates undertaking corporate internships can apply for an Extension under this route. It is not possible to switch into the GAE route from any other route.

Example

You can see an example of the various processes for the College of Optometrists here, which gives some idea of the importance of ensuring that the steps are taken in the right order: an applicant from the right kind of educational institution may switch from Appendix Student once they have obtained a degree of the right quality, obtaining a pre-registration place may be necessary before the CoS is issued, and then the CoS can be used to support an application for leave to remain, before the placement is taken up.

7.6.1.5 International agreement category

This category is for migrants who are coming to the United Kingdom under contract to provide a service that is covered under international law, including:

- the General Agreement on Trade in Services (GATS);
- similar agreements between the United Kingdom and another country;
- employees of overseas governments and international organisations; and
- private servants in diplomatic households (paragraph IA 7.6 is intended to prevent this route being used by diplomats bringing their family members);

Migrants entering the United Kingdom under the international agreement sub-category can apply for leave as follows.

- For private servants and employees of overseas governments or other international organisations:
    - entry clearance for a maximum of 24 months;
    - permission to stay for a maximum of the difference between the period already spent in the UK on a T5 (Temporary Worker) route and 24 months.
- For contractual service suppliers and independent professionals:
    - entry clearance for a maximum of 6 months, or 12 months for EU and Swiss nationals;
    - permission to stay for a maximum of the difference between the period already spent in the UK and 6 months, or 12 months for EU and Swiss nationals.

For contractual service suppliers and independent professionals there is a maximum limit of:

- 6 months in any 12-month period; or
- 12 months in any 24-month period for Swiss nationals; or
- no limit for EU nationals.

Their dependants will be allowed to work if they are accompanying or joining them in the United Kingdom.

Example

Your client wants to enter the UK with a view to taking up a job offer with the company that has issued them with a CoS to work as a Contractual Service Provider.

One of the things to check is that the contract was offered to their employer under an open tendering or other suitable procedure. Failure to carry out steps like this may mean that the CoS is deemed inadequate when a Home Office decision maker reviews it.

7.6.1.6 Seasonal worker category

This category is for migrants aged 18 or over who want to come to the United Kingdom to work in edible horticulture for up to 6 months. It was created from 10 January 2019 to cater for post-Brexit labour demands.

Sponsors must A-rated. The Guidance states that only two over-arching bodies have been approved: Concordia (UK) Ltd and Pro-force Limited.

The Certificate of Sponsorship must state that the role is in the edible horticulture industry. This means growing:

- Protected vegetables, i.e. those grown in glasshouse systems;
- Field vegetables, i.e. those grown outdoors;
- Soft fruit;
- Top fruit, i.e. trees bearing fruit;
- Vines and bines, e.g. hops is a bine and grapes is a vine;
- Mushrooms.

Work conditions must conform with all relevant UK and EU legislation, such as the National Minimum Wage Act, the relevant Agricultural Wages Order rate where this applies, and the Working Time Directive.

Permission will be granted for up to 6 months. Applicants may not hold more than 6 months' leave in any 12-month period.

There is no 'genuineness' testing for Seasonal Workers. Applications are for entry clearance only; there is no provision for extending leave.

7.6.2 Tier 5 (Youth Mobility Scheme)

This route is for people who want to live and work in the UK for up to two years. The Rules are found in both Appendix T5 (Temporary Worker) Youth Mobility Scheme and Appendix Youth Mobility Scheme: eligible nationals.

7.6.2.1 Eligibility

They have to be aged 18 to 30 and have £2,530 in savings.

They must be either:

- a British overseas citizen, British Overseas Territories citizen or a British national (overseas)
- Or they must be from Australia, Canada, Japan, Monaco, New Zealand, Hong Kong, Republic of Korea (South Korea), Taiwan or San Marino.

Citizens of San Marino must have a certificate of sponsorship reference number before they apply. A certificate of sponsorship is a unique reference number that holds information about the job they will do and their personal details. It's not a certificate or paper document.

All other countries have 'deemed sponsorship status'. This means applicants meet the sponsorship requirement simply by providing their passport.

7.6.2.2 Restrictions on eligibility

Some people who would otherwise be eligible cannot apply. These are:

- people whose children who live with them
- people who have children they are financially responsible for
- anyone who has already been in the UK under the scheme or in the former 'working holidaymaker' category

7.7 Specified evidence & evidential flexibility

Before the December 2020 modernisation of most routes, PBS applicants had to meet strict requirements regarding specified evidence and documents which had to be provided to support applications. Following reform in 2020, these requirements have largely been abandoned.

However, they continue to apply to the Tier 1 (Investor) and Entrepreneur routes, who have to come up with an exhaustingly precise set of documents. The Immigration Rules at r39B lay down the criteria for specified documents. They must be original documents, which are verifiable, and must be accompanied by a certified translation if not in English or Welsh. There is some limited provision for decision makers to use their initiative and discretion to seek further information where information is missing from the specified documents provided or a document is provided in the wrong format: see r245AA.

If the specified documents are not provided, the applicant will not meet the requirement for which the specified documents are required as evidence. You can speak brilliant English but if the appropriate evidence (eg of having studied to degree-level in the language is not provided), the application will fail.

For the modern PBS routes, there is a more mellow environment, though being slack with documents is never a good idea. For example the Skilled Worker Guidance repeatedly references the possibility of requesting more information or supporting documents, and explains that a '*fair and proportionate*' approach should be taken to evidence assessment generally. The proof of the pudding will be in the eating as lawyers monitor the progress of decision making under the modern system.

7.8 Other general considerations

7.8.1 Overstaying and extension applications; invalidity

The PBS rules explicitly allow for out of time extension applications where r39E applies. Up to 14 days of overstaying may be disregarded when considering an extension application – so an application may succeed. In addition, overstaying between 24 January and 31 August 2020 is automatically waived. This is clearly intended to reflect the circumstances of the Covid-19 pandemic; but it is not a requirement to prove that overstaying was caused by the pandemic.

However the applicant remains an overstayer who is subject to the hostile environment. Overstaying, even by one day, is always unwise. It is a criminal offence, albeit rarely one that is prosecuted. More importantly for PBS migrants, an overstayer cannot lawfully work in the UK, and may also have to leave any course of study. Working whilst in the UK with no leave was made a criminal offence under the Immigration Act 2016 as from 12 July 2016. There will be little point applying for leave as an overstayer where the sponsor has withdrawn their sponsorship as a result, or where the applicant is being prosecuted for working illegally.

Note that overstaying in excess of 30 days (or prior to 6 April 2017, 90 days) risks engaging immigration rules 9.8.1-2 if the person departs from the UK and seeks re-entry (i.e. the 12-month re-entry ban).

It is important therefore to make sure that the initial in-time application exactly conforms to the requirements of the Immigration Rules. An unsuccessful applicant may be able to repair a defective application by re-applying within the r39E tolerance period. But if they cannot get their application papers in order speedily, they may instead need to go home to apply for a visa to return, presuming the sponsor is content to keep an offer open for them.

Like other applications, PBS cases risk invalidity if the formalities are not complied with. A Notice of Invalidity will be sent when the application does not meet the requirements of r34 or route-specific validity requirements, though the applicant should first have been given a warning that their application appeared invalid, giving them a chance to correct it under rule 34B (see Module 1).

7.8.2 Payment of application fees

Many applicants find their applications returned as invalid because the Home Office alleges that they have not been able to collect the fee, or the correct fee was not paid.

Top Tip

It is possible to mitigate the effects of some of the stringent requirements of the PBS by lodging an administrative review against a decision to refuse an in-time application and, in the meantime, preparing a fresh application ensuring that the PBS requirements are fully complied with.

If the administrative review fails, or is withdrawn, an out of time application can then be made within 14 days with all the documents in order. It is always a good idea to check that any previous applications that were returned as invalid or refused were lawfully rejected.

7.8.3 PBS settlement applications

The simplified modern PBS routes must establish that the "knowledge of life in the UK" requirement is met via Appendix KOL UK rather than by Appendix KOLL. Applicants must provide a valid digital reference number from an approved educational institution or other approved person. There are exemptions for those aged 65+ or under 18, or with a disability (physical or mental condition) which prevents them from meeting the requirement.

Allowable absences – Appendix Continuous Residence

Appendix Continuous Residence sets out some general requirements regarding the meaning of *continuous residence* for Points Based System applicants seeking settlement. This Appendix entered into force from 1 December 2020 and applies to the following PBS routes:

- Skilled Workers
- Representative of an Overseas Business
- Global Talent and Exceptional Talent
- Innovator
- T2 Minister of Religion
- T2 Sportsperson
- T5 (Temporary Worker) International Agreement Worker (Private Servant in a Diplomatic Household)

Prior to the introduction of Appendix Continuous Residence, the meaning of *continuous residence* was addressed by Part 6A of the Rules, at r245AAA. R245AAA continues to apply to a small number of routes, most of which are closed to new applicants but still open for settlement. These are discussed further below.

The basic rule is that the continuous residence requirement is met if the applicant has spent the qualifying unbroken continuous residence period required by their route lawfully in the UK (CR 1.1).

The applicant must not have been outside the UK for more than 180 days in any 12-month period. Some absences do not count towards these 180 days, for example where travel was disrupted due to natural disaster, or where a period abroad was necessitated by helping with a humanitarian or environmental crisis, or where there were compelling and compassionate personal circumstances such as the death of a family member. Some excess absence due to pursuing research is also permitted for Skilled Workers who are scientists, academics and for those on the Global Talent route.

Continuous residence will be broken by the applicant being:

- Sentenced to prison
- Subject to a deportation or exclusion order
- Subject to removal directions
- An overstayer, or abroad without permission to enter or stay, unless
    - paragraph 39 E applies; or

   - the applicant had permission when they left the UK and successfully applied to extend permission before it expired, or within 14 days of its expiry
- Absent from the UK for longer than the permitted 180-day period.

The period of continuous residence is calculated by counting back from which ever is most beneficial to the applicant out of:

- The date of the ILR application
- Any date up to 28 days after the ILR application
- The date of the decision

There is a difference approach to taken to absences before and after 11 January 2018. For the latter, the rule requires that

> the applicant must not have been outside the UK for more than 180 days during any consecutive 12-month period, ending on the same date of the year as the date of the application for settlement.

Whereas for earlier periods, the periods of absence during each of the relevant calendar years would be taken *only* for the calendar year running up to the application date. This provided the useful possibility of timing the application so as to exclude periods of excess absence, or at least to share them between particular years, with a view to demonstrating that there was no excess absence in any of the five annual periods running up to the application date. However, one reading of the more recent wording is that applicants would have to calculate their absence during *every single possible* 12-month period over the last half decade.

If continuous residence is broken, then it will be necessary to rebuild it from scratch, making further extension applications

Allowable absences – r245AAA

As previously mentioned, Investors and Entrepreneurs have their continuous residence measured by reference to the old PBS system rather than Appendix Continuous Residence. The regime is not very different, though the grounds for when absences exceeding 180 days may be condoned are expressed more narrowly.

Further notes/ information

These issues are not to be dealt with by Level 1 advisors and must be referred on to a suitable accredited advisor.

Many people fall foul of the 'continuous residence' requirements, perhaps partly because they were tightened up in recent years, after many potential applicants obtained their leave to remain (e.g. earlier versions of the policy allowed discretion where residence was broken for 'reasons related to the applicant's employment or business in the United Kingdom').

Those migrants whose professional or academic commitments require a significant amount of travel may find themselves with a break in their leave.

The strategy of timing an application so that long periods abroad are spread over two calendar years no longer works from 11 January 2018, from which date the changed wording of the rule allows the decision maker to look at *any* 12-month period during the qualifying period (instead of the consecutive 12 month periods as distinct units).

Consider whether the part day absence proviso assists, or the new para 245AAA(d) (flexible end date to continuous residence).

Consider whether a further application for limited leave is possible in order to provide a further chunk of time over which continuous residence can be accumulated (if the application has already been refused, query whether the decision maker should have considered, or invited, an extension application rather than refusing the migrant outright and perhaps leaving them with no other application that they can make under the Rules).

Consider whether, if no application is viable under the Rules, there is an explanation for absence based on serious or compelling compassionate reasons that warrants an application outside the Rules or on human rights grounds.

7.8.4 Finance

Each PBS route states the level of funds an applicant must hold for the purpose of personal maintenance. Appendix Finance sets out general requirements regarding how these funds must be held and proved. The equivalent criteria for Entrepreneurs are found in Appendix C.

Appendix Finance provides:

- Amounts held in foreign currencies will be converted to pound sterling using the spot exchange rate on www.oanda.com.
- Where funds are held in a financial institution, the institution must be regulated and use electronic record keeping. It must be possible for the decision maker to conduct verification checks.
- Funds earned in the UK must have been acquired lawfully.
- Accounts must be in the name of the applicant, either singly or jointly, unless
    - the account holder is A's partner, who is applying for or already has permission
    - the account holder is A's parent or legal guardian applicant is applying as a dependant child or a Child Student
    - the account holder is a close relative or foster carer, if the applicant is applying as a Child Student
    - the relevant PBS route specifies that third-party accounts are acceptable.
- The account holder must have control of the funds.
- The most recent piece of financial evidence must be dated within 31 days before the application date. Evidence must cover the whole period for which funds must be held.
- It must be possible to access the funds immediately, subject to exceptions for Students benefiting from financial sponsorship or a student loan.

7.8.5 English language

English language requirements can be found in the PBS routes themselves, Appendix English Language, and Appendix B.

Appendix English Language was introduced when the PBS was reformed in late 2020. It applies to the following Appendices:

- Student
- Child Student
- Skilled Workers
- Representatives of an Overseas Business
- T2 Minister of Religion
- T2 Sportsperson
- UK Ancestry

- Start-up
- Innovator

The levels of English proficiency required will be found in the individual PBS route. There are exemptions for those aged 65+ or under 18, or with a disability (physical or mental condition) which prevents them from meeting the requirement. Proficiency can be established via various means set out in the Appendix:

- being a national of a majority English speaking country, or
- for a degree taught in English, or
- for passing an approved English language test (listed in the *Guidance for Secure English Language Tests* (SELT)) at the appropriate level, or
- having met the requirement in a previous grant of leave
- For students at institutions with a track record of compliance, via confirmation on the CAS that their sponsor has assessed their language skills
- For medical professionals who are applying as Skilled Workers, via an assessment by their relevant regulated professional body

7.8.6 Dependant Partners and Children

Most PBS routes allow dependant partners and children of applicants to apply for permission. There is a separate Appendix for Parents of Child Students.

The core requirement for dependants is the 'relationship requirement'. This specifies who is eligible to apply as a dependant partner or child.

Partners must be:

- Married to the principal applicant
- In a civil partnership with the principal applicant
- Living with the principal applicant in a relationship similar to marriage or civil partnership for at least the 2 years prior to the application

Partners must intend to live with the principal applicant in the UK.

Generally, child dependants may be the child of a principal PBS applicant, or a PBS dependant partner. They may not come to the UK as a dependant child if their other parent remains abroad, unless the parent in the UK has sole responsibility for their upbringing or there is some other serious and compelling reason.

Dependants must have sufficient funds, though the requirements are lesser than for principal applicants. Generally:

- Partners must show funds of £285
- Dependant children must show funds of £315 for the first child and £200 for each additional child.

Financial requirements are steeper for dependants of Students – the requirements are set out in Appendix Student.

Dependants will be granted permission ending on the same date as their principal's leave. In the case of child dependants, this will be the date of whichever parent's leave ends first.

Permission will be subject to the normal condition of no access to public funds. However, employment is generally permitted, as is study. Conditions are stricter for dependants of Students, who normally will not be permitted to work.

The following routes allow dependants to apply for settlement:

- Skilled Worker
- Global Talent
- Innovator
- T2 Minister of Religion
- T2 Sportsperson
- Representatives of an Overseas Business

The principal must have, or be applying for, settlement. If a partner, the dependant must have spent 5 years continuous residence in the UK with permission as a dependant partner. Applicants must demonstrate English language ability at B1 level and, if over 18, meet the Knowledge of Life in the UK requirement (see Appendix KoLL).

7.8.7 Curtailment of leave

In addition to the general grounds of refusal that are relevant to all applicants, there were specific grounds for the mandatory or discretionary curtailment (or variation of the duration of) leave granted under the PBS. These were at paragraphs 323A to 323C of the Immigration Rules.

Since 1 December 2020, when the new Part 9 came into force, "curtailment" was renamed "cancellation" and there is no longer one separate paragraphs covering it. Instead, cancellation appears as a subpara under each head of action under rr9.23.1-9.32.1:

- for failing to commence, or for ceasing, work or study
- where the sponsor ceases to hold a sponsor licence, or transfers the business to someone who does not have a licence and who fails to apply for one within 28 days of the date or is refused an appropriate licence
- where the migrant undergoes a prohibited change of employment.

Module 8: European Union Law

8.1 Underlying legal principles, retained and saved free movement law and the EU Settlement Scheme

Despite the UK having left the EU on 31 January 2020 and the Brexit transition period having ended at 11pm on 31 December 2020, most of the legal principles referred to in this module will remain relevant until at least 30 June 2021, the end of the "grace period", and in some respects well beyond that date. To summarise the continuing relevance of the following sections:

1. All of sections 8.1-8.5 in as far as they will assist to determine EEA free movement rights, whose effect is extended until the end of the grace period (and knowledge of which will continue to be relevant to naturalisation of EEA nationals and their family members for years to come)
2. Some of 8.6 on residence rights under the 2016 Regs (eg: to determine past entitlements to permanent residence by A8 nationals)
3. All of 8.8 on Excluding and removing EEA nationals from UK. These principles will continue to be applied to pre-2021 conduct.
4. All of section 8.7 on the EU Settlement Scheme will remain significant well beyond 30 June 2021 as there is no deadline for certain family members to join their sponsors under it. Module 8 may be restructured in due course after 30 June 2021 as the relative importance of its sections changes.
5. Section 8.9 on S2 Healthcare Visitors. Although applicants must have arranged healthcare before the end of transition, and the pool of potential applicants will dwindle, leave can be extended beyond the initial 6 months. Therefore, this section will remain part of this module for the foreseeable future.
6. Section 8.10 on service providers from Switzerland will remain a fixture as 31 December 2025 is the end date for any periods of 90-day leave granted on this route.

Familiarity with the underlying free movement- and other EU rights thus remains a vital competence area for any immigration practitioner. It will be relevant when dealing with a range of cases, not just under the EU Settlement Scheme but also, for example, when determining the lawfulness of a client's last 10 years of residence for good character in naturalisation cases, when dealing with appeal involving free movement rights or rights under the Withdrawal Agreement, or when advising European clients with deportation orders based on conduct committed before the end of the transition period.

So for the time being we are keeping the core structure for, Module 8 whilst ensuring it is up-to-date.

Introduction and current context

European Union (EU) law is sometimes referenced as European Economic Area (EEA) law, as it is to nationals of the EEA (and Switzerland) that the free movement regime applies. Free movement for EEA/Swiss nationals in the UK, and for UK nationals in the EEA/Switzerland ended with the transition period at 11pm on 31 December 2020, but some free movement rights and entitlements have been preserved during the "grace period" until 11pm on 30 June 2021.

The founding purpose of the European Economic Community was to create a common market and guarantee the four freedoms: freedom of goods, capital, services and people. That purpose has been set out in various Treaty and subordinate provisions of EC and EU law since 1957 and is currently found in the Treaty on the Functioning of the European Union (TFEU) and Directive 2004/38/EC, commonly referred to as the Citizens' Directive. These provisions allow EEA nationals and their family members to move freely among Member States to work, and study. The rights are not wholly unrestricted, particularly regarding the ability to secure stay for family members, but they are powerful nonetheless.

In simple terms, EU law on free movement of persons was intended to, and usually did, make it as easy to move from Bilbao to London as it is from Birmingham to London. As such it was the antithesis of immigration control.

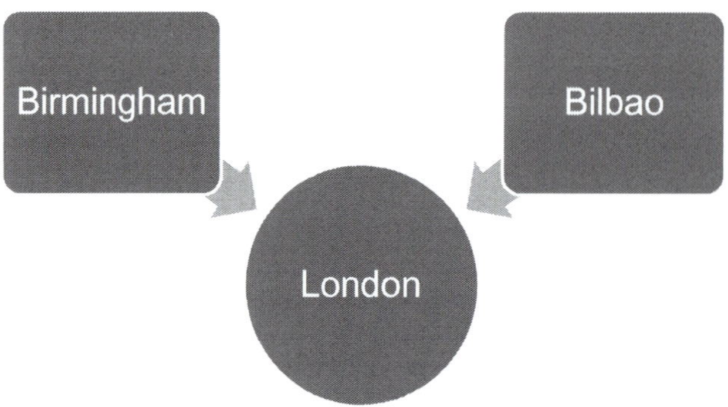

Directive 2004/38/EC of the European Parliament and of the Council of 29 April 2004 on the right of citizens of the Union and their family members to move and reside freely within the territory of the Member States, also referred to as the 'Citizens' Directive' contains the basis for the current rules of free movement within the EU.

Free movement rights also apply to the family members of EEA or Swiss nationals, whether those family members are EEA or Swiss nationals or not. Sometimes those rights would apply in the UK to the non-EEA national family members of UK nationals, where the UK national had exercised their free movement rights elsewhere in the EEA or Switzerland, and had returned to the UK.

As will be seen below, the principal advantage of reliance on EU law rather than UK immigration law was that EU law is designed to encourage movement and UK immigration law to restrict it.

At the end of transition, free movement ended. So we now find ourselves at stage 3 of the **three seminal periods created by Brexit:**

- Pre 31 January 2020: the EU Treaties and the Citizens Directive, largely transposed into UK law via the EEA Regs, regulated free movement rights
- Transition period following the UK's withdrawal from the EU at 11pm on 31 January 2020: the EU Treaties and the Citizens Directive (and EEA Regs) continued to apply, preserved in effect under the Withdrawal Agreement
- Grace period following the end of the transition period at 11pm on 31 December 2020 until 11pm on 30 June 2021: The **Citizens' Rights (Application Deadline and Temporary Protection) (EU Exit) Regulations 2020** (the "Grace Period Regulations") give effect to a Temporary Protection regime. These provide that

    - The Appendix EU regime will end on 30 June 2021 (Reg 2)
    - The period from the end of the transitional period until then (ie 11pm on 31 December 2020 to 30 June 2021) will be a **grace period** and some provisions of the EEA Regs 2016 will remain in force to secure their position (those specified in Regs 5-10, including protections for accessing benefits and public services: Reg 11)
    - So both EEA nationals and their family members living in the UK lawfully under the EEA Regs 2016 since before the end of the transition period are protected - including those who held permanent residence in the five years before 31 December 2020 (Reg 3) (and will not require leave to remain or remain: Reg 12)
    - Those who apply before the application deadline will continue to enjoy the protection of aspects of the EEA Regs 2016 pending their application being determined or any appeal rights being exhausted (Reg 4)
    - The burden of proof as to whether protection arises under the EEA Regs 2016 will be on the applicant (Reg 13)

The domestic law regime for EEA nationals, the EU settled status scheme, has been available throughout these periods. It is an (increasingly pressing) option to take up as the general deadline for applications is 30 June 2021. Thereafter, applications will only be accepted either by family members of existing EU Settlement Scheme status holders and by those upgrading their status, from pre-settled to settled status, or where the Home Office agrees that there were reasonable grounds to apply late. The only alternative for EEA/Swiss citizens and their family members not fitting any of those cases will be the domestic immigration routes.

Free movement rights vs the EU Settlement Scheme

Under EU law, essentially the exercise of Treaty ('*free movement*') Rights generated residence rights; as did the possession of an EU citizenship.

- This might either have been because the principal applicant was an EU national themselves (or a British citizen treated as such due to work in another EEA state). Or a family member might have relied on the EU national, who was in that sense a 'sponsor', to use a popular term from domestic immigration law.
- No application was generally needed to generate the rights, which existed by operation of law for EEA/Swiss nationals exercising treaty rights, and their direct family members, though it would of course normally be essential to physically reach the UK, to show one's status once here. Extended family members, by contrast, did not have such automatic residence rights but only benefited once an exercise of discretion was made in their favour to allow an application for a residence document.
- Over time, many new classes of EU right were identified in the case law of the CJEU, ranging from citizenship-driven rights to different derivative rights.
- The free movement scheme ended with the transition period. However there are some transitional protections flowing from the Withdrawal Agreement, which we address below.

The EUSS scheme (see section 8.7 below) is based on the same EU system. But there are some differences.

- It is a domestic Immigration Rule route and so to benefit, you have to make an application: there are no inherent rights.
- Applicants can be granted settled status (EUSS) or pre-settled status (EUPSS).
- And whilst the same idea of an EEA 'sponsor' for family members is required, the trigger is *not* that person's exercise of Treaty Rights, but simply the fact of residence in the UK. So to that degree it is much more generous than the free movement regime. Anyone who was residing on UK soil, however briefly, by 11pm on 31 December 2020 (which residence was not followed by a 6-month absence), can join the EUSS system.
- The scheme has had numerous amendments, aimed at capturing the development of free movement and citizenship rights. Sometimes these changes have been catching up with decisions from 2006 to the inception of the EUSS; others have been necessitated by case law during the EUSS's existence. By the end of 2020 it was difficult to find people who would have protection under the EEA Regs 2016 who lacked a route into the EUSS. At least if they were aware of the need to do so and properly advised. The Migration Observatory has written reports on the likelihood of individuals not learning of their rights in time: see eg ***Unsettled status***.
- The EUSS scheme has a sunset provision itself. To qualify as a sponsor, one has to have arrived before the end of the transitional period ie before 11pm on 31 December 2020. Or, to join as a family member, have been within (or born from) a relevant relationship that was formed by that date. The general deadline for applications is 30 June 2021 although there are categories of persons who can apply later.

As stated above, the 2016 Regs are saved with modifications during the grace period for EEA and Swiss nationals with pre-TP end UK residence, conferring rights of residence and other entitlements, and the status of clients now and retrospectively in the future will determine other entitlements. Free movement law therefore remains an essential part of a practitioner's knowledge for the remainder of 2020. This module aims to provide you with the comprehensive knowledge that is required.

8.1.1 EEA Member States

The EEA (European Economic Area) is made up of the EU member countries plus Iceland, Norway and Liechtenstein. Switzerland has a bilateral agreement with the EU adding it to the free movement regime. Nationals of all 31 countries enjoy free movement around the EEA and Switzerland.

The EU member states are:

Austria
Belgium
Bulgaria
Croatia
Cyprus
Czechia
Denmark
Estonia
Finland
France
Germany
Greece
Hungary
Ireland
Italy
Latvia
Lithuania
Luxembourg
Malta
Netherlands
Poland
Portugal
Romania
Slovakia
Slovenia
Spain
Sweden

It is important to remember that free movement rights are enjoyed by those moving or who have moved within the EEA or Switzerland, so will not normally be enjoyed by nationals of a country in whose territory they remain(even if they are dual nationals of another of the other countries, see 8.3.2 on 'dual nationals' below).

It should be noted that Croatian nationals from 1 July 2018,have had the same full free movement rights as all other EEA and Swiss nationals.

8.1.2 Interaction of UK and EU law

8.1.2.1 Rights not privileges

There is a very important difference of principle between UK immigration law and EU freedom of movement rights. In UK law, if a foreign national wishes to come to the UK, they must first make an application and await a positive decision. There is no pre-existing 'right' to enter the UK. Entry and stay in the UK is contingent on it being permitted by the Secretary of State: see section 1(2) of the Immigration Act 1971.

The position was very different under EU law. Certain individuals had a right to reside in the UK by virtue of their citizenship of another EEA country and their economic activities, or through their family relationship with such a person. The UK was bound by EU law to recognise and promote this right.

A great deal flowed from this distinction between inherent rights and discretionary privileges, and for those schooled in UK immigration law many aspects of EEA free movement law always seemed counterintuitive. The fact that family permit applications are free, that EEA documents (i.e. family permits and residence documents) were unnecessary for the exercise of free movement rights, and that Immigration Officers could not stamp the passports of EEA nationals were all natural consequences of the nature of pre-existing free movement rights in EU law.

The Immigration (European Economic Area) Regulations 2016 (now saved with modifications) contain further amendments, more restrictive than previously in place. We call them EEA Regs 2016 for convenience. These repealed and replaced the 2006 Regulations on 1 February 2017.

The Home Office require rather a lot of evidence before they are satisfied that EU rights are established, often more than was permissible under the Directive.

Those refused EEA entry and residence documents may still have a right of appeal to the First Tier Tribunal, whereas EU Settlement Scheme refusals of applications made from 1 February 2020 will attract a right to an administrative review *as well as* a right of appeal (applications lodged before that date attracted only a right to an administrative review.

8.1.2.2 Legal and procedural framework for EEA free movement law

When dealing with EEA applications and appeals, it was essential to consult the relevant sources of law and policy bearing in mind the above regarding the interplay between EU law, UK law and UK policy. For our purposes at OISC level 1, we will usually refer just to the EEA Regs.

- Immigration (European Economic Area) Regulations 2016 (check also for amendments as this free resource does not incorporate them). NB: for their current application, the duration of the grace period, the Regs are saved from the version immediately applicable before the end of transition (that consolidated version being available in the OISC exam resource **booklet** December 2020) with modifications for EEA/Swiss nationals resident lawfully since before the end of transition. The savings and modifications are found in the **Grace Period Regs**.
- EEA Immigration Staff Guidance
- EEA case law, summarised by UKVI: EEA Immigration Staff Guidance: EEA case law and appeals and available via other free case law sources, such as Bailii and UT decisions
- Citizens' Directive 2004/38
- Consolidated Version of the Treaty on the Functioning of the European Union (TFEU)

NB: we list free sources only here, but where legal subscription databases are available, these do have the great advantage of providing consolidated versions and should be used instead.

It is important to realise that where the EEA Regs (or UKVI guidance) were more restrictive than the principles they supposedly enshrined, then it would be the original EU version which will triumph. Any limitation on a general principle of EU law must be construed narrowly: Brey [2013] EUECJ C-140/12. The other side of the coin is that the UK's implementation of EEA law might occasionally be more generous than that of the EU. The EU does not prohibit a more generous approach than its own provisions.

Similar principles now apply in the relationship between the law on the EU Settlement Scheme which is intended to implement the Withdrawal Agreement; i.e. provisions in Appendix EU or its accompanying guidance which are stricter than the Withdrawal Agreement may be open to challenge (by a suitable accredited adviser) on that ground.

8.1.2.3 EU law: general principles and fundamental rights

The EU Charter of Fundamental Rights became part of the EU Treaties on 1 December 2009. The Charter contains rights that often equate to rights found in the European Convention on Human Rights, and some additional ones. The Charter is outside the OISC 1 curriculum. However, do note that the Charter itself does not form part of retained EU law for the UK, so its provisions can no longer be argued in cases, but UK courts may still have regard to some CJEU case law which may refer to its principles.

There are also general principles of European Union law: for example, the right to good administration and the proportionality principle.

8.2 Who benefited from EU rights?

It was the exercise or engagement of Treaty rights which underpinned EEA residence rights. Here are the main scenarios:

- an EEA national (and their family members) were themselves exercising Treaty rights giving a right to residence or permanent residence
- the EEA national enjoyed the right to EU citizenship (Article 20 of the Treaty).

These rights are found in the EEA Regs. We deal with each in significantly more detail later on, but for now it is useful to have an overview of the main categories.

8.2.1 Residence rights in summary

8.2.1.1 Residence rights under the Citizens Directive and the Immigration (EEA) Regulations 2016

This section provides only a brief outline of these rights, which are set out in detail in section 8.6. For the application in practice of 'settled status' or 'ILR under Appendix EU', and a comparison with the Regs, please refer to section 8.7.

The rights of residence under the Directive and the Regs were as follows:

Qualified persons and their family members – "extended" rights of residence – Reg 14

- as a person who was *economically active* as a jobseeker, worker or providing services, or who was *studying or self sufficient* (all 'qualified persons' as set out at Reg 6)
- those individuals had the right to enjoy the presence of various relatives such as *family members* their spouses and dependent children and relatives in the ascending line as of right (Reg 7), though students only had the right to have their spouses and dependent children here; and
- they had the right to have a discretionary consideration of whether their *extended family members* (unmarried partners, more remote dependent relatives who have been dependent or cohabiting with them in the past and present, and a person for whom the care of the EEA national is essential) should be allowed to reside with them here (Reg 8)

Permanent residents and their family members – Reg 15

- as a person who *was* present in one of those capacities but who gained *permanent residence* after five years' exercise of Treaty rights (Reg 15(1)(a)) or because they *ceased activity* in relevant circumstances (Reg 15(1)(c) read with Reg 5)
- as the family member of a person who had themselves *lived here for five years under the EEA Regs*, either consistently as the family member of a qualified person or down to a combination of entitlements, e.g. family membership followed by retaining a right of residence, who thus gained *permanent residence* (Reg 15(1)(b) and (f))

Further notes/information

The areas of retained- and derivative rights are outside OISC 1 scope and not part of its exam curriculum. The information in this box is provided to assist you in spotting and summarising these cases for referral.

Retained rights of residence – Reg 10

- as the family member of a person of an EEA national *worker or self-employed person* residing with them when they died, the EEA national having previously resided here for two years or dying because of an accident at work or occupational disease, who thus gained *permanent residence* (Reg 15(1)(e))

- as the *child of a person formerly exercising Treaty rights*, and as the primary carer of such a child
- as a person who has *retained a right of residence* because he or she *was* the family member of an EEA national who *was* economically active as a jobseeker, worker or providing services, or who was studying or self sufficient, or who was permanently resident here, specifically as the child who was in education when their EEA parent died or left the UK and their primary carer (Reg 10(3), (4))
- as the family member who had resided here for the year prior to the death of an EEA national who was a qualified person or who had permanent residence (Reg 10(2))
- as the spouse/civil partner whose marriage/partnership was terminated subject to it having endured three years' including a year of residence here, or had custody or access rights to their child, or whose relationship ended in particularly difficult circumstances including domestic violence (Reg 10(5))

Derivative rights of residence – Reg 16

- as a person who *enjoyed European citizenship*, the benefits of which they *could not be compelled to lose* – these people enjoyed the right to reside and to be accompanied by their primary carer, for example where they are self sufficient here (as in the Chen case, addressed domestically in Reg 16(2)) or when the departure of their primary carer would compel their own departure from the European Union and thus nullify their EU citizenship rights (as in the Zambrano case, whose primary carers are addressed domestically in Reg 16(5)
- as the primary carer ofa child of an EEA national in education, as in the **Ibrahim** and **Teixeira** cases, addressed domestically in Reg 16)

8.2.1.2 Residence rights found in the Treaty but not in the Citizens Directive – in summary

Family members of frontier workers

- as the family member of an EU national who is exercising the Article 56 Treaty right of freedom to provide cross-border services, which 'could not be fully effective if [he was] deterred from exercising it by obstacles raised in his country of origin to the entry and residence of his spouse' (Carpenter [2002] EUECJ C-60/00)
- **The Citizens' Rights (Frontier Workers) (EU Exit) Regulations 2020** provide for EEA nationals who, by 31 December 2020, are working or self-employed in the UK but living elsewhere (ie not primarily resident here) to continue to work in the UK for as long as they remain a frontier worker. They also provide for the restriction of those rights and establish a scheme for frontier worker permits.
- those Regs essentially replicate the regime familiar from the EEA Regs 2016 for EEA citizens generally to cater for the particular situation of frontier workers: they contain provisions for admission and protections against expulsion, and for retaining frontier worker status
- Guidance **Frontier workers in the UK: rights and status** deals with the situation before and after the transition period.

Further notes/information

The Surinder Singh and posted worker categories are outside OISC 1 scope and not part of its exam curriculum. The information in this box is provided to assist you in spotting and summarising these cases for referral.

Surinder Singh

- as the family member of an EU national who is exercising the Article 45 Treaty right of freedom of movement for workers, who must be given a *derivative right of residence* if the worker would otherwise be discouraged from effective exercise of their rights (Surinder Singh (C-370/90; [1992] ECR I-4265); S v Minister voor Immigratie [2014] EUECJ C-457/12)
  - as the family member of an EU national where the relevant family life was created or strengthened during genuine residence in the host Member State following the exercise of free movement rights, where the worker now wished that family member to accompany them on return to their EU state of origin (O v Minister voor Immigratie [2014] EUECJ C-456/12

Posted workers

- as the third country (i.e. non-EEA) national employee of a company (in EU legal language, as the *posted worker* of a relevant *undertaking*) established in another Member State exercising the Article 56 Treaty right of freedom to provide services, where they are lawfully and habitually employed in another Member State, will not take other employment in the UK and will leave the country at the end of their posting (Vander Elst v Office des Migrations Internationales [1994] EUECJ C-43/93), given grudging acceptance by the guidance *Non-EEA and Swiss nationals working in the EU (Van der Elst and Swiss posted workers* and entry clearance guidance **Non-EEA and Swiss nationals working in the EU: EUN04**.

8.2.2 Exercising Treaty rights

The term 'exercising Treaty rights' will often be inadequate to accurately define the rights and status of an EEA national or family member. A person exercising Treaty rights will have had a right of admission, an initial right to reside, and an extended right to reside; or a right to permanent residence. Each type of status had different requirements and may give rise to different rights at different times. We will address these in more detail later on, but to give a flavour of them now, the EEA Regs provided:

- There was an unconditional right of admission (Reg 11) and residence for an initial period of three months (Reg 13) for all EEA nationals and their family members. Note that the right of admission is one of the rights which are saved for EEA/Swiss nationals resident before TP end and their family members in modified and restricted form only during the grace period (see section 8.6.1).
- There was then an extended right to reside (Reg 14) thereafter for students and those who have entered the UK to seek work, who are economically active as workers or self-employed, or the self-sufficient - this right endured for so long as the criteria which gave rise to it are satisfied
- Those who have had a continuous right to reside for 5 years (and some others, e.g retired workers under Reg 5) will be permanently resident (Reg 15). Permanent residence provides a right to reside in itself (i.e. the person no longer needs to be a qualified person – thus Reg 15 beneficiaries are dealt with separately to qualified persons throughout the EEA Regs). Permanent residence can only be lost by an absence from the UK for a continuous period of two years or exclusion. The right of permanent residence will remain effective for the rest of the grace period only as the effect of the 2016 Regs is only saved until 30 June 2021.

8.2.3 Qualified persons and family members

Leaving aside the relatively unusual exercise of Treaty rights beyond the Citizens Directive, the main characters in the EU law story were:

- **qualified persons**, i.e. the EEA nationals themselves when engaged in the relevant forms of economic activity set out in Reg 6, i.e:
    - a jobseeker (Reg 6(1)(a));
    - a worker (Reg 6(1)(b));
    - a self-employed person (Reg 6(1)(c));
    - a self-sufficient person (Reg 6(1)(d)); or
    - a student (Reg 6(1)(e))
- their **family members** (defined in Reg 7)
- their **extended/other family members** ("extended" as called in the Reg 8; "other" as referenced in the Citizens' Directive).

8.2.4 Qualified persons and other EEA national beneficiaries

The gateway to most forms of residence under the EEA Regs based on free movement rights were owed to those who meet the definition of being 'qualified persons'. The definitions were set out at Regs 4 and 6.

8.2.4.1 Jobseekers

A jobseeker was defined in Reg 6. This used to be a straightforward provision to read and interpret because it simply asked whether a person was seeking work and assessed whether they had a reasonable chance of obtaining it. However, as the government policy has increasingly aimed to prevent access to benefits for those who have not worked, or were not working, various extra provisions were added, of which the central one was the reference to the 'relevant period', defined differently for jobseekers and out-of-work workers: 91 days for the former, six months for the latter. For a jobseeker to remain as such for longer than the 91 day period, it was necessary to show not merely that a person was 'seeking employment and has a genuine chance of being engaged', but rather that they could provide 'compelling evidence' of those requirements (Reg 6(7)).

- A jobseeker was defined as a person who entered the United Kingdom in order to seek employment, or a person who was seeking employment following a period of residence in the UK in one of the other categories of qualified person (Reg 6(4) onwards)
- To establish a right to reside as a jobseeker, the person had to either have entered the country to look for work or have been present in another category of qualified person (e.g. as a student), and be able to provide evidence that they were seeking employment and had a genuine chance of being engaged (Reg 6(6)). They could remain a jobseeker for no longer than 91 days (Reg 6(8)), subject to Reg 6(7).
- A person could remain a jobseeker for no longer than 91 days total, unless they had been absent for 12 months or more since the last period of job seeking (Reg 6(8))) The 2016 Reg made express provision for the same in Reg 6(1)

- After 91 days, they would lose their right to reside as a jobseeker unless they were able to show '*compelling* evidence that they are continuing to seek employment and have a genuine chance of being engaged' (Reg 6(7))
- If the jobseeker left the UK at the end of the 91 day period, they would not be able to return as a job-seeker within 12 months of having left unless they could meet the 'compelling evidence' test (Reg 6(9))
- If they left the country before they had exhausted their 91 days of job-seeking, they would have a right to reside as a job-seeker on return for the remainder of the 91 days: this discounted period lapses after one year (Reg 6(8)(b)).

Note the specific provisions on *workers* who were between jobs, who were subject to a less stringent regime, as opposed to *jobseekers* (see the next section, on workers, below).

Other points to bear in mind:

The EEA Regs were only the starting point as we are here discussing the implementation of Treaty rights: whilst the Citizens' Directive does not address the definition of 'jobseeker', case law did so. It decided in summary, that the period must be a 'reasonable period' and the assessment of what is 'reasonable' must be made in the context of each individual case. Thus, it may sometimes be less, sometimes more, than six months.

An EEA national jobseeker coming to the UK to look for work cannot, under the benefits regulations, claim out of work benefits for the first three months of residence in the UK. But they will be able to do so for the following 91 days (and for longer if they meet the 'compelling evidence' test). To that extent those coming to the UK to look for work will in fact have a right to reside whilst looking for work for six months (or longer).

What is *compelling evidence of seeking employment and having a genuine chance of being engaged*?

- the individual's intentions when entering the UK
- their job seeking history vis-à-vis the labour market (and the quality of their evidence of that)
- and their chances of getting employment reside as a jobseeker

Example

Pierre enters the UK to look for work. He has no job offers lined up.

Pierre is a jobseeker (Reg 6(1)(b)). He retains this status if he does not find work for 91 days (minus any period in which he has previously been present in the UK as a jobseeker without finding work) (Reg 6(1)(b)),

8.2.4.2 Workers

Important aspects of EEA 'worker' status include:

- the modest level of activities to be established to show that one is a worker
- the retention of worker status during certain periods of unemployment/inactivity
- the fact that there was no minimum period an EEA citizen had to work in order to be a worker, though employment for more than one year brings a stronger presumption under the EEA Regs that they retain that status notwithstanding temporary inactivity
- access to permanent residence where work ceases in certain circumstances

Level of activities to be a worker?

The definition is very broad indeed. The work need not be well paid nor full time so long as it is *effective and genuine* and *not marginal or ancillary*. On this basis a part-time music teacher giving 12 lessons a week topped up with Dutch Social Security payments was a worker for Community purposes and entitled to a residence permit even if he was also receiving public funds .The Immigration Staff Guidance states though that, "a student who gets a job behind the student union bar for two hours a week is actually a student, their work is marginal and supplementary to their actual role as a student."

The guidance required the decision maker to assess each case on its own merits to see whether the claimed employment was genuine and effective. Relevant considerations included:

- was there a genuine employer-employee relationship
- was the work regular or intermittent
- how long had the EEA national been employed for
- number of hours worked
- level of earnings.

If the work fell to be so defined it did not matter if the individual had to claim social assistance to top up their earnings. The guidance indicated the HO would make further enquiries of those earning below the HMRC's Primary Earnings Threshold (currently £162 per week) to assess whether the work was genuine and effective. An EEA national doing unpaid charitable work did not qualify as a worker but could be considered to be self-sufficient (see below). Those participating in the commercial activities of the charity and who had their living expenses and accommodation provided could be considered to be workers.

Compliance with the requirement to pay tax and NI is a domestic matter for the UK authorities and failure to comply does not stop an EEA national from qualifying as a worker. However, the guidance advised that non-compliance may indicate that the EEA national is in 'marginal and ancillary' employment. This could not be the sole basis for deciding that the EEA national was not exercising treaty rights as a worker, but was a factor which could be taken into consideration when making this assessment. A non-compliant worker would be reported to the HMRC.

In a similar way, rough-sleeping did not automatically stop someone from being a qualified person, but would be a relevant consideration.

Regulation (EU) 492/2011 on freedom of movement for workers within the Union sets out at Article 7 that

- workers may not be treated differently due to nationality regarding conditions of work and employment,
- workers shall enjoy the same social and tax advantages, and access to training in vocational schools and retraining centres, as national workers.

Example

Jose is a Spanish national present in the UK studying since 2013. He has worked for around 15 hours a week during term time, and longer hours in the holiday. He comes to see you to see if he has a claim for permanent residence; he is worried as he did not hold sickness insurance over this period.

As he did not hold sickness insurance his claim as a student is likely to fail: Reg 4(1)(d)(i). Jose has worked for a sufficient extent that he may well have established permanent residence as a worker. He need not be a full time worker so long as his work is 'genuine and effective': the SSHD treats the national insurance contributions level as the figure.

Maintaining worker status

A person could keep their worker status notwithstanding the following:

- Temporary inability to work owing to illness or accident (Reg 6(2)(a)) – for these purposes 'temporary' meant any non-permanent absence from work, see FMB (EEA reg 6(2)(a) – 'temporarily unable to work') Uganda [2010] UKUT 447 (IAC)
- That they were in 'duly recorded involuntary unemployment' and were registered as a jobseeker (Reg 6(2)(b)(i) & (c)(i)) (note that a person needed not show 'undue delay' in registering as such, see e.g. VP v Secretary for Works and Pensions (JSA) [2014] UKUT 32 (AAC))):

If employed here for more than a year, Reg 6(2)(b) applied and they could retain worker status:

- for six months provided the person provided *evidence of seeking employment and having a genuine chance of being engaged* (Reg 6(6)).
- after six months only if they could provide *compelling evidence* of seeking employment with a genuine chance of being engaged (Reg 6(7)(a)).

If employed here for less than a year, Reg 6(2)(c) applied and they could retain worker status only for a maximum of six months (Reg 6(3)), and only if the person provided *evidence of seeking employment and having a genuine chance of being engaged* (Reg 6(6))

However, do not forget that the important point made above where the CJEU found in summary, that the period must be a 'reasonable period' and the assessment of what is 'reasonable' must be made in the context of each individual case. Thus, it may sometimes be less, sometimes more, than six months.

Example

Pierre finds work as a bank clerk. He is not kept on after a 6 month probation period. He is worried about what status he has.

Pierre is a worker whilst working (Reg 6(1)(a)). Then as a person who is no longer working he has to go down one of the two avenues in Reg 6(2)(b) and (c): as he has been working for less than a year, this is Reg 6(2)(c). He then has to fulfil the three requirements therein: registering as a job seeker and fulfilling the cross-referenced conditions A and B, i.e. that

- he entered the UK to seek work or that he has worked during his time here, and

- provides evidence of seeking employment and a genuine chance of being engaged

Evidence that a person was seeking employment and had a genuine chance of being engaged could be provided in the form of:

- a letter from their former employer confirming the dates they were employed and that their unemployment was involuntary
- a letter from Jobcentre Plus or a recruitment agency confirming they had registered with them
- proof they are seeking work

Embarking on vocational training – if unemployment was voluntary then this must be related to the previous employment (Reg 6(2)(e)); if involuntary, then it could be of any kind (Reg 6(2)(d)).

Courses mandated by the DWP to assist a person in finding employment are vocational (and would thus qualify under Reg 6(2)(c) and (d) vis-á-vis the various forms of vocational training which do not cease worker status.

A special case – mothers and maternity leave

There is at least one class of worker who is not clearly catered for in the Citizens Directive: working mothers who take a career break for childbirth. This has been recognised in the case of *Saint Prix*: A mother:

1. leaving a job (or stopping actively seeking employment)
2. because of the physical constraints of the late stages of pregnancy and the (reasonably assessed) aftermath of childbirth,
3. provided she returns to work within a reasonable period of childbirth,
4. retains worker status

The thinking of the CJEU shows that there may be other scenarios where a migrant worker who is no longer in an employment relationship may nevertheless continue to benefit from that status.

Example

Laura is from Italy. Her husband Mohamad is from Pakistan. Laura works in the UK from January 2007 to April 2011. They have a child, Lynda, who is born in June 2011. Laura leaves work to care for her. She returns to work in April 2012.

Laura has stopped working for a significant period. The only protection that could apply to her is that identified by the Case Law in *Saint Prix*. ***Saint Prix* is one of those rare cases which basically create a class of residence right and so should have the same status as the EEA regulations.**

She will need to establish that she returned to work within a reasonable period of childbirth – it would be a good idea to explain precisely why she returned to work when she did. So long as this is accepted, she and Mohamad will be eligible for residence cards attesting to her being a worker and him being her family member throughout their stay, and they will attain permanent residence five years after her arrival in January 2007.

Even if she does not start work on arrival, the time for calculating permanent residence will still run from entry so long as she entered the country as a job seeker with real prospects of finding work after entering the country, see Regs 6(1)(a), 6(5)-(8).

Ceasing activities as a worker as a gateway to permanent residence

A worker or self-employed person became permanently resident under Reg 15(1)(c) if he or she ceased activity in one of the following circumstances (as specified in Reg 5):

- Retirement, if resident in the UK for at least three years and working for at least a year prior to retirement and having reached state retirement age or having taken early retirement if a worker: Reg 5(2)Permanent incapacity to work, if resident in the UK for at least two years immediately prior to this incapacity and the incapacity is the result of an accident at work or an occupational disease that entitles him or her to a pension payable in full or in part by an institution in the United Kingdom: Reg 5(3) (amended by EEA Regs 2019)
- Resident in the UK as a worker or self-employed person for at least three years and has retained a place of residence, to which he or she returns as a rule at least once a week: Reg 5(4), but also see Reg 5(5) which stated that prior residence in the UK is not necessary to benefit from this provision

In addition, Reg 5(6) stated that the above rules on periods of residence and activity do not apply where the person is married to or the civil partner of a UK national.

Example

Pierre has worked for his employer in the UK since arriving here four years ago. He has just retired aged 55.

Pierre has a claim to permanent residence as a person who has ceased working. He has lived and worked in the UK for more than three years and one year respectively and has taken early retirement in a context in which he was a 'worker'; so he satisfies the requirements of Reg 5(2) and thus the requirements for permanent residence for such a person under Reg 15(1)(c).

Had Pierre been married to a British citizen during his residence here would that have had any impact on his rights?

Not on the facts given; however, had he lived here for a shorter period before retirement that might have helped him, having a British citizen spouse would remove the requirements for particular periods of working: see Reg 5(6).

Would Pierre's situation have been different if he had stopped working not due to recent retirement but because of an accident in the kitchen where he worked?

Not materially: now he would satisfy the requirements of Reg 5(3) and thus the requirements for permanent residence for such a person under Reg 15(1)(c).

8.2.4.3 Self-employed persons

Those who wished to set themselves up in business or become self-employed (Article 43 TFEU) and to provide or receive services (Article 49 TFEU) had the right to move between EEA Member States to do so.

- Generally, the self-employed had the same rights as the employed: usually the EEA Regs recognised rights for 'a worker or self-employed person': occasionally a right was only recognised for workers, though, as with early retirement (Reg 5(2)(a)(ii))
- Self-employed persons who ceased activity enjoyed very similar subsequent access to permanent residence as did workers, as described above (Reg 5 read with Reg 15(1)(c), (d) and (e)). We address the test for self-employment under *Rights of Establishment* when we address the Ankara Agreement below.
- Because of the similarity of treatment of the employed and the self-employed, the distinction between them did not really matter when assessing the rights of EEA nationals and their family members: one area where it tended to assume importance is under the Turkish Association Agreement, which gave better rights of establishment to the self-employed than to the employed (who needed to establish lawful presence before they may start working)
- Self-employed status could be generated by a level of activity which was genuine and effective, whether or not it was full-time, by analogy to the approach taken to whether someone was working
- The Immigration Staff Guidance stated that 'marginal activity' (i.e. that which is not genuine and effective) was that which involves so little time and money as to be largely irrelevant to the lifestyle of the EEA national. It was supplementary because in this situation the EEA national was clearly spending most of their time on something else, not the self-employed activity. See more on this in the section on *Workers*, above.

Retention of self-employed status

The self employed are now recognised as owed the same protection as workers when it comes to periods out of work, so long as they have registered appropriately as a jobseeker: Reg 6(4).The Immigration Staff Guidance explained that reasonable evidence of self-employment may include:

- proof of registration for tax and National Insurance (NI) purposes with HMRC (e.g. letter of self-employed status or letter confirming payment of tax and NI contributions
- invoices for work done
- a copy of their business accounts
- an accountant's letter
- leases on business premises (if applicable)
- advertisements for their business
- business bank statements.

Any evidence submitted must be dated no more than six months before the application date.

8.2.4.4 Self-sufficient persons

The self-sufficient were qualified persons (Reg 6(1)(d)) and thus enjoyed the extended right of residence, leading to permanent residence after five years, for as long as they could show that

- they had sufficient funds not to become dependent on benefits and
- they had comprehensive private health insurance (Reg 4(1)(c): we address the requirements for this more specifically below, as it was also required by students).

Example

Artis is a French national present in the UK as the spouse of a British citizen. She has not worked or studied during her time here. She and her husband live off his pension and claim no benefits. She is covered by his sickness insurance.

Artis has a good case to be treated as a 'self-sufficient' person. She has the relevant health insurance and claims no public funds. One would need to check whether his pension exceeds the maximum level of resources before they would be entitled to social assistance: Reg 4(4)(a).

8.2.4.5 Students

EEA national students enjoyed a much more relaxed regime than third country nationals studying in the UK, as they could avoid the requirements for an educational sponsor and the set maintenance thresholds under Tier 4 of the PBS. Those seeking to enter another Member State solely for the purposes of study had to

- be enrolled at a relevant education establishment (not any college: it must have been either be accredited or financed from public funds: see the Home Office Guidance on *Qualified persons* which interprets 'accredited' as established by an endorsement from any educational regulatory body or by appearing on particular databases) for the principal purpose of following a vocational training course, and
- provide an assurance, in the form of a declaration or such like, that they were economically self-sufficient – if such an assurance is provided admission is unrestricted and there is no requirement to demonstrate means through the production of objective evidence (Reg 4(1)(d)(iii))
- have comprehensive sickness insurance cover (Reg 4(1)(d)(ii)) (we address CSIC as a generic requirement of EEA cases, below). Note that the requirement for CSIC for students was not a straightforward one).

Other features of residence as an EEA student are that:

- they could be joined by more limited family members than was the case with other qualified persons (see further below when we address *family members*)
- there could be no restriction on the student working in the UK so long as such work did not undermine the essential 'principal purpose of following a course of study' in Reg 4 (contrast the tight controls on students under the Student Appendices or, before that, Tier 4)
- EEA students studying in the UK could apply for loans to pay tuition fees and other forms of student support in some circumstances. The rules differed depending on whether the person was studying in England, Wales, Scotland or Northern Ireland. Detailed information is provided on the UKCISA
- students, whose rights were somewhat restricted under the Directive (e.g. on being joined by family members and requiring comprehensive sickness insurance cover), might also be workers or self-sufficient people and so benefit from the more generous rights afforded such persons (Reg 7(2)(a))

8.3 British citizens who benefit from free movement rights

As discussed earlier, the rights of EEA nationals to reside with their families are often stronger than those of British citizens. In some circumstances a British citizen residing in the UK can be treated as an EEA national by exercising their Treaty rights of free movement. One example of this is by going to work in another Member State and then returning to the UK.

8.3.1 British citizens exercising Treaty rights/Surinder Singh Route

Further notes/information

The *Surinder Singh* category is outside OISC 1 scope and not part of its exam curriculum. The information in this box is provided to assist you in spotting and summarising these cases for referral.

EU/EEA citizens always had the right to be joined in any country other than their own under EU Law. It was recognized that a person may not chose to exercise the right to move for a job, for example, if they could not take a family member with them. Or if, having lived abroad for a sustained period, they could not return to the UK with a new partner.

The central question which the CJEU poses in these cases is whether the exercise of Treaty rights might have been discouraged absent the ability to bring back a family member with whom one created or strengthened family life during one's residence abroad.

It was found in the judgement of *Surinder Singh*, that in order to give full effect to the right of an EU/EEA citizen to move from one member state to another, it was necessary to include the right for non-EEA family members to return to the home country with the EU/EEA citizen.

Reg 9 reproduced the SSHD's interpretation of *Surinder Singh*_into domestic law, and the EU Settlement Scheme cross-refers to its provisions. For OISC level 1 purposes we can treat this as correct, though we should always bear in mind the chance that a client's circumstances would fall within *Surinder Singh* thinking but not within Reg 9. Essentially Reg 9 requires

- the exercise of Treaty rights abroad
- over a period where the British citizen and family member resided together
- where that residence was 'genuine'
- having regard to whether the family member was part of the family throughout the whole of the residence abroad, and to whether family life was created or strengthened during residence there

Relevant considerations in assessing 'genuineness' are

- length of joint residence abroad
- the kind of accommodation abroad and whether it was the principal residence of the British citizen
- the degree of integration abroad
- whether this was the first principal residence
- whether the purpose of the exercise was to circumvent UK immigration controls

8.3.2 Dual (British and EEA) nationals

Though it was at one time thought that British citizens living in the UK who also held the nationality of

another Member State could benefit from the same free movement rights as EEA nationals who had moved here, that notion was dispelled by McCarthy v United Kingdom Case C-434/09. *McCarthy* ruled that dual nationals living in either country of their nationality but who had never exercised free movement rights could rely on neither the Citizens' Directive nor on Article 21 TFEU.

Transitional provisions existed for family members of dual EEA/British citizens who were residing in the UK on 16 July 2012, or had applied for residence documentation before that date, and who also held (or had applied for) a valid EEA residence document confirming this right on or before 16 October 2012. These are maintained in the saved provisions of the 2016 Regs without modifications, and are found at Schedule 6, para 9.

The ECJ in Lounes C-165/16 decided on 14 November 2017 that EU citizens who have naturalised as British citizens after moving to the UK keep their free movement rights, not under the Citizens Directive 2004/38 but Art 21 TFEU, and Reg 9A was introduced which sets out, essentially, that those who became British after exercising treaty rights could continue to be treated as EEA nationals in relation to sponsoring family members

8.4 Family members of qualified persons

8.4.1 Direct family members

Family members were defined at Reg 7 (consistently with Article 2.2 of the Citizens' Directive,and saved without modification for the grace period in respect of EEA/Swiss nationals resident lawfully before the end of transition, and their family members) thus:

> (1) Subject to paragraph (2), for the purposes of these Regulations the following persons shall be treated as the family members of another person—
> (a) his spouse or his civil partner;
> (b) direct descendants of his, his spouse or his civil partner who are—
> (i) under 21; or
> (ii) dependants of his, his spouse or his civil partner;
> (c) dependent direct relatives in his ascending line or that of his spouse or his civil partner;

8.4.2 Extended family members

Regulation 8 sets these out as follows:

> (2) The condition in this paragraph is that the person is–
> (a) a relative of an EEA national; and
> (b) residing in a country other than the United Kingdom and is dependent upon the EEA national or is a member of the EEA national's household; and either–
> (i) is accompanying the EEA national to the United Kingdom or wants to join the EEA national in the United Kingdom; or
> (ii) has joined the EEA national in the United Kingdom and continues to be dependent upon the EEA national, or to be a member of the EEA national's household.
> (3) The condition in this paragraph is that the person is a relative of an EEA national and on serious health grounds, strictly requires the personal care of the EEA national or the spouse or civil partner of the EEA national.
> (4) The condition in this paragraph is that the person is a relative of an EEA national and would meet the requirements in the immigration rules (other than those relating to entry clearance) for indefinite leave to enter or remain in the United Kingdom as a dependent relative of the EEA national.
> (5) The condition in this paragraph is that the person is the partner (other than a civil partner) of, and in a durable relationship with, an EEA national or the child (under the age of 18) of that partner, and is able to prove this to the decision maker.

A 5th route was added via Reg 8(1A) to reflect the CJEU decision in SM [2019] EUECJ C-129/18. This addressed the Islamic system of Kafala adoptions used in countries including Algeria, which do not carry all the legal implications of other systems of adoption.

There was no limit on the distance of the relationship between the EEA national and the extended family member as long as they could provide valid proof of the relationship between them.

Being an extended family member was a gateway to receiving residence rights.

Note that dependent relatives who do not hold an EEA or EUSS residence card in that capacity, since 1 January 2021 can no longer to apply to join their extended family members. Durable partners, however, still can.

8.4.2.1 Partner of an EEA national in a durable relationship

This proviso was the EEA equivalent of the unmarried partner route under the Immigration Rules.

Further notes/information

Complex cases, including those in which legal arguments must be made and fact-specific evidence must be provided, are outside OISC 1 scope and not part of its exam curriculum. The information in this box is provided to assist you in spotting and summarising these cases for referral.

- There is no European Union law definition of 'durable' so each case had to be looked at on its own facts. In YB [2008] UKAIT 00062, the Tribunal held that national law must not seek to define Community law terms and it would be wrong to equate this concept with '*living together in a relationship akin to marriage which has subsisted for two years or more*'.
- However the Home Office intermittently applied a rule of thumb of two years' cohabitation: the Guidance *Extended family members* did recognise 'If there is less than two years evidence, you can still accept this where there is evidence the relationship is durable'.
- A relationship could be durable whether or not it had entailed cohabitation (Dauhoo [2012] UKUT 79 at 19), though it would be very difficult indeed to make out durability where there has been no cohabitation.
- The 2016 Regs provided in Reg 2 that the definition of durable partner did not include a durable partner of convenience. We discuss the definition below where we address marriages of convenience.

The EEA Amendment Regs 2019 included the children of durable partners as extended family members. NB the subsequent version of Regulation 8 required an extensive examination of the best interests of the applicant, particularly if a child, as well as of the applicant's character and conduct.
Whilst not binding in UK law, the Supreme Court of Ireland's decision in Pervaiz [2020] IESC 27 is interesting its approach to durable relationships. The court opined that

- such relationships will typically be committed ones which have continued for some time and where each party would hope for it to continue for the foreseeable future.
- A committed relationship might exist between persons who had known one another for a short time, and so whilst lengthy duration might be an important factor it was not always essential.
- Decision makers could reasonably expect to see a relationship showing evidence of permanence and commitment, the couple being connected to one another by a number of identifiable threads, such as their social life and social network, finances and living arrangements, all of which would usually be recognised and acknowledged by their circle of family and friends.

8.5 Generic concepts: dependency, prior lawful residence and comprehensive sickness insurance

8.5.1 Dependency in EU law

A number of EEA family members had to establish dependency before satisfying the requirements of the EEA Regs: this applied both to direct and extended family members.

Direct family members are sometimes such as of right, as with children aged under 21 and spouses. And sometimes they are family members only via dependency: as where they are

- children aged 21 or more
- relatives in the ascending line: i.e. parents and grandparents

The same principles have been transposed into the EU Settlement Scheme.

Dependency criteria

The question of dependency is not reduced to a bare calculation of financial dependency, although that plays an important part in the consideration.

The courts have said over time that the essential focus has to be on the nature of the relationship concerned and on whether it is one characterised by a situation of dependence. This judgement should be based on an examination of all the factual circumstances, bearing in mind the underlying objective of maintaining the unity of the family.

It should be construed broadly to involve a holistic examination of a number of factors, including financial, physical and social conditions, so as to establish whether there is dependence that is genuine.

The HO will consider a family member to be dependent on the EEA national (or their spouse or civil partner) if they cannot meet their essential living needs without the financial support of that person.

This can be the case even if they also receive financial support or income somewhere else (but which is at a level not adequate to meet their essentials needs, expressed as including accommodation, utilities and food).

Dependency by choice is permitted and the reasons for this choice are not to be questioned.

Examples

Henrietta is a citizen of Ghana who lives with her French daughter Roopa. Roopa came to the UK to study and gained permanent residence here. Henrietta subsequently joined her having entered the UK as a visitor. Henrietta is reliant on Roopa for accommodation and maintenance.

Henrietta is dependent on Roopa. Accordingly she is her dependent for EEA purposes. There is no further test as there might be under the Immigration Rules of whether there are alternative sources of support for her. So she is the dependent relative in the ascending line, and can apply for a residence card.

Also residing with Henrietta and Roopa are Roopa's two Ghanaian sons Henry and William, who are aged 23 and 28. They have been working in the UK for two years having overstayed their visas. They each earn enough to subsist so long as someone else accommodates them.

Henry and William have a viable case for dependency, given that Roopa meets their accommodation needs. So they can apply for residence cards as direct family members, being the dependent children of a qualified person. In practice EEA dependency applications often face the risk of refusal because of Home Office suspicion that the dependency is not genuine, though the scope for such refusals is quite limited given the considerations we have discussed.

8.5.2 No requirement for prior lawful residence and prior presence

There was no barrier to illegal entrants and overstayers being recognised as family members (the same is the case under the EU Settlement Scheme).

Another example where case law laid down in findings of the CJEU has created accepted EU law is the Metock ruling. This decided that those who are in the UK irregularly – even those removable under UK law and facing imminent removal – would gain a right to reside immediately on becoming a genuine family member of a qualified person.

This thinking also applied to extended family members of EEA nationals. However they had an additional hurdle to jump. As discussed above, they had to show not just extended family membership, but had to also persuade the Home Office that discretion should be exercised in their favour.

NB cases involving the exercise of HO discretion are not Level 1 work and must be referred on to a suitable accredited advisor.

That consideration gave some wriggle room for the Home Office to take account of their immigration history. However, the overriding issue in all EEA cases was whether the grant of residence was essential to avoid directly or indirectly discouraging the exercise of Treaty Rights.

Examples

Think again about the cases of Henrietta, Henry and William above. Under conventional domestic immigration law they all faced significant barriers due to their immigration status. However the *Metock* principle means that the bare fact of immigration status could not be held against them. As just noted, it may be relevant for extended family members as part of the exercise of discretion.

Another example. Clare is French and permanently resident in the UK. She met and married Carl here in the UK. Carl is a failed asylum seeker who entered the UK unlawfully from a third country outside the EEA. Following Metock, Carl ought to obtain residence on the basis of his relationship with Clare.
The only provisions that might stop him obtaining residence would be the public policy, public security or public health clauses, which are unlikely to apply in most cases (see section 8.8).

8.5.3 Sham marriage/ marriage of convenience

Free movement rights for a spouse or civil partner did not extend to a party to a marriage or civil partnership of convenience (i.e. a 'sham'). The same is the case under the EU Settlement Scheme.

The Free Movement Directive defines a marriage of convenience as a relationship contracted for the sole purpose of enjoying the right of free movement and residence.

If it is suspected that a marriage or civil partnership is one of convenience, it is open to the Secretary of State to investigate individual cases.

Whilst an applicant must show they are the family member of an EEA national 'which would usually come from a valid marriage certificate' the Home Office may also ask the applicant and EEA sponsor for further information, invite the applicant and EEA sponsor for interview and/or arrange a home visit by the Immigration Compliance and Enforcement (ICE) team.

The burden of proof lies with the Secretary of State to prove that a marriage is one of convenience or sham.

> **Further notes/information**
>
> **Any case involving an allegation that your client's marriage/durable partnership/civil partnership is one of convenience or a sham is outside OISC 1 scope and not part of its exam curriculum.**
>
> Clearly you should, in your work, think about submitting proof of the genuineness of relationship where there may otherwise appear to be indicators of a possible sham, such as a short-lived relationship or a lack of a shared language.
>
> Where any such concerns could arise, you should refer the case to a suitable accredited adviser.

8.5.4 Comprehensive sickness insurance cover

The possession of comprehensive sickness insurance cover (CSIC) was a prerequisite of meeting the definition of some forms of qualified person or family member:

- Students and the self-sufficient require CSIC (Reg 4(1)(d)(ii, 4(1)(c)(ii))
- So do their family members (Reg 4(2)(b))

This was a very important requirement in relation to applications for documents under the 2016 Regs. Although the EU Settlement Scheme disapplied this requirement, it remains an issue in relation to the good character requirement in naturalisation applications by EEA nationals and their family members (or passport applications by their children, where their parents put forward a case of automatic acquisitions).

Many people may have thought themselves safely exercising Treaty Rights over time because they were studying or financially independent. But they could be derailed by a lack of CSIC. Wealthier individuals may have had private health insurance. Young people may have been covered by a parent's, or spouses may be covered by a partner's insurance. And where there was a history of cover but small gaps, the point made in Baumbast [2002] CMLR 23 (cited in Ahmad [2014] EWCA Civ 988) is important: there will be cases where

> "the host state should disregard minor discrepancies. These might arise when the cover was not totally comprehensive."

Leaving aside private health insurance, could national insurance schemes ever qualify?

A European Health Insurance card (EHIC) could be obtained from an EEA national's country of residence *prior* to coming to the UK.

The EHIC allowed EEA nationals to get the same medical treatment that was available free to residents of the country they are visiting without being charged.

The UKVI guidance on qualified persons states that the Home Office will accept an EHIC card (alongside some other types of certificates) issued abroad as amounting to comprehensive sickness insurance cover, but only if the applicant was living in the UK on a temporary basis.

Where a student was issued a Registration Certificate before 20 June 2011, they were excused from the CSI requirement retrospectively when applying for permanent residence.

8.6 Rights of admission and residence

The rights under the 2016 Regs were as follows:

8.6.1 Right of admission

Before the end of the transition period, all EEA nationals and EEA family members had a right of admission (without requiring leave to enter or remain, under s7 IA 1988).

That section, s7 Immigration Act 1988 was repealed on 31 December 2020 but was preserved to apply, during the grace period (by the "grace period" Regulations 2020/1209) to EEA/Swiss nationals who had resided lawfully in the UK before the end of the transition period, and to their family members. This means that, until the end of the grace period, all those individuals can ***reside*** in the UK without any other form of immigration leave until the end of the grace period on 30 June 2021 (and thereafter so long as by then they have applied for status under the EU Settlement Scheme).

Those EEA and Swiss nationals can also continue to ***enter*** the UK during the grace period with only their passport or national ID card under the preserved Reg 8. Admission if a removal decision under Reg 23(6)(b) was made against them in the past and remains extant.

However, family members who hold neither a document as such issued under the EEA Regs - or settled- or pre-settled status- will no longer have a right of admission. The right of admission without provision of residence documents was previously governed by Reg 11(4), which mandated immigration officers to "provide every reasonable opportunity [...] to prove by other means that" they were a family member with a right to accompany the EEA national or joint them in the UK. This subpara had been accepted as lifting the requirement for prior 'entry clearance' by way of family permit in CO) Nigeria [2007] UKAIT 00070. However, Reg 11(4) was deleted by the grace period Regs as part of the savings modifications. In short, the right of admission for family members without a UK-issued residence document no longer exists.

Prior to 1 January 2021, family members could also enter using an EEA residence document issued to them as a family member by another member state (Article 10 and 20 residence cards) but this is no longer possible (see updated guidance).

The UK has long operated and enforced the family permit scheme by which those asserting EEA rights should obtain a family permit before travelling. A family member wishing to travel to the UK can still apply to an Entry Clearance Officer for a family permit under Reg 12, but it will make more sense to apply for a family permit under the EU Settlement Scheme. Either type of family permit application is free and the permit must be issued as soon as possible if the person qualifies.

Not all applicants from 1 January 2021 have to apply for EUSS family permits. Some can apply under Appendix EU for settled- or pre-settled status from abroad (i.e. applying for Indefinite or Limited Leave to Enter), so long as they have the "required proof" for their entitlement to do so. The abridged definition of "required proof of entitlement to apply from outside the UK" in Annex 1 Appendix EU is as follows:

> (a) For EEA/Swiss nationals:
> (i) their valid passport; or
> (ii) their valid national biometric identity card
> (b) For non-EEA citizen, their valid "specified relevant document"
> unless SSHD agrees to accept alternative evidence of entitlement to apply from outside the UK, if the person is unable to produce the required document due to circumstances beyond their control or to compelling practical or compassionate reasons.
> 'valid' means that the document is genuine and has not expired, been cancelled or invalidated.

The abridged Annex 1 definition of 'specified relevant document' is as follows:

> (a) A biometric residence card, permanent residence card or derivative residence card issued by the UK under the EEA Regs on the basis of an application made on or after 6 April 2015; or
> (b) A biometric EUPSS residence card.

Guidance on procedures and requirements for EEA/Swiss nationals crossing the UK border from 1 January 2021 is here.

The Home Office has yet to confirm how immigration officers at the border are expected to distinguish between those EEA/Swiss nationals who continue to have the right of admission by virtue of their pre-TP end UK residence, and those EEA/Swiss nationals who lack such residence and should, therefore, be admitted as non-visa national visitors. .

Note that, for family members without a right of admission (i.e. without a residence document or family permit) the temptation may be to travel to the UK as visitors if they are non-visa nationals. They should be warned that visitors are barred from applying for leave under the EU Settlement Scheme as joining family members (unless they arrived on a marriage visitor visa and are now married to their 'sponsor' – see definition of 'visitor' in Annex 1 of Appendix EU).

8.6.2 Initial right of residence

All EEA citizens and their family members, before the end of the transition period, enjoyed what was referred to in the EEA Regs as an 'initial right of residence' (Reg 13). This enabled an EEA citizen to travel to the UK and reside in the UK for three months as if he or she were a qualified person (which therefore includes being accompanied by family members) but without having to establish that he or she is yet a qualified person.

This provision enhanced the possibilities of free movement around Europe by allowing for an unchallenged right to reside in order to become established (for example, whilst one earns money to fund a course of studies or to set up a business). In the UK before the end of transition, it could be asserted simply on production of a valid identity card or passport by the EEA national (Reg 13(1)) or of a valid passport by the third country national (Reg 13(2)).

The only caveats to the initial right of residence were:

- not to become 'an unreasonable burden on the social assistance system of the United Kingdom' (Reg 13(3))
- public policy: Reg 13(4) provided for circumstances in which a person is not entitled to this right where the following decisions have been made in relation to a person and which still has effect: removal on grounds of public policy/security/health; refusal to issue residence documentation,

cancellation of a right to reside, misuse of a right to reside, revocation of admission; and, from 24 July 2018, an exclusion order under Reg 23(5) or deportation under Reg 32(3).

8.6.3 Extended right of residence

Qualified persons had a right to reside in the UK as long as they remained qualified persons (Reg 14(1)). In addition, in some circumstances, they were permitted to retain a right of residence even though their qualifying activity has ceased, as is discussed above (i.e. temporary incapacity or temporary unemployment for workers and the self-employed: Reg 6).

This right was, under the 2016 Regs, subject to the same ineligibility criteria as the initial right of residence, under Reg 14(4) which mirrors Reg 13(4) (see section above).

During the 'extended right of residence', qualified persons could apply for and had to, immediately, be granted a Registration Certificate on production of a valid identity card or passport plus proof of their status us such (Reg 17). The application was made on form EEA(QP) and cost £65. This certificate was not essential by any means: it merely evidenced the right, it did not create it. Nevertheless, such certificates could be useful, particularly for EEA citizens likely to be travelling in and out of the UK who might otherwise suffer the inconvenience of regular questioning by HM Immigration Officers.

Similarly, the right to extended residence for family members was set out at Reg 14(2). However, the document to evidence their status and right of residence was referred to as a residence card, the details of which were set out at Reg 18. The application was made on form EEA(FM) or EEA(EFM)and costs £65.

Qualified persons could carry out qualifying activities and could not be subjected to any form of discrimination compared to the national workforce. This means that rights to benefits and other advantages enjoyed by the national workforce had to be made accessible in equal measure.

As long as a family member fell within the definitions of a family member set out in the Citizens' Directive and transposed into national law by the EEA Regs, that family member has a right to reside in the UK with the qualified person. There were no additional limitations relating to maintenance and accommodation, intention to live permanently with the other or subsisting marriage. The family members of qualified persons enjoyed the same rights to take up activities in Member States.

The children of nationals of a Member State who are or who had been employed in the territory of another Member State were entitled to that state's general educational, apprenticeship and vocational training courses under the same conditions as a national.

These rights had to be respected in an extremely proactive way by Member States. The rights were derived from the Treaty and were innate, meaning that it was for Member States to protect and promote these rights as far as possible. For example, when an EEA citizen or family member entered a Member State, the authorities must merely check that their documents were in order. The authorities are not entitled to ask further questions about intention, availability of funds, sponsors or the like – although, so long as they had a reasonable belief that there could be grounds for it, they may investigate exclusion on the grounds of public policy, public security or public health.

Examples

It is May 2019. Anya is German and has been working in the UK for two years. She has never applied for a registration certificate. Nevertheless, by virtue of her work, she has automatically acquired a right to reside.

It is May 2020. Herman is Canadian. He entered the UK as a visitor and overstayed his visa. He married Anya a year ago, and Anya has continued working. Despite the fact Herman has done nothing about his immigration status. he has automatically acquired a right of reside by virtue of his family relationship with Anya and Anya's position as a qualified person. Herman could have applied for a residence card before the end of the transition period if he wanted to but he did not have to. Were it not for the UK's exit from the EU, then, after five years of marriage he would automatically acquire a right to reside permanently, presuming Anya retains her right to reside for that period, whether or not he applied for the relevant paperwork.

However, because of the UK's exit from the EU both Anya and Herman must apply for status under the EU Settlement Scheme before 1 July 2021. During the grace period, so long as Anya has continued to work until before the end of transition and not lost qualified person status, they will both be protected by the same extended residence rights as they fall within the category of persons for whom the 2016 Regs have been saved.

8.6.4 Permanent residence

The relevant provision under the 2016 Regs was Reg 15. This has been saved without modifications for EEA/Swiss nationals lawfully resident in the UK since before the end of transition, and their family members, by the Grace Period Regs 2020. The right to permanent residence can no longer continue to accrue under this provision but knowledge of this right, and the operation of Reg 15, is still relevant, eg:

- to determining what other rights (to entry, residence and public services) your client may hold under the Grace Period Regs 2020 if they have not yet been granted settled status
- to advise and assist clients with outstanding PR card applications, lodged before the end of transition (perhaps lodged to assist with proving past lawful status in support of a naturalisation application)
- a right of permanent residence, accrued in the past, may need to be proven to remedy subsequent gaps in exercise of treaty rights or CSI as part of a naturalisation application which will assess 10 years' lawfulness of leave under the good character guidance.

Under the EEA Regs the following automatically acquired a permanent right of residence in the UK (Reg 15):

- EEA citizens who had lived here for five years in accordance with the EEA Regs (Reg 15(1)(a))
  - Third country family members of qualified persons who had lived here for five years in accordance with the EEA Regs (Reg 15(1)(b))

- A worker or self-employed person who had ceased activity in the circumstances defined under Reg 5 (retirement, illness and incapacity in various circumstances), and their family members (Reg 15(1)(c), (d)) One relevant question was whether they had "*resided in the United Kingdom continuously for more than three years prior to the termination*." In Gubeladze [2019] UKSC 31 the Supreme Court held that this referred to *factual residence* rather than "*legal residence*." So the fact that an Accession country national might have failed to register their employment in line with the relevant Regulations applicable (during the period which that country's nationals were subject to restrictions on accessing the labour market) did not prevent them from later acquiring permanent residence as a worker who had ceased activities.
- Family members of a worker or self-employed person
  - who had died,
  - where the family member had resided with him immediately before his death, and
  - where he had been living in the UK for at least the two years immediately before his death or the death had been the result of an accident at work or an occupational disease (Reg 15(1)(e)

- Those who had resided in the UK under the EEA Regs for five years ending with a period during which they retained a right of residence (former family members whose qualified person had died or from whom they had divorced)

Other relevant considerations in relation to permanent residence:

- As was the case for initial and extended rights of residence, Reg 15(4) again set out the circumstances in which a person was not entitled to this right: namely, where the following decisions had been made in relation to a person and which still had effect: removal on grounds of public policy/security/health; refusal to issue residence documentation, cancellation of a right to reside, misuse of a right to reside, revocation of admission; and, from 24 July 2018, an exclusion order under Reg 23(5) or deportation under Reg 32(3).
- Continuity of residence was not broken by periods of absence from the UK for six months or less per year, absence due to military service, or one absence not exceeding twelve months for an important reason (e.g. child birth, serious illness, study or an overseas posting) – though it would normally be broken by imprisonment or expulsion (Reg 3). In Viscu [2019] EWCA Civ 1052 it was found that a young offenders' institution counts as imprisonment, but could be recognised as less disruptive to integration than would be the case for an adult offender.
- Permanent residence lapsed with two years continuous absence from the UK (Reg 15(2))
- As the language suggested, the *serious reasons* allowing excessive absence mentioned were not exhaustive: Babajanov [2013] UKUT 513 (IAC). The case held that it would be possible to continue to be resident in the UK notwithstanding absence abroad where a person is integrated here, as where a minor is stranded abroad after a parent returns here, because there is no adequate accommodation in this country
- Residence under previous Directives would count towards permanent residence (Schedule 4: Transitional Provisions of the EEA Regs, also saved during the grace period)
- The right of permanent residence, which in all respects was equivalent to ILR, brought with it enhanced protection from removal, as is discussed below
- A permanently resident person, whether an EEA national or a family member, had that status unconditionally: once permanent residence was held, there was any requirement to be a qualified person or family member fell away thereafter
- Rights of residence under European Union law prior to the Citizens Directive entering force could still be relied on in acquiring a right of permanent residence: see 8.6.4.1
- Sometimes a person could have acquired a permanent right of residence some time ago, which could easily be overlooked, for example where the case has subsequently become more complicated and the focus has turned to questions such as a retained right of residence: Idezuna [2011] UKUT 00474 (IAC). So never forget to identify the basic rights of residence before going on examine if the more complicated ones are established.
- An EEA citizen could apply for a Document Certifying Permanent Residence and the non-EEA family member, a Permanent Residence Card on Form EEA(PR), both £65, issued under Reg 19. This was not essential but would sometimes prove to be convenient.
- Family members of workers who had obtained permanent residence under Article 17 of the Citizens' Directive on the grounds of retirement, permanent incapacity to work or three years of cross-border working, themselves enjoyed permanent residence from the time they became family members (i.e. the fact they were not family members when permanent residence was acquired by the worker did not count against them): RM (Zimbabwe) [2013] EWCA Civ 775. However, Reg15(1)(d) of the 2016 Regs (unlike the 2006 Regs) stated that only those who were family members for EEA purposes at the time the worker themselves qualified for permanent residence would qualify.

Example

Alberto is an Italian national. He has lived and worked in the UK for five years by 2017 and his Congolese wife Maria has lived with him for that time.

Alberto and Maria both obtained permanent residence in 2017: under Reg 15(1)(a) and (1)(b) respectively.

Think again about the example of Pierre above when we addressed *Ceasing activities as a worker as a gateway to permanent residence.* His ability to show himself as having ceased activities also brought access to permanent residence, as we explained: under Reg 15(1)(c). His family members also obtained such rights, so long as they enjoyed a right to reside as such at the time work ceased.

Louisa is a French national who established a business in the UK. She entered the UK in 2015 and ran the business thereafter. In 2018 she was killed in a car accident whilst delivering goods to a customer. Her twin daughters Lucy and Lucia want to know their situation; they both lived with her whilst they studied at university and were wholly supported by her.

Clearly Lucy and Lucia were dependent children so whatever their age they would be family members 'immediately before the death'. Louisa's demise is in circumstances which amount to an 'accident at work'. So they would get permanent residence under Reg 15(1)(e).

Marketa is a Czech national. Her American husband David divorced from her two years ago. At that time they had been married for three years over a period when Marketa had consistently worked in the UK.
David seems to have a viable right to permanent residence based on Reg 15(1)(f): he has resided in the UK for five years under the EEA Regs, firstly as the spouse of a qualified person for some three years and then with the retained right of residence for two years (we touched on this in outline only as retained rights are outside OISC 1 scope).

Manuel is a Spanish national working in the UK. He worked in the UK consistently from June 2012 to July 2017. Demoralised by Brexit, since then he has returned to Spain for several periods each of 3-4 months.

Manuel obtained permanent residence in June 2017 (five years as a worker: Reg 15(1)(a)). After that time he would only lose the continuous residence that underlies his permanent residence after two years of being consistently abroad: see Reg 3(2)(a).

During the grace period Manuel continues to benefit from his right to permanent residence and can return to the UK to apply for settled status on the basis either of a document certifying permanent residence, or simply on the basis of his past 5 years' residence, which should show up in his HMRC records from that time (and can be additionally proved via an employer letter, P60s, payslips etc.

Evidencing permanent residence

As explained above, this exercise will still remain a necessary competence for some time to come, for example when evidencing rights preserved during the grace period, or retrospectively in proving lawfulness of status under the good character requirement in a naturalisation application.

Evidencing permanent residence is not always easy. An EEA national may have had periods of economic inactivity in the relevant five year period, due to reasons that did not necessarily end their status as a qualified person, through illness, childbirth or unemployment, depending on the circumstances. Careful attention must be had to EEA Regs 4–15 to trace a five-year period of continuous residence entitlement, ensuring all relevant matters are fully evidenced. Absences from the UK during the five-year period will be considered under Reg 3.

EEA nationals from the A8 and A2 countries, and Croatia, may have had to meet certain documentary requirements to work lawfully in the UK during the accession periods (see next section). If they did not meet those requirements, they may only be able to rely on their right to reside in the UK from the date those accession periods ended when considering whether they have acquired permanent residence. For more on this, see the Immigration Staff Guidance, Qualified Persons.

The non-EEA family member's application will depend on themselves establishing five years of ***continuous residence*** under the EEA Regs, which will in turn depend on the evidence they can obtain of the EEA national's ***continuous right to reside*** in the UK during the same five year period.

Top Tip

Always remember that a person may have qualified for permanent residence if they have established five years residence in the UK as a qualified person or their family member

- this may include periods where a person is actually working, and

- periods where they retain worker status because of involuntary registered unemployment, vocational training and inactivity due to illness/accident (see above where we address *Workers*)
- the five-year period need not be the last five years – any continuous period of five years will qualify
- Evidence of a continuous five year period of residence in the UK can include (but is not limited to) tenancy agreements, utility bills, bank statements, school or nursery letters or immunisation records in support of applications for children
- Requests for HMRC records are free and can be made here (and the amount of earnings/NICs be reverse engineered by hourly rates to arrive at an average number of hours worked for each year), equally, a DWP subject access request, and client's GP and/or dentist appointment lists can help to prove residence.

8.6.5 Accession countries – the "A8", "A2" (Bulgaria and Romania), and Croatia

Further Member States acceded to the European Union throughout its history, and not every new member has received full rights of free movement at the moment of joining.

- Between 1 May 2004, when they joined the EU, and 1 May 2011, nationals of the Czech Republic, Estonia, Hungary, Latvia, Lithuania, Poland, Slovakia and Slovenia were required to register under the Workers Registration Scheme for the first 12 months of their employment. In all other respects they enjoyed free movement rights. In January 2015 the UT held, in **TG** [2015] UKUT 50 (AAC), that the extension of the WRS from 1 May 2009 to 30 April 2011 was unlawful. That means that workers who had failed to register under the scheme during that period were nevertheless lawfully employed in the UK. That decision was upheld on 7 November 2017 in Gubeladze [2017] EWCA Civ 1751.
- Two further countries, Bulgaria and Romania, (the 'A2') then joined the EU on 1 January 2007 and, again, were not immediately granted full access to the UK labour market. They were treated even less generously than the A8 countries, restricting those entitled to be employed in the UK to those granted work permits.
- The restrictions on A8 and A2 nationals no longer exist as the maximum period the UK could apply them was for seven years from the date of their country's accession. Failure to comply with those restrictions however may still have implications for A8 and A2 nationals who are seeking permanent residence documentation from the Home Office, or who seek to prove that they accrued a right to permanent residence in the past.
- Croatia joined the EU on 1 July 2013.
- Their nationals initially enjoyed limited free movement rights as, unless they were exempt (i.e. had been legally working here for a year before accession, or had no restrictions on their ability to work at that time), they required sponsorship under the Tiers 2 or 5 of the PBS for the first 12 months of their employment in the UK. See generally the Accession of Croatia (Immigration and Worker Authorisation) Regulations 2013. The scheme ended on 1 July 2018 since when they have had full free movement rights. Nevertheless one comes across the scheme in immigration histories sometimes, so it is still worth knowing about.
- Sponsored Croatians did not need to apply for visas or extensions under the PBS, but required Certificates of Sponsorship reference number and a purple registration certificate
    - There are three different types of registration certificate:
    - the blue registration certificate – to confirm unrestricted access to employment
    - the purple registration certificate –- to confirm permission to work for a particular employer or specific employment category, and
    - the yellow registration certificate – to confirm the holder is exercising treaty rights other than as a worker (for example, as a student, self employed or self sufficient person).

Croatians are dealt with here amongst the Immigration Staff Guidance for *EEA, Swiss nationals and EC association agreements Accession state countries*.

Further notes/information

Note: this subject area does not form part of the OISC 1 curriculum but is provided for background.

8.6.6 Association Agreements with Turkey and other non-EU states

Association Agreements are signed between the EU and third countries, usually states interested in becoming members. All of the Accession States had entered into EC Association Agreements before joining. The only agreement with meaningful immigration consequences was, until the end of the transition period, with Turkey.

The EU-Turkey Association Agreement gave self-employed persons a right to establish themselves in business in the EEA, and allowed for some Turkish workers lawfully employed in the UK to extend their stay to continue their employment. The idea was to promote integration of the economy prior to full membership. Following the closure for new entrants using this Agreement, there is now only provision for those Turkish nationals extending their leave under the ECAA rules.

In addition to the above Association Agreements, the EU has concluded a series of Association Agreements and Co-operation Agreements with countries such as Algeria, Tunisia and Morocco. The significance of these agreements in immigration terms is extremely limited in that they merely provide for non-discrimination clauses.

8.7 Settled and pre-settled status ('ILR/LTR under Appendix EU')

We have outlined the context and operation of Appendix EU above at 8.1. This section, 8.7, provides an overview over the application categories within it, and how they relate to residence rights under the Directive and the EEA Regs. The sections above, on the underlying residence rights under the EEA Regs have all been updated to provide the more detailed context for their EUSS equivalents, and examples provided cover both EEA Regs application- as well as EUSS scenarios.

Since Appendix EU became effective from 28 August 2018 it has been amended several times. These changes aim to capture the development of free movement and citizenship rights. Sometimes the result of a legal case has not stopped political realities requiring a particular approach to rights anyway. Thus from 24 August 2020 Northern Irish nationals were recently recognised as eligible 'sponsors' for EUSS purposes even though the case law had not gone that far. For current applications, all that really matters is that one's circumstances are presently covered. Where this is of interest or relevance, however, page 13 of the EUSS guidance can be consulted for a chronology of changes.

EEA and settled status guidance and policies

The development of a whole new body of immigration rules, that pertaining to settled status, and the continuing evolution of EEA free movement law, led to an exponential growth of the already voluminous amount of EEA guidance. In the newly re-named 'Immigration Staff Guidance' we find, contained in EU Settlement Scheme caseworker guidance (alongside the whole body of free movement rights guidance):

- EU Settlement Scheme: EU, other EEA and Swiss citizens and their family members
- EU Settlement Scheme: suitability requirements
- EU Settlement Scheme: derivative right to reside (Chen amd Ibrahim/Teixeira cases)
- EU Settlement Scheme: family member of a qualifying British citizen
- EU Settlement Scheme: person with a Zambrano right to reside
- EU Settlement Scheme (interim guidance): Gender identity and sex markers on documents

Separately, but referred to in the main EUSS guidance is the page Coronavirus (COVID-19): EU Settlement Scheme - guidance for applicants.

Grouped under the EEA guidance, we find the guidance document EU Settlement Scheme: family and travel permits.

In Immigration Staff Guidance – other cross-cutting guidance – Administrative review, is Administrative review: EU Settlement Scheme

The page 'EU Settlement Scheme: applicant information' currently contains the following:

- EU Settlement Scheme: evidence of UK residence
- EU Settlement Scheme: evidence of relationship to an EU citizen
- EU Settlement Scheme: applying from outside the UK
- Using the 'EU Exit: ID Document Check' app
- EU Settlement Scheme: apply as the family member of a frontier worker
- EU Settlement Scheme: apply for an administrative review

Support

- EU Settlement Scheme: ID document scanner locations
- EU Settlement Scheme: Assisted Digital service
- EU Settlement Scheme: community support for vulnerable citizens

Additional information

- EU Settlement Scheme: application processing times
- EU Settlement Scheme: how we use your personal information

The following was contained in the above but has been moved to a different location:

- EU Settlement Scheme: view and prove your rights in the UK

A separate guide for applicants is entitled Stay in the UK ('settled status'): step by step", with the steps linking to some of the above information.

Relevant Enforcement Instructions are:

- Guidance for Immigration Enforcement in respect of EU, other EEA and Swiss citizens and their family members
- Marriage Investigations (as to this topic also refer to the general guidance Suitability: Sham marriage or civil partnership and the European Commission's Handbook on dealing with the issue of marriages of convenience)
- Immigration Act 2014 Marriage and civil partnership referral and investigation scheme: statutory guidance for Home Office staff

On Frontier workers, the following guidance is available:

- **Frontier worker permit scheme caseworker guidance** and applicant guidance:

- **Frontier Worker permit**
- **Frontier worker permit for EU citizens**
- **Frontier Workers: apply for a review of your Frontier Worker permit decision**

On S2 Healthcare visitors:

- **S2 Healthcare Visitor caseworker guidance** and applicant guidance **Enter the UK as an S2 Healthcare Visitor**
- **S2 Healthcare Visitors: apply for a review of a decision**

On service providers from Switzerland:

- **Service Providers from Switzerland caseworker guidance** and applicant guidance **Apply for a Service providers from Switzerland visa**
- **Service Providers from Switzerland: apply for a review of a decision about your right to enter the UK**

As to practicalities, you may wish to consult the following:

- **Entering the UK as the holder of an Article 10 or 20 residence card**
- **Visiting the UK: information for EU, EEA and Swiss citizens** and more general guidance (also referring to EEa nationals) **Visiting the UK from 1 January 2021**
- Check someone's settled or pre-settled status
- View and prove your settled or pre-settled status
- Applicants who have difficulties with using the online form can seek local help through the Assisted Digital service. This service offers no immigration advice.
- Guidance for using the online system can be found here.
- To update, replace or transfer BRCs, use **this form**

8.7.1 The mechanics of the scheme

It is useful to broadly summarise the mechanics of the EUSS scheme before going into things in more detail, and to provide a roadmap as to how Appendix EU is applied to cases. Having done so we will itemise the conditions for "settled status" ("**EUSS**") at 8.7.3 and for "pre-settled status" ("**EUPSS**") at 8.7.4. As the definitions in Annex 1 to Appendix EU effectively contain the bulk of the rules, and are difficult to read, we have provided abridged versions of the most important definitions at 8.7.5 to which, it is recommended, readers should refer throughout.

The EU Settlement Scheme after the end of the transition period

Since the end of the transition period, applications are categorised, from the outset, by whether or not **the applicant** has been resident in the UK continuously since before the end of the transition period (which ended at 11pm on 31 December 2020). We refer to this point in time, by way of shorthand, as "**TP end**".

- If the applicant has continuous pre-TP end residence, they will apply
    - either as a "relevant EEA citizen" ("**REAACZ**") in their own right
    - or as a "family member of a relevant EEA citizen" ("**FM of a REAACZ**")
- If the applicant has no continuous pre-TP end residence, they will apply as a "joining family member of a relevant sponsor" ("**JFM of a RS**").

The definition of each category of person in Annex 1 to Appendix EU must be checked as to whether your client fits within it and is thus eligible to apply. Please refer to section 8.7.5 below

Two preliminary points:

- Some prospective applicants can apply directly for settled- or pre-settled status from abroad, thus eliminating the need for an extra application in the form of a family permit. To be entitled to apply from abroad, a person must hold "required proof of entitlement to apply from outside the UK" (definition in Annex 1), which is an EEA/Swiss passport/ID card, or a biometric residence document issued under the EEA Regs or the EU Settlement Scheme.

- *Surinder Singh* cases which are termed applications by "family members of qualifying British citizens" ("**FM of QBC**"), operate somewhat outside the new framework set out below, and the category is therefore addressed within a self-contained section at 8.7.3 (for settled status) and within the general section 8.7.4 on pre-settled status which is applicable to all categories. What is important to flag up in relation to the QBC category is that the deadlines by when the family relationship must have existed; when the family member must have returned to the UK with their sponsor; and the application deadline (which differs according to what type of family member the applicant is, are vital. Therefore, for QBCs and their family members, the relevant definitions containing those requirements, are all set out in section 8.7.3.

Categorising cases – joining family members of relevant sponsors vs relevant EEA citizens and their family members

This is the first stage in tackling EUSS cases, and the following structure is applied:

<table>
<tr><th colspan="3">Has <u>the applicant</u> resided continuously in the UK since pre-TP end?</th></tr>
<tr><th colspan="2">YES</th><th>NO</th></tr>
<tr><th></th><th colspan="2">Has <u>their sponsor</u> resided continuously in the UK since pre-TP end?</th></tr>
<tr><td>If the applicant is an EEA/Swiss national themselves, they will apply as a REAACZ</td><td>If the applicant is not themselves an EEA/Swiss national, they will apply as a FM of REAACZ"</td><td>The applicant will apply as a JFM of RS"</td></tr>
<tr><td colspan="2"><u>Settled status for REAACZ or their FM</u>:
• Eligibility conditions are in EU11
• grant is under EU2
<u>Pre-settled status for REAACZ or their FM:</u>
• Eligibility condition is condition 1. in EU14
• grant is under EU3</td><td><u>Settled status for JFM of RS</u>:
• Eligibility conditions are in EU11A
• Grant is under EU2A
<u>Pre-settled status for JFM of RS::</u>
• Eligibility conditions are in EU14A
• grant is under EU3A</td></tr>
</table>

Having categorised the application, the required status of the sponsor will need to be checked. The sponsor requirements differ according to whether the date of application is during or after the **grace period**. This period runs from TP end to 11pm on 30 June 2021. The required status of the sponsor in each case is set out in the Annex 1 definitions of "REAACZ" and "RS" represented as a table in section 8.7.5.

Some of the settled status eligibility conditions in EU11 and EU11A are again subdivided by whether the application is made during or after the grace period. These are set out below in section 8.7.3 side by side.

The general deadline for applications under the scheme is 11pm on 30 June 2021, the end of the grace period, but some categories of persons can apply later without having to prove "reasonable grounds" for doing so. The deadlines are set out in the Annex 1 definition of "required date", which breaks down as follows:

Annex 1 definition of "required date" (i.e. application deadlines)

If the applicant is/ arrives on (date):	...then the relevant application deadline is:
Not any of the below categories (i.e: this is the general deadline)	Before 1 July 2021
EUPSS (pre-settled status) holder	Before expiry of EUPSS
Where a JFM arrives, or where a child is born or adopted on or after 1 April 2021	Within 3 months of arrival, birth or adoption
Where a JFM is a "specified spouse or civil partner of a Swiss national" (i.e. the marriage or civil partnership was contracted between 1	Within 3 months of arrival and before 1 January 2026.

January 2021 and 1 January 2026) who arrives on or after 1 April 2021:	
Family member of a qualifying British national (*Surinder Singh*) **BUT not all categories – some must apply before 1 July 2021** (see section 8.7.3.3)	Before 11pm on 29 March 2022
Where an applicant holds leave under other parts of- or outside- the rules, which expires on or after 1 July 2021	Before leave expires. The HO will deem this to be a reasonable ground to apply after 30 June 2021. If made after expiry, evidence of reasonable grounds and consent by the HO are required as for all other categories.
Where a person ceases to be exempt from immigration control on or after 1 July 2021:	Within 90 days of ceasing to be exempt. The HO will deem this to be a reasonable ground to apply late. If made outside the 90 days, evidence of reasonable grounds and consent by the HO are required as for all other categories.

8.7.2 Key principles for understanding the EUSS following the changes in HC 813

It's easy to get lost in the dense EUSS provisions, particularly following the extensive changes which have been in force since the end of the transition period. We want to ensure our readers can navigate Appendix EU and Appendix EU-FP. We aim to cover most of the common issues in the set of principles identified below.

We address *Surinder Singh* applicants separately in s self-contained section at 8.7.3.3.

Extended family members – who's who?
This category can cause the most confusion as Appendix EU does not use the same language as the EEA Regulations. Below we summarise how the EUSS treats different kinds of cases, so you know where your client fits.

- **Extended family members** are not defined in Appendix EU. Instead, they are addressed separately as "**durable partners**" and "**dependent relatives**".
- **Dependent relatives** do not include "**dependent parents**" (definition in Annex 1) or **dependent adult children** (included in definition of "child" in Annex 1). These are direct family members.
- "**Dependent parents**" include grandparents, great grandparents etc; "**children**" include grandchildren, great-grandchildren etc, via their Annex 1 further definitions.
- **Children of durable partners**, and **children adopted by a sponsor under non-adoptive legal guardianship orders** are classed not as direct family members but alongside dependent relatives.
- **Dependent relatives** must hold an EEA residence document unless their sponsor is a relevant person of Northern Ireland (this is set out in the definition of "relevant document"). Dependent relatives who themselves lack pre-TP end continuous residence cannot apply under the EU Settlement Scheme.

Applicants

Where the applicant has been in the UK continuously since "**pre-TP end" (= before 11pm on 31 December 2020)**, and the family relationship existed pre-TP end, they apply as "family members of relevant EEA citizens" if their circumstances fit within one of the following scenarios.

The following are **"FM of REEACZ" (= family members of relevant EEA citizens)**:

- **Spouse/civil partner** where the marriage/civil partnership was contracted **pre-TP end**

- **Spouse/civil partner** where the marriage/civil partnership was contracted **post-TP end** but the **partnership was durable pre-TP end**. Usually applicants have to have already obtained an EEA residence document as a durable partner to establish durability pre-TP end, see the next point on durable partners.
- **Durable partners**: in all cases, the partnership must have been durable pre-TP end. The only classes of people who do not need to hold an EEA residence document as a durable partner are:
- durable partners of "relevant persons of Northern Ireland", and
- applicants who had leave in another category while in the UK with their partner
- **Children** (defined as including grandchildren, great grandchildren etc) **or dependent parents** (defined as including grandparents, great grandparents etc) of the REEACZ or their spouse/CP where **all the family relationships existed pre-TP end**. The spouse/CP can be one where the marriage/civil partnership was contracted post-TP end so long as the relationship was durable before TP end.
  NB: **dependency of parents or children aged 21** or over **need not have existed pre-TP end**, only the family relationship. A child born post-TP end can apply as a "**JFM**" (= joining family member) – see further below.
- **Dependent relatives of the REAACZ or their spouse/CP**. The spouse/CP can be one where the marriage/civil partnership was **contracted post-TP end** – so long as the **relationship was durable before TP end**.
- The family relationships must have existed pre-TP end
- So must the dependency/ membership of household/strict need for personal care on serious health grounds; and
- Both the family relationship and dependency must also continue to exist (or must have done so for the period relied on).
- An EEA residence document must be held or have been applied for pre-TP end: except where the sponsor is a relevant person of Northern Ireland.

Where the applicant has not been in the UK continuously since pre-TP end, they can apply as a **JFM of a RS (= joining family member of a relevant sponsor)**. The only differences to the above categories are:

- **Dependent relatives** (other than dependent parents or dependent children aged 21 or over) without continuous pre-TP UK residence **<u>are barred</u>** from applying under the EU Settlement Scheme.
- **Durable partners** who have no continuous pre-TP end residence in the UK pre-TP end **do not need to hold an EEA residence document** to be classed as durable partners. Neither do those who did reside in the UK but had lawful leave of another type (instead of an EEA residence card). They can simply provide evidence that the partnership was durable by pre-TP end, so the same kind of evidence of durability they would have brought in support of an EEA residence document or family permit in this capacity.
- A **durable partner whose sponsor is a relevant person of Northern Ireland** also **need not hold an EEA residence document**. This is set out in the definition of "relevant document" ((a)(i)(bb)).
- **Children born post-TP end** are one of the two exceptions to the rule that family relationships must have existed pre-TP end.
- **Specified spouse/CP of a Swiss citizen** are the second exception to the rule that the family relationship must have existed pre-TP end. This is an additional category of family member which does not exist under FM of REAACZ and are part of a special concession made under the separate Swiss/UK deal. To fit this definition, a person must be
- The spouse/CP of a Swiss national who is not also British
- The marriage/civil partnership must be contracted between 11pm 31 December 2020 and 1 January 2026

- The marriage/civil partnership must continue to exist on the date of application, unless the applicant relies on 5 years' residence including retained rights (EU11A condition.1) or on the death of their sponsor (EU11A condition 3)

The required status of the sponsor will differ according to whether an application is made before 11pm on 30 June 2021 or thereafter, i.e. during or after the grace period.

Below we will set out the other requirements of the sponsor, beginning with where they are the same for both REEACZ and RS, and then setting out the differences.

The sponsor status requirements

Remember:

- REAACZ can only sponsor "family members of REAACZ" (i.e. applicants who have their own continuous period of UK residence which started pre-TP end).
- RS, on the other hand, can only sponsor "joining family members of relevant sponsors" (i.e. applicants who lack such residence).

The sponsor status requirements are each set out in very lengthy detail in the Annex 1 definitions, but there is much repetition and overlap. Where the below points do not specify that one or the other definition only applies, this means both categories share the same requirements.

Note:

- The sponsor, in all cases except where they are a **frontier worker** or **a naturalised British citizen** must have pre-TP end continuous residence. The reasoning for frontier workers is clear: if they *had* been thus resident, they would not be frontier workers but REAACZ.

Sponsor status requirements – overlap between REAACZ and RS

All sponsor categories below must prove they have continuous UK residence which started pre-TP end. In addition, the following categories must also prove the following:

- **EEA/Swiss nationals,** where their family member applies during the grace period, that they have either been granted EUSS or EUPSS or would be granted this, if they applied during the grace period. If their family member applies after the grace period, they must either hold EUSS or EUPSS (except Irish nationals who need only prove that they *would have* been granted this had they applied during the grace period). Irish nationals are not singled out under the grace period conditions above, because they fall within EEA citizens who *would be* granted status if they applied within the grace period.
- Both **frontier workers** and **naturalised British citizens**:
- For applications during the grace period need only to prove their status as such.
- For applications thereafter:
- again frontier workers only need to prove their status.
- Naturalised British citizens after the grace period must also prove that (if they were not British) they *would have* been granted EUSS or EUPSS, had they applied during the grace period.
- **Relevant persons of Northern Ireland** (definition: the person has British/Irish/both nationalities, was born in NI and at least one parent had British/Irish/both nationalities, or was entitled to live in NI without restrictions)
- Where their family member applies during the grace period the sponsor must either have been granted EUSS or must show they would be granted EUSS (ignoring the fact they may be British).

- Where their family member applies after the grace period they can show that they hold EUSS *or EUPSS*, or that they would have been granted this, had they applied during the grace period (ignoring the fact that they may be British).
- **Those exempt from immigration control**
- Where their family member applies during the grace period the sponsor must show that (if they were not exempt) they would be granted EUSS.
- Where their family member applies after the grace period they must show that (if they were not exempt) they would have been granted EUSS *or EUPSS*, had they applied for this during the grace period.

  NB: yes, you have read correctly. Sponsors who are relevant persons of Northern Ireland and those exempt from immigration control do not qualify as sponsors during the grace period if they would only, in theory, qualify for EUPSS (rather than EUSS). Their family member's application during the grace period would fall to be refused as entitlement to EUPSS does not feature at that stage as a qualifying characteristic for one of these sponsor categories. After the grace period, however, both definitions allow the sponsor to have been entitled to either EUSS or EUPSS. It is not clear why this distinction is made but it is vital to be aware of it, to avoid advising a client to make an application too early, which would then clearly fall to be refused.

There is one category which only a relevant EEA citizen can fit into

There is no "relevant sponsor" equivalent of the following category.

- **A dual national British citizen, where the post-*McCarthy* transitional provisions in Sch 6 para 9 of the 2016 Regulations apply to the applicant as F (in those paragraphs)**. These paragraphs apply where a family member (F) whose residence rights depend on that person:
  - Was a permanent resident (before 16/7/12) and F has not lost that status or stopped being a family member
  - Had a right of residence before that date and an EEA registration certificate or EEA residence card was held/applied for/refusal appealed by 16/10/12 (and later issued)
  - Applied for a family permit or was appealing a FP refusal before 16/7/12; a FP was issued; and F travelled to the UK within 6 months of issue.

Can Appendix EU applications be made directly from abroad?

Yes ! Potential applicants are set out in the Annex 1 definition of "required proof of entitlement to apply from outside the UK". The benefit of attempting this is to cut out a potentially unnecessary extra application, namely for a family permit to travel to the UK.

The abridged definition is at 8.7.5. Essentially it says that

- EEA/Swiss nationals can apply from abroad if they have a valid passport or national ID card (either must be biometric);
- Non-EEA/Swiss nationals must have a valid biometric residence permit issued under the Regs or the EU Settlement scheme.

There is provision for the HO to accept alternative evidence of entitlement to apply from outside the UK "if the person is unable to produce" a document for reasons outside their control or compelling practical or compassionate reasons.

The EUSS guidance on page 29 sets out, within the section on entitlement to apply from outside the UK, a list of documents which are accepted by various member states as being of continuing validity, due to the pandemic.

EU Settlement Scheme step by step approach

The post-TP version of Appendix EU has complicated the process, of assessing a case to advise clients, so a step by step guide will hopefully assist:

- **CHECK** whether the applicant has pre-TP end continuous residence
  - **If yes**, they will apply either in their own right as **REAACZ**, or, if non-EEA/Swiss, as **FM of REAACZ**
  - **If no**, they will apply as "**JFM of RS**".
- **CHECK** whether the applicant fits the definition of either an REAACZ, a FM of a REAACZ or a JFM of a RS, which are all set out in abridged form in section 8.7.5

If the applicant meets the requirements of their person definition:

- **CHECK** whether the sponsor meets the requirements of their person definition, which set out what nationality the sponsor can be and what status they must have as a person with that nationality, in order to sponsor the applicant. The sponsor status requirements are found in the following Annex 1 definitions (all available in abridged form at section 8.7.5):
  - For FM of REAACZ, in the definition of REAACZ. Note there are two separate definitions, according to whether the application is made during or after the grace period.
  - For JFM of RS, in the definition of RS, which, instead of being two different definitions according to application date, is split into parts (a) (for applications made during the grace period) and (b)(for applications made thereafter)

    NB: all categories of sponsors except frontier workers (who can sponsor both, FMs of REAACZs and JFMs of RSs) must themselves have pre-TP end continuous UK residence. Obviously, if a frontier worker had such continuous pre-TP end residence, they would, by definition, not be a frontier worker! See definition of "frontier worker "in section 8.7.5

If the sponsor meets the requirements of the definition:

- **CHECK** the eligibility conditions for settled status. These are found
  - For REAACZ and FM of REAACZ in EU11 (see section 8.7.3.1 below)
  - For JFM of RS in EU11A (see section 8.7.3.2 below))
  - For FM of a QBC in EU12 (see section 8.7.3.3 below)

If the applicant would meet the condition which depends on 5 years' residence except for falling short of 5 years:

- **CHECK** the eligibility conditions for pre-settled status. These are found in section 8.7.4 below for all categories:
  - For REAACZ and FM of REAACZ in EU14 (condition 1)
  - For JFM of RS in EU14A
  - For FM of a QBC in EU 14 (condition 2).
- **CHECK** the suitability provisions for possible refusal grounds (see section 8.7.7)
- **CHECK** the requirements of the Annex 1 definition of "required evidence of family relationship" (abridged version in section 8.7.5)
- **CHECK** the application deadlines in the Annex 1 definition of "required date" (see above in this section)
- **CHECK** (if your client is abroad) whether an application under Appendix EU can be made from abroad (instead of a family permit) (this is possible where an EEA/Swiss passport/ID card is held, or a biometric residence document issued under the EEA Regs or the EUSS.

Differences between the EEA Regs and leave under Appendix EU and some general points

As already indicated, there is a great deal of symmetry between the EEA and EU Settlement Scheme routes. The latter is modelled on the former.

We address various technical differences throughout 8.7. However some particularly significant ones are:

For Sponsors:

- For EEA citizens who have come to the UK, there is no requirement to be exercising Treaty Rights to be a relevant sponsor
- Relevant persons from Northern Ireland, even those who are dual British/Irish nationals by birth or solely British nationals, are treated as EEA citizens and can thus sponsor family members, whether or not they have applied under the scheme

For family members

- Durable partners are included in the definition. For those relying on a pre-TP end continuous period of residence in the UK to prove their relationship, if they did not apply for EEA residence documentation before the end of transition, they are now barred from entry to the EU Settlement Scheme. This bar does not apply to durable partners of Northern Ireland (see Annex 1 definitions of "durable partner",then of ""relevant document" (a)(i)(bb) (abridged version below in section 8.7.5).
- Retained rights are generally modelled on the EEA Regs 2016: but family members beyond spouses can qualify following domestic abuse, and there is no requirement for the family member to be working, studying or self-sufficient after the relationship has ended. The requirement for domestic abuse victims to be divorced to be eligible for that category does not apply anymore: it is the date of the breakdown of the relationship due to domestic abuse which will determine from which point onward only the applicant's residence proof is required (which resolves what was always a serious evidential problem for this particular group of applicants).
- Dependency of parents (for applications before 1 July 2021) is *assumed* so does not have to be established by express evidence

Other general points on the EU Settlement Scheme

- Most routes to EUSS are barred by a **supervening event**. This is either a public policy expulsion or refusal, or having spent five consecutive years abroad since acquiring permanent residence. However supervening events do not bite on the children or ILR holders.

- The scheme is open to applicants who have resided in the Bailiwick of Guernsey, the Bailiwick of Jersey or the Isle of Man: hence many provisions refer *the Islands* and their laws as well as that of the UK

- There are some dates which permeate the system
- "specified date": the transition period's end, 11pm on 31 December 2020. In relation to *Surinder Singh* applications, the specified date in some respect is 11pm, 29 March 2022
- "date and time of withdrawal": ie Brexit, the UK's withdrawal from the EU, on 11pm 31 January 2020 – this is the date by which *Surinder Singh* family relationships must generally have been formed, to benefit from the later return date and application deadline.

- There are various dates of importance in the scheme.
- To enjoy rights as family members who are spouses/CPs, the marriage/CP must have been contracted by 31 December 2020, unless the couple were durable partners before that date and have married/contracted a civil partnership afterwards
- To enjoy rights as a family member who is a durable partner, the relationship must be evidenced as durable before 31 December 2020

- For the duration of the transitional period, both the rights under free movement law and under the settlement scheme existed side by side, and one could apply for, and hold, both simultaneously.

8.7.3 Eligibility for 'settled status'- all categories

Relevant EEA citizens (REAACZs) and their family members (FMs) vs joining family members (JFMs) of relevant sponsors (RSs)

The eligibility conditions for ILR/ILE under Appendix EU (collectively referred to as "EUSS" for "EU Settled Status") are contained in in EU11 and EU11A, which compare, by way of an overview, as follows:

Comparative table of settled status eligibility conditions Relevant EEA citizens (REAACZ) or their family members (FM) vs Joining family members (JFM) of relevant sponsors (RS)	
EU11 – EUSS for REAACZs or their FMs	**EU11A – EUSS for JFMs of RSs** *NB: essentially those lacking continuous pre-TP end UK residence*
1.PR holders (REAACZ or their FM)	*No equivalent*
2.ILR holders (REAACZ or their FM0	*No equivalent*
3.Five years' residence (REAACZ or their FM)	1.Five years' residence as a JFM of a RS
4.REAACZ who has ceased activity	*No equivalent*
5.FM of an REAACZ who has ceased activity	2.JFM of a RS who has ceased activity
6.FM of an REAACZ who has died	3.JFM of a RS who has died
7.Child FM of an REAACZ or their spouse/civil partner *early settlement*	4.Child JFM of a RS or their spouse/civil partner *early settlement*

Para EU11A has four conditions instead of 7, because:

- JFMs, being by definition those lacking continuous pre-TP end residence, cannot be PR holders, so condition 1. in EU11 is not reflected in EU11A; neither can they exchange ILR accrued in different immigration categories after arriving in the UK post TP end for settled status, hence condition 2. in EU11 is not reflected in EU11A
- There is no equivalent of condition 4. of EU11 (REAACZ being the applicant who has ceased activity) in EU11A as EU11A only applies to family members rather than the EEA national (the RS in that case) in their own right.

Other differences between FM of REAACZ and JFM of RS are:

- As the definition of JFM of a RS excludes those with Zambrano- or other derivative rights, those with no pre-TP end residence cannot qualify for settled or pre-settled status, using that status
- Dual British citizens whose other nationality is EEA/Swiss (to whom the pre-*McCarthy* transitional provisions apply) are not included as relevant sponsors under condition 2 and 4 of EU 11A (FM of person who has ceased activity and early child settlement, respectively) but they do appear as eligible sponsors in conditions 5 and 7 in EU11 (the corresponding conditions).

8.7.3.1 Para EU11 - Eligibility for EUSS for Relevant EEA Citizens and their family members

The seven conditions under which "relevant EEA citizens" ("REAACZ") and their family members will be eligible for settled status ("EUSS") are outlined in this section. We address the components of the various definitions in 8.7.5.

Where all requirements *except for the five years' residence* are met, an applicant will be eligible for a grant of 'pre-settled status' under EU14 (see section 8.7.4).

Conditions 1, 3, 4, 5 and 6 also include the '*supervening event*' proviso: ie entitlement is forfeited by absence for more than 5 years or public policy refusal grounds. Doubtless the thinking behind *not* applying this to conditions 2 (ILR holders) and condition 7 (early EUSS for children) being that where one has domestic ILR, there is no reason to hold this against you, there being domestic immigration sanctions if required. And that issues of these nature should not be held against children.

The conditions are:

- **Permanent residence holders:** A relevant EEA citizen, a current or former family member of one, or a family member who has retained the right of residence via a relationship with a relevant EEA citizen, and who holds a permanent residence document (issued under the Regs)
- **ILR holders:** A relevant EEA citizen, a family member of one, or a family member who has retained the right of residence via a relationship with a relevant EEA citizen, and there is valid evidence they hold ILR or ILE
- **EEA Citizens and their family members, and those with Zambrano or derived rights with 5 years' residence:** A relevant EEA citizen, a family member of one, or a family member who has retained the right of residence via a relationship with a relevant EEA citizen, or who is a person with a derivative or Zambrano right to reside; and who has accrued ***five years' residence*** in any (or any combination) of those categories.
- A **relevant EEA citizen who has ceased activity**
- A current or former **family member of a relevant EEA citizen who has ceased activity**; they were a family member when activity ceased and were resident continuously immediately before their sponsor ceased activity. In all cases, the applicant's sponsor must have resided continuously in the UK since pre-TP end. The status requirements for the sponsoring REAACZ differ according to whether the application is made within or after the grace period:

Under condition 5. in EU11, if REAACZ is:	... then the REAACZ must have the following status for:	
	Applications during grace period	**Applications from 1 July 2021**
EEA/Swiss national	Holds EUSS/would be granted EUSS	Holds EUSS
Relevant naturalised British citizen	Would be granted EUSS if they were not British	Would have been granted EUSS if they were not British
Dual national (non-"relevant naturalised BC")	Has resided since pre-TP end OR would be granted EUSS if they were not British	Would have been granted EUSS if they were not British
RPNI (Irish only)	Holds EUSS/ is being/ would be granted	Holds EUSS/ would have been granted EUSS
RPNI (Irish/ British or BC only)	Would be granted EUSS if they were not British	Would have been granted EUSS if they were not British
Exempt from immigration control	Would be granted EUSS if they were not exempt	Would have been granted EUSS if they were not exempt

NB: there is no reference here to EUPSS as those who cease activity are eligible for EUSS.

- A **family member of a relevant EEA citizen who is deceased** and who was at time of death a worker or self-employed; the EEA citizen was resident in the UK and Islands for two years before death or the death was due to an accident at work or an occupational disease; the family member lived with them immediately before the death. ***NB:*** *Where the EEA citizen was neither a worker nor self-employed at time of death (nor held PR or ILR), the applicant may still come within condition 3, as a person who has retained a right of residence, so long as they resided in the UK as the family member of the deceased for one year before death – see definition of 'family member who has retained the right of residence' in Annex 1 to Appendix EU.*
- **A child (under 21) of a relevant EEA citizen, or of their spouse or civil partner (early EUSS)**. Where the parent is the partner of the REAACZ, the marriage/civil partnership must precede TP end or that parent must have been the REAACZ's durable partner pre-TP end and remained so at TP end. The status requirements for the sponsoring REAACZ or their spouse/civl partner differ according to whether the application is made within or after the grace period:

Under condition 7. in EU11, if REAACZ is:	... then the REAACZ must have the following status for:	
	Applications during grace period	Applications from 1 July 2021
EEA/Swiss national	Holds EUSS/would be granted EUSS	Holds EUSS
Irish national (this is the only additional category compared with the table under condition 5.)	*Would be granted EUSS*	*Would have been granted EUSS*
Relevant naturalised British citizen	Would be granted EUSS if they were not British	Would have been granted EUSS if they were not British
Dual national (non-"relevant naturalised BC")	Has resided since pre-TP end OR would be granted EUSS if they were not British	Would have been granted EUSS if they were not British
RPNI (Irish only)	Holds EUSS/ is being/ would be granted	Holds EUSS/ would have been granted EUSS
RPNI (Irish/ British or BC only)	Would be granted EUSS if they were not British	Would have been granted EUSS if they were not British
Exempt from immigration control	Would be granted EUSS if they were not exempt	Would have been granted EUSS if they were not exempt

NB: there is no reference in condition 7. to EUPSS as this category provides early EUSS for children whose relevant parent settles.

8.7.3.2 Para 11A – Eligibility for EUSS by joining family members of relevant sponsors

The four conditions under which a "joining family member of relevant sponsor" (i.e. a person lacking pre-TP end continuous residence) will be eligible for settlement in the UK are outlined in this section. Please refer to the relevant definitions in 8.7.5.

Where all requirements *except for the five years' residence* are met, an applicant will be eligible for a grant of 'pre-settled status' under EU14A.

Conditions 1, 2 and 3 below also include the '*supervening event*' proviso: ie entitlement is forfeited by absence for more than 5 years or public policy refusal grounds.

The conditions are:

- **Five years' residence:** the person is (or was, for the relevant period) a JFM of a RS or a person with retained rights of residence via a relationship with a RS. They must have 5 years' continuous residence in any combination of these.
- A current or former **family member of a relevant sponsor who has ceased activity**; they were a family member when activity ceased and were resident continuously immediately before their sponsor ceased activity. As this is the JFM category, their residence must have started ***after*** TP end. In all cases, the applicant's sponsor must have resided continuously in the UK since pre-TP end. The status requirements for the sponsoring RS differ according to whether the application is made within or after the grace period:

Under condition 2 in EU11A, if RS is:	... then the RS must have the following status for:	
	Applications during grace period	Applications from 1 July 2021
EEA/Swiss national	Holds EUSS/would be granted EUSS	Holds EUSS
Irish citizen	*NB: Would come under the above category during the grace period*	Would have been granted EUSS
Relevant naturalised British citizen	Would be granted EUSS if they were not British	Would have been granted EUSS if they were not British
RPNI (Irish only)	Holds EUSS/ is being/ would be granted	Holds EUSS/ would have been granted EUSS
RPNI (Irish/ British or BC only)	Would be granted EUSS if they were not British	Would have been granted EUSS if they were not British

Exempt from immigration control	Would be granted EUSS if they were not exempt	Would have been granted EUSS if they were not exempt

NB: there is no reference here to EUPSS as those who cease activity are eligible for EUSS.

- A **family member of a relevant sponsor who is deceased** and who was at time of death a worker or self-employed; the EEA citizen was resident in the UK for two years before death or the death was due to an accident at work or an occupational disease; the family member lived with them immediately before the death. As this is the JFM category, this residence must have started ***after*** TP end. ***NB:*** *Where the EEA citizen was neither a worker nor self-employed at time of death, the applicant may still come within condition 1, as a person who has retained a right of residence, so long as they resided in the UK as the family member of the deceased for one year before death – see definition of 'family member who has retained the right of residence' in Annex 1 to Appendix EU.*
- **A child (under 21) of a relevant sponsor, or of their spouse or civil partner (early EUSS)**. Where the parent is the partner of the RS, the marriage/civil partnership must precede TP end or that parent must have been the RS's durable partner pre-TP end and remained so at TP end (see our summary of the "durable partner" definition)

  Where the applicant is the child ***of the spouse or civil partner*** of the RS, the spouse/CP must either hold or, be in the process of being granted, EUSS.
- The marriage or civil partnership must either have been contracted pre-TP end or the now spouse/CP must have met the definition of a 'durable partner' pre-TP end; and
- The parent can either
- ***have*** been resident in the UK continuously since pre-TP end as a FM of an REAACZ and holds or is being granted EUSS under EU2; or
- ***not have*** been resident pre-TP end as a FM of an REAACZ and has been or is being granted EUSS under EU2A; or
- have been so resident but their continuous residence was broken by absence or imprisonment; or
- have been so resident but a supervening event has occurred

The status requirements for the sponsoring RS or their spouse/ civil partner differ according to whether the application is made within or after the grace period:

Under condition 4. in EU11A, if RS is:	... then the RS must have the following status for:	
	Applications during grace period	**Applications from 1 July 2021**
EEA/Swiss national	Holds EUSS/is being granted EUSS	Holds EUSS
Irish citizen	Has not applied but would be granted EUSS	Would have been granted EUSS
Relevant naturalised British citizen	Would be granted EUSS if they were not British	Would have been granted EUSS if they were not British
RPNI (Irish only)	Holds EUSS/ would be granted EUSS	Holds EUSS/ would have been granted EUSS
RPNI (Irish/ British or BC only)	Would be granted EUSS if they were not British	Would have been granted EUSS if they were not British
Exempt from immigration control	Would be granted EUSS if they were not exempt	Would have been granted EUSS if they were not exempt

NB: there is no reference in condition 4. in EU11A to EUPSS as this category provides early EUSS for children whose relevant parent settles.

As with EU11, children under condition 4 are excluded from the application of supervening events.

8.7.3.3 Eligibility for settled status for family members of Qualifying British Citizens

Further notes/information
This is the EUSS version of the *Surinder Singh* route, which is outside OISC 1 scope and not part of its exam curriculum. The information in this section is provided merely to assist you in spotting and summarising these cases for referral. For details on the underlying EU rights and their application under the free movement regime before 2021, please refer to section 8.3.1.

The four conditions, under which family members of 'qualifying British citizens' will be eligible for settled status are in EU12. They require that the applicant is a **family member of a qualifying British citizen** or **a family member who has retained the right of residence** via a relationship with such a person.

Post-TP end, deadlines, which are particularly important in this category, have now been put into the rules and they are best set out as part of the definitions in which they feature:

Annex 1 definitions of "qualifying British citizen" and "family member of a qualifying British citizen"

Qualifying British citizen

A QBC is a British citizen who:

- Has or for the relevant period had returned to the UK with the applicant:
- Before 11pm on 29 March 2022): or
- For the relationship categories in (a)(ii), (a)(iv), (a)(vii) or (a)(viii) of the definition of 'FM of a QBC' before TP end. **[these are the categories in the left-hand column in the next table below]**

  or later if the HO is satisfied there were reasonable grounds for missing that deadline; and
- satisfied regulation 9(2), (3) and (4)(a) of the EEA Regulations (i.e.the *Surinder Singh* requirements for residence in another member state – see section 8.3.1 on *Surinder Singh*)
- before TP end; and
- immediately before returning to the UK with the applicant
- was continuously resident in the UK under Reg 3 of the 2016 Regs

Family member of a qualifying British citizen

Annex 1 definition of Family Members of a Qualifying British Citizen (FM of a QBC) – *("withdrawal date" = 11pm on 31 January 2020, when the UK left the EU)*	
Deadlines for arrival in the UK to enter the EU Settlement Scheme in that category	
Before 11pm on 31 December 2020	**Before 11pm on 29 March 2022**
(a)(ii) Post-withdrawal date **spouse/CP** *with pre-TP marriage or civil partnership, where partnership was not durable pre-withdrawal*	(a)(i) Pre-withdrawal date **spouse/CP**, or current spouse/CP who was a durable partner before and on withdrawal date
(a)(iv) Post-withdrawal date **durable partners** *where partnership was durable pre-TP end and remains durable on date of application*	(a)(iii) Pre-withdrawal date **durable partner** who remains a durable partner at the date of application
(a)(vii) Pre-withdrawal date **dependent parent; or a child of a QBC's spouse/CP** *where marriage/civil partnership was formed between withdrawal and TP end and was not durable pre-withdrawal*	(a)(vi) Pre-withdrawal date **dependent parent; or a child of a QBC's spouse/CP** *where marriage/civil partnership existed pre- and on withdrawal date*

(a)(viii) **Other dependent relative of the QBC or of their spouse/CP** *The family relationship and person's dependency/membership of the household/strict need for personal care on serious health grounds existed before returning to the UK together and continues to exist at date of application or existed for the period relied on.*	(a)(v) Pre-withdrawal date **dependent parent of QBC; child of QBC**

Application deadlines for family members of QBCs

These are found in the Annex 1 definition of "required date" (see 8.7.5 for full abridged definition).

For *Surinder Singh* applicants to enter the EU Settlement Scheme, the deadlines are:

- Before 11pm on 29 March 2022 ***but only*** for the relationship categories in the right hand column in the table immediately above this paragraph
- Before 1 July 2021 for the relationship categories in the left hand column.

Eligibility for settled status for family members of QBCs – rEU12

- **Permanent residence holders:** ie those who already hold a permanent residence document (issued under the Regs) or
- **ILR Holders**: ie those with valid evidence of ILR or
- **Family members with 5 years' residence: those who have** accrued five years' residence in any (or any combination) of those categories, and residence was lawful under Reg 9 (although the British citizen need not have been a qualified person) or
- **Children**: the applicant is a child (under 21) of the spouse or civil partner of a QBC who would be in the UK lawfully under Regs 9(1)-(6) (disregarding exercise of Treaty rights by the British citizen), and that spouse or civil partner has been/is being granted settled status. The marriage or civil partnership must either have been contracted before 11pm on 31 January 2020 (withdrawal date) or the applicant's parent was the durable partner of the QBC before that date).

Conditions 1 and 3 also include the '*supervening event*' proviso: ie entitlement is forfeited by absence for more than 5 years or public policy refusal grounds. As with the other settled status categories, this proviso is not applied to ILR holders or children.

Qualifying for settled status via a combination of categories – para EU13

EU 13 clarifies that, for the categories in which five years' residence must be accrued, applicants can combine periods of residence as:

- a relevant EEA citizen, their family member or a person with derivative or Zambrano rights to reside
- the family member of a qualifying British citizen (*Surinder Singh* cases)
- a family member with a retained right of residence based on a relationship with one of the above

Whether to apply under EU11 or EU12 in those cases is determined by the relevant status at the time of the application.

8.7.4 Pre-settled status – "leave to remain under Appendix EU" – all categories

EU14 allows for pre-settled status to be granted to REAACZ or their family members under the following conditions

- Condition 1: five years' residence have not yet accrued by the time of the application, where all other requirements of EU11 condition 3 are met (REAACZ or FM of REAACZ); or
- Condition 2: five years' residence have not yet accrued by the time of the application, where all other requirements of EU12 condition 3 are met (*Surinder Singh* cases)

EU14A, which applies to JFM of RS, has only one condition, which is again that they would be granted settled status if they did not fall short of the 5-year residence requirement.

8.7.5 Definitions from Annex 1 of Appendix EU Part 1

From the first edition of Appendix EU, it has always appeared as if its structure under which the Annex 1 "definitions" in fact contain many complex substantive requirements, may have been intended to make the rules themselves appear relatively short and straightforward. In practice, Appendix EU is now extremely difficult to navigate and the definitions are thick with cross references. To assist our readers we have abridged the most important definitions and, where appropriate, grouped them together, where they cross refer to one another substantively and are best read together.

As cross-referencing within Appendix EU is so ubiquitous, we have preserved section numbering within the definitions except where this results in the text becoming too expansive. In those instances, definitions have been presented as tables.

As referred to throughout in this Module, the 2016 Regs were repealed at TP end but saved with modifications. Within the sections on residence rights above, Appendix EU continues to refer to the Regs, and the Annex 1 definition n of "EEA Regulations" sets out how this is to be done in that context:

Annex 1 definition of "EEA Regulations"

- The 2016 Regulations in relation to something done pre-TP end
- The 2016 Regulations in relation to something done post-TP end. Although revoked, these continue to have effect with modifications

Annex 1 definitions of "Joining Family Members" of "Relevant Sponsors", and "family member of a relevant EEA citizen" side by side

The first two of these definitions were introduced, and the third changed, by HC813. The new provisions have been in force since 11pm on 31 December 2020, the end of the transition period (referred to as the "specified date" in Appendix EU).

Essentially, a Joining Family Member of a Relevant Sponsor ("JFM of a RS") is a national of any country except the UK who lacks continuous residence which started before the end of the transition period ("pre-TP end"). If they are EEA/Swiss nationals, they will no longer be able to commence UK residence to eventually qualify for leave under Appendix EU in their own right as, lacking pre-TP end continuous residence, they do not fit the definition of a relevant EEA citizen ("REAACZ"). Instead, they would have to apply under other immigration rule categories – unless, that is, they have a family member who is a Relevant Sponsor ("RS"), enabling them to apply as a Joining Family Member of a Relevant Sponsor ("JFM of an RS").

A person *with* pre-TP end continuous residence:

- If an EEA/Swiss national, can qualify in their own right for leave as a REAACZ, or as a Family Member of a Relevant EEA Citizen ("FM of a REAACZ").
- If not an EEA/Swiss citizen, can only qualify as a FM of a REAACZ, not in their own right.

Family members for new applications are now defined as follows:

<table>
<tr><th colspan="2">Comparative table of definitions</th></tr>
<tr><th>Family member of a Relevant EEA Citizen ("FM of a REAACZ")</th><th>Joining Family Member of a Relevant Sponsor ("JFM of a RS")</th></tr>
<tr><td>A person who is not a JFM of an RS</td><td>NB: a JFM is essentially a person lacking continuous UK residence which started pre-TP end</td></tr>
<tr><td colspan="2">A person who is (or was, at the relevant time) a spouse/civil partner since pre-TP end; or a spouse/CP who was the durable partner pre-TP end and remained so at TP end. Check definition of "durable partner" as to whether in the circumstances an EEA Regs document must be held.</td></tr>
<tr><td></td><td>Specified spouse or civil partner of a Swiss citizen (see definition below)</td></tr>
<tr><td colspan="2">A person who is or was (for the relevant period) a durable partner, and the partnership was durable since pre-TP end.</td></tr>
<tr><td>A child or dependent parent of the REAACZ,or of their spouse/CP, and all the family relationships existed pre-TP end</td><td>A child or dependent parent of the RS, or of their spouse/CP, and all the family relationships existed pre-TP end, unless the child was born/adopted thereafter</td></tr>
<tr><td>A dependent relative of REAACZ or their spouse/CP where dependency/ membership of household/strict need for personal care on serious health grounds existed pre-TP end and continues to exist (or did so for the period relied on). A relevant document (under the EEA Regs) must be held or have been applied for pre-TP end apart from where their sponsor is a relevant person of Northern Ireland. Check the definition of "relevant document".</td><td></td></tr>
</table>

A few comments before looking at the definitions in the table below, side by side:

- Any leave under Appendix EU which REAACZs or RSs must, to sponsor family members, show they hold, or which would be granted, will inevitably be under either EU2 or EU3 as they must have pre-TP end continuous residence. The definition repeats this but to ease readability, this can be generally stated here. The only other paragraphs under which Appendix EU grants of leave *could* be made are EU2A and EU3A, which cover, respectively, grants of settled- or pre-settled status for JFMs of RS, as a category, *lack* residence which is continuous and started before TP end. The two categories are mutually exclusive.
- In the post-grace period definition of REAACZs and RSs, wherever that person is required to hold, *or show that they would have been granted*, any form of leave under Appendix EU, they must also demonstrate that such leave has not/would not have lapsed, been cancelled, revoked/curtailed or invalidated.
- In the grace period definition of REAACZs and RSs, that requirement only applies to EEA/Swiss nationals and Relevant Persons of Northern Ireland (RPNIs) who have single Irish nationality. Within these categories, the requirement applies only those who *have been* granted EUSS, not those who *would be* granted EUSS.

Additional comments:

Dependent relatives include:

- Those dependent on the EEA Sponsor
- A member of the EEA Sponsor's household
- Those who strictly require the EEA Sponsor's care on health grounds
- Those subject to a *non-adoptive legal guardianship order* (an example of how the EUSS aims to track the most recent CJEU case law, here **SM Algeria** [2019] EUECJ C-129/18)

- The children and adopted children of durable partners

Family members include those with retained rights. Those are essentially residence rights following the death or departure of the EEA citizen, or where the relationship has ended with divorce after a certain period (or where child access rights are at stake). See for an outline of the version under the 2016 Regs: 8.2.1.1.

- Retained rights are generally modelled on the EEA Regs 2016. Thus we can see that generally the Annex 1 definitions for *family member who has retained the right of residence* from (a)-(e) are the same for those benefiting from retained rights under the Regs, Reg 10(2)-(5)

- However one significant difference is that not only *spouses* can qualify following domestic violence. Thus a person can benefit where the applicant '*or another family member has been a victim of domestic violence or abuse before the relevant family relationship broke down permanently*'

- There is no requirement for the family member to be working, studying or self-sufficient after the relationship has ended (because there is no equivalent provision to Reg 10(6) of the EEA Regs 2016)

- The Appendix EU equivalent of Reg10(5) explicitly states that, where termination proceedings (divorce or dissolution of a civil partnership) are initiated but the EEA citizen leaves the UK before termination, they are *deemed* to have remained until termination.
- And of course, consistent with the general scheme of EUSS which looks to a sponsor's residence rather than any Treaty Right exercise, the EEA citizen need not have worked or studied etc

Further notes/information

Zambrano and retained rights cases are outside OISC 1 scope and not part of its exam curriculum. The information in this box is provided to assist you in spotting and summarising these cases for referral.

Annex 1 definition of a "person with a Zambrano right to reside"

The EUSS includes Zambrano rights holders amongst its beneficiaries. It does so without choosing to provide any definition of its own. Rather it cross references to Reg 16(5) and (6) of the EEA Regs 2016. Please refer to section 8.2.1.1 for an outline on Zambrano rights. Thus those who can benefit are

- Primary carers of British citizens where the latter could not live in the UK or EU without the former's care (Reg 16(5))
- Other children of such primary carers so long as they are under 18 and otherwise lack leave under the Rules (Reg 16(6)): and once granted leave under Appendix EU such children can be granted further leave (presumably EUSS itself) notwithstanding that they have reached majority and that they have now held leave under Appendix EU)

Note that the derivative rights guidance, as well as the EUSS guidance on Zambrano mandate refusals of all applications on Zambrano grounds:

- where the applicant has never made an application under Appendix FM or any other Art 8 claim, or
- where such a claim was refused but circumstances have changed so as to, now, allow for success.

This is explicitly based on (we would say, a misinterpretation of) Patel [2017] EWCA Civ 2028. The SSHD considers that that decision suggested that all domestic routes under the Rules had to be exhausted before a Zambrano application can be made. The Supreme Court in the onwards appeal in Patel [2019] UKSC 59 did not deal with the question as to whether Art 8 applications must be made before *Zambrano* rights are open to an applicant. The Court of Appeal decision observes the relationship and overlap between the two routes, but did not hold that an Article 8 application having failed is a prerequisite.

The FTT in Zambrano is known to have rejected there being any such prerequisite.

Any time spent in the UK with leave to remain under the rules (other than pre-settled status) cannot count towards the 5-year residence period. See the definition of 'a person with a Zambrano right to reside' in Annex 2 to Appendix EU Part 1, at (5)(b).

Annex 1 definition of a "person with a derivative right to reside"

Similarly to Zambrano cases, here again derivative rights are defined by a cross reference to Reg 16 of the EEA Regs 2016. Again, for the detail on these rights, please refer to section 8.6.3.3. So the same classes of beneficiary exists as under those Regs (save for Zambrano cases who of course have their own route). Essentially they are primary carers of self sufficient children, the children now in education of EEA nationals formerly exercising Treaty Rights here, and their primary carers.

Under the EUSS primary carers of self sufficient children need not establish that the child holds comprehensive sickness insurance.

Annex 1 definitions of "relevant EEA citizen" and "relevant sponsor" side by side

<table>
<tr><th colspan="2">Comparative table of definitions</th></tr>
<tr><th>Relevant EEA Citizen ("REAACZ")</th><th>Relevant Sponsor ("RS")</th></tr>
<tr><th colspan="2">For applications made during the grace period</th></tr>
<tr><td>An EEA/Swiss national, resident continuously since pre-TP end</td><td></td></tr>
<tr><td colspan="2"><u>NB:</u><ul><li>The above REAACZs can apply for EUSS/EUPSS in their own right.</li><li>All further REAACZ categories below are for REAACZs in the capacity as a sponsor for a FM of a REAACZ.</li><li>All RS categories are intended for sponsorship of JFMs.</li></ul></td></tr>
<tr><td>An EEA/Swiss national<ul><li>Resident continuously since pre-TP end; and</li><li>Has been granted EUSS/EUPSS; or</li><li>Would be granted EUSS/EUPSS if applied before 1/7/21</li></ul></td><td>An EEA/Swiss national<ul><li>Resident continuously since pre-TP end; and</li><li>Has been granted EUSS/EUPSS; or</li><li>Would be granted EUSS/EUPSS if applied before 1/7/21</li></ul></td></tr>
<tr><td colspan="2">A relevant naturalised British citizens</td></tr>
<tr><td>A dual national BC (whose other nationality is EEA/Swiss) (where the post McCarthy transitional provisions in Sch 6 para 9 of the 2016 Regulations apply to the applicant as F):<ul><li>Resident continuously since pre-TP end; or</li><li>Who, having been so resident, would be (but for the fact they are a BC) granted EUSS if applied before 1/7/21</li></ul></td><td></td></tr>
<tr><td colspan="2">A relevant person of Northern Ireland (RPNI – this includes those with Irish, Irish/British or just British citizenship)</td></tr>
</table>

<table>
<tr><td colspan="2"><ul><li>Resident continuously since pre-TP end; or</li><li>Having been so resident, has been/would be granted EUSS if applied before 1/7/21 (if they were not BCs, should that be the case)</li></ul></td></tr>
<tr><td colspan="2">A person exempt from immigration control<ul><li>Resident continuously since pre-TP end; or</li><li>Having been so resident would be granted EUSS if applied before 1/7/21 (but for the fact they are exempt from immigration control)</li></ul></td></tr>
<tr><td colspan="2">A frontier worker</td></tr>
<tr><th colspan="2">For applications made from 1 July 2021</th></tr>
<tr><th>REAACZ</th><th>RS</th></tr>
<tr><td>An EEA/Swiss national, resident continuously since pre-TP end</td><td></td></tr>
<tr><td>An Irish national, resident continuously since pre-TP end</td><td></td></tr>
<tr><td colspan="2"><u>NB</u>:<ul><li>The above two REAACZ categories are those applying in their own right.</li><li>All further REAACZ categories below are for sponsorship of an FM of an REAACZ.</li><li>All RS categories are for sponsorship of JFMs only.</li></ul></td></tr>
<tr><td colspan="2">An EEA/Swiss national who has been resident continuously since pre-TP end, and who has been granted EUSS/EUPSS</td></tr>
<tr><td colspan="2">An Irish national who has been resident continuously since pre-TP end, and who would have been granted EUSS/EUPSS, had they applied before 1/7/21</td></tr>
<tr><td colspan="2">A relevant naturalised British citizens who would (but for the fact they are a BC) have been granted EUSS/EUPSS had they applied before 1/7/21</td></tr>
<tr><td>Dual national BCs (whose other nationality is EEA/Swiss) (where the post-McCarthy transitional provisions in Sch 6 para 9 of the 2016 Regulations apply to the applicant as F):<ul><li>Resident continuously since pre-TP end; and</li><li>Would be (but for the fact they are BCs) granted EUSS/EUPSS had they applied before 1/7/21</li></ul></td><td></td></tr>
<tr><td colspan="2">A relevant person of Northern Ireland<ul><li>Resident continuously since pre-TP end; and</li><li>Has been granted EUSS/EUPSS; or</li><li>Would have been granted EUSS/EUPSS (if applied before 1/7/21, and but for the fact they are a BC, if that is the case)</li></ul></td></tr>
<tr><td colspan="2">A person exempt from immigration control, who has been resident continuously since pre-TP end and who would (but for the fact they are exempt from immigration control) have been granted EUSS/EUPSS had they applied before 1/7/21.</td></tr>
<tr><td colspan="2">A frontier worker</td></tr>
<tr><td></td><td>In addition: unless the JFM applies under retained rights based on the death of their sponsor, the RS must be alive(!)</td></tr>
</table>

Annex 1 Definition "durable partner"

This category of persons appears in identical terms within the definitions of FM of a REAACZ and JFM of a RS. Whether or not a residence document/family permit is required depends on the nationality of the sponsor, and on whether or not the person resided in the UK continuously since pre-TP end, and in what circumstances:

- Person in a durable relationship (with an REAACZ, a QBC or a RS) at the relevant time, having lived with them in a relationship akin to marriage for at least 2 years unless there is other significant evidence of durability; **and**

- The person holds a BRC/family permit as the durable partner of an REAACZ, QBC or RS for the period of residence relied on. Such a document is deemed to have been granted pre-TP end if it had been applied for pre-TP end; **or**
- The person does not hold such a card. Where applying as a durable partner or where marriage/ civil partnership was formed post TP end but the applicant was durable partner pre-TP end:
  (aa) The date of application is after TP end; and
  (bb) the person
  (aaa) was not in the UK as a durable partner without a BRC/family permit in that capacity and without other leave; or
  (bbb) was in the UK before TP end but their continuous residence was broken through absence or imprisonment and after this, they were not resident in the UK again before TP end; or
  (ccc) was in the UK before TP end but were then absent for 5 years and not resident again before TP end. The relationship must have been durable before TP end (or for *Surinder Singh* cases before 31 January 2020).

- The partnership is not one of convenience
- Neither partner has (or had, for the relevant period) another durable partner, spouse or civil partner with immigration status on the basis on that relationship.

The definition adds that where the application is on the basis of being a family member of a person who is deceased (i.e. an application under either condition 6. in EU11 or condition 3. In EU11A) this definition must have been met at the time before death rather than the date of application. Both definitions require that the family member lived with the deceased person before the death, and clearly by the date of application they no longer do.

Annex 1 definition of "relevant person of Northern Ireland"

a person who:
(a) is:
(i) a British citizen; or
(ii) an Irish citizen; or
(iii) a British citizen and an Irish citizen; and
(b) was born in Northern Ireland and, at the time of the person's birth, at least one of their parents was:
(i) a British citizen; or
(ii) an Irish citizen; or
(iii) a British citizen and an Irish citizen; or
(iv) otherwise entitled to reside in Northern Ireland without any restriction on their period of residence

Annex 1 definition of "required evidence of being a relevant person of Northern Ireland"

- Birth certificate or passport showing the person was born in NI; and
- Evidence that when they were born one parent was
- A British citizen; or
- An Irish citizen; or
- Both; or

Entitled to reside in NI without restriction on their period of residence

Annex 1 definition of "frontier worker"

a person who:
(a) is an EEA or Swiss national; and
(b) is not a British citizen; and

(c) satisfies SSHD by relevant evidence of this that they fulfil the relevant conditions of being a frontier worker set out in regulations made under section 8 of the European Union (Withdrawal Agreement) Act 2020, and that they have done so continuously since TP end; and
(d) has not been (and is not to be) refused admission to, or removed from, the UK by virtue of regulations of the type to which (c) above refers

The cross reference in (c) is to the Citizens' Rights (Frontier Workers) (EU Exit) Regulations 2020, which defines frontier workers at Reg 3, as someone who:

- Was, pre-TP end, and has been continuously since then, an EEA national worker or self-employed person (or someone who has retained that status under Reg 4)
- Is not primarily resident in the UK i.e. they have been in the UK for less than 180 days in the preceding year; or have returned to their country of residence at least once in the preceding 6 months; or twice in the preceding 12 months (unless there were exceptional circumstances why they did not)

Annex 1 definition of "specified spouse or civil partner of a Swiss citizen"

This class of persons is a special category of JFM of a RS, which has no equivalent for applicants with prior continuous UK residence. A specified spouse or civil partner of a Swiss citizen is defined as:

(a) the spouse/CP of a RS; and
(b) the RS is a national of Switzerland and is not also a British citizen; and
(c) the marriage or civil partnership was formed between 1 January 2021 and 1 January 2026; and
(d)

(i) the marriage or civil partnership continues to exist, unless the application is for EUSS on the basis of 5 years' residence in general or under retained rights, or death of the sponsor; or
(ii) if applying on the basis of 5 years' residence, it must have existed for the relevant period; or
(iii) where applying for EUSS on the basis of the death of the sponsor, the marriage or civil partnership existed immediately before death

Note that the use of the word "exists" is in contrast to "subsists". A subsisting relationship would normally require cohabitation, indicating that, to meet the definition, no cohabitation is required. However, for applications as a partner of a deceased person, of course, cohabitation immediately before the death *is* required.

Annex 1 definition of "specified date"

(a) 2300 GMT on 31 December 2020; or

(b) 2300 GMT on 29 March 2022 for *Surinder Singh* family members (FMs of QBCs) ***but only***

- spouses/CPs
- durable partners
- dependent parent of QBC/their spouse/CP
- child of QBC/their spouse/CP (unless born or adopted after 29 March 2022).

NB: This later date for some *Surinder Singh* family members is the specified date, before which the "continuous qualifying period" starts for FMs of QBCs who qualify for either EUSS or EUPSS on the basis of their own residence (i.e. under EU12 condition 3 for settled status or EU14 condition 2 for pre-settled status)

Annex 1 definition of "required proof of entitlement to apply from outside the UK"

Not all applicants from 1 January 2021 have to apply for family permits. Some can apply under Appendix EU for settled- or pre-settled status from abroad, so long as they have the "required proof" for their entitlement to do so. The abridged definition is as follows (and immediately below are the further definitions referred to therein):

(a) For EEA/Swiss nationals:
  (i) their valid passport; or
  (ii) their valid national biometric identity card
(b) For non-EEA citizen, their valid "specified relevant document"

unless SSHD agrees to accept alternative evidence of entitlement to apply from outside the UK, if the person is unable to produce the required document due to circumstances beyond their control or to compelling practical or compassionate reasons.

'valid' means that the document is genuine and has not expired, been cancelled or invalidated.

Annex 1 definition of "specified relevant document"

(a) A biometric residence card, permanent residence card or derivative residence card issued by the UK under the EEA Regs on the basis of an application made on or after 6 April 2015; or
(b) A biometric EUPSS residence card.

Note the difference to the broader definition of "relevant document" (immediately below), which is referred to more widely throughout Appendix EU. The latter category includes documents issued to EEA/Swiss nationals, whereas "specified document" only includes those issued to non-EEA/Swiss nationals.

Annex 1 definition of "relevant document"

(a)
  (i)
    (aa) Any document issued under the EEA Regs applied for pre-TP end (or, for family permit of durable partners before 1 July 2021)
    (bb) For extended family members or durable partners of an RPNI: other evidence which would have led to the grant of a document issued under the EEA Regs, is deemed to be equivalent of a document in (aa)
  (ii) *[mirrors (i) for the Islands]*
  (iii) A EUPSS BRC (pre-settled status BRC)
(b) Which has not been revoked or fell to be revoked, because the relationship/dependency never existed or had ceased
(c) Unless (d) applies, it has not expired or otherwise ceased to be effective and had remained valid for the period relied on
(d) for dependent relatives and durable partners, the relevant document may have expired, where:
  (i) the new document was applied for before the old one expired. It must be on the basis of the same family relationship.
  (ii) this new document must be issued by the date of decision on the Appendix EU application

Annex 1 definition of "required evidence of family relationship"

To facilitate cross-referencing from other sections when dealing with the actual provisions in Appendix EU, we have retained the structure and numbering of this definition. However, the below is an abridged version where cross references contained in its subparas have been explained rather than retained, for readability.

- Spouses without a documented right of PR:
- A relevant document issued on that basis, or a valid document of record of marriage recognised in the UK; and

(aa) for marriages contracted after TP end, a relevant document issued as a durable partner of the sponsor. Specified spouses/CPs of Swiss citizens are excluded from this requirement. Post-TP spouses of RNPIs and JFMs of RSs (i.e. those without pre-TP residence) can evidence their durable relationship pre-TP end via the relevant evidence. They do not need to have a relevant document.

(bb) for spouses of QBCs who married post-31 January 2020, evidence of the durable relationship before and on 31 January 2020

- Civil partners without a documented right of PR:
- A relevant document issued on that basis or a valid civil partnership certificate recognised by the UK; or an overseas registration document which can be treated as a civil partnership under the Civil Partnership Act 2004
-

(aa) for civil partnerships contracted after TP end, a relevant document issued as a durable partner of the sponsor. Specified spouses/CPs of Swiss citizens are excluded from this requirement. Post-TP civil partners of RNPIs and JFMs of RSs (i.e. those without pre-TP residence) can evidence their durable relationship pre-TP end via the relevant evidence. They do not need to have a relevant document.

(bb) for civil partners of QBCs who married post-31 January 2020, evidence of the durable relationship before and on 31 January 2020

- A child without a documented right of PR: a relevant document issued to them on that basis or their birth certificate, and
- Children aged 21 and over, not previously granted EUPSS as a child: evidence of dependence
- A JFM of a RS, born or adopted (or otherwise became a 'child') after TP end: , evidence that either their parent is Swiss or a spouse/civil partner of a Swiss national; or that both parents are an RS; or one is an RS and the other a BC; or one parent is an RS with joint or sole custody under UK, EEA or Swiss law, or recognised by those states (particularly as regards best interests of the child)
- A dependent parent without a right of PR: a relevant document issued on that basis; or evidence of birth. Evidence of dependence is only required in applications from 1 July 2021 where no previous leave as a dependent parent is held.
- A durable partner:
  (i) a relevant document as the durable partner of the REEAC (or of the QBC or of the RS). If this does not confirm the right of permanent residence, also: evidence which satisfies SSHD that the partnership remains durable at the date of application (or did so for the period of residence relied upon); or
  (ii) for applications after TP end and where no relevant document is held: evidence of durability if the applicant was not in the UK with continuous leave since pre-TP end.
  The evidence must show that the partnership was durable pre-TP end (or before 31 January 2020 for *Surinder Singh* cases)
- Dependent relative:
- A relevant document as the dependant relative of their sponsor. If this does not confirm a right to PR, also: evidence that the relationship and dependency/membership of the household/strict need for personal care exist at the date of application (or did for the relevant period); or
- In the case of a FM of a QBC: evidence that the relationship and dependency/membership of the household/strict need for personal care existed at TP end and at the date of application (or that it existed for the period relied on)

In addition, the definition provides:

- A death certificate or other evidence of death is required where the application is in a category relating to the death of a person
- Any family member applicants of any nationality without a documented right of PR, the evidence of family relationship must include:
- Proof of ID and nationality of the sponsoring person (REAACZ. QBC or RS)

(aa) valid passport; or

(bb) valid national ID card or confirmation they have been/are being granted EUSS/EUPSS

(cc) for naturalised British citizens or those to whom the pre-*McCarthy* transitional provisions apply, their valid EEA/Swiss passport or national ID and "information or evidence which is provided by the applicant, or is otherwise available to the [SSHD] that the person is a British citizen" (dd) for relevant persons of Northern Ireland (RPNI): the required evidence of being a RPNI (see below), and:

(aaa) If British: information or evidence which is provided by the applicant, or is otherwise available to the HO that the person is a BC

(bbb) If Irish: valid passport or national ID card or confirmation that they have been/are being granted EUSS/EUPSS

(ccc) If British *and* Irish: either of the above (not both)

unless (in any case) the Secretary of State agrees to accept alternative evidence of identity and nationality where the applicant is unable to obtain or produce the required document due to circumstances beyond their control or to compelling practical or compassionate reasons; and

- Evidence that a sponsoring family member does (or did for the relevant time) fit the relevant family member definition. This applies to:
  - (aa) REAACZ
  - (bb) QBC
  - (cc) RS (i.e. someone sponsoring a JFM)
- 'Valid' means a document is genuine and has not expired or been cancelled or invalidated
- Where a copy is provided the HO can request the original where there is doubt as to authenticity

The HO can require a certified translation of (or a Multilingual Standard Form to accompany) any document which is not in English, where this is necessary to decide the application

8.7.6 Losing continuity of residence; 'supervening events' which terminate permanent residence and EUSS; and cancellation, curtailment and revocation of EUSS/EUPSS

Both the EUSS and the EEA Regs 2016 have specific measures for

- Breaking continuity of residence for the purpose of acquiring permanent residence
- Losing permanent residence/EUSS once it is granted

Breaking continuity of residence

For exclusion from the benefits of the schemes

Continuity of residence is required to establish a right to permanent residence under the EEA Regs 2016 or ILR under the EUSS.

- Under the EEA Regs 2016, a person will lose continuity of residence for the purpose of acquiring permanent residence if they are imprisoned (Reg 3(3)(a))
- Though if they have lived in the UK for more than 10 years and had forged integrating links here, continuity may be retained (Reg 3(4))
- Under the EUSS those whose eligibility requires 5 years of residence need to show residence for a *continuous qualifying period* (eg Condition 3 of EU11) : continuity is broken if '*the person served or is serving a sentence of imprisonment of any length*'

Losing permanent residence/EUSS

Under the EEA Regs 2016, permanent residence may be lost through '*absence from the United Kingdom for a period exceeding two years*'.

Under the EUSS, only a '*supervening event*' suffices, defined in Annex 1 as follows:

- An absence from the UK and Islands for five consecutive years since the applicant last acquired permanent residence or completed a continuous qualifying period of five years; or
- The making of one of the following decisions, which remains effective: removal or exclusion under Regs 23 or 32, other exclusion decisions, cancellation of a right of residence, revocation of admission under Reg 11; deportation outside the EEA Regs

Note that in terms of time outside the UK under the EEA Regulations permanent residence will lapse after two years continuous residence outside the UK (Reg 15(2)). Under Appendix EU settled status will remain in place unless five years is spent continuously outside the UK (Annex 1-definitions). The Appendix EU is more accommodating than the Regs. Note that pre-settled status is lost only after 2 consecutive years outside the UK, but eligibility for settled status will be lost if continuous residence is broken during the 5-year period on which the applicant will be relying. It is important to advise clients of this carefully to avoid misunderstandings.

Cancellation, curtailment and revocation of leave granted under Appendices EU and EU (Family Permit)

Until 1 December 2020, the following paragraphs in Part 9 applied to leave granted under the appendices: 321B, 323(i), 323(ia) and 323(ii) (which are now replaced by the new Part 9 provisions, in force from that date.

321B provided that leave to enter or remain may be cancelled on arrival or while the holder is outside the UK

- On grounds of public policy, public security or public health
- On conducive grounds in relation to conduct committed after the end of the transition period
- If, where material to the grant, and whether or not the holder knew, false/misleading information, representations or documents were used in the application; or false/misleading information was put to someone else to obtain a supporting document.
- The holder no longer meets the requirements of the relevant rules

323 provided that LTE/LTR may be curtailed if:

- (i) in this or a previous application, or to obtain a supporting document, the person made false representations of failed to disclose material facts
- (ia) the person uses deception (successfully or not) to obtain LTR or a variation of LTR
- (ii) the person no longer meets the requirements of the rules under which leave was granted

From 1 December 2020, these provisions have been moved into new Annex 3 in both appendices.

Essentially:

Annexes 3 in both Appendices allow for cancellation, curtailment or revocation, in all cases only where proportionate.

On or before arrival in the UK, any leave granted under the Appendices can be cancelled:

- On grounds of public policy, public security or public health
- On conducive grounds in relation to conduct committed after the end of the transition period
- If, where material to the grant, and whether or not the holder knew, false/misleading information, representations or documents were used in the application; or false/misleading information was put to someone else to obtain a supporting document.
- The holder no longer meets the requirements of the relevant Appendix

They also allow for curtailment of EUPSS or LTE as a Family Permit holder:

- If, where material to the grant, and whether or not the holder knew, false/misleading information, representations or documents were used in the application; or false/misleading information was put to someone else to obtain a supporting document.
- On the ground that it appears on the balance of probabilities the holder, after the end of the transition period, entered or tried to enter a sham marriage/-civil-/-durable partnership or assisted someone else to do so

EUPSS can also be curtailed where the holder no longer meets the requirements of Appendix EU

EUSS can be revoked where:

- The holder is liable to deportation but cannot be deported for legal reasons
- EUSS was obtained by deception

The main differences are:

- The addition of sham marriage involvement as a ground for curtailment
- Deception used in previous applications is no longer a ground for curtailment, but instead false/misleading information, representations or documents having been submitted *without the knowledge of the person* is now a ground for curtailment (whereas previously it was only a ground for cancellation prior to or during entry). This ground was, however, already a ground for refusal of an application (see EU16(a)).
- The addition of revocation of EUSS for deception in this part of the rules

8.7.7 Suitability under Appendix EU

As in other parts of the Rules, applications can be refused for not meeting substantive requirements of the Rules, which is what we have dealt with so far. But they can also be refused on the basis of misdemeanours of various kinds. This is the concept of Suitability. Some refusal grounds are mandatory, others are discretionary.

The mandatory suitability criteria under rEU15(1) are where at the date of decision there is in place one of the following (which has not, at the date of decision, been set aside or become ineffective – rEU17):

- an extant decision to deport, or a deportation order
- an extant exclusion order, or an exclusion decision

That same ground is not mandatory- but discretionary where the decisions arise under the law of the Islands: rEU15(2).

Discretionary refusal grounds are found in rEU16 , meaning an application *may* be refused, if it is proportionate to do so, where:

- Materially false or misleading information, representations or documents have been submitted in relation to the application, including false or misleading information provided to anyone in obtaining a supporting documents, (regardless of whether the applicant was aware of this) Europe or
- There is an extant removal decision under the Regs on grounds of non-exercise or misuse of rights
- The applicant has previously been refused admission to the UK under Reg 23 of the EEA Regs (ie public policy, public security or public health grounds).
- The applicant has had EUSS or PSS cancelled under the General Refusal reasons (r321B(b)(i) or 321(b)(ii)) under paragraph A3.1.(a) or A3.1.(b) of Annex 3 to Appendix EU or under paragraph A3.1.(a) or A3.1.(b) of Annex 3 to Appendix EU (Family Permit), i.e.

- on *public policy, public security or public health* grounds for conduct pre-dating 11pm on 31 December 2020, and
- on grounds *conducive to the public good* for conduct after that date

- The application falls for refusal as a "relevant excluded person" based on conduct pre-dating or post-dating 11pm on 31 December 2020: and the same differentiation as to threshold applies as per the last bullet point

From 1 December 2020, Part 9 no longer applies to Appendix EU or Appendix EU (Family Permit) as set out in the preceding section, as the new Annexes 3 now contain the relevant provision for the two appendices.

Prior to that, there were some grounds for cancelling leave under Appendix EU on arrival in the UK found in the General Refusal reasons:

- Due to the same proviso for materially false information/documents as above (r321B(iii))
- Or cancelled for a material change in circumstances (r321B(iv))
- Or cancelled due to no longer meeting the Rules' requirements (r321B(v))

Under the old Part 9 provisions, leave could also be *curtailed* post-arrival on the basis of the false representations/document as above (r323(i)). :

8.7.7.1 EUSS applicants with criminal records

Further notes/information

Cases involving problematic issues such as this are outside OISC 1 scope and not part of its exam curriculum. The information in this box is provided to assist you in spotting and summarising these cases for referral.

The EUSS Suitability guidance sets out cases of applicants with criminal records which *must* be referred for immigration enforcement, and cases which *must not* be referred. If a removal or deportation decision is then made, this would additionally give rise to a suitability refusal. Therefore, as a representative, it is vital to know when UKVI could make such a referral within the policy. Where the guidance states that a client's case should *not* be referred to IE, this should perhaps be pointed out in the covering letter.

Under the guidance, cases ***must*** be referred for deportation or exclusion, which is to be considered on a case by case basis, where the applicant has had:

- Any prison sentence in the last 5 years
- Any 12 month prison sentence for one offence at any time
- Three or more convictions in the last 3 years, where the person has been resident for under 5 years. At least one of these must have occurred in the last 12 months.
- Involvement in serious deception such as assisting unlawful immigration or sham marriages/partnerships
- Being 'of interest', meaning the CCD were already considering issuing a deportation or exclusion order, for example where a prison sentence is currently being served

Cases ***not to be referred*** are where:

- A recorded decision has been made not to pursue deportation or to revoke a deportation order
- A tribunal has overturned a deportation decision, the HO has not appealed and there are no further offences meeting the referral criteria
- While in prison a conviction did not meet the referral criteria and there are no further offences meeting the referral criteria
- A past conviction or convictions were not referred for deportation under the policy in place at the time and there are no further offences meeting the referral criteria

The previous referral criteria were:

- Before 1 April 2009: a single prison sentence of 24 months
- From 1 April 2009: a single prison sentence of 12 months for a violent, drug-related or sexual offence
- From 14 January 2014: a single prison sentence of 12 months and/or 6 or more prison sentences for any offence in the last 3 years
- From 1 April 2015: a single prison sentence and/or 3 or more convictions for any offence in the last 3 years
- From 6 October 2015: all foreign national offenders are referred for deportation consideration

Clearly there are many cases falling into neither category, particularly where there are additional, more recent, if minor offences, and thus it is not certain at this point how best to advise clients.

In any case, you should refer these cases to a suitable accredited adviser as soon as possible.

8.7.8 Application procedure and guidance

Aside from the Immigration Staff Guidance EU Settlement Scheme caseworker guidance, a body of online guidance is available under EU Settlement Scheme: applicant information. The latter appears to be aimed at applicants without representatives but contains a wealth of useful information which may be of use to advisers, too. A full list of all EEA and settled status guidance is provided at 8.7.

The HO takes the view across immigration law generally, including EEA applications, that the burden of proof is on the applicant. So it is rather rare for the HO to actively help an applicant to obtain evidence in these cases (see further Amos directions from the FTT discussed in module 8.6.3.2),

However under the EUSS (including the EU(FP) Appendix) there is a more proactive approach. Under Annex 2 decision makers will have regard both to

> '(a) the information and evidence provided by the applicant, including in response to any request for further information or evidence made by the Secretary of State; and
> (b) any other information or evidence made available to the Secretary of State (including from other government departments) at the date of decision.'

There is some scope under the PBS and Appendix FM for decision makers to request further documents and information. The range of enquiry is fuller under the EUSS: Annex 2 provides

> 'they may (a) request that the applicant provide further information or evidence that they meet those requirements; or
> (b) invite the applicant to be interviewed by the Secretary of State in person, by telephone, by video-telecommunications link or over the internet.'

In relation to the eligibility requirements:

- the applicant may be invited to provide further information or evidence or to be interviewed
- the sponsor may be invited to provide further information or evidence about the relationship or be interviewed
- interviews may be conducted in person, by telephone, by video communication or over the internet

Where applicant or sponsor fail to respond or at least twice fail to comply with an interview invitation, the ECO may draw factual inferences about eligibility and refuse the application, but not on the sole basis of failure to comply at least twice with an interview invitation (A 2.2(3)-(5)).

Note that no such procedural safeguards apply to the meeting of the suitability requirements.

Online application, using the EU Exit ID app

This procedure is used by EEA and Swiss nationals with current biometric passports or national ID cards and non-European family members with current valid Biometric Residence Cards. The same process can be used from abroad by those applicants who meet the Annex 1 definition of "required proof of entitlement to apply from outside the UK" (see section 8.7.5 – in short, they must have an EEA/Swiss passport or ID card and if non-EEA/Swiss, a biometric residence card).

The submission procedure is via the EU Exit ID app, which can only be downloaded to phones with Near Field Communication. This function scans the biometric information from the chip in passports and BRCs, and will take and submit directly to the Home Office a facial image. The rest of the application can then be completed online, here: https://www.gov.uk/settled-status-eu-citizens-families/applying-for-settled-status

Online and postal application

This procedure is open to European applicants holding current, but non-biometric and non-machine readable documents. The application form is filled online, a digital photo uploaded, and once the online form is submitted the document must be sent to the address as notified by the online system.

Online form & biometrics appointment

Non-European applicants who do not hold a current valid Biometric Residence Card complete the online form as above, with a digital facial photograph, but once submitted the online application will direct the applicant to book an appointment with Sopra Steria. If it is impossible, due to a client's specific vulnerabilities (eg if they are currently residing at a mental health facility having been 'sectioned' under the Mental Health Acts) you can ring the resolution centre for alternative solutions. The HO has committed to facilitating applications from the vulnerable. Where warranted by the circumstances, it is even possible for the mobile biometrics unit to be deployed without charge.

Application by paper form

The system for beneficiaries of derivative- and Zambrano rights, Surinder Singh applicants and for those unable to obtain ID documentation, is paper-based.

8.7.9 Application from abroad under Appendix EU(FP)

This Appendix was added to the Immigration Rules on 30 March 2019; there is accompanying Immigration Staff Guidance EU Settlement Scheme Family Permit. The objective is to provide a route for non-EEA family members of EEA citizens to apply for entry clearance to come to the UK in order to make an application under the EUSS.

Under Appendix EU (Family Permit) para FP3 a grant of six months from the date of decision will be made if the application is valid, meets the eligibility requirements and the applicant is not refused on suitability grounds in FP7.

The eligibility requirements in FP6 are that:

- The applicant is a "specified EEA citizen" (defined in Annex 1 to Appendix EU (Family Permit) as a, EEA/Swiss national who is not also British) or a "non-EEA citizen" (a person who is neither EEA/Swiss nor a British national)
- The applicant is a "family member of a relevant EEA citizen" or a "joining family member" (the latter being a person with no pre-TP end continuous residence – note this definition cross-refers to that of a "family member of a relevant EEA citizen and not all categories of family members appearing there are included here)
- The relevant EEA citizen resides in the UK or will travel to the UK within six months of the application
- The applicant will accompany or join them in the UK

- The applicant is not the spouse, civil partner or durable partner where such a partner (of the applicant or the EEA citizen) has already been granted entry clearance under Appendix EU(FP) or under Reg 12 of the EEA Regs

The suitability requirements in FP7 are almost identical to those at EU15 & EU17 of Appendix EU, except that under Appendix EU (Family Permit)

- the existence of a removal decision on the ground of non-exercise or misuse of rights is not one of the suitability grounds for refusal
- the ground under Appendix EU for relevant excluded persons does not appear

Annex 1 contains the definitions which apply to Appendix EU (Family Permit). A 'relevant EEA citizen' here is defined as:

- an EEA citizen (including persons from Northern Ireland)
- who has been granted settled or pre-settled status
- which has not lapsed, been cancelled, curtailed or revoked
- which is evidenced by a Home Office reference number

A 'family member of a relevant EEA citizen' is defined similarly to under the mainstream EUSS in so far as it caters for close family members of EEA citizens:

- Spouses/CPs and durable partners where the relationship was contracted, or durability achieved, by the end of December 2020.
- And the children and dependent parents of their spouses/CPs.

But not dependent relatives beyond parents: so there is no route for extended family members. Nor for derivative rights holders. As mentioned above in the similarities and differences between EUSS and the EEA Regs 2016, there are more generous provisions for seeking further information.

8.7.10 Challenging EU settled status refusals – appeals and administrative review

Administrative review of EUSS decisions

Administrative review is available under Appendix AR(EU). The process is via an online form and the fee of £80 will be refunded if the review is successful. The page on which the form appears states as follows:

> You can apply if you think there has been an error in your application decision:

- under the EU Settlement Scheme
- under the Frontier Worker Permit Scheme, or if your Frontier Permit has been revoked
- as an S2 Healthcare Visitor
- as a Service Provider from Switzerland
- for entry clearance, leave to remain or indefinite leave to remain
- for cancellation of your entry clearance, leave to enter or leave to remain (including leave granted under the EU Settlement Scheme, as an S2 Healthcare Visitor or as a Service Provider from Switzerland) at the UK border

> If you are not eligible for a review, you may have a right of appeal. If you do, your decision letter will tell you so.

Note that decisions in relation to applications under Appendices S2 Healthcare Visitors and Service Providers from Switzerland (see sections 8.12 and 8.13 below) are now included in eligible decisions under Appendix AR(EU).

Appendix AR(EU) is more generous than Appendix AR in that

- any information and evidence submitted with the application for the review, including information and evidence that was *not* before the original decision-maker can be considered
- there is no automatic withdrawal if AR was applied for in-country and the applicant leaves the UK
- the time limit to apply is in new 34R(1A) in Part one, and is 28 days from receipt of the refusal.Under Appendix AR, the shorter limit of 14 days applies for in-country applications for AR

However, the time to apply for those in detention was brought back to 7 days under Appendix AR(EU).

Administrative review under Appendix AR(EU) is only available to challenge

- refusals on eligibility grounds, to grant EUSS or EUPSS
- grants of EUPSS instead of EUSS
- cancellation of EUSS/EUPSS on grounds of no longer meeting the requirements
- cancellation of LTE/PTE where EC is held, or refusal of LTE/PTE, due to change of circumstances (family permits, S2 healthcare visitors and service providers from Switzerland – the latter two term this "permission to enter", not "leave to enter")

Rejections of applications as invalid are not eligible for administrative review. Suitability refusals are also excluded.

Further notes/information

The area of appeals is outside OISC 1 scope and not part of its exam curriculum. The information in this box is provided to assist you in spotting and summarising these cases for referral.

In relation to Administrative Review, the OISC guidance on competence states that OISC 1 advisers can lodge and deal with these for any Level 1 type application (basic applications were all the requirements can be met without exceptional or discretionary arguments-, or complex evidence needing to be presented) with the exception of applications refused on the basis of credibility or a fundamental issue of genuineness of documents, or relationships.

EUSS appeals

The Immigration (Citizens' Rights Appeals) (EU Exit) Regulations 2020 ("ICREx Regs 2020") introduce appeal rights for individuals receiving negative decisions in relation to the EU Settlement Scheme or frontier workers.
Appeal rights are only available where a decision is made in relation to an application submitted after Exit Day: ie from 1 February 2020 (Reg 3(2)).

Forum and appeal deadline

Appeals will be to the FTT with onward appeals to the UT on points of law. Where the appeal is certified on grounds of national security, the appeal is to SIAC.

Reg 19 of the FTT Procedure Rules 2014 provides that notice of such appeals must be received 14 days after *being sent* the decision, unless the appellant is abroad, in which case the deadline is 28 days after *receipt* of the decision.

Option to apply for administrative review first *and* appeal later

The same deadlines apply again from the date a negative decision on an Administrative Review is either sent or received (depending on whether the appellant is inside or outside the UK). AR is available as an additional option here, but cannot be applied for once an appeal has been lodged. This regime is achieved by r3C-r3D of the IAPRs 2014.

The decision which will be appealed in these circumstances is not the AR decision but the original decision.

8.8 The public policy exclusions

Further notes/information

The area of … is outside OISC 1 scope and not part of its exam curriculum. The information in this box is provided to assist you in spotting and summarising these cases for referral.

EEA law is very different to domestic immigration law when it comes to refusing applications and expelling individuals down to misconduct. In domestic law the SSHD has a broad discretion to refuse applications for just about any kind of misconduct, as discussed above when we addressed the general refusal reasons.

And there is then no challenge to that conclusion – except to argue that it is based on a mistake (for example, there was in fact no dishonesty in an immigration application) or that the refusal is disproportionate to private and family life. And of course bad immigration history can often justify a refusal.

But in EEA law things are different. Applications may be refused only where public policy, public security or public health would otherwise be threatened: see generally Reg 27. This rules out generalised public policy considerations based on perceived threats to public policy due to defying immigration control.

The key principles are:

- Decisions may not be based on economic reasons (Reg 27(2))
- There is elevated protection for individuals with the right of permanent residence (Reg 27(3)) by way of
  - a narrowing of grounds (only public policy and public security)
  - a heightening of threshold: only **serious grounds** will suffice
- There is super-elevated protection for EEA nationals (Reg 27(4))
  1. with permanent residence who have resided in the UK for 10 years OR
  2. who are minors
  3. In either case only **imperative grounds of public security** will suffice
  4. (i.e. in general there needs to be **a risk of reoffending** or subject to a truly exceptionally serious offences test)

2. Decisions must be (Reg 27(5)):
   a. proportionate
   b. based on the individual conduct of the person concerned
   c. only conduct representing a **genuine, present and sufficiently serious threat to a fundamental interest of society will suffice**
   d. previous criminal convictions are not enough (i.e. in general there needs to be **a risk of reoffending**, subject to a truly exceptionally serious offences

On 31 December 2020, the 2016 Regulations were repealed but saved for certain purposes, including expulsions. From 11pm on that day, Part 4 is saved with the following added paragraph:

Decisions taken on conducive grounds

Examples

Herman is a German citizen. He has lived in the UK for four years and has consistently worked here. He is convicted of a string of burglary offences and sentenced to three years' imprisonment.

Herman has no obvious claim on permanent residence and so he is at the lowest level of protection. However this is still significant: this kind of offending is of only limited severity and so the SSHD will have to establish a future offending risk to justify his expulsion.

Rachel is a Polish national who has been in the UK working for one year and has been convicted of shoplifting on two occasions a few months apart. She has been fined and given a community sentence.

Rachel enjoys the lowest level of EEA protection. But it is hard to see that her offending is sufficiently serious to threaten a fundamental interest of society, at least without a real threat of an escalation in her offending.

Jean, a national of the DRC, is the spouse of a French national, Joanne, who has consistently worked here as a chef. They have lived together in the UK for six years. Jean has been convicted of grievous bodily harm following a brawl in a pub.

Given Jean has permanent residence having lived in the UK for five years, only serious grounds of public policy of security will suffice for his exclusion. So although this is a more serious offence, the SSHD has to leap a higher hurdle to justify expulsion. And proportionality is relevant, which includes both the proportionality of interfering with the couple's family life and the proportionality of interfering with Joanne's ability to work in the UK.

Elena, an Italian national, has lived in the UK for 11 years. She has just been convicted of two offences of serious fraud.

Elena has lived in the UK for more than 10 years and so only imperative grounds of public security would suffice to justify her exclusion.

> **27A.**—(1) An EEA decision may be taken on the ground that the decision is conducive to the public good.
> (2) But a decision may only be taken under this regulation in relation to a person as a result of conduct of that person that took place after IP completion day

This means that any EEA/Swiss national and their family member who would otherwise have benefited from the above regime will fall within the domestic deportation rules in relation to any conduct committed after TP end. Note that during the grace period, deportation orders will still be made under the 2016 Regs, but under application of Reg 27A, the additional protections from expulsion no longer apply.

8.9 Appendix S2 Healthcare visitors

The introduction to this Appendix outlines its purpose as relating to persons who before 11pm on 31 December 2020 had requested authorisation to receive planned healthcare under the S2 route, pursuant to Regulation (EC) No 883/2004. The S2 route entitles UK nationals to NHS-funded state healthcare treatment in another European Economic Area (EEA) country or Switzerland, and entitles EEA nationals to reciprocal rights here. The treatment in question must be provided under the national health scheme and must not be experimental or emergency; its need must be backed by a consultant's report. As the introduction adds, such persons may be accompanied by a person to provide care or support during the treatment. Caseworker guidance is published here.

As the Rules goes on, they use the abbreviations "P" for patient and "AP" for accompanying person.

The appendix is structured under the following headings and with the following paragraph numbers:

5. HV 1.1-7 Validity requirements for entry clearance or permission to stay as an S2 Healthcare Visitor
6. HV 2.1-4 Suitability requirements for an S2 Healthcare Visitor
7. HV 3.1-8.3 Eligibility requirements for an S2 Healthcare Visitor
    - HV 3.1-4 Entry requirements for an S2 Healthcare Visitor
    - HV 4.1-3 Financial requirement for an S2 Healthcare Visitor

- o HV 5.1 Treatment requirement for an S2 Healthcare Visitor
- o HV 6.1-2 Patient (P) requirement
- o HV 7.1-5 Accompanying person (AP) requirement
- o HV 8.1-3 Consent requirement for child S2 Healthcare Visitor

8. HV 9.1 Decision on application as an S2 Healthcare Visitor
9. HV 10.1-2 Period and condition of grant for an S2 Healthcare Visitor
10. HV 8.1 Cancellation and curtailment

There are no fees for applications under this route and applicant guidance, linking to the form, is here. Guidance for applicants on requesting administrative reviews of refusals is here.

HV 1.1-7 Validity requirements for entry clearance or permission to stay as an S2 Healthcare Visitor

EC applications must be made on online form "Apply for an exempt, diplomatic or official visit vignetter or S2 Healthcare Visitor visa" (HV 1.1) while outside the UK and to a post designated to accept such applications (HV 1.2).

PTS applications must apply on form FLR(IR) and must have or have last held, permission in this category (HV 1.3).

A must provide biometrics (HV 1.4(a)); and a passport or satisfactory national ID card (b); or, if a non-EEA national, a passport or satisfactory travel document (c).

Where someone enters the UK from Ireland having travelled from outside the common travel area holding a certificate of entitlement to S2 treatment or proof of S2 leave, they are permitted to remain for 6 months by virtue of a statutory instrument. So they need only apply for PTS at the end of that period (and indeed, under Appendix S2, may only apply at that point) (art 5 of the Immigration (Control of Entry Through Republic of Ireland) 1972 Order read with HV 1.5).

One can only extend leave by obtaining further PTS (HV 1.6(a)) where one holds or last held, permission in this category (b).

An application not meeting all validity requirements is invalid and ***may*** be rejected and not considered (HV 1.7).

HV 2.1-4 Suitability requirements for an S2 Healthcare Visitor

An application ***must*** be refused where A is subject to a deportation/exclusion order or decision (HV 2.1 (a)&(b)). However, where such an order or decision relates to conduct before transition ends (ie before 11pm on 31 December 2020), it must be justified on the grounds of public policy/security/health under Reg 27 of the 2016 Regs. This is regardless of whether the EEA Regs otherwise apply to A (HV 2.2).

Under HV 2.3, an application ***may*** be refused, if proportionate, in the following scenarios:

(a) In relation to the application and whether or not to A's knowledge, false/misleading information, representations or documents have been submitted including to obtain a supporting document, and this is material to a decision on the application; or

(b) For pre-11pm 31 December 2020 conduct, on grounds of public policy/security/health in accordance with Reg 27 of the 2016 Regs whether or not they apply to A ("EEA decision" to be read as "a decision under HV 2.3")

(c) For conduct thereafter on domestic law grounds (ie "conducive to the public good")

The same exclusion regime as for the UK applies where the deportation/exclusion decision relates to one of the Islands. Grounds HV 2.3 (d) and (e) are that A is subject to an Islands deportation order (d) or an Islands exclusion decision on direction by the relevant minister or other authority on conducive grounds (e), subject to the proviso in HV 2.4 which repeats the reference in (b) to the EEA standard to be applied.

HV 3.1-8.3 Eligibility requirements for an S2 Healthcare Visitor

<u>HV 3.1-4 Entry requirements for an S2 Healthcare Visitor</u>

HV 3.1. A person seeking to come to or stay in the UK as an S2 Healthcare Visitor must be a person to whom one of the following applies:

(a) Article 32(1)(b) of the withdrawal agreement [EU nationals]; or

(b) Article 31(1)(b) of the EEA EFTA separation agreement [citizens of Norway, Iceland and Liechtenstein]; or

(c) Article 26a(1)(b) of the Swiss citizens' rights agreement.

HV 3.2 provides for mandatory refusal of non-visa nationals lacking entry clearance. Non-visa nationals, however, may apply for PTE on arrival in the UK (HV 3.4)

<u>HV 4.1-3 Financial requirement for an S2 Healthcare Visitor</u>

A must have sufficient funds to cover all reasonable costs in relation to their visit (inc cost of return journey) without working or access to public funds (HV 4.1). These must be shown in accordance with Appendix Finance (HV 4.2). A third party can cover the cost of travel, maintenance and accommodation if the decision maker is satisfied that they can and will do so for the intended duration of the stay (HV 4.3).

<u>HV 5.1 Treatment requirement for an S2 Healthcare Visitor</u>

The course of planned treatment must have been arranged prior to travel to the UK.

<u>HV 6.1-2 Patient (P) requirement</u>

The patient must provide their valid S2 certificate (HV 6.1).

Under HV 6.2, for PTS to complete a course of treatment, the patient must provide this valid S2 certificate demonstrating that the length of treatment extends beyond the period of EC granted (a); or a renewed or extended S2 certificate covering the extension period (b); or the original S2 certificate and a letter from the treating healthcare professional detailing the further treatment required (c).

<u>HV 7.1-5 Accompanying person (AP) requirement</u>

The accompanying person must evidence a right to reside in the EEA or Switzerland (HV 7.4) and be accompanying the patient (the S2 Healthcare visitor) on entry to the UK (HV 7.1(a); or joining P in the UK (b).

The relationship must be evidenced via proof of the patient's PTE as an S2 Healthcare Visitor (HV 7.2(a)); or their S2 certificate (b); and their passport of EEA national ID card (or other satisfactory travel document if P is not an EEA national).

For PTS applications, the accompanying person must also provide the person's S2 documentation (HV 7.4, 6.2).

The accompanying person can provide copies of documents but must provide originals where the decision maker has reasonable doubts as to their genuineness (HV 7.5).

HV 8.1-3 Consent requirement for child S2 Healthcare Visitor

If the patient is a child their parent or legal guardian must give consent who is not travelling with them (HV 8.1). The consent must cover the application (HV 8.2(a)); living and care arrangements (b); and, if for an EC/PTE application, the travel and reception arrangements in the UK (c). This consent must be available in writing on request (HV 8.3).

HV 9.1 Decision on application as an S2 Healthcare Visitor

If all suitability and eligibility requirements are met, the application ***will*** be granted, otherwise it ***will*** be refused.

HV 10.1-2 Period and condition of grant for an S2 Healthcare Visitor

PTE/PTS will be granted for up to 6 months (HV 10.1&2). The conditions on grants are no access to public funds (HV 10.3(a)); no work (b); no study (c); and police registration is required by Part 10 (d).

HV 8.1 Cancellation and curtailment

EC/PTE/PTS in this category ***may*** be cancelled, where it is proportionate to do so:

- In relation to the conduct of the patient or accompanying person preceding the end of the transition period on grounds of public policy/security/health grounds under Reg 17 of the 2016 Regs. Decisions on Appendix S2 cases are treated as EEA decisions for this purpose; or
- In relation to conduct thereafter on conducive grounds
- On grounds of misleading or false information having been provided, whether or not to the applicant's knowledge and including for a supporting document, where this is material to the decision on the application
- On the ground the applicant ceases to meet the requirements of this category
- On the ground they have breached a condition in HV 10.3 unless EC or further permission was granted in knowledge of the breach.

8.10 Appendix Service Providers from Switzerland

This Appendix is in force from 1 December 2020. The introduction to this appendix summarises the route as allowing eligible employers, companies or self-employed individuals to carry out contracts with a UK based party for 90 days per calendar year in total (regardless of how many contracts are held). The contract must have been signed and commenced before 11pm on 31 December 2020. There is no provision for dependants to accompany migrants on this route.

This Appendix is structured under the following headings and with the following paragraph numbers:

1. SPS 1.1-4 Validity requirements for Service Providers from Switzerland
2. SPS 2.1-4 Suitability requirements for Service Providers from Switzerland
3. SPS 3.1 Eligibility requirements for Service Providers from Switzerland
4. SPS 4.1-10 Services requirement for Service Providers from Switzerland
5. SPS 5.1 90 day limitation requirement for Service Providers from Switzerland
6. SPS 6.1-2 Genuineness requirement for Service Providers from Switzerland
7. SPS 7.1-2 Decision on an application as a Service Provider from Switzerland
8. SPS 8.1-4 Period and conditions of grant for Service Providers from Switzerland
9. SPS 9.1 Cancellation of entry clearance or permission of a Service Provider from Switzerland

There are no fees for applications in this category. Applicant guidance, linking to the form, is available here and caseworker guidance Service Providers from Switzerland here. Further applicant guidance on requesting an Administrative review is here.

SPS 1.1-4 Validity requirements for Service Providers from Switzerland

Applications are to be made on online form "other work visas for the UK (non points-based working visas)" on the "Find and apply for other visas from outside the UK" form (SPS 1.1).

The applicant must pay the fee and provide biometrics and a passport, Swiss national identity card or, if non-Swiss a satisfactory travel document (SPS 1.2). They must be aged 18 or over at application date (SPS 1.3).

An application not meeting all these requirements is invalid and ***may*** be rejected and not considered (SPS 1.4).

SPS 2.1-4 Suitability requirements for Service Providers from Switzerland

An application ***must*** be refused if at the date of decision the applicant is subject to a deportation or exclusion order or decision (SPS 2.1), but where such a decision related to conduct before 11pm on 31 December 2020 the order or decision must be justified on the grounds of public policy, public security or public health in accordance with Reg 17 of the 2016 Regulations, whether or not those Regulations apply to that person. In applying this provision, "an EEA decision" read "a decision under SPS 2.1" (SPS 2.2).

Under SPS 2.3, application ***may*** be refused, if proportionate, in the following scenarios:

1. In relation to the application and whether or not to A's knowledge, false/misleading information, representations or documents have been submitted including to obtain a supporting document, and this is material to a decision on the application; or
2. For pre-11pm 31 December 2020 conduct, on grounds of public policy/security/health in accordance with Reg 27 of the 2016 Regs whether or not they apply to A ("EEA decision" to be read as "a decision under SPS 2.3")
3. For conduct thereafter on conducive grounds

The same exclusion regime as for the UK applies where the deportation/exclusion decision relates to one of the Islands Grounds SPS 2.3 (d) and (e) are that A is subject to an Islands deportation order (d) or an Islands exclusion decision on direction by the relevant minister or other authority subject to the usual proviso (SPS 2.4) distinguishing between when EEA and domestic legal standards are applied.

SPS 3.1 Eligibility requirements for Service Providers from Switzerland

The applicant must apply for EC before their arrival in the UK.

SPS 4.1-10 Services requirement for Service Providers from Switzerland

If the applicant is a Swiss national they must be either established in self-employment or habitually employed in Switzerland (SPS 4.1) and if self-employed must be registered as such with the appropriate Swiss tax authority (SPS 4.2).

Non-Swiss nationals must be legally integrated into the regular Swiss labour market, be habitually employed there and if required must provide a copy of their Swiss residence or work permit (SPS 4.3).

SPS 4.4 provides that the applicant is legally integrated where they are an EEA national with the relevant residence status enabling them to work in Switzerland (a) or if a non-EEA, non-Swiss national they have permission to reside and have been working for an extended period within the regular labour market of Switzerland (b).

EEA or Swiss nationals need not evidence permission to reside in Switzerland if their country of nationality remains within the free movement system (subject to transitional provisions) (SPS 4.5).

An employer or company is eligible if legally formed in Switzerland (SPS 4.6 (a)); has their registered office, central administration or principal place of business in Switzerland (b); and remains active and trading (c).

Under SPS 4.8, a contract will be eligible if it is written (including electronically) and between a Swiss employer or company and a UK employer or company (formed legally in the UK) or an individual established in the UK (a); it is signed and dated before 11pm on 31 December 2020 (b); and performance has started before then (c).

SPS 4.7 cross refers to the evidence required by SPS 4.9&10 for A to show they are required to travel to the UK.

The evidence required for employees to show they are required to travel to the UK, is set out at SPS 4.9: a letter (a), signed by a senior member of the organisation (b); including the author's credentials (c); a copy of the contract (d); including reasons why A is required to travel to the UK to execute it (e), confirming A has the professional qualifications to do so (f); and confirming the employer or company has not already used the 90 days per year to execute this or other contracts (g).

Self-employed Swiss nationals must provide a letter of self-certification meeting the same requirements as in SPS 4.9 except (a)&(b), and confirmation that the 90-day limit has not already been exceeded.

SPS 5.1 90-day limitation requirement for Service Providers from Switzerland

The employer, company or self-employed person must not have used up their 90-day annual limit.

SPS 6.1-2 Genuineness requirement for Service Providers from Switzerland

There is scope for "genuineness" testing. To be satisfied the route is not being abused, the decision maker must ensure that the applicant does not remain in the UK after the end of their permission (SPS 6.1 (a)), will not live in the UK for extended periods through frequent and successive visits or make the UK their main home (b); and is genuinely seeking entry as a Service Provider from Switzerland (c).

A must not, while in the UK, intend to access public funds or NHS treatment (apart from emergencies) (SPS 6.2(a)&(b)); study (c), marry/enter a civil partnership (d) or give notice thereof (e).

SPS 7.1-2 Decision on an application as a Service Provider from Switzerland

If all the requirements are met, the application ***will*** be granted, otherwise it ***will*** be refused (SPS 7.1). On refusal, administrative review is available under Appendix AR(EU: Admin Review (SPS 7.2)

SPS 8.1-4 Period and conditions of grant for Service Providers from Switzerland

Under SPS 8.1, grants will end on whichever is soonest: the end date of the eligible contract (a); the end date of the employee's fixed term work contract (b); the day before the expiry date of the applicant's permission to reside in Switzerland (c); or 31 December 2025 (d).

Multiple entry during the permission period is allowed, subject to the 90 day proviso (SPS 8.2). The company or employer (or self-employed person) must ensure the total number of days in the UK in this category does not exceed 90, regardless of the number of staff granted permission (SPS 8.3).

Grants are subject to the conditions in SPS 8.4: no more than 90 days' work in each calendar year (a); no work other than on the eligible contract (including self-employment and voluntary work (b); no study (c) and no access to public funds (d).

SPS 9.1 Cancellation of entry clearance or permission of a Service Provider from Switzerland

EC in this category ***may*** be cancelled, where proportionate, if

- Justified in relation to pre-TP end conduct on grounds of public policy/security/health grounds under Reg 17 of the 2016 Regs, regardless whether these apply to A. For an "EEA decision", read "a decision under SPS 9.1"; or
- Justified in relation to conduct thereafter on conducive grounds
- Justified on grounds of misleading or false information having been provided, whether or not to A's knowledge and including for a supporting document, where this is material to the decision on the application
- Justified on the ground the applicant has breached one of the conditions in SPS 8.4 unless further permission was granted in knowledge of the breach
- Justified on grounds that the applicant, the company or the employer cease to satisfy the Service Requirement at SPS 4.1-6 or the 90 day limit; or
- An agreement is concluded between the UK and Switzerland dealing with movement of natural persons for supply of services under WTO terms.

Module 9: British Nationality Law

Further notes/Information

This course covers a brief history of nationality law to explain the context of the current system. It is very useful background material to help a full understanding of how the present legislation was developed.

9.1 A brief history of nationality law

Broadly, the subject of nationality law for our purposes covers two central questions; firstly, am I a British citizen and, secondly, if I am not, how do I become one?

The key stages of development are broadly as follows:

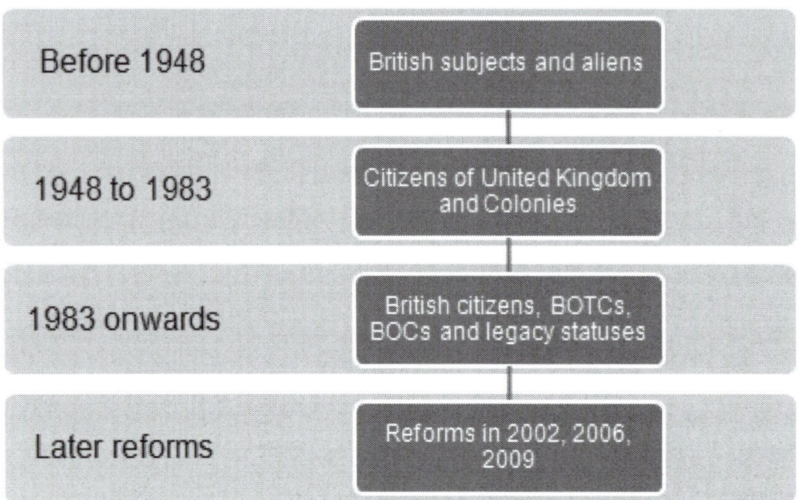

Top Tip

It is useful briefly to review the historical development of different forms of British nationality to ensure familiarity with the key terminology of nationality law. An old passport, or the passport of someone who has died, may be for a category of British nationality that is no longer current but may be useful to establish a person's current entitlements.

9.1.1 Pre 1948

Until 1948 the terminology used in law was 'British Subject'. The world was divided into British subjects, who were in the UK and overseas, and aliens, with the exception of British protected persons who were connected not to colonies but to British protectorates. Both were not subject to immigration control.

9.1.2 1948 to 1983

The British Nationality Act 1948 created the status of a '**Citizen of the UK and Colonies**', often abbreviated to CUKC. All CUKCs had a right of abode in the UK. They were also, at the same time, British Subjects.

Citizens of colonies which had become independent were not CUKCs but they retained the status of British Subject and with it the right of abode. The term Commonwealth Citizen was also used for this group.

No change was made to British Protected Persons and the status of British Subject Without Citizenship was created for those who had not acquired the citizenship of the independent country, but were not CUKCs either.

As more colonies became independent after 1948 their citizens lost their CUKC status if they gained citizenship of the new country, and became British Subjects/Commonwealth citizens.

From the 1960s onwards, some CUKCs and some British Subjects began to lose their right of abode. The IA 1971 introduced the term 'Patriality. Patrial citizens were those who had a right of abode and thus were not subject to immigration control:

- **Patrial CUKCs** – who had acquired their CUKC citizenship in the UK (by birth, registration or naturalisation) had a parent or grandparent who had similarly acquired CUKC status in the UK, or had lived in the UK for five years or more;
- **Non-patrial CUKCs** – all CUKCs not in the category above.

The right of abode was also withdrawn from certain British Subjects and Commonwealth citizens during this period.

In summary, the following people born before 1 January 1983 are British Citizens:

- Those born in the UK pre 1 January 1983 (save the children of diplomats)
- Those born abroad pre 1 January 1983 whose father was born in the UK
- Those born abroad pre 1 January 1983 whose father was registered or naturalised as British before their birth
- Those adopted in the UK by a British father.

9.1.3 1983 onwards

With the coming into force of the British Nationality Act 1981 on 1 January 1983, what mattered primarily was parentage, rather than place of birth. The Act created three new categories of British nationals:

- **British Citizens** – these were people who, on 31 December 1982, were patrial CUKCs. As British citizens they retained their rights of abode and are recognisable as the British Citizens of today.
- **British 'Dependent' Territories Citizens** (renamed '**Overseas**' in the British Overseas Territories Citizens Act 2002) for people who, on 31 December 1982, were CUKCs because of their connection with a British Dependent Territory (e.g. Bermuda). Those who had the right of abode retained it.
- **British Overseas Citizens** for non-patrial CUKCs who did not fit into the category of British Dependent (Overseas Territories) Citizens.

Meanwhile,

- **British Protected Persons** retained their status.
- **Commonwealth Citizens'** status did not change. Those who had the right of abode retained it.
- **British Subject** changed its meaning. It became the new name for British Subjects without Citizenship as defined in the BNA 1948.

As you can see, there are therefore several types of British national currently in existence. This guide is intended as an introductory text and therefore focuses on British citizens.

Section 11 of the BNA 1981 made provision for certain CUKCs to become British citizens on passage of the Act. The principal requirements were that a person, on 31 December 1982:

- Was a citizen of the UK and colonies
- Had a right of abode in the UK

9.1.4 2002 legislation

In 2002, the British Overseas Territories Act 2002 was passed. This Act renamed British Dependent Territories, British Overseas Territories. People became British Overseas Territories Citizens automatically on 26 February 2002 and on the 21 May 2002 they all became British Citizens with a right of abode in the UK, with the exception of those connected with the Sovereign bases.

In the same year, the Nationality, Immigration and Asylum Act 2002 were passed. It did not change the list of categories of citizen, but enlarged some and did make changes to entitlements to move between categories.

9.1.5 Children of unmarried fathers; good character requirement

The 2002 Act also finally abolished the patrial-centric approach of previous nationality laws and in section 9 of the Act made unmarried fathers the transmitters of British nationality just as much as unmarried mothers.

From 6 April 2015, s65 of the Immigration Act 2014 amended the BNA 1981 (by adding ss 4F to 4I) to provide for the registration as a British citizen, by right, subject to the good character requirement, for all those who missed out on being a British citizen at birth because their mother was not married to their father.

Further:

> For individuals who are overseas the impact may be on their ability to come to the UK. Where we are made aware of individuals affected, we will consider their individual circumstances on a case-by-case basis.

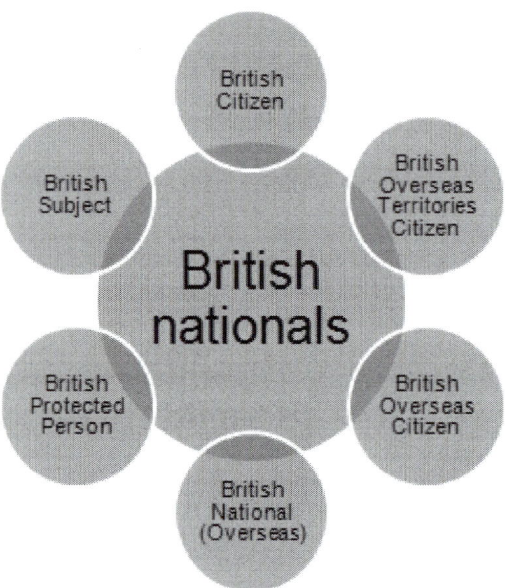

9.1.6 2006 legislation

The Immigration, Asylum and Nationality Act 2006 made further changes to nationality law, widening the power to deprive a person of citizenship (s.56) or the right of abode (s.57) to include 'conducive to the public good' and also to remove registration as a British citizen as of right by inserting a good character test for all applicants. An Order passed in January 2010 also includes children aged 10 and over in the 'good character requirement'.

9.1.7 2009 legislation

The BCIA 2009:

- Enables registration as British of the children born outside the UK of members of the armed forces and confirms automatic British citizenship of children born in the UK of members of the armed forces.
- Allows registration of children born outside the UK under s.3(2) of the BNA 1981 up to their 18th birthday (extended from 12 months after their birth or six years in exceptional circumstances).
- Permits registration of otherwise stateless BN(O)s.
- Enables registration of those born before 7 February 1961 with British mothers, if they would have become a British citizen at birth had women been able to pass on citizenship in the same way as men.

9.1.8 2014 legislation

The Immigration Act 2014

- Enables registration of those born before 1 July 2006 and previously excluded from acquisition of British nationality on the ground their parents were unmarried at the time of their birth by insertion, via s65 IA 2014 of sections 4E to 4J into the BNA 1981
- Extends powers to deprive a person of their British nationality by insertion, via s66 IA 2014, of s40(4A) into the BNA 1981

9.1.9 Windrush scheme – uncharged nationality applications and waiver of certain requirements

In April 2018 media exposure of the impact of the hostile environment on members of the Windrush generation and their descendants, some with entitlements to citizenship, led to a public outcry, a change of Home Secretary and the launch of the Windrush scheme on 30 May 2018. Where this applies, nationality fees and certain requirements are waived. For all the essential details of the policy see Module 4 at 4.2.14 of MIL.

9.2 Nationality Guidance

The Nationality Instructions were, in late July 2017, archived here http://web.archive.org/web/20170425005852/https:/www.gov.uk/topic/immigration-operational-guidance/nationality-instructions

They were replaced by a set of documents, all posted 27 July 2017, as a set entitled 'Nationality Guidance', accessible here https://www.gov.uk/government/collections/nationality-policy-guidance

Where the new 'Nationality Guidance' set of policy documents is silent on a topic previously covered by the Nationality Instructions, or where coverage is in much more vague terms, you may wish to consult the archived NIs (link above) in preference to proceeding with no guidance at all.

Other guidance, fees and forms

Additional guidance is often available either in separate booklets appearing on the same page as the relevant nationality application form, or on the form itself. All citizenship application forms and fees are accessibleon UKVI page "forms and fees".

In the case of PRCBC[2019] EWHC 3536 (Admin) (see PRCBC Press Release for details) it was held that the child citizenship registration fee of £1,012, when the processing costs only £372, is unlawful on the ground that the government had failed to consider the best interests of children in setting the fee levels. The case will, however, progress further and any reduction in the fee is unlikely until a final outcome is reached. In the meantime, clients interested in child registration should be advised of this position.

Those seeking advice on behalf of child clients who are separated from their parents, such as children in care, should of course also be advised of the fact that all immigration and nationality immigration cases have been brought back within legal aid scope, meaning they can now seek free legal advice and assistance from legal aid providers (without the need for these to apply for Exceptional Case Funding). *This reopening of funding for immigration cases explicitly includes nationality cases.*

Organisations considering taking on such cases now should refer to new LAA guidance Separated migrant children - transitional guidance for organisations making civil legal aid applications for immigration matters concerning separated migrant children.

9.3 Birth or adoption in the UK on or after 1 January 1983

The routes by which a child born in the UK is a British citizen by birth or can become so by registration under s1 of the BNA 1981 are as follows:

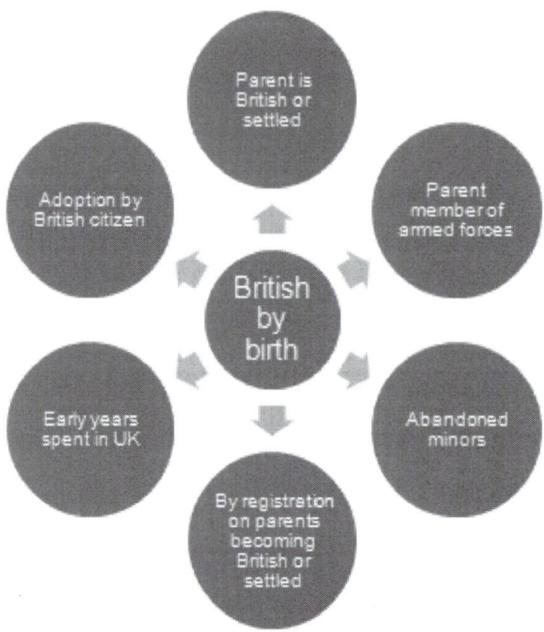

9.3.1 Automatic Acquisition – Parent is British or settled at time of birth s1(1) British Nationality Act (BNA) 1981

The plain fact of birth in the United Kingdom since 1 January 1983 does not usually create any entitlement to citizenship unless it is combined with a parental link to a person settled in the United Kingdom:

s.1(1) A person born in the United Kingdom after commencement, or in a qualifying territory on or after the appointed day, shall be a British citizen if at the time of the birth their father or mother is:

(a) a British citizen; or

(b) settled in the United Kingdom or that territory.

This form of acquisition of citizenship operates by law, so no registration or other forms need be completed. However, proof that a person meets the above criteria will be required to prove citizenship and apply for a passport.

Settlement is defined in the Immigration Act 1971 as 'being ordinarily resident in the United Kingdom … without being subject under the immigration laws to any restriction on the period for which he may remain.' Effectively this means that the parent in question must have indefinite leave to remain.

Example

David is a US citizen present in the UK as a Tier 4 student. He has a child, Gemma, with a British citizen, Frances. The child is born in London.

Frances is a British citizen. She was born in the UK and her mother is a British citizen.

Imagine that David remains a Tier 4 student, but Frances was not British citizen but also a US citizen, and she has been present in the UK for seven years. She has obtained ILR here. Gemma would still be a British citizen: she was born in the UK to a person settled in the UK.

Until 1 July 2006, a child could establish his right to nationality via either parent so long as they were born within marriage. 'Illegitimate' children (for this was the effect of this provision) could trace entitlement only via their mother. Under s47 of the British Nationality Act 1981, a person born out of wedlock was to be treated as if they had been born legitimate (i.e. retrospectively) for the purposes of nationality law if their parents subsequently married.

This old fashioned and discriminatory approach came to a partial end as of 1 July 2006, though only for children born after that date, with the coming into force of amended s50(9A) of the BNA 1981, which redefined father as either:

- (a) the husband of the mother (until recently, regardless of who is the biological father – but see below at 9.3.3), or
- (b) & (ba) the person treated as the father under s28 of The Human Fertilisation and Embryology Act 1990, or under s35, 36, 42 or 43 of The Human Fertilisation and Embryology Act 2008, or
- (c) *only* where (a) to (ba) do not apply: the person who satisfies the requirements of The British Nationality (Proof of Paternity) Regulations 2006 – either the person named as the father of the child in a birth certificate issued within one year of the date of the child's birth, or the person who otherwise satisfies the Secretary of State that he is the father (e.g. by way of a DNA test report – a list of HO approved DNA testing companies is available here: https://www.gov.uk/get-dna-test). In Alake [2020] EWHC 1956 (Admin) the Judge held that there would be some cases where HMPO should consider whether it was appropriate to assist an applicant with requesting their father to provide DNA evidence voluntarily.

Note that for birth certificates issued after 10 September 2015, being named as the father will no longer be sufficient to prove paternity. Under the British Nationality (Proof of Paternity) (Amendment) Regulations 2015, it will be left to the Secretary of State to determine who is the 'natural father' of the child.

A further step was taken to right this historic wrong by s65 of the IA 2014, which from 6 April 2015 provides the right to register for all those who missed out on British citizenship, by operation of law or registration, because their natural father was not recognised as their father for the purposes of nationality law because of the pre-July 2006 discrimination against children born illegitimately.

Example

Beatrice was born in the UK in 2005 to a French national mother, Sandra, and a British father, James. Sandra has only been present in the UK for 18 months and was not therefore settled here. The parents were not married.

Beatrice was not therefore automatically born British. This is a pre-1 July 2006 where the parents were not married. So she would be reliant on an exercise of discretion by the SSHD.

Now imagine another child, Bertie, was born in the UK in 2007 to Sandra and James. Sandra remains non-settled and they have still not married. Bertie, however, would be treated as born British so long as James could prove paternity (e.g. via DNA) because of the change in the law effective from 2006.

9.3.1.1 Nationality and EU law rights: the Good Friday Agreement

The Good Friday Agreement recognises "*the birthright of all the people of Northern Ireland to identify themselves and be accepted as Irish or British.*" In De Souza [2019] UKUT 355 (IAC) the UT considered whether this provision had any material effect on British nationality law, such that persons born in Northern Ireland might be able to access Treaty Rights on the basis of self-identifying as Irish.

The UT concluded that, whether or not an individual so identifies, they are still excluded from benefitting from the EEA Regs 2016 if they are also a British citizen. It was not reasonably possible to read section 1(1) of the British Nationality Act 1981, conferring British citizenship on individuals born in the UK to a British citizen parent, such that the words "*if they consent to identify as such*" appeared there. The UT rules out this possibility. To do so would represent a radical departure from the existing law of British nationality, and an international Treaty such as the Good Friday Agreement could not have such effects.

The EUSS scheme was subsequently amended in order to ensure the Good Friday agreement was properly reflected in UK law: see Module 8/

9.3.2 EEA nationals treated as 'settled' in the past – notes on *Capparelli*

For a very long time it has been understood that EEA nationals exercising Treaty Rights in the UK may be treated as 'settled' here. The old Nationality Instructions, Chapter 3, Part 1, para 3.5.1.4 provided that children born in the United Kingdom before 2 October 2000 would need only to evidence that one of the parents was an EEA national who, at the time of the birth, was exercising EC Treaty rights in the United Kingdom. This reference is not replicated in the current guidance. This factor can be relevant to the acquisition of British nationality by birth, as under section 1 of the British Nationality Act 1981, a person born in the UK after the Act's commencement is a British citizen if at that time a parent was a British citizen or settled here. Settlement is defined under section 50(2) of the BNA 1981 as being, ordinarily resident in the United Kingdom or … without being subject under the immigration laws to any restriction on the period for which he may remain.

Accordingly, it will be seen potential candidates for British citizenship, must show that:

(1) They were ordinarily resident in the UK; and

(2) They were not subject to a restriction under such immigration laws

In one controversial Upper Tribunal decision, it was found that because section 33(1) of the Immigration Act 1971 defines the 'immigration laws' as domestic ones only, EEA nationals are ruled out from being settled, because they cannot ever be subject to a restriction under UK immigration laws. Thus, as they could not establish condition (2) above, they did not count as settled here.

In any event, for many years the Home Office treated persons present on a long-term basis exercising Treaty rights as settled in the UK and many people have been ostensibly recognised as British citizens on the basis of that stance.

The implications of the judgement on those registered or naturalised based on the incorrect definition of 'settled status' are as follows: where a person is wrongly recognised as a British citizen and there is a discretion under which it can be maintained, the Home Office will normally do so. In cases of child registration under s1(3) or 'automatic acquisition' by birth, the general discretion in s3(1) enables the Home Office to maintain recognition. For naturalisation of adults, no equivalent discretion is available to waive the 'settled status' requirement. This means that, theoretically, recognition could be declared a nullity.

9.3.3 Who is the father?

This is a vexed question in nationality law, where proving paternity may render a person British by birth or give them an opportunity to register. Unsurprisingly, the HO set a high bar for proving who the father is.

Section 1(1) of the British Nationality Act 1981 ('BNA') sets out that a person born in the United Kingdom is automatically a British citizen at birth if at that time their mother or father was a British citizen or settled in the United Kingdom.

Section 50(9A) provides various routes by which fathers qualify to confer nationality via fatherhood (see section set out under 9.3.1).

There is a difficulty with s50(9A)(a), read with (c), in that, where the child's mother was married to someone other than the biological father at its date of birth, it seems that the true father cannot be the basis for any entitlement to British citizenship for their child.

The Administrative Court in K (A Child) [2018] EWHC 1834 (Admin) (18 July 2018) finds that this state of affairs represents unjustifiable discrimination against the affected children. Being born to a mother married to a person other than one's biological father represented an 'other status', given the need to treat people in a fundamentally equal manner as to their dignity and rights. So anti-discrimination protection had to be considered.

Although the Home Office could rectify the problem by actively exercising discretion in the child's favour, the Judge decided this was not enough: a child deserved a legal guarantee rather than having to rely on executive discretion. Accordingly, s50(9A) represented a disproportionate interference with rights protected by Article 8 of the Human Rights Convention and a declaration of incompatibility was necessary to record this.

Otherwise, if the child loses out from being born British in these circumstances, or being able to register as British, it is likely the HO will allow the child to register as of discretion, under s3(1) BNA 1981 but at the current fee of £1,012 this is expensive.

For children born on or after 1 July 2006 to a British father where the mother was married to someone else, there is now a fee waiver available. The fee waiver is not automatic and must be applied for. The application is made on form UKF(M). There two relevant sets of guidance which need to be consulted as to the practicalities of the fee waiver application:

- the form guidance
- general child registration guidance (updated in April 2020)

9.3.4 Qualifying territories

The references to qualifying territories throughout the Act are not of great importance for our purposes, being references to specific entitlements for those born on or after 21 May 2002 in a 'qualifying territory' – which means a British overseas territory other than the Sovereign Base Areas of Akrotiri and Dhekelia in Cyprus, if a parent is a British citizen and settled in the UK or that qualifying territory.

Nevertheless, for ease of reference where this is relevant, the qualifying territories are: Anguilla; Bermuda; British Antarctic Territory; British Indian Ocean Territory; British Virgin Islands; Cayman Islands; Falkland Islands; Gibraltar; Montserrat; Pitcairn Islands; Saint Helena, Ascension and Tristan da Cunha; South Georgia and the South Sandwich Islands; Turks and Caicos Islands (see list here: https://www.gov.uk/types-of-british-nationality/british-overseas-territories-citizen)

9.3.5 Automatic acquisition – children born inside UK to members of the armed forces – s1(1A) BNA 1981

Section 42 of the Borders, Citizenship and Nationality Act 2009 provides a statutory basis for the acquisition of British citizenship for children born in the UK to members of the armed forces. This removes the need to treat parents of such children as if they were settled here, as the previous legal regime had done.

In 2010 s1(1A) was inserted into the BNA 1981, which provides that a person born in the United Kingdom or a qualifying territory on or after the relevant day (13 January 2010) shall be a British citizen if at the time of the birth his father or mother is a member of the armed forces.

9.3.6 Automatic acquisition – new born infants found abandoned in the UK – s1(2) BNA 1981

Under s1(2), a new born infant found abandoned in the United Kingdom on or after 1 January 1983 can be regarded, for the purposes of s1(1), if:

- born in the United Kingdom on or after 1 January 1983; and
- to a parent who at the time of the birth was a British citizen or settled in the United Kingdom,

unless the contrary can be proven by the Home Office. So, the presumption will be that such a child is a British citizen.

9.3.7 Acquisition by registration of children born in the UK upon parents becoming British or settled – s1(3) BNA 1981

Minors are entitled to registration under s.1(3) of the British Nationality Act 1981 if:

- they were born in the United Kingdom on or after 1 January 1983; and

- they were not British citizens at birth because at the time neither parent was a British citizen or settled here; and
- while they are minors, either parent becomes a British citizen or becomes settled in the United Kingdom (NB: unlike for naturalisation of adult EEA nationals, no prior issue of permanent residence documentation is required, only evidence of acquisition of PR by the parent); and
- they are minors on the date of application

Examples

1st example

Lets go back to the situation of David and Frances above, and their child Gemma. Now imagine that Frances had only lived in the UK for four years when Gemma was born. She herself is a Tier 2 migrant and is on a route to settlement. Gemma would not be born a British citizen. However, once Frances settled in the UK, Gemma would become one.

2nd example

Algernon is a citizen of Canada, which makes him a Commonwealth citizen. Two years ago he has a child, Ramneek, with Farhat, a citizen of Pakistan, whilst he and Farhat are studying in the UK.

Of course Ramneek is not born British: neither parent is a British citizen or settled here.

Now Algernon joins the British Army, which as a Commonwealth citizen he is eligible to do. Now we can see that Ramneek's father has become a member of the armed forces: so Ramneek can register as a British citizen under s1(3A).

3rd example

To continue with the example of Beatrice, above, if her mother becomes settled in the UK after five years of residence under EU law, Beatrice could be registered as British. Unlike with Bertie, this is a positive step that must be taken and it must be taken before Beatrice turns 18.

Alternatively, Beatrice could probably have been registered under s.1(3) after 1 July 2006, once her father was recognised in law as her father for nationality purposes, i.e. when one of her 'parents' became British.

9.3.8 Acquisition by registration of children or adults born in the UK due to early years spent in UK – s1(4) BNA 1981

Adults or minors are entitled to registration under s.1(4) of the BNA 1981 if they:

- were born in the United Kingdom on or after 1 January 1983; and
- were not a British citizen at birth because at the time neither parent was a British citizen or settled here; and
- were aged 10 years or more on the date of application; and
- have lived in the United Kingdom for the first 10 years of their life; and
- during that 10 years have not been out of the United Kingdom for more than 90 days in any one of those years

The lawfulness of residence is irrelevant for this provision. The statute (s1(7)) gives a discretion to condone longer absences than 90 days. This discretion is explained in the Nationality Guidance *Registration as British citizens: children*, which indicates that non-intentional longer absences may be permitted:

> You should normally waive excess absences if: • the number of days absent from the UK in any one of the years does not exceed 180 days and the total number of days over the 10 year period does not exceed 990 days • the number of days absent exceeds 180 or 990 respectively but was due to circumstances beyond the family's control, such as a serious illness

Note the form is the same for adults and children (Form T) but the fee differs £1,012 for children, £1,206 for adults see Nationality Fees list.

Example

Horatio is the child of Nelson and Augusta, citizens of Ghana who have been lawfully present as students in the UK for many years. He was born in the UK nine years ago.

Horatio's parents, as students, have no apparent settlement route open to them. So Horatio has not been born to British citizens or persons settled here, nor to people likely to become settled here. However so long as they remain in the UK for another year then he will have lived in the UK for the first 10 years of his life, and by then he will be aged more than 10 years. Providing he has not clocked up excess absence abroad of more than 90 days annually, he will qualify for registration.

9.3.9 Acquisition by registration of stateless persons – Sch 2 BNA 1981

Schedule 2 of the 1981 Act makes some provision for reducing statelessness, where:

- there is a link with the UK via parental possession of one of the lesser forms of British nationality such as being a British Overseas Territories citizen, a British Overseas citizen and a British subject where the child would be otherwise stateless, and the child is born in the UK or in a British Overseas Territory
- Paragraph 3 enables a person born in the UK after commencement who is and has always been stateless to be registered as a British citizen if under the age of 22 and resident in the UK for a period of five rather than 10 years (as long as absent for no more than 450 days during that period).

Evidential requirements were added in new Nationality Guidance Stateless Persons on 26 Sep 2017.

9.3.10 Automatic acquisition – minors adopted by British citizens – s1(5) BNA 1981

Section 1(5) of the British Nationality Act 1981, as amended, explains which children adopted on or after 1 January 1983 acquired British citizenship automatically because of their adoption. Under s1(5), a child who is not already a British citizen becomes a British citizen from the date of an adoption order if

EITHER:

- the adoption is authorised by order of a court in the United Kingdom on or after 1 January 1983 or, on or after 21 May 2002, by an order of a court in a qualifying territory; and
- the adopter or, in the case of a joint adoption, one of the adopters is a British citizen on the date of the adoption order

OR

- it is a Convention adoption under the 1993 Hague Convention on Intercountry Adoptions; and
- the adoption is effected on or after 1 June 2003; and
- the adopter or, in the case of a joint adoption, one of the adopters is a British citizen on the date of the Convention adoption; and
- the adopter or, in the case of a joint adoption, both of the adopters is habitually resident in the United Kingdom on the date of the Convention adoption.
- The current guidance is set out in Nationality policy Registration as a British citizen: children
- For adoptions non-compliant with the requirements set out in the policy, the old policy recommended registration if demonstrably in the child's best interests, whereas the new policy allows registration only if there are exceptionally compassionate or compelling circumstances.

Example

Eric is a British citizen, who lives in the UK with his wife who is settled here; she is of Chilean nationality. They adopt a daughter, Esmerelda, a Chilean national, in an order made formally by a Chilean court.

There are two routes to an adoption's recognition: one authorized by a family court in the UK or a Hague Convention one. Chile is a Hague Convention country which is promising. As both adopters are UK resident and one is a British citizen, section 1(5) gives an avenue to British citizenship for Esmerelda. Note there is no need for registration: citizenship takes effect from the date of the adoption order.

9.3.11 Applications to change nationality by Local Authorities for children in their care

Local authorities have significant powers to take steps for the welfare of the children in their care. In Y (Children In Care: Change of Nationality) [2020] EWCA Civ 1038 the Court of Appeal held that whilst a local authority's powers which might include taking steps to change the nationality of a child in its care against the wishes of the child's parents, it must first seek the approval of the court.

9.4 Birth outside the UK

The routes by which a child born outside the UK can become British are as follows:

At birth

- To a parent who is a British citizen otherwise than by descent

On registration

- Any time up to age of 18
- On residence in UK with British citizen parents for 3 years
- If parent is or becomes a member of the armed forces

9.4.1 Automatic acquisition by descent – s2(1) BNA 1981

Section 2(1) of the BNA 1981 reads as follows:

> A person born outside the United Kingdom after commencement shall be a British citizen if at the time of the birth his father or mother:
>
> (a) is a British citizen otherwise than by descent; …

This form of transmission of nationality operates by law, so no registration form need be completed, but evidence may be required that the person does meet the above requirements.

Example

Chris is a British citizen who emigrates to Australia with his Australian girlfriend, Clarissa. They do not get married. They have a baby boy, Clarence, in 2005, who was born in Australia. Clarence had no entitlement to British nationality when he was born, because his birth preceded the change in the law of 1 July 2006. However, following the further change of 6 April 2015, he can now register under s4G BNA 1981. The application is free but in his case will confer citizenship by descent only (because this is the status he would have had, if his parents had been married, because of his birth outside the UK – s4G(2)).

Chris and Clarissa have another child, a baby girl called Carrie, who is born in 2007. Carrie is automatically born British and does not need to take any further steps to become British.

9.4.2 Acquisition by registration of children under the discretion in s3(1) BNA 1981

Section 3(1) can be used to register a variety of problem cases as it is a very wide discretion:

3(1) If while a person is a minor an application is made for their registration as a British citizen, the Secretary of State may, if they think fit, cause them to be registered as such a citizen.

Applications may be made either outright (on Form MN1) or argued as an alternative, for example where some of the evidence for registration by entitlement cannot be obtained.

Note that these applications are very often refused as the evidential threshold applied by the HO is very high. They are not basic citizenship applications, thus fall outside OISC 1 remit and should therefore be referred to a suitable accredited adviser. The rest of this section is provided by way of further information only.

The exercise of discretion under s3(1) should be conducted under the policy set out in Nationality Guidance Registration as British citizen: children.

What must be shown is that the child lives in the UK and their future clearly lies here. Generally, the Home Office will exercise its discretion in favour of registering the child as British if the child has settled status and either both parents are British citizens or one is while the other is settled. However, if the child has lived in the UK for many years, it may be argued that, whatever the parents' circumstances, the child's future clearly lies in the UK and that it would be in the child's best interests to be registered as British. Where such an application is contemplated, advice may be sought from the Project for the Registration of Children as British Citizens (PRCBC).

A suggested checklist of documents for this type of application is as follows:

- Original old and new passports or any biometrics card/immigration status documents
- Original full birth certificate may be necessary to prove identity and/or relationship with parents
- Proof of continuous residence in the UK since first arrival (baby book, confirmation letters from nursery, schools, GP, etc original signed and dated)
- If child is aged 10 or over, a Police National Computer check should be requested https://www.acro.police.uk/Subject_Access_Apply_By_Post.aspx
- Medical/ educational/social services details/reports of any serious medical condition(s)/special needs
- As many letters of support from tutors, British friends, peers, support workers any other professionals and non-professionals involved in the child's life in the UK.
- Awards, Certificates of achievements, diplomas, photos of medals etc.
- Photos covering as much as possible of the child's life since arrival in the UK, e.g. with school and British/settled friends/tutors/extra- curricular activities etc.
- Certified copy of any current immigration status document/biometrics or British passport(s)/registration/naturalisation certification of parent/s or legal guardian and siblings etc.

PRCBC [2019] EWHC 3536 (Admin) found that the fee regime for at least some s3(1) cases was unlawful for failing to lawfully consider the best interests of the child. This required a rethink in Parliament, and the Immigration and Nationality (Fees) Regulations 2018 were amended from 6 April 2020. Now the SSHD may waive a fee re children born after 1 July 2006

- where the child's mother was married to, or in a civil partnership, with a man other than the child's natural father at the time of the child's birth,
- whereas had she been married to the natural father the child would have automatically become a British citizen.

9.4.3 Acquisition by registration of children born outside the UK due to a connection with the UK – ss3(2), (4) &(5), and s4D BNA 1981

9.4.3.1 Section 3(2)

This section permits registration where there is a sufficiently strong link with the UK, looking back across the generations, as to make it unfair to decline access to full British citizenship. The requirements, in the normal case, are as follows:

- As of 13 January 2010, the child to be registered must be under the age of 18. The previous rule until the relevant section of the BCIA 2009 came into effect was that registration had to take place within 12 months of birth or six years in exceptional circumstances.
- The child's parent has the weak form of nationality ('by descent') but their grandparent has the strong form of nationality ('otherwise than by descent').

- The child's parent has a residential link with the UK, in that they have lived here for a three year period some time prior to the birth of the child, and did not leave the UK for more than 270 days within that period (however, for a child born stateless, this requirement is waived).

9.4.3.2 Section 4D

With effect from 13 January 2010, s4D of the BNA 1981 permits registration of certain children born outside the UK to a parent serving overseas in the UK armed forces.

9.4.3.3 Section 3(5)

This section permits another form of registration. This does not require the *grandparent connection* that we saw in s3(2), nor does it require the *historic* three-year stay in the UK that that section demands – however, it does require that the family including the child were in the UK *for the three years leading up to the application for registration*, and did not leave the UK for more than 270 days within that period. The application can only be made whilst the child is a minor.

Example

To continue with the story of the family of Chris and Clarissa, we saw earlier that Carrie was born British by descent by virtue of section 2(1) of the Act. Section 14 of the Act sets out a definition of a British citizen 'by descent' and Carrie falls within that definition.

When Carrie grows up she has a child of her own, Colin, who is born in Australia. Colin is not automatically born a British citizen under the same section as Carrie, because section 2(1) states that the parent must be a British citizen 'otherwise than by descent'.

However, Colin could be registered as a British citizen under section 3(2) if the proper procedures are followed, or could be registered under section 3(5) if he was later to qualify (see below).

When Colin grows up, he has two children, Claude and Cedric. They have no entitlement at all to British citizenship by descent.

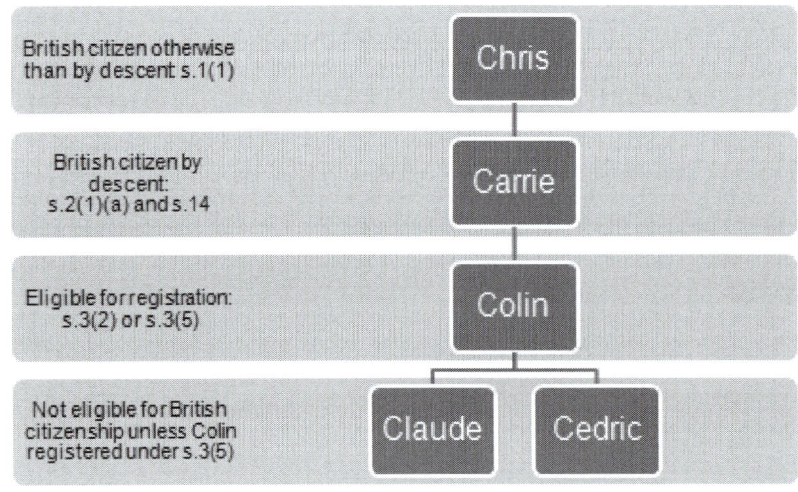

9.4.4 Acquisition by registration as an adult – ss4(2), s4(4), ss4A-C & ss4E-I BNA 1981

Certain adults are also able or entitled to register as British citizens:

Under s 4(2), a person who is a British Overseas Territories citizen, British National (Overseas), a British Overseas citizen, a British Subject or a British Protected Person may register as a full British citizen under s4(2) if he or she meets the same residence requirement as for naturalisation and, since the advent of the 2006 Act, a good character requirement

Under s4(4) & (5) there is a discretion to register as a British citizen the above persons, even if the residence requirements are not met.

Under s4A, there is a discretion to register (as British citizens otherwise than by descent) a British Overseas Territories citizen (refer to list of qualifying territories above) and who does not have the citizenship only by a virtue of a connection with the sovereign base areas of Akrotiri and Dhekelia, who has not previously renounced citizenship.

Under s4B, there is an entitlement to register (as British citizens by descent) BOTC, BN(O) BOC, British subjects or BPPs who have no other nationality. The applicant must not have renounced, voluntarily relinquished or lost through action or inaction any citizenship or nationality after the relevant day which is for BN(O) 19 March 2009 and for the rest 4 July 2002.

Under s4C, there is an entitlement to register (as British citizens by descent) those born outside the UK to British mothers before 1983. This is on Form UKM.

It has been acknowledged that to give effect to s4C(3A) BNA 1981, the consular registration condition in s5(1)(b) 1948 Act is to be treated as being inapplicable in cases where citizenship is claimed by descent from a mother. The relevant updated Nationality Guidance Registration as British citizen: children of British parents, puts it in the following terms: 'Where you are considering whether a person who was born outside the UK between 1 January 1949 – 31 December 1982 (inclusive) to a British mother you must disregard the requirement that their birth must have been registered with a UK consulate in the 12 month period after their birth.'

Under ss4E-I (inserted by s65 of the Immigration Act 2014, see above there is now the option to register for those disadvantaged by the law's pre-2006 discrimination against those born outside wedlock. This is on form UKF.

9.4.5 Applications

Registration applications involve the completion of a form and payment of a fee (except UKM and UKF applications which are free). Applications for the registration of people living abroad will normally be made through a visa application centre. Applications for people living in the UK are made to the Home Office. Registration is evidenced by a certificate and the person can subsequently apply for a British passport.

For details of the various routes that are available and how to proceed please see https://www.gov.uk/british-citizenship

If on receipt of an application the Home Office detect that a person does not need to register because they are already a British Citizen, they will inform the applicant of this and refund the application fee. The public Citizenship Ceremony requirements apply to applicants for registration as for naturalisation but there are exemptions (see next section).

9.5 Acquisition by Naturalisation as an Adult – ss6(1) & 6(2)

Section 6 of the BNA 1981 deals with naturalisation, the process by which most adults will become British citizens. There are two routes for naturalisation, under s6(1) BNA 1981) or, where the applicant is the spouse of a British citizen, s6(2). The requirements for each route are then set out in Schedule 1 to the BNA 1981.

In addition to requirements as to length and continuity of residence and immigration status,

- an individual must be of good character,
- have sufficient knowledge of the English, Welsh or Scottish Gaelic language, and of life in the UK; and
- intend to make their principal home in the United Kingdom (if they are not married to a British citizen), or, if they intend to live abroad, that they work in Crown service or for a UK enterprise.

Provisions in the 2009 Act were set to change the route to naturalisation in a major way. They were enacted but never commenced, and the subsequent government scrapped them. Advisers should be careful though as some books and websites might include the 2009 amendments without clearly setting out that they are not in force.

The criteria are explained in Naturalisation as a British citizen by discretion: nationality policy guidance as well as the HO's Booklet AN and Guide AN available on the same page as application form AN.

The criteria for naturalisation are as follows:

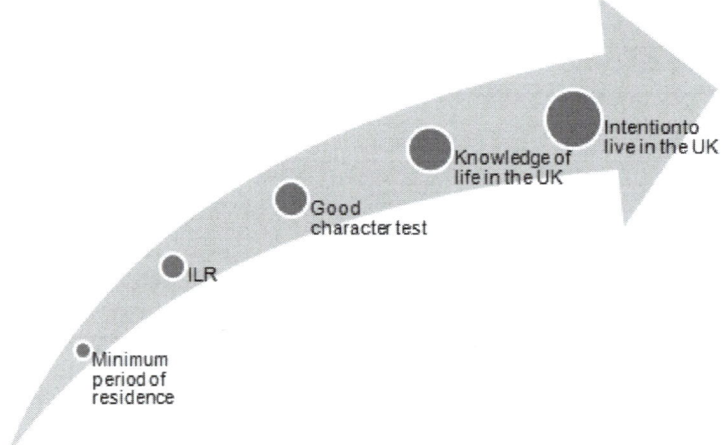

9.5.1 Period of residence

9.5.1.1 Non-spouse cases

The requirements of residence for those not applying as spouses are set out at Schedule 1 paragraph 2.

- subject to subsection (3), that he was in the United Kingdom at the beginning of the period of five years ending with the date of the application and that the number of days on which he absent from the United Kingdom in that period does not exceed 450; and
- that the number of days on which he was absent from the United Kingdom in the period of twelve months so ending does not exceed 90; and
- that he was not at any time in the period of twelve months so ending subject under the immigration laws to any restriction on the period for which he might remain in the United Kingdom;
- that he was not any time in the period of five years so ending in the United Kingdom in breach of the immigration laws.

So effectively these break down into these requirements:

- residence for the last five years without having been outside the country for more than 450 days;
- including residence for the last year without having been away for more than 90 days;
- possessing indefinite leave to remain or permanent residence for the year leading up to the application;
- not having been present unlawfully in the five years leading up to the application.

However, there is discretion to treat these conditions as satisfied despite insufficient periods of time being accumulated.

Example

Herbert is Bolivian. He arrived in the UK five years ago as an Investor and has mostly lived here since then. He was granted ILR recently. He wants to naturalise as soon as possible and intends to continue living here for the foreseeable future.

When we work through the four time-related residence requirements Herbert is in a promising situation. He has been living in the UK for five years so hopefully has not clocked up excess absence abroad during that time, though of course this must be checked. Equally hopefully he has not been away for more than 90 days in the last year. Clearly he has had leave for five years, so has not been present unlawfully over that period. So the only barrier is the need for a year's ILR when he applies.

Of course you would also need to ensure that he is of good character and can speak English. We can already see that he has effectively stated an intention to make the UK his home.

9.5.1.2 Spouse cases

Section 6(2) deals with applications of persons 'married to a British citizen'. The required residence period is 270 days, with the references to five years replaced by three years, in sub-paragraphs (a) and (d).

The restriction at 3(c) is lifted, so that there is no requirement to be free from immigration control (i.e. to have indefinite leave to remain) for 12 months prior to the date of application, with the practical consequence that a spouse can apply from the grant of indefinite leave to remain without waiting for a further year.

There is no requirement to make the UK their permanent home, though spouses must still meet the requirements of good character, English language proficiency, and have the requisite knowledge of life in the UK.

9.5.2 EEA nationals

There are three important considerations for EEA nationals and their family members who wish to naturalise.

Firstly, is naturalising a good idea? This matters for those whose country of nationality does not provide for dual nationality (e.g. Austria and the Netherlands). They should carefully weigh up the pros and cons of naturalisation, given Brexit and the loss of their free movement rights which this would entail.

Secondly, when can they apply? It had long been understood that permanent residence is recognised by the issue of a permanent residence card – not created by the card. So you might have thought that the question was entitlement to permanent residence, not possession of a card that matters.

However, the British Nationality (General) (Amendment No. 3) Regulations 2015 (SI 2015/1806) require that applicants must be issued with a permanent residence (PR) document to establish they are free from immigration control restrictions. This requirement could unfairly delay a nationality application, if a person was required to show one year's freedom from immigration control before making the nationality application. However, this was addressed by the SSHD, who when issuing a permanent residence card will provide a letter stating the date on which permanent residence is deemed to have been acquired. For the rest of the grace period, proof of permanent residence can be used to meet the ILR requirement, but from 1 July 2021 settled status is required. Clients should be advised to apply for settled status in any case, should the naturalisation application not be decided by the end of June 2021.

Thirdly, from May 2020, the UKVI Guidance on naturalisation changed, to raise the possibility of refusal of naturalisation to EEA nationals present with EUSS but who had not consistently exercised Treaty Rights over the previous five years. Gaps in 'qualified person' status may be treated as unlawful residence:

> 'You must only exercise discretion to disregard a period of unlawful residence if there are reasons for this which were clearly outside the applicant's control, or if the breach was genuinely inadvertent and short.
>
> A person may also be in breach if they have not complied fully with all the requirements of the route they are on. Following the introduction of the EU Settlement Scheme you may increasingly see applications from EEA or Swiss nationals who have not fully complied with additional requirements under the EEA regulations, such as having comprehensive sickness insurance where they needed it, and who may therefore have been in breach of immigration

law. When considering such applications you should take into account all the facts surrounding such a breach and make a full assessment about whether discretion should be exercised in their favour.'

9.5.3 In breach of the immigration laws

Where there are qualifying periods to be met, periods spent in the relevant territory 'in breach of the immigration laws' do not count. The meaning of 'in breach of the immigration laws' for the specific purpose of calculating residence is set out in s50A(4) of the BNA 1981.

The Nationality policy: Naturalisation as a British citizen by discretion sets out the circumstances in which one is considered to be in breach of immigration law in the qualifying period, and this, notably, includes those who have claimed asylum whilst in the UK illegally. Even if granted temporary admission or immigration bail during the consideration of their claim, the policy considers them in breach until leave to remain was granted. There is some discretion to disregard such 'unlawful residence', however, where the claim was made within one month of clandestine arrival or longer if there were 'extenuating circumstances'. Other circumstances in which unlawful residence may be disregarded include where the applicant

- Was a minor at the time, or a victim of domestic violence whose abusive partner prevented a renewal of leave
- Had an application invalidated but a fresh application was submitted within 28 days if before 24 November 2016
- Made a late application, subsequently granted, no more than 28 days after overstaying began (14 if overstaying ended on or after 24 November 2016)

Unlawful residence during the qualifying period, unless exempt by discretion, do not count towards the qualifying period; but these, as well as other breaches of immigration law, are also taken into account in assessing 'good character'.

9.5.4 The good character requirement

This is not in the scope of level 1 work and must be referred to a suitable qualified advisor.

Good character will be in issue in applications to naturalise and register for those aged 10 years or over (by reason of s41A of the BNA 1981). 'Good character' is not defined in legislation and the policy is now contained in Nationality Policy Good character requirement. This leaves the Secretary of State with enormous discretion.

The good character test gauges a person's behaviour before and after they arrived in the UK. It is not unusual, for instance, for a person recognised as a refugee to be refused citizenship due to events they disclosed as part of their asylum claim.

As good character is the most common ground of refusal, it would be negligent for an adviser to make an application without carefully taking their client through the provisions of the good character: nationality policy linked above.

All criminal convictions, however minor, including spent convictions, must be declared (immigration and nationality decisions being exempted from section 4 of the Rehabilitation of Offenders Act 1974). Broadly, convictions will be dealt with as below:

Sentence	Impact on Nationality applications
4 years or more imprisonment	Application will normally be refused, regardless of when the conviction occurred.
Between 12 months and 4 years imprisonment	Application will normally be refused unless 15 years have passed since the end of the sentence.
Up to 12 months imprisonment	Applications will normally be refused unless 10 years have passed since the end of the sentence.

A non-custodial offence or other out of court disposal that is recorded on a person's criminal record	Applications will normally be refused if the conviction occurred in the last 3 years.

The guidance explains that some minor convictions may be disregarded, and useful advice is given as to the effect of receiving a fixed penalty and similar notices which 'do not form part of a person's criminal record as there is no admission of guilt'. It also clarifies that the 'end of the sentence' is not the release date but the end of the sentence imposed, and that a suspended prison sentence is treated to fall within row 4 of the table above.

Checks are made on financial impropriety. A bankrupt will, where there has been fraud or they were discharged less than 10 years ago, be of insufficiently good character.

The person's immigration history will also be considered. In a major amendment to the good character guidance introduced in December 2014, citizenship will normally be refused 'if within the 10 years preceding the application the person has not been compliant with immigration requirements'. All breaches will be taken into account, including illegal entry, failure to report, breach of conditions, overstaying, and failure to report.

The good character requirement has been extended to include children aged 10 and over (who will be applying to register rather than naturalise). The specific position these individuals find themselves in has now been addressed in Nationality guidance Naturalisation as a British citizen by discretion: nationality policy guidance.

9.5.5 Sufficient knowledge of language and life in the UK

Under Schedule 1 of the BNA 1981, all applicants for naturalisation must show sufficient knowledge of English, Welsh or Scottish Gaelic, and 'sufficient knowledge about life in the UK'.

The British Nationality (General) (Amendment) Regulations 2013 provide that the language and life in the UK tests are met in pretty much the same way as under Appendix KoLL for a person applying for settlement. Where the Appendix KoLL provisions have been met, an applicant for naturalisation will not have to meet them again. If they have not, guidance about English for citizenship is available on this page.

To pass the English language requirement, applicants will need to, either, come from an English-speaking country listed in Schedule 2A to the Regulations or have a degree taught in English, or pass a test specified in Schedule 2A (excluding those provided by the Educational Testing Service). For the life in the UK element, the applicant must have passed the Life in the UK test.

The Home Office possesses a discretion to waive the language requirement where it would be unreasonable to expect the applicant to fulfil it because of age or physical or mental condition. The language requirement will normally be waived where the applicant is aged 65 or over.

The grounds for exemption of younger people need to be compelling, such as where the applicant:

- is suffering from a long-term illness or disability which severely restricts mobility and ability to attend language classes; or
- suffers from a speech impediment which limits ability to converse in the relevant language; or
- has a mental impairment which means that they are unable to learn another language.

9.5.6 Intention to live in the UK

If a person is abroad or about to go abroad it may be important to explain this. For example, caring for a person overseas who is ill or dying is likely to be a temporary absence and should not be treated as evidence that a person has no intention to live in the UK. For guidance, consult Naturalisation nationality policy guidance.

9.5.7 Citizenship ceremonies

The BNA 1981 at s42 to 42B and Schedule 5 provides that anyone over the age of 18 who acquires British citizenship, whether by registration or naturalisation, must do so at a public ceremony and is required to take the Oath of Allegiance (there is an affirmation to be used by people of different religions and of none) and now a new pledge as set out in these provisions. Section 6 of the Become a British citizen guidance has further details. Ceremonies are normally held in groups, although arrangements can be made (at a price) to have individual ceremonies. People can invite guests. A fee is payable.

Some people are exempted from the requirement by Section 42(2) of the 1981 Act. These are:

- those not of full age; or
- those who are already:
    - British citizens; or
    - British Overseas Territories citizens; or
    - British Nationals (Overseas); or
    - British Overseas citizens; or
    - British subjects under the 1981 Act; or
    - citizens of any country of which Her Majesty is Queen (Antigua and Barbuda, Australia, the Bahamas, Barbados, Belize, Canada, Grenada, Jamaica, New Zealand, Papua New Guinea, St Christopher and Nevis, St Lucia, St Vincent and the Grenadines, Solomon Islands and Tuvalu.)

Where an applicant is required to take an oath of allegiance s/he must normally do so within the time limit of three months prescribed by the British Nationality (General) Regulations 1982 (or the British Nationality (General) Regulations) 2003, as appropriate). Otherwise the applicant cannot be registered or naturalised unless the Home Secretary decides to extend the period. Notification letters will advise the applicant to contact the local authority to arrange a ceremony. The Home Office will also notify the local authority.

If a person does not attend a citizenship ceremony within the time limit permitted, the Home Office should notify them that it will not be possible to become a British citizen because the Home Secretary is not able to register or naturalise a person who has not attended a ceremony and taken an oath/pledge. If the applicant still wishes to become a British citizen, and had an entitlement at the date of application, a certificate may be issued at any time on the basis of the original application on payment of the balance of fee and attending a citizenship ceremony and making an oath/pledge. In all other cases, the applicant will need to re-apply under an appropriate provision of the legislation.

In exceptional circumstances an exemption may be made in respect of any or all of the following:

- the requirement to attend a citizenship ceremony
- the requirement to make an oath of allegiance and pledge
- the time limit for attending a ceremony

Module 10: Refugee Law - Overview

Further notes/Information

NB Asylum Claims are outside the scope of level 1 work and these must be referred on to a suitable accredited advisor, however it is important that Level 1 advisors are aware of:

-the requirements of the Refugee Convention

-the procedure for making applications

-the consequences of a grant of refugee status or humanitarian protection

10.1 Definition of a refugee

The international definition of a refugee is found at Article 1 (A) (2) of the 1951 Convention and Protocol Relating to the Status of Refugees (The Refugee Convention).

Taking the Convention and the Protocol together the definition is as follows:

> Owing to well-founded fear of being persecuted for reasons of race, religion, nationality, membership of a particular social group or political opinion, is outside the country of his nationality and is unable or, owing to such fear, is unwilling to avail himself of the protection of that country; or who, not having a nationality and being outside the country of his former habitual residence as a result of such events, is unable or, owing to such fear, is unwilling to return to it.

The principle underlying the Refugee Convention is one of establishing a system of international protection to persons who are in need of it.

10.1.2 Asylum Claim

The UK definition of an 'asylum claim' is detailed at section 113 of the Nationality, Immigration and Asylum Act 2002.

> 'asylum claim' means a claim made by a person to the Secretary of State at a place designated by the Secretary of State that to remove the person from or require him to leave the United Kingdom would breach the United Kingdom's obligations under the Refugee Convention.

10.2 The procedure for making applications

Asylum claims should be made in person at the port of entry or by appointment at the Asylum Screening Unit in Croydon. It is possible to have a claim for asylum processed if a claim has been made elsewhere but it will only be registered as an asylum claim at a screening interview.

Asylum support is available to asylum seekers and people who have made a protection claim under Article 3 of ECHR plus their dependents if they are over 18 and would otherwise be destitute and/or homeless.

It can be claimed immediately upon claiming asylum and will be processed by the same officials dealing with the asylum application.

Unaccompanied children under 18 will be supported by their local authority.

10.2.1 Screening interview

Once a claim has been made the next step is the screening interview. At this interview the applicant will be photographed and have their fingerprints taken. The fingerprints will be entered in the EURODAC database to check for multiple applications in the UK or in other EU countries.

The applicant will then be interviewed to check who they are and where they are from and will be asked to submit any passports, travel documents, police registration certificates, or any other ID documents they may have e.g. ID cards, birth or marriage certificates, school records etc.

They will also be asked to say why they want asylum and will be able to submit written evidence to support the claim if they wish.

The applicant may request for a male or a female interviewer but the choice may not always be respected. They should request a male or female caseworker at this interview if they wish.

They will receive a form of induction.

10.2.2 Post screening

The applicant will receive an Application Registration Card (ARC) which contains their personal details and serves as a form of ID.

The revised ARC and associated process, introduced in July 2017, enables an ARC to be issued to asylum claimants and their dependants within three working days of the claim being registered as in paragraph 359 of the Immigration Rules regardless of where the claim for asylum is made.

Asylum claimants will be sent their ARC by post following the successful enrolment of biometric details on Home Office terminals (livescan or cardscan). A successful enrolment requires the capturing of fingerprints for all claimants and dependants aged five and over and a facial image of all claimants and dependants regardless of age.

After the screening interview the case will be referred to a caseworker in one of the regional asylum teams. These are situated in Cardiff, Glasgow, Leeds, Liverpool, Central London, West London and Solihull.

They may be given a 'preliminary information questionnaire'. If an asylum applicant receives one of these it is important that it is filled in and returned by the deadline. Failure to do this will result in the Home Office assuming the asylum application has been withdrawn.

10.2.3 Asylum interview

The asylum interview should take place shortly after the screening interview. This is what is known as the substantive asylum interview and will concentrate on the substance of the asylum claim. They will be asked to explain how they have been persecuted in their country and why they are afraid to return to their country.

They are allowed to take a legal representative to this interview and legal aid is available if they qualify which can be checked out here https://www.gov.uk/check-legal-aid

10.2.4 The decision

The Home Office aim to make the decision within 6 months but add that it may take longer if it is complicated. The examples given by the Home Office are:

1. The Home Office needs to check documents

2. the applicant needs to attend for further interview(s)

3. the Home Office want to check on personal details like existing criminal convictions or if the applicant is being prosecuted.

10.2.4.1 Refugee

If the applicant is recognised as a refugee, they are given permission to stay as a refugee for five years.

After five years they can apply for settlement protection (ILR) in the UK.

They can apply for family reunion to sponsor pre-flight immediate family members to join them in the UK. Immediate family members are defined in the Immigration Rules as a spouse or partner and children under the age of 18, who formed part of the family unit before their refugee sponsor fled their country of origin or former habitual residence to claim asylum in the UK.

Refugees can apply for a travel document to travel outside the UK as they must not apply for a passport of their own nationality (this could jeopardise their refugee status!). This is an online application https://www.gov.uk/apply-home-office-travel-document. Before they travel, they need to check that the country they want to visit will accept a travel document and if they need a visa.

10.2.4.2 Humanitarian Protection

The applicant may not be granted permission to stay as a refugee but may still get permission to stay for humanitarian reasons. This will also result in permission to stay in the UK for protection for 5 years.

After five years they can apply for settlement protection (ILR) in the UK.

Applicants can apply for family reunion to sponsor pre-flight immediate family members to join them in the UK. Immediate family members are defined in the Immigration Rules as a spouse or partner and children under the age of 18, who formed part of the family unit before their refugee sponsor fled their country of origin or former habitual residence to claim asylum in the UK.

They can apply for a certificate of travel (more expensive than a refugee travel document) to travel outside the UK. This is an online application https://www.gov.uk/apply-home-office-travel-document. Before they travel, they need to check that the country they want to visit will accept a travel document and if they need a visa.

10.2.4.3 Permission to stay for other reasons

If an application is not recognised as a refugee or in need of humanitarian protection, they may get permission to stay for other reasons.

How long they get permission for will depend on their circumstances. One typical example is where asylum seeking children are given permission to stay until their 18th birthday when a decision will be taken on their substantive asylum claim.

They can apply for a travel document to travel outside the UK. This is an online application https://www.gov.uk/apply-home-office-travel-document. Before they travel, they need to check that the country they want to visit will accept a travel document and if they need a visa.

10.2.4.4 Refusal

Most asylum applicants have their claim refused in the first instance. Decisions to refuse claims for asylum and/or humanitarian protection generate a right of appeal to the First Tier Tribunal. See Module 10.1 for further detail in MIL.

Module 11: Appeals and Administrative Review

This is important information but it is outside the scope of Level 1 work and any appeal case must be referred on to a suitable accredited advisor.

11.1 Appeals in the First Tier Tribunal, rights and grounds of appeal

Under the 2002 Act, certain decisions of the Home Office give rise to an independent right of appeal before a judge of the First-tier Tribunal (Immigration and Asylum Chamber). The First-tier Tribunal judge has the power to allow or dismiss an appeal, subject only to a further challenge on points of law to the Upper Tribunal (Immigration and Asylum Chamber).

The appeals system created by the extensive amendment of the NIAA 2002 by the IA 2014 entered full effect on 6 April 2015. There a few old appeals in the system still.

The SSHD has to notify a person whose application has been refused of the right of appeal under the Immigration (Notices) Regulations 2003. If there is a right of appeal, and it is not notified, then the refusal has not been made lawfully. So it would not stop s3C leave running, and would not render a person liable to removal, whatever the SSHD's computer records might suggest.

11.1.1 Rights of appeal

Appeals arise under the system which fully came into effect on 6 April 2015 (following a staged implementation). Section 15 of the Immigration Act 2014 substantially amended Part 5 of the 2002 Act. This was a very major change, and reduction, in appeal rights.

The practical operation of the appeals system, from the Home Office perspective, is explained in a series of Modernised Guidance documents, including a 'Keeling Schedule' (i.e. a consolidated up-to-date version) of the amended Part 5.

Rights of appeal are at s82 of the 2002 Act, the full text of which reads:

> 82 Right of appeal to the Tribunal:
>
> (1) A person ('P') may appeal to the Tribunal where—
>
> > (a) the Secretary of State has decided to refuse a protection claim made by P,
> > (b) the Secretary of State has decided to refuse a human rights claim made by P, or
> > (c) the Secretary of State has decided to revoke P's protection status.

11.1.2 Protection claims

A protection claim is one where a person alleges their removal would contravene the Refugee Convention or the UK's obligations in relation to Humanitarian Protection (s113 NIA 2002). Such a claim is refused where the Home Office makes a decision that removal would not breach the relevant Convention (in the form of a Notice of Decision accompanied by a Reasons for Refusal letter).

The protection claim must usually have been made in person at the port on entry to the UK, at the Asylum Screening Unit, or by delivering further submissions to the Further Submissions Unit of the HO in Liverpool. It can also be made on encountering an Immigration Officer having already entered the UK, or whilst the person is detained by the HO.

11.1.3 Human rights claims

Relatively few people will have a viable asylum claim, so the only way that most people will be able to access the appeals system will be via a human rights claim. A 'human rights claim' means a claim made by a person that to remove him from or require him to leave the United Kingdom or to refuse him entry into the United Kingdom would be unlawful under s6 of the HRA1998) as being incompatible with his Convention rights (s113 NIA 2002).

Note that although these claims will usually arise under Article 8 ECHR and involve family or private life, they may involve other Articles. For example, Article 3 (non-health) claims: i.e. where someone is excluded from international protection because of criminality but nevertheless has a decent claim to fear inhuman and degrading treatment from powerful forces in their country of origin. There are other Articles, such as Article 1 of Protocol 1, the right to property, which might conceivably arise.

A human rights claim under the 2002 Act can be made by way of a 'valid application', relying on the family and/or private life provisions in the Immigration Rules or outside the Rules, or as 'further submissions' under the Immigration Rules, by completion of a s120 notice, or simply by representations, depending on the circumstances in which the person finds themselves.

Identifying a human rights claim

Usefully the Home Office Rights of appeal guidance explains (summarising Appendix AR) that the following applications made under the Immigration Rules are automatically treated as human rights applications so will bear the right of appeal against refusal.

Immigration Rule (Category of application)

- Paragraph 276B (long residence)
- Paragraphs 276ADE (1) or 276DE (private life)
- Paragraphs 276U and 276AA (partner or child of a member of HM Forces)
- Paragraphs 276AD and 276AG (partner or child of a member of HM Forces) where the sponsor is a foreign or Commonwealth member of HM Forces and has at least four years' reckonable service in HM Forces at the date of application
- Part 8 of these Rules (family members) where the sponsor is present and settled in the UK or has refugee or humanitarian protection in the UK

But not: paragraphs 319AA to 319J (PBS dependents), paragraphs 284, 287, 295D or 295G (sponsor granted settlement as a PBS Migrant)

- Part 11(asylum)
- Part 4 or Part 7 of Appendix Armed Forces (partner or child of a member of HM Forces) where the sponsor is a British Citizen or has at least four years' reckonable service in HM Forces at the date of application
- Appendix FM (family members)

But not: section BPILR (bereavement) or section DVILR (domestic violence)

So, we can see that applications made under the above listed categories will be accepted by the HO (and consequently the FTT) as being human rights claims.

Where human rights claims are made outside the rules, the guidance explains that:

> It is only where the applicant ticks the box 'Other purposes or reasons not covered by other application forms' that it should be treated as a human rights claim. Even if this box is ticked, the application may not be a human rights claim.

You should consider the following three questions:

> Does the application say that it is a human rights claim?
> Does the application raise issues that may amount to a human rights claim even though it does not expressly refer to human rights or a human rights claim?
> Are the matters raised capable of engaging human rights?

Where question 1 or 2, and 3 can be answered in the affirmative, the HO will accept the application is a human rights claim and acknowledge that a right of appeal is available if the application is refused.

The Home Office Rights of Appeal guidance also provides that, in general, cases raising medical issues should be considered as claims under Article 3 or Article 8, and cases seeking leave to remain to participate in legal proceedings as a witness should be considered as Article 6 claims.

Outside the UK, applications based on a human rights claim outside the Immigration Rules must form part of a valid application for entry clearance.

Where the person's circumstances might engage Article 8, but they are applying under categories of the rules that do not specifically refer to Article 8 (e.g. student extensions cases) or which the HO do not otherwise accept are human rights claims (e.g. domestic violence) or where they raising another Article (e.g. Turkish business cases which might engage the right to property under Article 1 of Protocol 1 to the ECHR), applicants will have to either: make the case in their accompanying representations that the application is also being made on human rights grounds, in so doing hope to survive the ban on simultaneous applications, if they are to have any chance of engaging the new rights of appeal if refused. Otherwise the sole remedy will be the administrative review regime: see Appendix AR.

It appears that the SSHD largely ignores representations made on human rights grounds which try to piggy-back on non-human rights-type applications. This raises a potential problem, as the right of appeal arises from the *refusal* of a human rights claim (etc.) rather than from merely ignoring one.

The UT has considered what is needed for a human rights claim outside of the standard immigration routes which are automatically treated as such. Essentially the respondent must treat an application as including a human rights claim where it appears from the totality of the information supplied that the appellant was advancing a case which requires a discretionary decision to be made by reference to Article 8 issues.

Examples

Fatima makes an application for asylum because she fears persecution for defying her powerful family's wishes as to who she should marry.

This is a claim for international protection: its refusal carries the right of appeal. This is clear from s82 of NIAA 2002 itself.

Gopal is present as a Tier 4 student. He has got married and his Appendix FM application has just been refused because he provided inadequate evidence of the financial requirements.

Gopal has the right of appeal: as shown above, the SSHD treats most Appendix FM refusals as human rights claims and so there is automatically a right of appeal.

Maryam has been present in the UK as a spouse but her British citizen Sponsor has just died during the currency of Maryam's limited leave.

Now this is an Appendix FM application: so you might expect a right of appeal. However, the HO policy is to expressly exclude these 'bereaved partners' applications from being treated as appealable on refusal. Administrative review is the only remedy.

Imagine now that you review Maryam's application paperwork and supporting evidence and note that there are very many references to very strong UK ties and that she has serious mental health problems.

You might consider lodging an appeal anyway to test the water.

11.1.4 Grounds of appeal

Section 84 of the 2002 Act, provides the grounds (or legal reasons or basis) for an appeal:

The grounds of appeal are found in s84 NIAA 2002:

- For refused Protection claims: Refugee Convention, Humanitarian Protection, or Human Rights Convention grounds (s84(1))
- For refused human rights claims: that the decision is contrary to the Human Rights Act 1998 (which effectively means, contrary to the ECHR) (s84(2))
- For revocation of protection cases: Refugee Convention or Humanitarian Protection grounds (s84(3))

In line with s82, the only available grounds for appeal are ones raising protection or human rights issues.

Before the current appeal system (which generally entered force from 6 April 2015), appeals could be brought on more technical legal grounds. However now the sole focus is on whether there is a breach of one of the Conventions, or the Rules on Humanitarian Protection.

11.1.5 First-tier Tribunal Procedure Rules

Immigration appeals in the First-tier Tribunal (IAC) are, as from 20 October 2014, governed by the Tribunal Procedure (First-tier Tribunal) (Immigration and Asylum Chamber) Rules 2014 (the 'Rules').

Immigration appeals to the Immigration and Asylum Chamber of the UT are governed by the amended Tribunal Procedure (UT) Rules 2008, addressed below.

The procedure rules are supplemented by both Practice Directions, Practice Statements and Guidance Notes.

The Rules for the First-tier deal with many issues about the listing and conduct of appeals, but for our purposes at OISC level 1 we only need to deal with one Rule:

- The deadline for lodging appeals (r19)

Deadline for appeal

The deadlines for receipt by the Tribunal of the Notice of Appeal are specified at rule 19:

- 14 days after being sent the notice of decision if appellant is in the UK
- 28 days after departure where appellant was in the UK when decision made, but appeal is out of country
- 28 days from receipt of the decision in other cases

The distinction between business and calendar days has largely disappeared, as have the deemed receipt provisions; there is no longer any difference between deadlines for those detained as opposed to those at liberty. Days are calendar days, finishing at midnight; but where a deadline falls on a day other than a working day, the act is done in time if it is done on the next working day (rule 11).

Example

Rahul comes to your office having received a decision from the Home Office on Tuesday 12 May; the notice of decision is dated Friday 8 May. He wishes to identify the deadline to appeal.

He is in the UK so the relevant provision is r19(2): 'the notice of appeal must be received not later than 14 days after they are sent the notice of the decision ...'

These are 'days' not 'working days'. Sometimes the rules do refer to working days, but not here. The primary focus is on when he was sent the decision (thus prudent legal offices always keep copies of the envelopes in which decisions are sent on file where there is a difference between the stamped date of posting and the date on the notice of decision itself).

If the refusal letter was sent on Friday 8 May, the notice of appeal must be sent not later than 14 calendar days later: this means he has until Friday 22 May, until midnight that day (r11(1)). If the refusal letter was sent on Saturday 9 May, whilst the calculation would initially produce the date of Saturday 23 May, r11(2) allows the application to be treated as in time when done on the next working day, i.e. Monday 25 May.

This is outside the scope of Level 1 work and must be referred on to a suitable accredited advisor

11.1.6 Barring the right of appeal

Sometimes an immigration decision may involve the refusal of a human rights claim but there is no appeal. This will be where the Immigration Rules or the immigration legislation bars the right of appeal. This is all beyond the scope of OISC level 1, but we will just mention the scenarios, as you will see them in your casework.

- NIAA 2002 s94 allows the SSHD to **certify** a human rights or asylum claim as **clearly unfounded** – there is then a right of appeal, but only from abroad
- NIAA 2002 s94B allows the SSHD to **certify** a human rights as out-of-country if the SSHD believes the person can pursue their appeal from abroad and to do so would not involve any **serious irreversible harm** – so again there is then a right of appeal, but only from abroad
- NIAA 2002 s96 allows the SSHD to **certify** a human rights claim as **made too late**: basically after an appeal has been run and lost, or a s120 notice has been given, and the matters now relied on were previously available but not raised
- Immigration Rule 353 says that any further representations that follow the exhaustion of appeal rights must pass the **fresh claim test**: i.e. they must be sufficiently different to what was previously argued to have a real prospect of success. There is no need to certify a case where there is no fresh claim: because there will be no human rights or asylum claim made in the first place

11.2 Appeals and administrative review

Level 1 can lodge and deal with an application for Administrative Review for any Level 1 type of application with the exception of applications refused on the basis of credibility or a fundamental issue of genuineness of documents or relationships.

11.2.1 Overview of the process

Human rights aside, for most people whose immigration applications are refused, or whose leave is cancelled at the port of entry or return, an 'administrative review' (AR) will be available to challenge the decision. The administrative review process was introduced at the same time as the new appeals regime, particularly aimed at those who had lost their right of appeal under that act. An AR involves the HO reconsidering its own decision to refuse leave, or to cancel leave at the border.

HJT offers an e-book *Administrative review* with more detailed examples, and specimen pieces of drafting, for those wanting more detail than is available here.

As explained in the Explanatory Memorandum to the Statement of Changes HC693, that introduced AR(HC693), published on 16 October 2014:

> The new administrative review process will resolve case-working errors and will do so more quickly than the appeals process it replaces. The reviewer will be a different person from the original decision maker. The Home Office service standard is to determine an administrative review application within 28 days whereas the average time for a Points Based System appeal to be concluded is 12 weeks.

The AR process is provided for in the Immigration Rules (HC693):

- Rules 34L-34Y in Part 1 discuss the procedures such as time limit, form and fee,
- Appendix AR explains the scope of the remedy, and
- Appendix SN provides for the service of AR decisions, and for notifying the person that an application is invalid

There is also Modernised Guidance administrative review (now at version 10.0).

The Rules define an administrative review as (Appendix AR, paragraph AR2.1):

> the review of an *eligible decision* to decide whether the decision is wrong due to a *case working error.*

An administrative review is available where the HO makes an 'eligible decision'. An eligible decision cannot be appealed to the FTT (IAC). The only remedy will be to seek AR (and/or, sometimes, to make a fresh application for leave). Eligible decisions are listed in AR3.2, AR4.2, and AR5.2, dependent on where the eligible decision is made (i.e. outside, at the border, or inside the UK). The list of potential 'case working errors' is at AR2.11-2.12.

Paragraph AR2.8 of Appendix AR confirms the Home Office will not seek to remove the applicant from the United Kingdom where administrative review is pending (as defined in AR2.9).

AR normally looks only at the decision to refuse an application, and not at post-decision facts.

The Independent Chief Inspector of Borders and Immigration published a report on the AR process in May 2016, one year after the process was introduced. The review was ordered in response to concerns of MPs and peers during the passage of the Immigration Bill about the effectiveness and independence of the proposed new process as a replacement of the right of appeal. The Chief Inspector was highly critical. It is notable, for instance, that ARs succeeded in a far lower proportion of cases than similar cases under the old appeals regime. However, a person cannot choose their remedy, so that where only an AR is available, they will have to pursue it (and then consider a judicial review if warranted).

In line with the new appeals regime, the process of AR for in-country applications was brought in progressively, in four stages, for various types of application, becoming fully operable for all eligible decisions made on or after 6 April 2015. For the relevant dates, see AR3.2. For decisions at the border, and out of country applications, AR was introduced on the same date.

11.2.2 Extension of leave to remain

One important feature of the remedy is that it brings with it a statutory extension of leave to remain, as section 3C of the IA 1971 to cover administrative review as well as pending 'in-time' applications and appeals, such that leave to remain is statutorily extended where:

(d) an administrative review of the decision on the application for variation—
(i) could be sought, or
(ii) is pending.

Because this automatic extension of leave bars the making of another application once an application has been refused, it will be necessary for a person who wants to make a speedy further application rather than pursue the administrative review route to complete an 'Administrative review waiver form' (AR2.10). In any event the making of a further application of any kind is deemed as withdrawing any pending administrative review (r34X(4)) and thus bringing 3C leave to an end of the day before the application is made (AR2.10(b)).

11.2.3 Administrative review – the principles

There are two key concepts found in the administrative review process: **eligible decision** and **case working error.** Essentially the practitioner will be looking to see their client's problem arises from an eligible decision (i.e. something which can be the subject to the administrative review process) in circumstances where the complaint involves a 'case working error' (effectively, a ground of appeal).

Both **refusals** of leave and **grants** may be challenged. Grants can be challenged on the basis that the period or conditions of leave are inconsistent with the Immigration Rules (AR2.12).

11.2.4 Eligible decisions

Eligible decisions in relation to leave to remain (AR4.1):

An eligible decision is either a decision to refuse an application for leave to remain or a decision to grant leave to remain where a review is requested of the period or conditions of leave granted. They include decisions in regard to:

- applications under the Immigration Rules generally (e.g. PBS, UK ancestry etc.) except:

  NOT Short-term students under the Part 3 rules, and Visitor cases (where the only remedy will be to apply again or seek JR), or

NOT Asylum, including family reunion; and applications and human rights claims under Appendix FM, Rules 276B (long residence) 276ADE (private life), Part 8 of the Rules (except for PBS dependants), and various similar 'family routes' for members of the Armed Forces: but also excluding from this list bereaved partners and domestic violence cases (so that refusal of applications made by PBS dependants, bereaved partners and domestic violence cases *are* eligible decisions and not therefore appealable)

- Turkish Association Agreement applications.

Eligible decisions in relation to leave held on arrival in the United Kingdom (AR4.1)

- decisions to cancel leave to enter or remain due to change of circumstances, false representations or non-disclosure of material facts

Eligible decisions in relation to entry clearance (AR5.1)

- All entry clearance cases except for the exceptions which apply as for leave to remain, above
- There is no reference to refugee family reunion cases under Part 11 as an exception, unlike the other routes which might readily be presumed to involve human rights issues: perhaps this is an oversight. In any event, it is hard to see that a refusal of such an application would not involve refusal of a human rights claim, and thus amount to an appealable decision

AR2.11 provides a complete list of *'Case working errors'*:

These are the case working errors:

- Refusing applications generally (including Turkish ECAA applications), or cancelling leave at the port of entry (including for visitors) because of **allegations of dishonesty** (AR2.11(a))
- Refusing applications because a time limit has been miscalculated (AR2.11(b))
- Refusing applications because a document should have been requested but wasn't (AR2.11(c))
- Applying the Immigration Rules incorrectly (AR2.11(d))
- Failing to apply published Guidance (AR2.11(e))

Many kinds of challenge can doubtless be brought under these provisions, including:

- Most often, overlooking relevant documents, or misunderstanding them
- Arguments over the meaning of the rules, including the possibility that the interpretation of the rules does not conform to principles established by case law ('applied the Immigration Rules incorrectly').
- Disputes as to the correct exercise of discretion ('applied the Immigration Rules incorrectly')
- Challenges to the length of stay granted, which might be relevant to students where the HO has misunderstood the course's start and finish dates, and conditions placed on the grant of leave.

<u>However, one has to be realistic as to how these Rules are likely to be interpreted by the Home Office</u>.

- Applications are much more likely to succeed where they involve unequivocal overlooking of evidence that was previously supplied on an application, or where the wrong Immigration Rule has been applied.
- AR is not a promising remedy for debates about what the Immigration Rules or Home Office policy means.
- The SSHD also tends to stick their heels in once a dishonesty allegation has been made, unless really strong new evidence is produced.

11.2.5 When can I rely on new evidence in administrative review?

In some cases, fresh evidence can be admitted. This is where the relevant ground of review is under AR2.11(a), (b) or (c) above, i.e. where:

- the refusal or cancellation made on the basis that there was deception used in the application, or a previous application, under the general grounds of refusal was incorrect (or the application

has been refused for other mandatory grounds relating to a previous breach of immigration control)
- the original decision as to the application being made outside a relevant time limit in the Rules was incorrect (i.e. beyond the period of 28 days of overstaying that is disregarded for such applications)
- the original decision maker's decision not to request specified documents under paragraph 245AA of these Rules was incorrect

Where an application for leave to remain is refused under the general refusal reasons at r9.7, based on an allegation that deception was used in an earlier application of leave, new evidence will only be considered if that allegation had not also been made at the time that previous application was refused (AR2.4(b)).

So one cannot rely on new evidence merely because the *genuineness* of a student (r245ZX(o)) application is challenged, but only where the challenge is made expressly by reference to the mandatory general refusal reasons relating to deception.

However in those cases refused because the SSHD is "*not satisfied that you genuinely wish to establish in business as proposed*" the Court held in Karagul [2019] EWHC 3208 (Admin) this accusation by the SSHD amounts to alleging misconduct or bad faith. In any such case, it would be essential to give the chance to make representations in response to the allegation made, either via written representations following a letter, or via a formal interview. The administrative review procedure would only be lawful in such cases if a fair opportunity was given to provide further evidence.

A procedure at AR2.5 provides that 'the Reviewer' can contact the applicant to request relevant evidence is provided within seven days of the date of request where such a case working error has been identified. No fresh evidence will be considered other than that requested by the HO, so that any such evidence submitted with the AR application will be ignored.

11.2.6 Administrative review – procedure

Features of the process are that

- Rule34L provides that written notice of an eligible decision must be given (which will need to conform to the requirements of the Immigration (Leave to Enter or Remain Order 2000 (as amended). As with an appeal, a refusal must be accompanied by a statement of reasons, and information about how to apply for administrative review, including the time limit. A refusal that does not do this will be invalid and an applicant could argue that they should receive a fresh notice of an eligible decision.
- Only one valid application for administrative review may be made in respect of an eligible decision, unless the administrative review does not succeed, but for different or additional reasons to those specified in the decision under review (34N(2)): in such a case, there may be a further application (AR2.2(d)).
- The application must be made in the relevant location – whilst the applicant remains in the United Kingdom in relation to 'in-country' refusals, whilst they remain abroad vis-á-vis entry clearance applications, and whilst they remain here if it is a decision made on their arrival, though no application may be brought whilst they remain in the control zone (of the Channel Tunnel)
- Dependants can be included in the AR application where they were dependants on the application which resulted in the eligible decision (34S).
- It must be made in accordance with 34U if made online, or 34V if made by post. The guidance states that Tier 4 AR applications must be made online. The paper form will only be available where the initial application was made on a paper form, and will only apply to a Tier 4 migrant who has more than 10 dependants, or used the super-premium route.
- An application will be treated as withdrawn on the Applicant's notification to such effect, or if they request the return of their passport for the purposes of travel outside the United Kingdom, or if they actually travel abroad, or if they make a fresh application for leave (34X).
- Where an application is made online any specified fee must be paid, any section of the online application which is designated as mandatory must be completed as specified; and documents

specified as mandatory on the online application or in the related guidance must be submitted in the specified manner (34U).
- A notice of the outcome of an administrative review application, or a notice of invalidity informing an applicant that their application is invalid, must be given in writing.

11.2.7 Fees

The current fee for an AR is £80.00. **This figure is correct at the time of printing, please note that this may have changed and the link below should be followed to confirm:**

See Schedule 6 of The Immigration and Nationality (Cost Recovery Fees) (Amendment) Regulations 2014.

According to the Guidance:

- Fee exemptions will be available for those who were fee-exempt on the original application, or where the application to a decision that has been re-issued following administrative removal with different or additional reasons to the original decision; or otherwise in exceptional circumstances
- The fee will be refunded if the original decision is withdrawn and leave is granted, or varied as to duration or conditions

11.2.8 Time limits for the application

Where notice of the eligible decision is sent by post to an address in the UK, it is deemed to have been received, unless the contrary is shown, on the second working day after the day on which it was posted.

The AR application is treated as being made on the marked date of posting, or on the date it is delivered by a courier or submitted online.

The application must be made (34R):

- where the applicant is not detained, no more than 14 calendar days after receipt by the applicant of the notice of the eligible decision (7 days if they are detained); or
- where the applicant is abroad, no more than 28 calendar days after receipt by the applicant of the notice of the eligible decision;
- where the challenge is to the conditions of a grant, no more than 14 days after the biometric residence document is received

The AR application may be accepted out of time if the Secretary of State is satisfied that it would be *unjust not to waive the time limit* and the application was made as *soon as reasonably practicable*. **If this arises it should be referred on to a suitable accredited advisor**

The Home Office policy guidance Administrative Review sets out that

- It is recognised that some applicants may accept that documents were missing and therefore that the refusal was correct overall, but they may still wish to request administrative review if they can show that the documents were genuine, even though this would not change the overall outcome of the original application
- Administrative review is not available for EEA applications, human rights applications or protection claims, or to try and apply for leave on another basis from the refused application (as is evident from the Rules themselves and their limited list of eligible decisions)
- As the online administrative review application does not allow for the submission of further documents, where an online application is accepted as valid, an opportunity should be given at that point to provide any further documents which Appendix AR permits, before the case is reviewed
- Applications should be made online if possible; a postal application must, to be valid, use the appropriate application form, pay the specified fee, fill out all mandatory sections of the form (either identified as such in the form or in associated guidance), be appropriately signed, any mandatory documents must be supplied, and the form must be sent to the specified address
- Extensions of time will not be given for minor oversights, internet connection problems, minor illnesses or needing to discuss the matter with an advisor who was not available

- Further evidence, where requested by the HO, must be supplied within 7 working days, plus 2 extra days for it to pass through internal mail, unless there are exceptional reasons justifying an extension of time
- If the Applicant's leave has expired and they remain in the UK, a section 120 notice must be provided when the original decision is upheld
- The administrative review process should proceed notwithstanding any challenge by way of judicial review
- If a challenge is brought by way of appeal to a decision which is liable to administrative review, the Home Office will defend the appeal on the basis that there is no jurisdiction for the appeal
- Where a person launches a JR following the refusal of an AR, time for the JR (i.e. the 3 month limit) will start running from the date the person receives the AR decision (and not the date of the original decision).

The guidance also gives a useful set of 'example scenarios' as to whether a particular complaint amounts to a case working error and whether new evidence can be requested.

Example

These are possible administrative review avenues given the possible case working errors, leading to a refusal, that are identified in AR2.11.

An application is refused because enquiries of a bank lead to a response that the bank statements are not genuine. The applicant produces further evidence by way of a letter from the bank central office confirming an error in the original letter. This may be reviewed under Appendix AR2.11(a) and fresh evidence is admissible.

An application is refused because it is believed that the applicant previously overstayed for 31 days. However they produce the original grant of further leave to remain which shows they were granted leave to a later date than Home Office records showed. This may be reviewed under Appendix AR2.11(b) and fresh evidence is admissible.

An application is refused because a resident labour market test has not been carried out where the vacancy is in fact on the 'shortage occupation' list and so does not require such a test: This may be reviewed under Appendix AR2.11(c) – fresh evidence is not admissible.

An application is refused because of an insufficient number of points but the decision maker overlooked the highest qualification submitted by the applicant: This may be reviewed under Appendix AR2.11(c) – fresh evidence is not admissible.

A student's extension application is refused because the decision maker checks the sponsor register and finds that their college is not on it. They therefore refuse the application because this invalidates the CAS. However they have overlooked the Tier 4 Guidance which says that a student in this situation should be given an opportunity to find an alternative place within sixty days: This may be reviewed under Appendix AR2.11(d) as relevant Home Office guidance has been overlooked – fresh evidence is not admissible.

Top Tip

When planning your strategy vis-á-vis administrative and judicial review, at least until there is authority to the contrary, always presume that you are bringing a challenge against the original decision, not the decision made on administrative review. The Home Office lawyers may argue that the earlier decision is effectively unchallenged otherwise, or that the assault on the administrative review decision is a disguised challenge to the original one as to which time has now expired.

Module 12: Offences under the Immigration Act 1971

This is important information, but it is outside the scope of Level 1 work and must be referred on to a suitable accredited advisor.

The 1971 Act is one of the main sources of offences under immigration law. The key offences are as follows:

Section 24 criminalises entry into the UK in breach of a deportation order or without leave; overstaying and failing to comply with the conditions on which leave is granted without reasonable excuse. By s24(1A) an overstayer is committing an offence throughout the period of overstaying, but can only be prosecuted once in respect of overstaying the same leave. It is for the defence to prove that the person did in fact have leave, or that a stamp in a passport or travel document is wrong.

The s.24 offence as a whole is subject to an extended time limit for prosecution as set out in s.28. The offence can be tried if information is laid within three years of the commission of the offence provided that a senior police officer certifies that this is within two months of the date on which there is sufficient evidence to justify proceedings. Otherwise, the more usual six month time limit for trial in the magistrates' court applies.

Section 24A, inserted by the Immigration and Asylum Act 1999, again applies to a person who is not a British citizen. It criminalises obtaining or seeking to obtain leave to enter or remain, or securing or seeking to secure avoidance postponement or revocation of the giving of removal directions, making a deportation order, or actual removal, by deception. It can be tried either way and before the Crown Court the maximum penalty is two years imprisonment and a fine.

In practice the SSHD usually prefers to try to remove people in these situations rather than prosecute them. But you still need to advise your clients that they are liable to prosecution otherwise they may not appreciate the seriousness of their situation.

Example

Pablo, a Colombian national, enters the UK in the back of a lorry.

This is a clandestine entry, a form of illegal entry. He is liable to prosecution.

12.1 Assisting: s25 to 25D

Section 25 means that it is an offence to do anything

- to facilitate
- the entry, transit or stay in the UK
- of a person who is not an European Union national
- in breach of the immigration law of any member State of the EU (the Asylum and Immigration (Treatment of Claimants etc.) Act gives the Secretary of State powers to add states to the list covered if it is necessary to do so to comply with UK obligations under EU law)
- if you know, or have reasonable cause to believe that the person is not an EU national

AND

- if you know or have reasonable cause to believe that your act facilitates a breach of immigration law.

Anyone can be prosecuted for an act done in the UK. All forms of British nationals can be prosecuted for acts done outside the UK and so can corporate bodies incorporated under UK law. The maximum penalty is 14 years in prison and a fine.

- It is not an offence to make an application to regularise a person's status where that person is an overstayer, or has entered illegally. Such an application would assist the person to attempt to stop being in the UK in breach of immigration law.
- Nor does the section override normal duties of confidentiality. If a person comes to you and you advise them that they are, or may be, in the UK in breach of immigration law, you have not facilitated their stay by giving them that advice.
- Nor would you be liable if you gave your advice and the client said 'thank you very much' and disappeared.
- Where you would be in trouble would be if YOU took steps to facilitate their remaining in the UK in breach of immigration law; for example by knowingly misleading the authorities.

Section 25A makes it an offence to

- facilitate the arrival in the UK of a person
- knowingly
- and for gain
- if you know or have reasonable cause to believe that the person is an asylum-seeker (the definition of an asylum seeker also covers those who say that their removal would be contrary to the Human Rights Act 1998).

<u>There is an exception to 25A.</u>

To benefit from the exception, you must be

- acting on behalf on an organisation
- which aims to assist asylum-seekers and
- and which does not charge for its services.

Gain is not limited to financial gain. The exception is narrowly drafted. It will not help a person who is working for a 'not for profit' organisation if they are not acting in the course of their employment, and it will not help a person who works for an organisation existing to help people seeking asylum if the organisation charges for its services.

Example

Roger is a British citizen. Whilst on a wine-buying jaunt to Calais, he accepts the invitation of two Afghan youngsters to give them a ride in the boot of his car; they offer him £50 as their share of the petrol costs. They are discovered as he passes through UK immigration control on the return journey.

Roger is very likely to have committed an offence under s25A. He has certainly facilitated the youngsters'' arrival in the UK for gain, and he is acting as an individual, not as a charitable organisation. And moderate knowledge of world current affairs might well have given a clue as to the possibility of their being asylum seekers.

Section 25B means that it is an offence to do anything

- to facilitate a breach of a deportation order
- by an EU national
- if you know or have reasonable cause to believe that your act facilitates a breach of a deportation

OR

- to assist a person who has been excluded from the UK
- on the grounds that this is conducive to the public good
- to arrive in, enter, or remain in the UK
- if you know or have reasonable cause to believe that your act assists the person to arrive in, enter or remain in the UK
- and if you know or have reasonable cause to believe that the person is excluded from the UK because this is considered conducive to the public good.

All three offences carry a maximum sentence of 14 years in prison. Section 25D deals with related powers to detain ships aircrafts and vehicles.

12.1.2 General offences: s26

Section 26 lists a whole series of offences, all of which carry a maximum sentence of six months imprisonment and a fine, and to all of which the extended time limit for prosecution (s.28) applies (see note above to s.24). The offences are all linked to the administration of the immigration acts.

Those under examination under Schedule 2 to the 1999 Act (i.e. clients) are criminalised if:

- they fail to submit to such examination without reasonable excuse
- they fail without reasonable excuse, or refuse, to produce documents in their possession or control which they are under examination to produce
- they fail to complete and produce a landing or embarkation card in accordance with an order made under Schedule 2 of the 1971 Act
- without reasonable excuse they fail to comply with reporting restrictions (or certificates of registration or payment of fees for same – i.e. requirements of regulations made under s.4(3) of the IA 1971).

The last two offences in the section could catch anybody:

- Altering without lawful authority a certificate of entitlement, entry clearance, work permit or other document issued or made under or for the purposes of any of the Acts named; or (this later part for clients and third parties, probably under immigration control) using or having in one's possession for a document for such use which one knows or has reasonable cause to believe to be false.
- Obstructing an immigration officer or other person acting lawfully in the execution of one of the named Acts, without reasonable excuse.

NB All of these must be referred on to a suitable accredited advisor

12.2 Giving Immigration Advice: The OISC

Section 91 of the Immigration and Asylum Act 1999

Section 91 states as follows:

91(1) A person who provides immigration advice or immigration services in contravention of s84 or of a restraining order is guilty of an offence

Immigration advice' is defined in s.82 as advice which:

- Relates to a particular individual
- Is given in connection with one or more relevant matters
- Is given by a person who knows that he is giving it in relation to a particular individual and in connection with one or more relevant matters
- By a person in the UK (wherever the client is)
- In the course of a business carried on whether or not for profit, by him or another

AND

- Is not given in connection with representing an individual before a court in criminal proceedings or in matters ancillary to criminal proceedings.
- Immigration services are defined as the making of representations on behalf of a particular individual:
- In connection with one or more relevant matters
- In civil proceedings before a judicial decision maker in the United Kingdom or
- In correspondence with a Minister of the crown or government department
- By a person in the UK (wherever the client is)

- In the course of a business carried on whether or not for profit, by him or another.

Relevant matters are – just about every kind of encounter with the UK immigration authorities including the Home Office that you could imagine: asylum, removal, deportation, and applications for entry clearance or for leave to enter or leave to remain.

Example

Roger runs a travel agency. Normally he deals with outbound travel, but he has started to take some inbound clients. An Ecuadorean national asks Roger to give him some information about how to ensure his tourist visa application succeeds. Roger tells him. Trouble ahead?

Roger seems to have crossed the line. He has advised a particular individual in the course of his business in relation to a relevant matter, i.e. 'an application for … entry clearance or leave to enter'.

Roger had better book his HJT OISC Level 1 course pronto!

Acknowledgements

Many thanks go to Mark Symes for his editorial flare and incredible law knowledge. Thank you to Jane Aspden and Agnete Gribkowski for their huge contribution in producing this resource. Thank you to Melanie Porte and Lippy Begum for their valued help and support. Special thanks go to Androulla Demetriou for her design expertise, her patience and hard work in producing the printed edition.